Praise for *Information Literacy Through Theory*

'Bringing together a wide range of distinguished scholars – both in terms of methodology and geography – the editors of this volume have fostered the kind of conversation between various forms of scholarship and applications that has long been the unrealized potential of Library and Information Science as an interdisciplinary academic field. Each of the contributors specifically describes how "theory" informs the research they do in the context of its application to Information Literacy. The reader is thereby encouraged to make connections and identify points of commonality and tension between the approaches. Highly recommended as an introduction to the scholarship of information literacy as a research domain as well as an introduction to Library and Information research more broadly.'
James Elmborg, Professor Emeritus, Library and Information Science, University of Iowa, USA

'To better understand information literacy in the intricate social, political, and technological situations of contemporary society, it is crucial for students, researchers, and practitioners to recognize the broad repertoire of theoretical frameworks at hand. *Information Literacy Through Theory* offers precisely that by showcasing how the theories we employ shape the knowledge we gain from our research and practice in information literacy. Authored by a team of experts with in-depth expertise in various methodologies and theories, this book is an invaluable resource for advancing our understanding of an essential phenomenon.'
Eystein Gullbekk, PhD, Head of Teaching and Learning Services, The University of Oslo Library, Norway

'*Information Literacy Through Theory* presents a broad palette of theories for exploring and understanding the multifaceted concept of information literacy. It provides a much longed-for toolbox for research, including social and practice-oriented as well as critical approaches, enabling studies from a variety of angles. Together, the thirteen chapters provide a rich choice of research lenses, where findings from various studies will combine to add to more in-depth understandings of this unruly concept. The book further offers valuable knowledge and ideas for teaching and learning in the professional practices, where we find the origin of the concept.

The team of authors represents an international research community with contributions from the UK, the Nordic countries, the USA, South America, and Australia. Taken as a whole, this book offers strong potential for deepening and broadening on-going and future information literacy research.'
Louise Limberg, Professor Emerita, Swedish School of Library and Information Science, University of Borås, Sweden

'Disinformation, misinformation, trivia, alternative truths, lies, ideology, propaganda, pseudo-science, conspiracy theories – all thrown at us in a dizzying 24/7, wall-to-wall, multimediated information environment – no wonder that societies and economies, institutions and cultures shudder in and out of gridlock and paralysis, lurching towards tribalism and fascism, hate and violence. We as social scientists are left like proverbial blind people shuffling around an

elephant – each bringing our own disciplinary perspectives, epistemic standpoints and embodied histories to bear. *Information Literacy Through Theory* is a unique and rich multidisciplinary toolkit – offering diverse theoretical models and normative approaches to our current crises and discontents. Libraries – as physical and virtual archives, as trustworthy human resources, as convivial and welcoming systems of exchange – remain essential sources of human and planetary stories, knowledges, wisdom, memories, histories. Without them, we can neither survive nor flourish.'
Allan Luke, Emeritus Professor, Queensland University of Technology, Australia

'*Information Literacy Through Theory* provides a much-needed, accessible overview of key theories in information literacy research. It will be invaluable to students and practitioners interested in moving beyond rational, instrumental perspectives and approaches to information literacy research (and practice) to engage in critical interrogations of the information literacy project itself. This book fills an important gap in the information literacy literature and I can't wait to see what new ideas and projects it inspires.'
Karen P. Nicholson, Western University / University of Guelph, Canada

'Written by leading scholars in the field, this long-awaited book provides a multifaceted perspective on the theoretical developments within the domain of Information Literacy. Each of the 13 chapters of the book reflect how particular theoretical approaches to information literacy can be used to enhance research in this field. Examples of the rich tapestry of theoretical approaches include practice theory, positioning theory, critical literacy, sociomateriality, consciousness and cognition, and institutional ethnography. Each chapter explains clearly what assumptions the theoretical approach makes about key concepts and the ways in which the theory enables or constrains our understanding of information literacy. Recommended reading for researchers, practitioners, and students interested to dig deeper into the theoretical and methodological issues of information literacy research.'
Reijo Savolainen, Professor Emeritus, Tampere University, Finland

'Not only an invaluable collection of leading theorists in the field of information literacy, this title includes unique and provocative insights into how people engage with and make sense of information environments using sound theoretical bases. Hicks, Lloyd, and Pilerot have assembled a landmark volume that makes a resounding case for applying theory to information literacy research in a meaningful way, thereby allowing the field to truly grasp the complex social nature of information literacy. Chapter authors each introduce and analyse a different theory in accessible but rigorous manners, making this book of great interest to library and information science students, researchers, and practitioners who seek to understand information literacy theories and apply them to their work.'
Eamon Tewell, Head of Research Support and Outreach, Columbia University Libraries, USA

**Information Literacy
Through Theory**

Every purchase of a Facet book helps to fund CILIP's advocacy, awareness and accreditation programmes for information professionals.

Information Literacy Through Theory

Edited by
Alison Hicks, Annemaree Lloyd
and Ola Pilerot

© This compilation: Alison Hicks, Annemaree Lloyd and Ola Pilerot 2024
The chapters: the contributors 2024

Published by Facet Publishing
c/o British Library, 96 Euston Road, London NW1 2DB
www.facetpublishing.co.uk

Facet Publishing is wholly owned by CILIP: the Library and Information Association.

The editors and authors of the individual chapters assert their moral right to be identified as such in accordance with the terms of the Copyright, Designs and Patents Act 1988.

Except as otherwise permitted under the Copyright, Designs and Patents Act 1988 this publication may only be reproduced, stored or transmitted in any form or by any means, with the prior permission of the publisher, or, in the case of reprographic reproduction, in accordance with the terms of a licence issued by The Copyright Licensing Agency. Enquiries concerning reproduction outside those terms should be sent to Facet Publishing, c/o British Library, 96 Euston Road, London NW1 2DB.

Every effort has been made to contact the holders of copyright material reproduced in this text and thanks are due to them for permission to reproduce the material indicated. If there are any queries please contact the publisher.

British Library Cataloguing in Publication Data
A catalogue record for this book is available from the British Library.

ISBN 978-1-78330-589-6 (paperback)
ISBN 978-1-78330-590-2 (hardback)
ISBN 978-1-78330-591-9 (PDF)
ISBN 978-1-78330-592-6 (EPUB)

First published 2024

Typeset from editors' files in 10/13 pt American Garamond and Frutiger
by Flagholme Publishing Services.
Printed and made in Great Britain by CPI Group (UK) Ltd, Croydon, CR0 4YY.

Contents

Notes on Contributors ix

Introduction: Themes, Patterns and Connections xiii
    Alison Hicks, Annemaree Lloyd and Ola Pilerot

1   **Democracy and Information Literacy**   1
    John Buschman

2   **Information Literacy and the Social: Applying a Practice Theory View to Information Literacy**   27
    Annemaree Lloyd

3   **Information Literacy in a Nexus of Practice: A Mediated Discourse Perspective**   39
    Noora Hirvonen

4   **The Radical and the Radioactive: Grasping the Roots of Theoretically Informed Praxis in Brazilian Studies on Critical Information Literacy**   57
    Arthur Coelho Bezerra and Marco Schneider

5   **Locating Information Literacy within Discursive Encounters: A Conversation with Positioning Theory**   71
    Alison Hicks

6   **Plural Agonistics**   91
    Johanna Rivano Eckerdal

7   **Critical Literacy and Critical Design**   111
    Veronica Johansson

8   **Information Literacy Through an Equity Mindset**   131
    Amanda L. Folk

9   **Sociomateriality**   149
    Jutta Haider and Olof Sundin

10   **Surfacing the Body: Embodiment, Site and Source**   165
    Annemaree Lloyd

11	**Variation Theory: Researching Information Literacy Through the Lens of Learning** Clarence Maybee	**183**
12	**Information Literacy: What Consciousness and Cognition Can Teach Us** John Budd	**197**
13	**Information Literacy Theorised Through Institutional Ethnography** Ola Pilerot	**215**

Conclusion: Alerting Us to Difference — **233**
   Alison Hicks, Annemaree Lloyd and Ola Pilerot

Index — **241**

Notes on Contributors

Editors
Alison Hicks is Assistant Professor and Programme Director, Library and Information Studies, at University College, London (UCL). Her research primarily focuses on the information literacy practices that help people to cope with uncertainty, including risk and transition, within academic, health, everyday and work contexts. She is additionally interested in qualitative, visual and participatory information literacy research methods. She is the Editor-in-Chief of the *Journal of Information Literacy*.

Annemaree Lloyd is professor at the Department of Information Studies, University College, London (UCL) and a social science researcher who conducts research into information literacies and contemporary information practices in formal and informal learning connected to workplaces, community settings and in education. Her research programme focuses on the intersection between information, learning and the performance of practice from theoretical and empirical perspectives. Annemaree is the leader of the FOIL (Forum of Information Literacy) and has published over 100 refereed journal articles and conference proceedings. She is the author of *Information Literacy Landscapes* (2010, Chandos) and *The Qualitative Landscape of Information Literacy Research* (Facet Publishing, 2021) and has co-edited several titles focused on information literacy and research methods.

Ola Pilerot is Professor at the Swedish School of Library and Information Science, University of Borås, where he is a member of the research group Information Practices and Digital Cultures. He teaches and publishes within the field of information practices. During recent years, a great part of his research work has concerned issues related to information practices of librarians. Ola has published in, for example, *Journal of Documentation*, *Information Research*, *Journal of the American Society for Information Science and Technology*, *Library Trends* and *Journal of Librarianship and Information Science*.

Contributors
Arthur Coelho Bezerra is a tenured researcher at the Brazilian Institute of Information in Science and Technology (IBICT) and professor at the Post-Graduate Program in Information Science (PPGCI IBICT UFRJ). He is currently co-chair of the International

Centre for Information Ethics (ICIE) and represents the Latin America and Caribbean Chapter of ICIE. He was a visiting researcher at the Université Toulouse – Jean Jaurès (Latin American Chair) in 2018. He co-ordinates the research group Critical Studies in Information, Technology and Social Organization (Escritos). He is the author of *Cultura Ilegal: as fronteiras morais da pirataria* (2014), co-author of *iKritika: estudos críticos em informação* (2019) and co-editor of *Competência Crítica em Informação: teoria, consciência e práxis* (2022).

John Budd is Professor Emeritus with the School of Information Science and Learning Technologies of the University of Missouri. He has also been on the faculties of Louisiana State University and the University of Arizona. He is the author of more than 150 publications, including 15 books. He has also presented at well over 100 conferences. He has been the recipient of the American Library Association's Highsmith Library Literature Award and the Beta Phi Mu Award. He continues to be active in the American Library Association, the Association for Library and Information Science Education and the Association of Information Science and Technology.

John Buschman is Associate Provost for Research & Innovation and Dean of University Libraries at Seton Hall University, New Jersey, USA. Buschman is author of *Dismantling the Public Sphere: situating and sustaining libraries in the age of the new public philosophy* (2003). His most recent book is *Libraries, Classrooms and the Interests of Democracy: marking the limits of neoliberalism* (2012) and he is the author of numerous chapters and articles in *Library Quarterly*, *Journal of Documentation* and other leading journals. He holds an MLS from Ball State, an MA in American Studies from St Joseph's University and a Doctor of Liberal Studies from Georgetown University.

Amanda L. Folk is an associate professor and Head of the Teaching & Learning Department at the Ohio State University Libraries. She earned her PhD in social and comparative analysis in education from the University of Pittsburgh's School of Education. In addition to serving as the editor in chief for *The Journal of Academic Librarianship*, Amanda has been published in *College & Research Libraries*, *portal: Libraries and the Academy*, the *Journal of Information Literacy* and *International Information & Library Review*. Amanda was the recipient of the 2020 ACRL Instruction Section's Ilene F. Rockman Instruction Publication of the Year Award.

Jutta Haider is Professor at the Swedish School of Library and Information Science (SSLIS), University of Borås. She has published widely on information practices and digital cultures' emerging conditions for production, use and distribution of knowledge and information. This includes work on algorithmic information systems and on knowledge institutions, including encyclopedias and search engines. She is co-author of *Invisible Search and Online Search Engines: the ubiquity of search in everyday life* (Routledge, 2019) as well as of *Paradoxes of Media and Information Literacy: the crisis of information* (Routledge, 2022).

NOTES ON CONTRIBUTORS

Noora Hirvonen is Professor in Information Studies at the Research Unit of History, Culture and Communication Studies, Faculty of Humanities, University of Oulu, Finland. Her research has focused on people's competencies and practices to seek, evaluate, use and create information in everyday life and in connection to health and wellbeing. Currently, her work concentrates on the ways the everyday information practices and competencies of young people are shaped as they interact with intelligent technologies.

Veronica Johansson is Senior Lecturer in Library and Information Science at the Swedish School of Library and Information Science (SSLIS), University of Borås and a regional editor at *Information Research*. She has been a guest lecturer in visual learning and communication at the Department of Science and Technology, Linköping University and Visualization Center C, Norrköping and served as academic advisor to the European Commission in the Horizon 2020 Commission Expert Group to advise on specific ethical issues raised by driverless mobility (EU CAD). Her main research interests concern societal perspectives on data and visualisations, with particular focus on aspects related to ethics, privacy, critical literacy and critical design.

Clarence Maybee is a professor and the W. Wayne Booker Endowed Chair in Information Literacy at the Purdue University Libraries and School of Information Studies. He is the Director of the Institute for Information Literacy at Purdue. Dr Maybee publishes widely and presents internationally on his research investigating experiences of information literacy in higher education. In 2019, he received the Librarian Recognition Award from the American Library Association. Dr Maybee is the author of the book *IMPACT Learning: librarians at the forefront of change in higher education,* published by Chandos Publishing.

Johanna Rivano Eckerdal is Associate Professor, Archives, Libraries, Museums and Digital Cultures, Department of Arts and Cultural Sciences, Head of Centre for Oresund Region Studies, Lund University, Sweden. Her research concerns relations between information and democracy. Her dissertation explores young women's information literacy practices when choosing a contraceptive: analysing information literacy as depending on the view of democracy. Current research concerns public libraries and librarians' social role, suggesting that it is fruitful to understand libraries as verbs rather than as nouns. Librarising brings out the continuous making of the library. She has proposed libraries as important societal institutions in which agonistic debates can unfold.

Marco Schneider is a tenured researcher at the Brazilian Institute of Information in Science and Technology (IBICT), Professor at the Post-Graduate Program in Information Science (PPGCI IBICT UFRJ), Professor of Social Communications at the Fluminense Federal University (UFF) and at the Post Graduate Program in Media and Everyday Life (PPGMC UFF), Chair of the International Center for Information Ethics (ICIE). He is the author of the books *The Dialectic of Taste: information, music and politics* (2015) and *The Age* of *Disinformation: fake news, post truth and other traps* (2022), besides several book chapters and papers published in scientific journals. He is co-author of *iKritika: estudos críticos em informação* (2019) and co-editor of *Competência Crítica em Informação: teoria, consciência e práxis* (2022) and leader of the research group Perfil-i (Perspectivas Filosóficas em Informação).

Olof Sundin is Professor in Information Studies at the Department of Arts and Cultural Sciences, Lund University, Sweden. He has long experience of researching the configuration of information in contemporary society, the construction of trustworthiness as well as practices of media and information literacy in schools and in everyday life. He is co-author of *Invisible Search and Online Search Engines: the ubiquity of search in everyday life* (Routledge, 2019) as well as of *Paradoxes of Media and Information Literacy: the crisis of information* (Routledge, 2022). Both books are written within a sociomaterial perspective on information.

Introduction: Themes, Patterns and Connections

Alison Hicks, Annemaree Lloyd and Ola Pilerot

What is the work of theory? Theory is a critical element of research and provides the intellectual scaffolding that is necessary for the development, implementation, analysis, interpretation and critical evaluation of research. Theory provides the necessary concepts that can be employed to describe a phenomenon or practice as it is experienced and/or performatively enacted. Knowledge from theory is always a view from somewhere (Barad, 1996) and the knowledge provided by social theory draws attention to certain forms of knowledge and ways of knowing, i.e. different contexts, different concepts and different truths (Lloyd, 2005). Theory makes our standpoint or our assumptions and beliefs visible – our ontological and epistemological positions – and it scaffolds our decisions about methodology (Lloyd, 2021, 18).

Currently there is only one theory of information literacy practice, the Theory of Information Literacy (Lloyd, 2017). However, the employment of social theory, which is drawn from wider disciplinary arenas and applied to understand information literacy as a socially situated practice and lived experience, has been prodigious in the last 20 years. Sociocultural, postmodern and post-structuralist perspectives that underpin these social theories act as counterbalance to the provision and attainment view of information literacy, which continues to advocate an autonomous (Street, 2003), skills-based, measurement-focused approach to practice. The autonomous view fundamentally satisfies the instrumental rationality of education systems and the continued need for librarians who operate within those systems to stake their claims as experts in the field.

The use of social theory allows researchers to dive under the surface of the attainment perspective and turn their attention to understanding and explaining what information literacy is, as well as how it happens and how its operationalisation contributes to the shaping of social life.

This volume

The inspiration for this book arose from the realisation that a significant proportion of information literacy research remains focused on technical, practical or problem-solving topics. In addition, attempts to conceptualise the topic often take place without a comprehensive understanding of the ontological or epistemological foundations of theoretical work. Theoretically focused information literacy research has also been poorly treated within existing theoretical scholarship, with the information literacy focus of recent publications addressing theory development and use within library and information studies (LIS) being limited to Kuhlthau (Sonnenwald, 2016) or loose understandings of Freirean thought (e.g. Leckie, Given and Buschman, 2010). This volume aims to address these issues by providing a space for key theorists in the field of information literacy to discuss, interrogate and reflect on the applicability of theory within information literacy research. The continued growth of information literacy research as well as the publication of Lloyd's (2021) recent book on information literacy methods and methodologies provides a good example of the appetite for this more robust engagement with theory development and use in the field. The volume will consequently be of interest to (a) students and practitioners who are looking to design more theoretically robust information literacy research projects or read existing work more critically and (b) more experienced researchers who are looking to extend their understanding of theoretical approaches in the field.

The book comprises 13 chapters, each of which interrogates how a particular theory has been used within information literacy research. These chapters are book-ended by an introduction, which provides an initial analysis of theoretical information literacy research to date and a conclusion, which constitutes a meta-analysis of each of the 13 chapters of the book. Each of the 13 chapters follows a similar template, which includes an introduction to the featured theory to situate the work before explaining the theory in relation to information literacy. Each author has been free to develop their chapter as they saw fit but has been encouraged to respond to the same set of key guiding questions, namely:

- What assumptions does this theory make, for example, about people, activities, contexts, knowledge, information, learning or information literacy (implicitly or explicitly)?
- What understanding about information literacy does this theory open us to and what does it close us to?
- How does the theory we use shape our methodological choices?

Authors have then been encouraged to reflect on how the theory in question might be enhanced by other theoretical perspectives. Aiming to open information literacy theory up to ontological, epistemological and methodological interrogation, these questions further endeavour to build connections between theoretical considerations. Each chapter was subsequently submitted to a separate peer-review and editor-review process, which further extended each author's thinking.

Chapter authors were invited to participate in this project based on two main criteria: advanced study in the field, as represented by PhD completion, and prior engagement with theoretical information literacy work. While these criteria may be seen as limiting and there are many overlaps (and confusion) about the connections between information literacy and information behaviour research, we also recognised the lack of opportunities to focus on the rich theoretical complexity that lies at the heart of information literacy research. While information literacy is a practical field and theory and practice are always entwined, we argue that there must also be space for purely conceptual information literacy reflection and development, too. Beyond these two criteria, careful consideration was given to ensuring that a wide range of authors was invited to participate in this volume, including authors at different career stages and from practitioner and researcher backgrounds, as well as from diverse regions and research traditions. Attention was also paid to the range of theories represented in this book to ensure that research from cognitive, sociocultural and critical traditions was included. However, we note that while this process has ensured a more equal gender and career-stage author representation, it has also resulted in a lack of other forms of diversity, including those in relation to race and ethnicity. We acknowledge this shortcoming and the gaps or oversights that this lack of representation creates; we also acknowledge that a 'race for theory' constitutes a culturally loaded decision in itself (Christian, 1988). These omissions further acknowledge that the field has yet to answer uncomfortable yet vital questions about the whiteness of information literacy theory and practice – questions that we believe must be at the forefront of all future theoretical and practical work.

Theoretical research to date

The purpose of this introductory chapter is to map and review theoretical information literacy work to date. A rich palette of theoretical approaches has emerged since Limberg, Sundin and Talja (2012) described the three main theoretical perspectives and methodologically driven approaches to information literacy that had been employed by the early 2010s. In scoping the literature for the introduction to this book we are now able to recognise a wider corpus of theories. However, this rich palette also creates tensions about how theories fit with (or challenge each other), all of which comes down to questions about truth and knowledge. These issues are also reflected in how information literacy is understood as an object of research.

Table 1 provides an initial attempt to categorise existing literature. Providing examples of theoretical perspectives that have been used to frame empirical research and analysis of information literacy, the table also offers examples of conceptual papers where theory has been used to clarify concepts employed in information literacy (represented in the table in italics). The literature that informs this table was gathered through an extensive search process, including within LIS, social science and educational databases, key books and existing literature reviews in the field, reference chaining and through consultations with chapter authors. Each of these papers was subsequently read and coded for themes related to what the author says about theory in relation to information literacy and how each author puts the theory to work. At the same time, we note that this is not a comprehensive list and there will be key authors and studies missing from this table.

Table 1 *Theory employed in information literacy research*

Cognition	Personal construct theory	Kuhlthau, 1993; Smith, 2015
	Phenomenology	Budd and Suorsa, 2019 Limberg and Sundin, 2006
	Variation theory	Bruce, Edwards and Lupton, 2006
Criticality	Critical pedagogy	Elmborg, 2006 Jacobs, 2008
	Critical race theory	Morrison, 2017; 2018 Rapchak, 2019
	Critical theory	Bezerra, 2021 Johansson, 2012 Flierl and Maybee, 2020 Kapitzke, 2003 Pawley, 2003
	Validation theory	Quiñonez and Olivas, 2020
Discourse	Genre theory	Simmons, 2005
	Positioning theory	Hicks and Lloyd, 2021a; 2021b Lloyd and Hicks, 2021 Rivano Eckerdal, 2011
	Nexus analysis	Multas and Hirvonen, 2019
Materiality	Sociomateriality	Haider and Sundin, 2022 Sundin, 2015
	Actor network theory	Carlsson and Sundin, 2017 Schreiber, 2017 Sundin and Carlsson, 2016
	Practice theory	Pilerot, 2016
	Embodiment	Lloyd, 2007
Practice	Practice theory	Gullbekk, 2016 Hicks, 2018 Lloyd, 2010 Moring and Lloyd, 2013 Schreiber, 2014
	New literacy studies	Buschman, 2009 Hicks, 2016 Nicholson, 2014 Papen, 2013
	Community of practice	McCluskey-Dean, 2020
Sociocultural	Cultural capital	Folk, 2019
	Social capital	Lloyd, Pilerot and Hultgren, 2017 Widén, Ahmad and Huvila, 2021
	Sociocultural	Limberg, Sundin and Talja, 2012 Lloyd, 2010 Lundh, Limberg and Lloyd, 2013 Lupton and Bruce, 2010 Wang, Bruce and Hughes, 2011

Continued

Table 1 *Continued*

Sociopolitical	Plural agonistics	Rivano Eckerdal, 2017
	Resistant spectatorship theory	Tewell, 2016
	Theory of public sphere	Andersen, 2006; Whitworth, 2014
Sociotechnical	Activity theory	Abdallah, 2013; Hall, Cruickshank and Ryan, 2018; Kurttila-Matero, Huotari and Kortelainen, 2010
	Sociotechnical	Tuominen, Savolainen and Talja, 2005

Key themes in the literature

The ideological approach (Street, 2003) to information literacy represents a variety of conceptual standpoints and ways of understanding about how the practice emerges and is enacted as a situated practice. These perspectives have opened up the subject area to a deeper understanding about the intricate layers that constitute the landscape of information literacy research. Analysis of theoretical literature to date demonstrates that these layers are represented by several overarching themes, including tension between agency and enactment; the legitimacy of information; the moral imperative of information literacy; the socially situated shape of information literacy and marginalisation. These themes are represented in Table 2 and explored in detail below.

Table 2 *Themes from theoretical literature*

1. Tensions between agency and enactment	Abdallah, 2013; Haider and Sundin, 2022; Hall, Cruickshank and Ryan, 2018; Pilerot, 2016; Schreiber, 2017; Sundin, 2015
2. The legitimacy of information	Hicks, 2018; Lloyd, 2007 and 2017; Lloyd and Hicks, 2021; Lloyd, Pilerot and Hultgren, 2017; Moring and Lloyd, 2013; Rivano Eckerdal, 2011; Schreiber, 2014; Widén, Ahmad and Huvila, 2021
3. The moral imperative of information literacy	Bezerra, 2021; Bruce, Edwards and Lupton, 2006; Buschman, 2009; Budd and Suorsa, 2019; Elmborg, 2006; Flierl and Maybee, 2020; Hicks, 2016; Jacobs, 2008; Kuhlthau, 1993; Limberg and Sundin, 2006; Lupton and Bruce, 2010; Nicholson, 2014; McCluskey-Dean, 2020; Smith, 2015; Tewell, 2016; Walton, 2017; Wang, Bruce and Hughes, 2011
4. The socially situated shape of information literacy	Andersen, 2006; Gullbekk, 2016; Hicks and Lloyd, 2021a and 2021b; Johansson, 2012; Kapitzke, 2003; Limberg, Sundin and Talja, 2012; Lloyd, 2010 and 2017; Lundh, Limberg and Lloyd, 2013; Multas and Hirvonen, 2019; Papen, 2013; Pawley, 2003; Rivano Eckerdal, 2017; Simmons, 2005; Tuominen, Savolainen and Talja, 2005; Whitworth, 2014
5. Marginalisation	Folk, 2019; Morrison, 2017 and 2018; Quiñonez and Olivas, 2020; Rapchak, 2019

Themes

1 Tension between agency and enactment

Questions about how agency is exercised are central to information literacy research and often implicit in research discussions. They can be addressed and discussed in relation to both actors and the contexts in which they act or the material objects that they interact with. Sociocultural theories embrace agency through claims of subjective and/or intersubjective construction. Subjects unavoidably act in relation to various communities that strive for intersubjectivity. Such communities are infused by collectively and historically shaped rules, norms and conventions. Adhering to these necessitates ongoing negotiation between subjective and intersubjective knowledge claims. According to such a stance, information literacy is a socially negotiated practice enacted in relation to what is deemed important to know in a specific community. Information literacy is thus socioculturally shaped and collectively expected to be carried out in a more or less specific way that correlates with the interests of the community in which it is enacted.

The notion of agency, furthermore, must be understood in relation to rationality. If the autonomous skills-based approach to information literacy assumes a logic characterised by rational instrumentality, where people solely act in line with preconceived goals for what to accomplish, sociocultural theories, as well as practice and critical theories, question rational instrumentality as the main driver of human action. The epistemic conditions and ontological arrangements of information literacy practice are cast – and recast over again – in a dynamic ecology of subjectivity and intersubjectivity, where agency is dispersed over people and material objects. In particular, according to theories of sociomateriality, the ways in which a certain setting is ordered, arranged and equipped with material objects – i.e. information and communication technologies and their configurations, contribute to shape information literacy practices. Including the notion of distributed agency in analyses of information literacy practices allows for observation of how events such as breakdowns, manipulations and supervision contribute to enable and constrain information literacy practices. A common strand in social theorising of the sort dealt with here is consequently to conceptualise information literacy as a practice that is mutually shaped by the setting in which it is enacted, including the tools used for searching and using information and the subjectivities among those who engage in the practice.

2 Legitimacy of information

A second theme identified in the literature, albeit one that is often only implied, is the discussion about what counts as information within information literacy research and which truths or ways of knowing about the world stabilise information into knowledge. Traditionally, information literacy research has favoured rational forms of knowledge, which has centred the mind and cognitive approaches to learning. The legitimisation of these forms of knowledge has subsequently created a tension in information literacy research because it disregards or relegates other forms of knowledge as less important, including social, nuanced and corporeal and embodied knowledge, as less important (Lloyd, 2014).

More recent research has, however, demonstrated that these 'secondary' forms of knowledge are essential to lived experiences and to developing a way of knowing about the paths, nodes and edges that constitute an information landscape (Lloyd, 2017). Within this literature, theory is consequently employed to draw out and challenge the traditional emphasis on rational knowledge, including by exploring how information literacy is negotiated in relation to the dynamics of social relations and the presentation and reading of the human body. This research, in turn, challenges understandings about the accepted information activities and outcomes of information literacy practice, including the conditions that structure the establishment of prevailing discursive practices.

3 The moral imperative of information literacy

A third theme found within theoretical work relates to the moral imperative of information literacy or the idea that being informed constitutes an inherent 'moral good' for society. Information literacy has always been imbued with a wide variety of social aims; from the nation-building goals that were referenced within early information literacy documents (e.g. National Commission on Excellence in Education, 1983) to developmental and wealth-creation goals referenced in international policy briefs (Pilerot and Lindberg, 2011). More recently, attention has been focused on the contributions that information literacy makes to the advancement of human rights, as well as broader claims of social justice (e.g. Goldstein, 2020). Theory is consequently employed to extend these claims, including improving the ways in which these benefits are made available or taught to people. At the same time, the underlying premise that information literacy constitutes a uniquely affirmative (Hicks and Lloyd, 2022) or virtuous activity remains unchallenged, even when information literacy is employed within contexts and for purposes that directly challenge many of the espoused goals found in standards and frameworks (Haider and Sundin, 2022). Relatedly, there is little interrogation of the benefits of becoming informed or of whether the advantages that these pedagogies bring can be attained in any other way. While research is starting to challenge inferences about the connections between information literacy and empowerment (e.g. Hicks and Lloyd, 2022; Lee et al., 2021), it is clear that there is scope for theoretically informed responses to these questions.

4 The socially situated shape of information literacy

A fourth theme within theoretical literature is the positioning of information literacy as a socially situated practice that is shaped by normative values relative to the context and setting. Focusing attention on the discursive norms and understandings that shape information literacy rather than the specific modalities of information that are legitimised within these spaces, research in this vein encompasses the social and political aspects of information literacy's emergence, including the discourses and genres that shape conditions for learning. Often mobilised in opposition to the early positioning of information literacy as a neutral and apolitical concept, this literature also challenges thinking about how library and wider information literacy discourses are distributed, as well as the open-ended shape of social practices. As a result, theory forms the means to unpack infrastructures that shape information literacy practice, while further interrogating how these ideas are reified and assimilated into everyday practice, including in the creation of inward or outward narratives (Hicks and Lloyd, 2021a). Drawing attention to collective enterprise, a focus on the accepted ways of doing information literacy means that theory also highlights the social conditions that enable and constrain practice. Theory is additionally employed to introduce a distinct political or ideological framing to information literacy, which further embeds questions of authority and power within the field.

5 Marginalisation

The final and least-explored theme within theoretical information literacy research relates to marginalisation within information literacy, including how key aspects of research and practice have (and continue to) actively discriminate against certain groups and communities. Centred on questions of power and privilege, this area of research is fraught with tensions as researchers begin to unpack how the 'othering' of lived experience has relegated culturally, socially, physically, or economically disadvantaged and disenfranchised groups within the community. This includes how specific forms of knowledge (including indigenous, oral and local) have been consigned to the sidelines of information literacy practice, which has effectively suppressed ways of knowing that are significant to a community. The privileging of information literacy as a product of western library-based research and educational practices, for example, has been little acknowledged within scholarship, even as critical information literacy becomes more established in the field (Leung and López-McKnight, 2020). Other areas of marginalisation still remain underexplored, including those relating to ableism and disability (Hicks, 2022). Within this framing, theory is used to critique or ask pointed questions about existing understandings of information literacy, including drawing attention to oversights and gaps within the field as well as challenging accepted approaches to social justice. However, the potential scope of this work as well as broader sociopolitical tensions related to questions of diversity and inclusion means that recent applications of critical race theory and theories of social capital to information literacy research are a single step forward in this space.

Next steps

The purpose of this Introduction is to examine how theory enables us to conceptualise information literacy practice from different social and material perspectives and to account for the lived experience, conditions and arrangements that enable information literacy to be enacted. Findings from this brief review demonstrate that, unlike what may be assumed, theory has a long history within information literacy research and encompasses various themes and emphases. Furthermore, the suggested gap between scholars and practitioners may be less pronounced than has previously been implied (Williamson and Julien, 2011); with practitioners being represented in each of the five themes and the marginalisation theme being almost entirely driven by practitioner activism. At the same time, it is interesting to see what grows or diminishes in importance when non-theoretical information literacy literature is stripped away. Whitworth's (2014) content analysis of information literacy literature, for example, suggests that the field is dominated by themes of 'competency' and 'learning to learn', which are themes that do not appear in theoretical literature, with 'social impact' and 'practice' forming the only overlaps with findings from this study. Similarly, there is little synergy between theoretical literature reviewed for this study and Onyancha's (2020) categorisation of information literacy literature as marked by an evolution from computers through the internet to learning, although the importance of context is shared across both studies. Demonstrating the importance of qualitative reviews of information literacy work, these findings also highlight the need for a more nuanced consideration of the role that theory plays within information literacy research and practice.

The book will now provide an opportunity for each chapter author to present, interrogate and discuss their theory in relation to information literacy. Drawing on many of the themes that have been identified through this brief survey of information literature, chapters also establish the groundwork for new areas of interest. These themes and contributions will be explored through a meta-analysis of all 13 chapters in the Conclusion. In performing this additional analytical work, we will continue to challenge outdated assumptions about the role that theory plays within information literacy research and practice, while further advancing the contributions that conceptual work can make to the development of understanding about informed ways of knowing. As part of this process, we hope that readers of this book will take away a deeper understanding of theory, a greater knowledge of theory as it is applied to information literacy and a more complex understanding of the sociality of information literacy more generally.

References

Abdallah, N. B. (2013) Activity Theory as a Framework for Understanding Information Literacy. In Kurbanoğlu, S., Grassian, E., Mizrachi, D., Catts, R., Špiranec, S. (eds) *Worldwide Commonalities and Challenges in Information Literacy Research and Practice*, ECIL 2013. *Communications in Computer and Information Science*, 397, 93–9.

Andersen, J. (2006) The Public Sphere and Discursive Activities: information literacy as sociopolitical skills, *Journal of Documentation*, 62 (2), 213–28.

Barad, K. (1996) Meeting the Universe Halfway: realism and social constructivism without contradiction. In *Feminism, Science and the Philosophy of Science*, Springer, 161–94.

Bezerra, A. C. (2021) From Critical Information Literacy to a Critical Theory of Information, *International Review of Information Ethics*, 30 (1).

Bruce, C., Edwards, S. and Lupton, M. (2006) Six Frames for Information Literacy Education: a conceptual framework for interpreting the relationships between theory and practice, *Innovation in Teaching and Learning in Information and Computer Sciences*, 5 (1), 1–18.

Budd, J. M. and Suorsa, A. (2019) A Phenomenological Imperative for Information Literacy. In *Information Literacy in Everyday Life*, ECIL 2018. *Communications in Computer and Information Science*, 989, 233–43.

Buschman, B. J. (2009) Information Literacy, 'New' Literacies and Literacy, *Library Quarterly*, 79 (1), 95–118.

Carlsson, H. and Sundin, O. (2017) Searching for Delegated Knowledge in Elementary Schools, *Information Research*, 22 (1).

Christian, B. (1988) The Race for Theory, *Feminist Studies*, 14 (1), 67–79.

Elmborg, J. (2006) Critical Information Literacy: implications for instructional practice, *Journal of Academic Librarianship*, 32 (2), 192–9.

Flierl, M. and Maybee, C. (2020) Refining Information Literacy Practice: examining the foundations of information literacy theory, *IFLA Journal*, 46 (2), 124–32.

Folk, A. L. (2019) Reframing Information Literacy as Academic Cultural Capital: a critical and equity-based foundation for practice, assessment and scholarship, *College & Research Libraries*, 80 (5), 658–73.

Goldstein, S. (ed.) (2020) *Informed Societies*, Facet Publishing.

Gullbekk, E. (2016) Apt Information Literacy? A case of interdisciplinary scholarly communication, *Journal of Documentation*, 72 (4), 716–36.

Haider, J. and Sundin, O. (2022) *Paradoxes of Media and Information Literacy: the crisis of information*, Routledge.

Hall, H., Cruickshank, P. and Ryan, B. (2018) Exploring Information Literacy Through the Lens of Activity Theory. In Kurbanoğlu, S., Boustany, J., Špiranec, S., Grassian, E., Mizrachi, D., Roy, L. (eds) *Information Literacy in the Workplace*, ECIL 2017. *Communications in Computer and Information Science*, 810.

Hicks, A. (2016) Reframing Librarian Approaches to International Student Information Literacy Through the Lens of New Literacy Studies. In McNicol, S. (ed.) *Critical Literacy For Information Professionals*, 43–56, Facet Publishing.

Hicks, A. (2018) The Theory of Mitigating Risk: information literacy and language-learning in transition, PhD dissn, Högskolan I Borås, Sweden.

Hicks, A. (2022) A Difference that Matters: disability activism, scholarship and community, *Journal of Information Literacy*, 16 (1), 1–3.

Hicks, A. and Lloyd, A. (2021a) Deconstructing Information Literacy Discourse: peeling back the layers in higher education, *Journal of Library and Information Science*, 53 (4), 559–71.

Hicks, A. and Lloyd, A. (2021b) Relegating Expertise: the outward and inward positioning of librarians in information literacy education, *Journal of Librarianship and Information Science*, 54 (3), 415–26.

Hicks, A. and Lloyd, A. (2022) Agency and Liminality During the COVID-19 Pandemic: why information literacy can't fix vaccine hesitancy, *Journal of Information Science*, https://doi.org/10.1177/01655515221124003.

Jacobs, H. L. M. (2008) Information Literacy and Reflective Pedagogical Praxis, *Journal of Academic Librarianship*, 34 (3), 256–62.

Johansson, V. (2012) A Time and Place for Everything? Social visualisation tools and critical literacies, PhD dissn, University of Borås, Sweden.

Kapitzke, C. (2003) (In) Formation Literacy: a positivist epistemology and a politics of (out) formation, *Educational Theory*, **53** (1), 37–53.

Kuhlthau, C. C. (1993) A Principle of Uncertainty for Information Seeking, *Journal of Documentation*, **49** (4), 339–55.

Kurttila-Matero, E., Huotari, M. L. and Kortelainen, T. (2010) Conceptions of Teaching and Learning in the Context of a School Library Project: preliminary findings of a follow-up study, *Libri*, **60** (3), 203–17.

Leckie, G. J., Given, L. M. and Buschman, J. (eds) (2010) *Critical Theory for Library and Information Science: exploring the social from across the disciplines*, Libraries Unlimited.

Lee, C., Yang, T., Inchoco, G. D., Jones, G. M. and Satyanarayan, A. (2021) Viral Visualizations: how coronavirus skeptics use orthodox data practices to promote unorthodox science online. In *Proceedings of the 2021 Chi Conference on Human Factors in Computing Systems*, https://doi.org/10.1145/3411764.3445211.

Leung, S. Y. and López-McKnight, J. R. (2020) Dreaming Revolutionary Futures: Critical Race's centrality to ending white supremacy, *Communications in Information Literacy*, **14** (1), 12–26.

Limberg, L. and Sundin, O. (2006) Teaching Information Seeking: relating information literacy education to theories of information behaviour, *Information Research*, **12** (1).

Limberg, L., Sundin, O. and Talja, S. (2012) Three Theoretical Perspectives on Information Literacy, *Human IT: Journal for Information Technology Studies as a Human Science*, **11** (2), 93–130.

Lloyd, A. (2005) Information Literacy: different contexts, different concepts, different truths? *Journal of Librarianship and Information Science*, **37** (2), 82–8.

Lloyd, A. (2007) Learning to Put Out the Red Stuff: becoming information literate through discursive practice, *Library Quarterly*, **77** (2), 181–98.

Lloyd, A. (2010) Framing Information Literacy as Information Practice: site ontology and practice theory, *Journal of Documentation*, **66** (2), 245–58.

Lloyd, A. (2014) Informed Bodies: does the corporeal experience matter to information literacy practice? In Bruce, C. (ed.) *Information Experience: approaches to theory and practice*. Emerald Group Publishing.

Lloyd, A. (2017) Information Literacy and Literacies of Information: a mid-range theory and model, *Journal of Information Literacy*, **11** (1), 91–105.

Lloyd, A. (2021) *The Qualitative Landscape of Information Literacy Research: perspectives, methods and techniques*, Facet Publishing.

Lloyd, A. and Hicks, A. (2021) Contextualising Risk: the unfolding information work and practices of people during the COVID-19 Pandemic, *Journal of Documentation*, **77** (3), 1052–72.

Lloyd, A., Pilerot, O. and Hultgren, F. (2017) The Remaking of Fractured Landscapes: supporting refugees in transition (SpiRiT), *Information Research*, **22** (3).

Lundh, A. H., Limberg, L. and Lloyd, A. (2013) Swapping Settings: researching information literacy in workplace and in educational contexts. In *Eighth International Conference On Conceptions of Library and Information Science (Colis8)*, Copenhagen, Denmark, 19–22 August.

Lupton, M. and Bruce, C. (2010) Windows on Information Literacy Worlds: generic, situated and transformative perspectives. In Lloyd, A. and Talja, S. (eds) *Practising Information Literacy: bringing theories of learning, practice and information literacy together*, 4–27.

McCluskey-Dean, C. (2020) Identifying and Facilitating a Community of Practice in Information Literacy In Higher Education, PhD dissn, Robert Gordon University, UK.

Moring, C. and Lloyd, A. (2013) Analytical Implications of Using Practice Theory in Workplace Information Literacy Research, *Information Research*, 18 (3).

Morrison, K. L. (2017) Informed Asset-Based Pedagogy: coming correct, counter-stories from an information literacy classroom, *Library Trends*, 66 (2), 176–218.

Morrison, K. L. (2018) Counter-Story as Curriculum: autoethnography, critical race theory, and informed assets in the information literacy classroom, PhD dissn, Queensland University of Technology.

Multas, A. M. and Hirvonen, N. (2019) Employing Nexus Analysis in Investigating Information Literacy, *Information Research*, 24 (4).

National Commission on Excellence in Education (1983) *A Nation at Risk: the imperative for educational reform*, US Department of Education.

Nicholson, K. (2014) Information Literacy as a Situated Practice in the Neoliberal University. In *Proceedings of the Annual Conference of CAIS/Actes du Congrès Annuel de l'ACSI*, https://doi.org/10.29173/cais864.

Onyancha, O. B. (2020) Knowledge Visualization and Mapping of Information Literacy, 1975–2018, *IFLA Journal*, 46 (2), 107–23.

Papen, U. (2013) Conceptualising Information Literacy as Social Practice: a study of pregnant women's information practices, *Information Research*, 18 (2).

Pawley, C. (2003) Information Literacy: a contradictory coupling, *Library Quarterly*, 73 (4), 422–52.

Pilerot, O. (2016) A Practice-Based Exploration of the Enactment of Information Literacy among PhD Students in an Interdisciplinary Research Field, *Journal of Documentation*, 72 (3), 414–34.

Pilerot, O. and Lindberg, J. (2011) The Concept of Information Literacy in Policy-Making Texts: an imperialistic project?, *Library Trends*, 60 (2), 338–60.

Quiñonez, T. L. and Olivas, A. P. (2020) Validation Theory and Culturally Relevant Curriculum in the Information Literacy Classroom, *Urban Library Journal*, 26 (1).

Rapchak, M. (2019) That Which Cannot be Named: the absence of race in the framework for information literacy for higher education, *Journal of Radical Librarianship*, 5, 173–96.

Rivano Eckerdal, J. (2011) To Jointly Negotiate a Personal Decision: a qualitative study on information literacy practices in midwifery counselling about contraceptives at youth centres in southern Sweden, *Information Research*, 16 (1).

Rivano Eckerdal, J. (2017) Libraries, Democracy, Information Literacy and Citizenship: an agonistic reading of central library and information studies' concepts, *Journal of Documentation*, 73 (5), 1010–33.

Schreiber, T. (2014) Conceptualizing Students' Written Assignments in the Context of Information Literacy and Schatzki's Practice Theory, *Journal of Documentation*, 70 (3), 346–63.

Schreiber, T. (2017) E-learning Objects and Actor-Networks as Configuring Information Literacy Teaching, *Information Research*, 22 (1).

Simmons, M. H. (2005) Librarians as Disciplinary Discourse Mediators: using genre theory to move toward critical information literacy, *portal: Libraries and the Academy*, 5 (3), 297–311.

Smith, L. (2015) Critical Information Literacy and Political Agency: a critical, phenomenographic and personal construct study of young people's experiences of political information, PhD dissn, University of Strathclyde, UK.

Sonnenwald, D. H. (ed.) (2016) *Theory Development in the Information Sciences*, University of Texas Press.

Street, B. (2003) The Limits of the Local: 'autonomous' or 'disembedding', *International Journal of Learning*, 10 (1), 2825–30.

Sundin, O. (2015) Invisible Search: information literacy in the Swedish curriculum for compulsory schools, *Nordic Journal of Digital Literacy*, 10 (4), 193–209.

Sundin, O. and Carlsson, H. (2016) Outsourcing Trust to the Information Infrastructure in Schools: how search engines order knowledge in education practices, *Journal of Documentation*, 72 (6), 990–1007.

Tewell, E. (2016) Toward the Resistant Reading of Information: Google, resistant spectatorship and critical information literacy, *portal: Libraries and the Academy*, 16 (2), 289–310.

Tuominen, K., Savolainen, R. and Talja, S. (2005) Information Literacy as a Sociotechnical Practice, *Library Quarterly*, 75 (3), 329–45.

Walton, G. (2017) Information Literacy is a Subversive Activity: developing a research-based theory of information discernment, *Journal of Information Literacy*, 11 (1), 137–55.

Wang, L., Bruce, C. and Hughes, H. (2011) Sociocultural Theories and their Application in Information Literacy Research and Education, *Australian Academic & Research Libraries*, 42 (4), 296–308.

Whitworth, A. (2014) *Radical Information Literacy: reclaiming the political heart of the IL movement*, Elsevier Science & Technology.

Widén, G., Ahmad, F. and Huvila, I. (2021) Connecting Information Literacy and Social Capital to Better Utilise Knowledge Resources in the Workplace, *Journal of Information Science*, https://doi.org/10.1177/01655515211060531.

Williamson, K. and Julien, H. (2011) Discourse and Practice in Information Literacy and Information Seeking: gaps and opportunities, *Information Research*, 16 (1).

1
Democracy and Information Literacy

John Buschman

Introduction

Both democracy and information literacy are, in an intertwined way, severely challenged now (see Taylor et al., 2022; Jaeger and Taylor, 2021), calling for some reflection and analysis. The well-established connection between them serves as a political and civic *reason for* information literacy in democratic societies: a 'theory in the form of the dominant paradigm' (Wolin, 1968, 151). Information literacy so construed is a building block of one theoretical construction of citizenship. Establishing the dominant paradigm and its persistence will generate a reflection and unpacking of the IL–democratic theory relationship that will be theoretically richer. To accomplish this, the first section identifies a work in library and information science (LIS) that captured and axiomatically stated the information literacy paradigm. That theory-in-the-form-of-a-dominant-paradigm is then briefly traced back and through its persistence in LIS thinking about democracy and libraries. In the second section a democratic theory is identified as the rootstock of the dominant IL–democracy paradigm. It is interrogated to unpack its assumptions and empirical lacunae of particular relevance. The third section will produce a more complex theoretical understanding of the evidence, the normative values of information literacy in democratic societies and the actual role of libraries and information literacy in them and then will offer a conclusion.

Information literacy and democracy: the dominant LIS paradigm

It is important to state clearly a working assumption: the gigantic changes from 1776 to 1914 – the American, French and Industrial Revolutions, colonialism, socialism, the British Empire and the rise of secularism to name a few – demand a focus on Britain to adequately understand them. It is the same for the USA from World War 1 to the fall of the Soviet Union, and is arguably still core to knowing the state of democracy and the world (Buschman, 2022, 11). Political science and political theory (from which this chapter draws) follows this pattern (Katznelson and Milner, 2002, 3–5), as does LIS, broadly. *Libraries and Democracy: the cornerstones of liberty* (Kranich, 2001), a volume described as 'prophetic' (Waters, 2001, 61) in its contemporaneity with the 'recent tragic events in New York and Washington' on 9/11 (Cope, 2001, 383), was recognised at the time as a capstone to the IL–democracy paradigm for its 'aggressive advocacy' (Moon, 2001, 183) for 'the relationship of libraries and democracies' (Dugan, 2001, 486), earning a recommended place in all professional and LIS collections (Waters, 2001, 61). The topic was Nancy Kranich's American Library Association (ALA) presidential year theme in 2000–2001 and in the 20-year retrospective on the book she stated it set out the 'defining narrative' on 'the relationship between libraries and democracy' (Kranich, 2020, 122). The book represented a distillation of ideas about both information literacy and democracy long deployed in the LIS literature. They are condensed as five axioms in the preface (Kranich, 2001, v):

1 'An informed public constitutes the very foundation of a democracy'
2 libraries 'provide opportunities for citizens to develop the skills needed to gain access to information of all kinds and to put information to effective use'
3 libraries 'disseminate information so the public can participate in the processes of governance', which includes 'access to government information [to] monitor the work of its elected officials and benefit from the data collected and distributed'
4 'democracies are about discourse . . . Ultimately discourse among informed citizens assures civil society'
5 'Democracies need libraries. . . . They are the cornerstone of democracy'.

McCook (2001) and Lenker (2016, 512) give particularly good précis of the policies around these axioms.

The axioms display the branding of modern LIS, but these ideas were widespread in the late 18th century and in fact existed for more than three centuries (Schudson, 1998, 69–72; 2018, 143). Thomas Jefferson in 1787 argued to:

> give [the people] full information of their affairs through the channel of the public papers and to contrive that those papers should penetrate the whole mass of the people. . . . [W]ere it left to me to decide whether we should have a government without newspapers, or newspapers without a government, I should not hesitate a moment to prefer the latter. But I should mean that every man should receive those papers and be capable of reading them.
> (Koch and Peden, 1944, 411–12)

Over his lifetime Jefferson contemplated something akin to information literacy by linking literacy, publicly supported education and the practical goods of transacting business and protecting one's interest and rights in the process (in 1782) and later (in 1809) linking those ideas to lending libraries to foster a 'tolerable knowledge' of history in order for the people to be the 'safe guardians of their . . . rights' – and he founded the Library of Congress, the University of Virginia and its library (in Buschman, 2012, 26–7). James

Madison similarly wrote in 1822 that 'A popular government without popular information, or the means of acquiring it, is but a Prologue to a Farce or a Tragedy; or perhaps both . . . a people who mean to be their own Governors must arm themselves with the power which knowledge gives' (Meyers, 1973, 437).

These ideas evolved through the 19th century and the development of representative democracy, emblematically in ballot reforms and 'informational' and 'educational' campaigning (Schudson, 2018, 141–3) and then in early 20th-century reforms of 'direct primaries, the initiative, the referendum and the recall' as the tools 'only an informed and empowered populace could [use to] truly win the battle to regulate and control capital in the interests of the country as a whole' (Goodwin, 2013, 629). The mid-20th century brought LIS scholarship from Ditzion (1947) and Shera (1949) that sought to establish the link between the development of American democracy, early public education and public libraries' founding. 1947 and 1952 saw the *Public Library Inquiry* cast LIS as a 'sustaining contributor to American democracy' and complementary national library policies for the remainder of the century (McCook, 2001, 30–1). 'Library professionals . . . prefer to envision a society in which information literacy plays a positive role in enhancing the quality of public engagement' (Pawley, 2003, 443) and the axioms and their surrounding ideas dominate Kranich's 2001 volume. For instance, 'citizenship' and its variations appear in it over 200 times. These ideas recur and remain stable (see Buschman, forthcoming; Taylor et al., 2022; Cloudesley, 2021; McCook and Bossaller, 2018; Downey, 2016). When researching information literacy–democracy concepts, one quickly reaches data saturation both 'when data collection ceases to provide new information and when relationships and patterns . . . are fully developed' and theoretical saturation when the 'data categories are 'full' (i.e. fully depicted . . .) in terms of their properties and dimensions' (Powers and Knapp, 2011, 166, 185).

Public dissemination of information and a free press linked to knowledge gathered from library reading to know one's interests and rights and reformed politics subject to informed voters are not difficult themes to find in current publications. Cooke's (2022) discussion of fake news, biased/inaccurate news, misleading/ambiguous news, false connections, false context, manipulated content (48–9) is countered, she argues, by multiple literacies for citizens: critical information literacy, digital literacy and visual literacy, cultural literacy (cultural competence), news literacy and metaliteracy (53–4). Others argue that 'Teaching students to think independently, by pursuing multiple sources of knowledge, is the gateway to engaged learning and a critical citizenry. . . . Students need knowledge and skills that afford a threefold approach to participation in public life: becoming informed, debating ideas and taking action' (Jovanovic, Damasceno and Schwartzman, 2021, 133, 139; see also Mehra, 2021) and that 'Information literacy is a fundamental contribution of libraries to their patrons and to their communities for education, employment, engagement and enjoyment. It is also a contribution that supports the health and robustness of democratic societies' (Jaeger and Taylor, 2021, 23; see also Jaeger et al., 2022). So as not to be left implied, the argument here is that separately delineated literacies share a critical-intellectual foundation that is not effaced by differing modalities: 'critical reflexivity became the central point of efforts in dealing with information and information systems in all their formats' (Buschman, 2009, 110).

LIS professional organisations also weigh in: 'The International Federation of Library Associations has . . . taken on the topic of fake news . . . with statements highlighting digital literacy as 'essential to a democratic society and an engaged citizenry' and the role of librarians as information evaluation experts' (Singh and Brinster, 2022, 116–17). They do so because 'Generations of people feel disconnected from democratic values because they do not see their practical relevance. . . . More than ever, young people need to know . . . how to take a more critical approach to the information they find and how to communicate effectively within society's new virtual realm' (Derbaix, 2021; see also Stauffer, 2022). As the Public Library Association put it (in Mehra, 2021, 143), the idea is that 'acting on behalf of the public library to increase public funds and ensure that it has the resources needed to be up to date' is a form of advocacy for democracy and its citizens. An extensive discourse analysis is unnecessary to identify Kranich's five LIS axioms underwriting this literature: an informed public, democratic decision making, monitoring of government, informational skill development, access to information and effective use of it, active citizenship, democratic discourse and civil society. This ongoing narrative tradition appears frequently, representing a welding of information literacy to democracy resulting in a theory-in-the-form-of-a-dominant-paradigm.

From information literacy to a democratic theory, from a democratic theory to information literacy problems

Civic republicanism: the democratic theory underwriting information literacy axioms

A way to unpack this dominant paradigm is to turn to the rich theoretical literature of democracy – a topic which must be narrowed. In the 1980s, political theory 'even narrowly defined, encompasses an unmanageably large literature' (Galston, 1993, 27) and growth has only accelerated since. This effort will focus only on the democratic theory from which it draws. Unlike political philosophy, which attempts to give concepts and language precision to test relationships, compatibilities and outcomes for logical clarity and logically coherence (Hampton, 1997; Wolin, 2004, 8, 12), democratic theory is about the workings and failings of democracy (Shapiro, 2002, 235; Wolin, 2004, 504), blending theoretical and empirical realities of politics in the world. Separated, empirical description is empty and method-driven and theoretical prescription banal. For instance, empirically we know there has been a decline in political participation, but simply documenting the phenomenon does not tell us why we should care about that (Schlozman, 2002). (For a very short example describing a purely theoretical debate, see Hogan, 2000, 17.) Each productively informs the other and links to actual democratic practices and contexts (Benhabib, 2002, 411; Galston, 1993, 33; Shapiro, 2002, 235; Walt, 2002, 199; Robbin, Courtright and Davis, 2004, 462). An active, informed citizenry is the connective tissue between information literacy and democracy and our pathway into a democratic theory. Classically, 'citizen' has two differing meanings: chronologically first is the *subject* of a state of whatever type with attendant privileges and duties; second are citizens in democratic societies with a heritage of political rights (Crick, 2007, 243). The second meaning is the dominant modern understanding of citizenship, but the democratic theory information literacy draws upon inflects it with the 'importance of virtues . . . required by the priorities and functions of democratic practices' – that is, responsibilities to be *good* citizens in the interests of both their rights and democratic society (Mara, 2008, 238).

John Stuart Mill's thinking on representative democracy illustrates the idea. A modern précis of his thought states that 'ordinary citizens should be actively involved in the governance of local public institutions and voluntary associations and participation was more than just a means to protect the interests of the governed from the arbitrary exercise of power by the government. It was also a mechanism of moral education and a means of promoting the public good' (Hogan, 2000, 24). This is by now familiar: stir in information-seeking skills and the institution to support it (libraries) and one arrives at Kranich's IL/LIS axioms. They are derived from this root and form the dominant LIS paradigm functioning as a theory. Mill's ideas in turn are a modern version of civic republicanism, a very old ideal of citizen 'active participation in the exercise of political power' as intrinsically valuable and a necessary burden to secure liberties (Kymlicka, 2002, 294–5). It is no longer characterised by the ancient Greek and Roman duties of military service or holding office, but the theoretical link remains between civic activity, the virtue of citizens, the common good, securing liberty and contemporary democracy (Honohan, 2007; Gey, 1993; Hogan, 2000). 'That democratic self-government requires an actively engaged citizenry has been a truism for centuries. . . . [T]he health of . . . democracy requires citizens to perform our *public* duties and . . . the health of our *public* institutions depends . . . on widespread participation in *private* voluntary groups [in] networks of civic engagement' (Putnam, 2003, 157). Restated, this is the 'premise . . . that involvement makes better people', primarily through voting and activities like serving in voluntary organisations, neighbourhood watches, helping the less well-off, local political activities and observing basic duties such as reporting a crime or serving on a jury (Robbin, Courtright and Davis, 2004, 418; Dalton, 2006; Galston, 2007; Putnam, 2003). Civic republicanism seeks to create cohesive political values and civic virtue, often through educative institutions like schools and libraries; it is not neutral about how people go about shaping their lives and discovering and sorting values (Kymlicka, 2002, 307–15; Gey, 1993; Callan, 2004). Information literacy clearly draws from modern civic republicanism and grafts it on to 'institutions that provide predictable and effective means for influencing and monitoring public policy' (Mara, 2008, 93), in this case libraries informing democratic citizens. Entangled as it is with civic republicanism, information literacy will share in many of its challenges.

Challenges to civic republicanism – and by extension, to IL
Size and complexity
The 'state has simply outgrown the human reach and understanding of its citizens' (Walzer, 1970, 204). This takes two forms. First, *geographic size* challenged the Greek ideal of face-to-face interaction: shared institutions and culture across expanses in the Roman Republic and Italian city states became the model before the shift to representation in the nation-states of modern democracy accompanied by bureaucracies to manage complexity (Honohan, 2007; Urbinati and Warren, 2008). Second, the size and complexity of modern *mass electorates* diminish the efficacy of civic republicanism's active citizens. Federalism in the USA was specifically meant to address these two interrelated issues. Eighty years ago, Joseph Schumpeter (2001) demonstrated that achieving any coherent notion of the common good or common agreement was nearly impossible in modern mass democracy. Judge Learned Hand expressed that when he wrote in 1932 that 'My vote is one of the most unimportant acts of my life; if I were to acquaint myself with the matters on which it ought really to depend, if I were to try to get a judgment on which I was willing to risk affairs of even the smallest moment, I should be doing nothing else and that seems a fatuous conclusion to a fatuous undertaking' (Berelson, 1970, 69). There are four resulting democratic difficulties that have been around for a while: generating equality, accountability, effective participation and finding a balance between maintaining order and liberty (Przeworski, 2009, 72).

The quintessential act of the active citizen – voting for one's representative in *representative* democracy – is 'information poor' (Urbinati and Warren, 2008, 402). One is not voting for a specific set of policy outcomes but rather for a broad orientation to policy by a representative who serves many thousands of people and a political party. Scale and sociotechnical complexity also mean it takes considerable resources, time and organisation to create political change (Warren, 2017, 50; Cunningham, 2002; Robbin, Courtright and Davis, 2004, 422). To function, a wide diversity of expertise among political elites who deploy specialised discourses is needed, thereby increasing democratic difficulties (Urbinati and Warren, 2008; Warren, 1996). Last, the simplification of a complex reality such that any large bureaucracy (governmental or corporate) must undertake in order to make a problem capable of being addressed with the tools it possesses means it will often be unresponsive to specific groups and individuals being served (Scott, 2006). This sociological truism can be illustrated with the common example of work-to-rule: '[T]he formal rules and regulations . . . are never an adequate guide to the actual practice [and] to follow the rules . . . to the letter is, in fact, to bring the work to a virtual standstill' (Scott, 1999, 273). These exist before we consider globalised corporate and finance power that challenges national-level democratic controls and practices (Held, 2006, 292–3, 296 *passim*). Formal democracy is now an abstract, distant thing and 'the sense that agency is impossible is powerfully alienating, whenever citizens have pressing reasons for dissatisfactions with political outcomes', as they will (Dunn, 2010, 109). Democratic governing in any direct, meaningful sense is simply beyond the ken of the active, informed citizen, evacuating much of the substance of civic republicanism and the LIS tradition and leaving only rights.

LIS examples of the problems are not difficult to find. Dervin (1994) expands both Schumpeter and Scott in a contemporary description of the infrastructure information literacy depends upon: 'Information is defined as that which instructs and so . . . information systems are defined as transmission systems, not participation systems. This is as true for formal systems (e.g. . . . libraries . . .) as for informal procedures (e.g. town meetings . . .). When introduced into system design and operation, diversity exists in isolation without any theoretical guidance for contrast or comparison. . . . Dialogue becomes conceptualized as a throwing around of differences [and] . . . the Babel of voices . . . makes information availability and accessibility contradictory' (380). People use efficient-but-information-poor heuristics (cognitive shortcuts) 'in the face of difficult, complex issues' like information seeking for democratic policy choices (Ryfe, 2005, 51) and these widespread mechanisms often rely on groups, likeability and advertising exacerbating the problems (Carmines and Huckfeldt, 1996, 244–8; Schudson, 2006; Held, 2006, 234; Crowley, 2022; Singh and Brinster, 2022).

Those who do set out to do their own research 'can quickly become unreasonably confident after just a small amount of exposure' to finding; such beginners 'often end up becoming more misled than informed' (Ballantyne and Dunning, 2022). The choice of information in the act of research is now transactional: people choose their facts because they choose the context into which they fit, have meaning, or reinforce identities: 'The key to an intelligent assessment of a given state of affairs used to lie in seeing information in an adequate context [but] the very concept . . . falls apart. . . . Information travels across contexts and it is not clear at all which of them is the adequate one' (Slačálek, 2021; see also Cottom, 2022; Solnit, 2022). Information seeking is influenced by self-selection, making for homogenous groups (Ryfe, 2005; Singh and Brinster, 2022) and exacerbated by social technologies that reinforce identity and polarisation (Cyr, 2022; Klein, 2020). A fundamental challenge to the combined democratic values of civic republicanism and the LIS narrative tradition, these are at cross-grains to how information systems are designed (see also Chapter 7 by Johansson), how people actually seek information, how they think, decide and identify as citizens.

Disengagement and the nature of contemporary engagement

Since contemporary democracy produces strong feelings that active participation (including voting) is ineffective, the normative standards of civic republicanism are 'confronted by the reality of substantial empirical evidence. . . . Large numbers of people do not participate in the political process or civic life; civic engagement and trust have declined; and most people . . . are not well informed about political issues and have low levels of interest in politics' (Robbin, Courtright and Davis, 2004, 423; Warren, 2002, 679–80; Galston, 2001; 2007; Schlozman, 2002). If one key benefit of democracy is the liberty to make choices and shape one's life plan, many people conclude that there are better, more interesting and fulfilling things to choose than becoming active, informed citizens when faced with the barriers. Realising the goals of civic knowledge and participation closely tracks white, middle-class and college-educated people who can 'afford' the costs (Schlozman, 2002, 442–6; Galston, 2001, 222; Ryfe, 2005, 52), following the pattern of technology, information access, library programming and use (Lievrouw and Farb, 2003; Wiegand, 2015; Harris, 1986). These constrictions produce power differentials in deliberative contexts, with social class warping participation and outcomes (Young, 2001; Benhabib, 1994; Ryfe, 2005; Urbinati and Warren, 2008; Robbin, Courtright and Davis, 2004, 429–30). Civic republican and LIS/IL avenues of participatory expansion may ironically *limit* democratic participation. Significant tides within modern democracy run against the goods of civic participation and the information literacy narrative tradition.

Some political thought reflects those realities. If politics is about conflict, struggle and forging new political identities of democratic citizens (Mouffe, 1992; 2005; Rivano Eckerdal, 2017) the deliberative, informational, communal and participatory goals of civic republicanism and the information literacy axioms are not a comfortable fit. In turn, a more passionate, intensely engaged politics can be dangerous (Taylor, 2017; see also Chapter 6 by Rivano Eckerdal) and raises 'the question of how [we] might judge different exercises of political energy' when 'deliberative citizenship is continuously challenged by passionate attachments . . . under conditions that are turbulently unsettled' (Mara, 2015, 314, 326). The 6 January 2021 insurrection in the USA is the obvious example. Conversely, the political quietude anathema to active citizenship, civic republicanism and information literacy can be a sign of satisfaction, there being no compelling political reason to become informed or active (Berelson, 1970; Held, 2006, 162, 166). New political identities, conflict and engaged politics can produce unintended reactions and exclusions: political intolerance (Gibson, 2008; Edsall, 2021), pushback on remediating the legacy of systematic racism (Katznelson, 2006; Iati, 2021), or outright racial denials of citizenship rights and resources of self-sufficiency (Shklar, 1990; Blake, 2021; Bouie, 2021). Those represent political engagement too and their results are not contemplated in either civic republicanism or the LIS axioms. US schools and libraries are, as of this writing, on these very front lines with state and local pushes to take over boards, censor materials and exclude topics from libraries and curricula, leaving librarians, historians and teachers 'scrambling to respond to this legislative onslaught . . . tantamount to a state-mandated denial of foundational aspects of American history' (Hajdarpasic, 2021; see also Gowen, 2022; Bader, 2021; Natanson, 2022). A form of informed, active citizenship is now deployed to *restrict* information and inquiry in democracy, a reminder that social conflict is always lurking beneath the surface of democracies (Walker, 1970, 237).

Fake news

Fake news – we know the term is problematic and a topic LIS has extensively written on: competing and complex definitions, elements, methods, variations, sources, technology, history, effects and LIS responses to name the obvious (see Buschman, 2019; Jaeger and Taylor, 2021; 2022; Cooke, 2017 and sources already cited). Used here as a generic term (like Kleenex or Xerox), 'Fake news is now viewed as one of the greatest threats to democracy' (Zhou et al., 2019, 836) and a clear challenge to the IL–citizenship–democracy paradigm. Fake news 'can spread in part because people spreading it do not know that it is' such that, or because, 'bad-faith actors . . . motivated by profit' or power 'rather than a desire to contribute to public discourse' crowd out or diminish accurate information; libraries combat this with critical information literacy adapted to the environment (Cyr, 2022, 95, 97; Singh and Brinster, 2022; Sullivan, 2019a; 2019b). But LIS 'can't go on believing that the issue can be solved simply by flooding [people] with public service announcements or hectoring' them to believe the facts (Sreedhar and Gopal, 2021) or investigate within approved channels, as librarians tend to do. There are many factors at play that attenuate the civic republican–active citizen imaginary driving the information literacy axioms.

Citizens were more likely to share fake news they *knew* was false if it represented their political views; they did so because they were more attuned to receiving positive social media feedback for signalling their allegiances than they were to accuracy (Pennycook et al., 2021). Fake news thrives *because* people can choose their own contexts into which facts fit (Slačálek, 2021). Thus 'researching' the 'facts' mimics consumer choice (Solnit, 2022) and 'when thinking as a consumer, people tend to downplay social obligations in favour of a narrow pursuit of self-interest' (Sreedhar and Gopal, 2021). The result is a 'growing disagreement among voters over what the obligations of a good citizen are' (Edsall, 2022) since politics and government itself are themselves increasingly akin to market transactions (Cottom, 2022). These 'examples have the same social DNA: failing institutions' (Cottom, 2022) operating under the relentless market ethos of neoliberalism – just like libraries, schools and colleges (Buschman, 2022). Civic republicanism–active citizenship relies upon such institutions to shape and inform citizens, but also on the institutions of democracy itself: routine, safe and fair elections and the basic willingness to honour the results (Edsall, 2022). The evidence around fake news indicates it is as much a symptom as cause of the democratic difficulties described.

Diminution of public spheres

LIS lacks a political theory of *the fake* in fake news, a theory of political lying. Arendt (2006, 223, 247) wrote that 'No one has ever doubted that truth and politics are on rather bad terms with each other and no one . . . has ever counted truthfulness among the political virtues', secrecy and deception long being tools of politics and statecraft. The 18th-century public sphere changed the principle: 'the state [was] called upon to make its decisions before the open gaze of the reasoning citizenry [by] 'disclosure' (in business) or 'freedom of information' (in government) today. The concept was used to attack the state as a carrier of secrets. . . [and the] collective of private citizens acquires considerable power as a critical influence . . . giv[ing] birth to the democratic ideas which make constitutional states trustworthy and . . . legitimate' (Peters, 1993, 548, 544). That is, arguably the development of public spheres – as much as the civic republican tradition – produced our modern concepts of active, engaged and informed citizenship.

The 'traditional political lie' concealed recognisable 'true secrets' or intentions, but 'modern political lies deal . . . with things that are not secrets at all but are known to practically everybody' – shared meaning is threatened instead (Arendt, 2006, 247). For Arendt (who died in 1975), the outstanding example was the US government during the Vietnam War: all the facts were well known – the *Pentagon Papers* did not contain any classified military information – but 'the policy of lying was hardly ever aimed at the enemy; [it] was destined chiefly, if not exclusively, for domestic consumption' (Arendt, 1972, 14; Maret, 2013). Modern political lies are an 'attempt to change the whole context' and the 'fabric of factuality' – a radical move, since 'our apprehension of reality is dependent upon our sharing' a perception of the world with our fellow citizens: that is, in public spheres (Arendt, 2006, 248–9).

The years since have only enhanced the diminution of public spheres through lying – 'what use is fact-checking against "fact-free politics"?' (Hajdarpasic, 2021) – and fake news, the campaign for Brexit being a notable example (Dittert, 2021). US Middle East wars were fuelled over the years on political lies not dissimilar to the Vietnam era, (re)launching in the process some of the polarisation and nativism that led to 'our own citizens assault[ing] the Capitol building that al-Qaeda hoped to strike on Sept. 11, 2001' (Lozada, 2021). Equally disturbing are the similarities between fake-news methodologies used in democracies (Jaeger and Taylor, 2022) and authoritarian regimes like China to paper over the inefficacy of their own COVID vaccines and to justify massive, stringent lockdowns (Krugman, 2022) and in Russia to squash dissent, bolster Putin's dictatorial control and invade Ukraine (Koposov, 2022; Krugman, 2022). These same methods are deployed in support of anti-democratic, authoritarian and nativist politicians in parts of Eastern Europe as well (Hajdarpasic, 2021). With 'communication abundance' there are always bits and pieces easily picked up and aggregated as fake news to 'utilize as confirmation of the overall' perfidy of opponents (Slačálek, 2021). The Russian public's support of Putin during his disastrous, criminal invasion of Ukraine points to its efficacy: if the populace does not 'have access to relatively reliable information' and cannot 'openly discuss its situation, formulate various action plans and promote them in the public space [then] agreed-upon decision-making mechanisms to determine which plan is the best' means they are not 'free to make rational and responsible decisions' as democratic citizens and develop public spheres (Koposov, 2022). Fake news erodes democracy, public spheres and active citizenship in and beyond the horizon of information literacy efforts. 'Librarians are virtually unanimous in their conviction that they have a central role to play in the fight against fake news' (Sullivan, 2019a, 96). '[G]iven that the problem . . . is largely constructed in opposition to traditional library values and services, it comes as no surprise that the proposed solutions entail reaffirming those values and doubling down on those services', but 'librarians are not effectively combatting' fake news and 'in reality . . . they might not be able to do so in principle' (Sullivan, 2019b, 1148).

A reset: the empirical and the normative

Is the IL–democracy paradigm hopelessly compromised or naïve – or both? There is much evidence that suggests just that, implying that the role information literacy crafted for itself in democratic society is also vulnerable, if not a theoretical failure. If civic republicanism fails as a democratic theory, the IL–democracy paradigm also fails, since it draws so heavily from that account of democracy and citizenship. Here we arrive at a conundrum. Some version of civic republicanism has persisted for well over two millennia. Why would it have staying power if the evidence consistently contradicted it? Another political theory – monarchical divine rights – disappeared because its grounding assumptions and claims became obviously untrue. We must pull back and reframe the issue.

Democracy: a reset

Rather than essentialising information literacy (Pawley, 2003, 445) and the particular form of democratic citizenship that it implies, we must account for realities of democratic life that transcend a model built on very different assumptions: 'ancient and early modern republics were layered, hierarchical status orders [consisting of] the equality of all who are of noble birth. . . . Certainly, it was thought that martial virtue should extend throughout the community [and was a] central principles of republics from the earliest days. Over the centuries that has translated into "the underlying vision . . . of frequent participation and deliberation in the service of decision . . . about the sorts of values according to which the nation will operate." So say virtually all contemporary [civic] republicans' (Goodin, 2003, 62; 66; 67). This is untenable and calls for a reset to civic republicanism. Reframed, democracy currently:

1 is as much a culture – '"internalized rules of life that reflect a reasonable confidence" in the ability of the [democratic] political system to guarantee' rights, liberty and democratic outcomes – as it is a set of formal procedures and institutional arrangements like the rule of law or free elections (Laidi in Robbin, Courtright and Davis, 2004, 417; Blokker, 2018
2 needs – for better or worse – experts and expertise to make decisions work at scale in complex systems (Mansbridge et al., 2012)
3 must/should rely on representation because of that (Warren and Castiglione, 2004; Mansbridge 2004)
4 is the result 'not of a legislative design . . . on behalf of a coherent system of values, but of conflicts among individuals and groups acting on behalf of diverse values and ambitions' (Cohen, 1986, 465; see also Mouffe, 1992 and Rivano Eckerdal in Chapter 6); therefore it
5 often takes place outside formal politics, instead taking place in local, social and institutional settings like libraries, schools, business associations, etc. (Warren, 2017, 43; 45)

6 is 'enacted and reproduced through social actions' such as voice, recognition, resistance and protest, pressure, deliberation, voting, representing groups, joining and exit in those venues (Warren, 2017, 43, 45–51; Warren, 1996; Mansbridge et al., 2012) as well as 'dispositions and skills' like deliberation and openness or quotidian activities like running a meeting or giving a presentation (Kymlicka, 2002, 323 n. 7; 288–9; Putnam, Feldstein and Cohen, 2003, 157–9)
7 also takes place – for better or worse – through political and other media that intersect with representatives, diverse values, institutional settings, complex systems, etc. (Mansbridge et al., 2012); while it
8 must still rely upon its formal institutions as well, like elections, voting, transfer of power, rule of law, rights, juries, representation, etc. (Warren, 1996); through which it
9 is influenced by electoral politics and the appearance of agendas, issues and pressures in public spheres (Buschman, 2022; Hove, 2009) via a 'robust domain of associational interaction' (Dahlgren, 2006, 272; Schlozman, 2002, 450–1).

In the light of contemporary conditions and the backdrop of power exercised through government secrecy, democratic calls for 'access to information [as] a necessary precondition for public reason' (Mathiesen, 2015, 440), 'information literacy [as] necessary [but] not sufficient', and education to promote 'critical informational scrutiny' (Budd, 2013, 18; Gutmann, 1998) are not empty slogans. Citizenship itself still carries substantial value and protections (Howard, 2006b). Arendt noted that to be stateless or a refugee is to be without the protections of citizenship, open to radical vagaries (Arendt, 1968, 99; 149; Benhabib, 2015). Further, all societies – democratic or otherwise – must *produce* its citizens (Galston, 2001, 219), even if only 'for the sake of cultural coherence' (Gutmann, 1998, 30). In producing citizens, a democracy must be concerned with protecting rights and liberty, the legitimacy of its governing and creating the capacity for self-government; those jobs have partially fallen to institutions like schools and libraries (Gutmann, 1987; Galston, 2001; Robbin, Courtright and Davis, 2004, 423; Warren, 1996), even though both have a chequered history of fulfilling the task (Stevens and Wood, 1995, 115–35; Wiegand, 2020).

In communist countries pre-1989, the *absence* of public spheres – unfettered discourse that creates a public space of exchange – meant that 'there was no real place . . . for a spontaneous, self-started, painstaking clarification of . . . political consciousness' or historical experience (Habermas, 2020). Public spheres and their publics are 'something other than merely media audiences' (Dahlgren, 2006, 274) and the substitution of one for the other has democratic and cultural consequences. The theoretical question of the efficacy of the IL–democracy relationship should be evaluated against the other ways to conduct political life such as autocracy, monarchy, aristocracy, totalitarianism, violence, or divine revelation to give the historical examples (Kahane, 2000, 524; Arendt, 1968, 158–77). Information literacy programmes 'designed with the aim of strengthening . . . information literacy within the community to ensure that people master the abilities required for learning and engag[ement] as students, employees and citizens' (Rivano Eckerdal, 2017,

1011; see also Robbin, Courtright and Davis, 2004) look less naïve in their effects on democratic *culture*. Abandonment of these very ideas among the educative professions have been damning historical incidents paving the way for inequality, injustice and tyranny (Snyder, 2017, 38–40; Wiegand, 2020; Galston, 2001, 231–2). The effects of media-saturated flows of information in democracy was thoroughly questioned by Postman (1988) almost 40 years ago, but the stakes of rolling over and playing dead when it comes to the varieties of media and their dissemination of misinformation are simply too high (Ignatius, 2019; Maldonado, 2017). Theoretically, information literacy has as a relationship to the democratic *culture* that active citizenship implies.

Evidence for the reset: democratic politics

More nuanced ideas about democratic culture, formal democratic institutions and the effects of localities and institutions like libraries and schools on democracy result in a reset of the *theoretical* relationship between information literacy and democracy. Is there evidence to back up this account? Yes, but a qualified yes. Evidence is mixed, with hopeful signs tucked in among the worrisome ones. People still argue dialogically about democracy and politics in contemporary letters to a newspaper's editor in one large US study (Hart, 2018): 'What is said in a letter is obviously important, but the writing of the letter is even more important' . . . 'A number of options have been available to them . . . but they have chosen to stand and fight. . . . They are . . . the nation's secret weapon' for democracy (10; 24). In terms of the ups-and-downs of civic knowledge and voter participation, 'voters do not differ from non-voters in their partisan leanings or their opinions on policy matters' (Schlozman, 2002, 446) and 'levels of political knowledge among US citizens did not change over the past fifty years' (Kuklinski and Peyton, 2007, 53). Furthermore, 'in comparative terms, civic engagement in America is still alive and well', including among the young, with new venues and patterns outside traditional organisational structures (Howard, 2006a, 18; Panageotou, 2018; Stolle, 2007, 662–3). Trust in democratic government has been eroding for some time, but that may not affect democratic functioning, or may spur political engagement and worries may be misplaced because democracy relies more on *interpersonal* – not institutional – trust (Citrin and Stoker, 2018, 62; Warren, 1999, 353–4). And 'There is no systematic evidence that younger Americans are more (or less) likely to trust government than are older Americans' (Galston, 2007, 626).

The link between information, education and citizenship is not and has not been entirely severed as they are 'slow-moving sociological factors' (Citrin and Stoker, 2018, 63). Voters 'ground their beliefs and attitudes in reality': consistent with their interests, US Black voters are more liberal and all voters reflect new information in their thinking (Kuklinski and Peyton, 2007, 53). Further, 'being a member of an ethnic minority is not inimical to trust' and those who are 'more informed and educated tend to be the more trusting' of government (Patterson, 1999, 191; Galston, 2001, 224). Though now more difficult, 'given sufficient time and motivation, people [can and do] think self-consciously and reflectively' about evidence around their beliefs, especially in deliberative political environments (Kraft, Lodge and Taber, 2015, 129, 131; Warren and Gastil, 2015). Media *per se* 'do not have largely negative effects on civic participation; rather, news use appears to contribute' to it and 'news media . . . have stronger and more direct effects on . . . civic participation than entertainment television' (Keum et al., 2004, 383). This is mirrored in the effects of social media in the division between engagement and organisation for democratic debate or action and entertainment and consumer surveillance (Maldonado, 2017; Clarke and Koçak, 2019; Fuchs, 2014), which characterised social media and the COVID-19 pandemic environment (Honneth, 2020; Smith, 2020). While there are variations among democratic societies, the 'democratic deficit' and declining trust are reflected in European and other societies, too (Mansbridge, 2004; Stolle, 2007, 662; Panageotou, 2018), but political engagement and membership is still higher in more established democracies than in newer ones (Howard, 2006a, 18). The dispersion of political participation across non-electoral (social) venues and in technologies is taking place in most modern democracies (Panageotou, 2018) and globalisation makes the withdrawal of investments and consumption a powerful political tool in all of them (Panageotou, 2018; Beck, 2007). The response to the pandemic 'became an indicator for the democratic quality of . . . political systems' with those following the patterns of modern democracy (openness, expertise, public debate) performing better (Honneth, 2020).

Evidence for the reset: libraries and IL

With all the bad news, we might miss the fact that libraries are popular and much used, a theme that resonates across democratic societies. Well more than 'half the British population are members' of their local public libraries and those see 'more than ten times the total attendances at professional football games' (Webster, 1999, 376; Huysmans and Oomes, 2013). This echoes Weigand's (1999, 2) long-recited data that there are more American libraries than McDonald's restaurants, three times more questions are answered in libraries than people who attend college football games and the same ratio reflects library visits v. movie attendance. The data and underlying idea hasn't changed much in the intervening 20 years: the public still values libraries and pushes back at proposals to do away with them (Ingraham, 2018; Fiels, 2011, 12). Deploying political theory, a review of Weigand's (2015) history of American public libraries found that he documented substantial evidence of democratic values such as equality, citizenship, community, civil society and public spheres (Buschman, 2018). Other international studies at scale provide evidence of these same themes:

- *Equality*. Library usage fosters education and equity of information resources and tools, for instance in 'support for vulnerable populations' (Stenstrom, Cole and Hanson, 2019, 356, 359; Jaeger et al., 2011; Huysmans and Oomes, 2013, *passim*; Chow and Tian, 2021, 6–7) and 'findings have universally shown that students in schools with libraries, staffed by' a librarian, do better (Fiels, 2011, 12).
- *Citizenship*. Citizens themselves recognise libraries as 'critical to democracy' (Fiels, 2011, 12) and supportive of acquiring civic literacy and government information at

all levels (Huysmans and Oomes, 2013, *passim*; Jaeger et al., 2011; Milner, 2002, 128–33), which they value.
- *Community*. Many studies show library usage fosters social connection, trust and 'the quality of life in the community' (Fiels, 2011, 12; Huysmans and Oomes, 2013, *passim*; Stenstrom, Cole and Hanson, 2019, 356; Chow and Tian, 2019, 7). The 'first public act of many newcomers . . . is to get a library card. It is the first official document that connects them to their new home' (Putnam, Feldstein and Cohen, 2003, 45).
- *Civil society*. Data show that library usage is an indicator of a variety of civic engagement (Huysmans and Oomes, 2013, *passim*; Putnam, Feldstein and Cohen, 2003).
- *Public spheres*. People identified libraries as 'public space and a low threshold social meeting space', a place to find information and as a 'public sphere in its own right' in many studies (Huysmans and Oomes, 2013, 173, *passim*; Stenstrom, Cole and Hanson, 2019, 356; Putnam, Feldstein and Cohen, 2003).

The common act of defending (or founding or re-founding) a library is in itself civic engagement, engaging civil society, community and public spheres (Jaeger et al., 2013, 168; Ingraham, 2015; Halpern, 2018). And it is worth remembering that books, reading and access to information – the attributes of information literacy democratic axioms – are prime targets of repressive political regimes (White, 2019). Aggregated surveys can face the challenge of accommodating too many rivalrous explanations (Citrin and Stoker, 2018, 61), but the data are consistent and take us to civic republican citizenship and IL. The interpretation here is that these attributes are not a straight line from libraries to information to citizens to active democratic participation, but rather as indicators of democratic culture still extant in democratic societies.

Conclusion: the empirical, the normative and IL

It would be irresponsible not to acknowledge that this chapter is being written at a liminal moment: a toxic form of informational populism infecting democracy (Citrin and Stoker, 2018, 63–4) and the House Congressional hearings on the 6 January 2021 insurrection. Historically, LIS research had significant gaps in analysing the source of publications and information, how they were produced, came to be selected, what values were embedded in them and the financial underpinnings of it all (Harris, 1986). There is now significant emphasis in information literacy on the production of information, categories of mis/disinformation (Cooke, 2022; Taylor and Jaeger, 2022; Singh and Brinster, 2022; Haigh et al., 2022), epistemology, how information is structured for searching in libraries (Lenker, 2016, 522) and what cannot be found or is missing (Lilburn, 2017). Evidence indicates that democratic *cultures* receive considerable support from their libraries for the functioning of democratic *societies* and publics support and recognise library practices for the goods they do.

This is good for libraries, but in theoretical terms, what good does this do for *democracy*? Information literacy effects democracy not in the form of deep citizen knowledge of local government initiatives, who the Minister for Climate and the Environment or the Secretary of Labour is, or what the 5th Amendment or the Public Health Act of 1848 does. Rather, 'if citizens trust the institutions that they interact with most closely' in democratic societies like libraries, then 'their confidence in these close-to-home representations of government [can] mitigate distrust of more remote . . . institutions' (Citrin and Stoker, 2018, 64). Trust is implied in the active citizenship that both information literacy and civic republicanism deploy. The combination – trust and informed engagement – produces 'better places to live: the schools are better, crime rates are lower', community connections are stronger and so on (Schlozman, 2002, 437). It is why democracy is attractive: people can exercise autonomy to carry out life plans and the active citizen personally gains social and civic skills to realize them, helping to create social conditions of more equality and equal protections *en route* (Schlozman, 2002, 437–8).

When we de-link (a) financial support of libraries, (b) information literacy efforts, (c) knowledge of specific democratic information and (d) surveys about those lacks (Wiegand, 2015, 263–4), we clear the theoretical underbrush of LIS. It allows messy empirical realities to actually meet the normative goods of active citizenship in our field. If we are expecting a one-to-one result, we will be disappointed. The reset makes information literacy efforts look different in their relationship to democratic cultures in democratic societies. Analogies are helpful. Automobile accidents do not mean that driver training is useless or should be abandoned. It is meant to reduce the quotient of serious injuries and property damage under constantly changing conditions of travel. The same goes for public health measures or compulsory public education and so on. Declaring them inefficacious would be nuts. Likewise, information literacy practices are one of an ensemble of things libraries *just do* under the values and conditions of democracies. Libraries are themselves one ensemble of practices among many: schools, courts, churches, newspapers, business associations, universities, soccer clubs, parent–teacher associations, etc. Information literacy and libraries are part of an ensemble of ensembles that reinforce democratic values, practices, habits, effects and outcomes (Warren, 2017). That is what is meant by a democratic *culture* in a democratic *society* and it still exists and solves social and political problems (Allen, 2022). The information literacy axioms and the normative prescriptions they draw from civic republicanism are unrealistic. The data tell us that. We simply must come to theoretically understand better what characterises contemporary democratic societies and cultures and the ensembles of practices that support those cultures and societies. LIS efforts in information literacy are a part of *that*.

References

Allen, D. (2022) 'I Ran for Office Full of Anger and Despair. I Felt Hope When I Dropped Out', *Washington Post*, 8 June,
   www.washingtonpost.com/opinions/2022/06/08/danielle-allen-run-office-massachusetts.

Arendt, H. (1968) *The Origins of Totalitarianism: part three*, Harcourt, Brace and World.

Arendt, H. (1972) *Crises of the Republic*, Harcourt Brace & Company.

Arendt, H. (2006) *Between Past and Future*, Penguin Books.

Bader, E. J. (2021) Librarians to the Defense: groups form to fight a conservative-led attack on libraries' efforts to promote social justice, *Progressive Magazine*, 19 October, https://progressive.org/magazine/librarians-to-the-defense-bader.

Ballantyne, N. and Dunning, D. (2022) Skeptics Say, 'Do Your Own Research.' It's Not That Simple, *New York Times*, 3 January, www.nytimes.com/2022/01/03/opinion/dyor-do-your-own-research.html.

Beck, U. (2007) A New Cosmopolitanism is in the Air, *signandsight*, 20 November, www.signandsight.com/features/1603.html.

Benhabib, S. (1994) Deliberative Rationality and Models of Democratic Legitimacy, *Constellations*, 1, 26–52.

Benhabib, S. (2002) Political Theory and Political Membership in a Changing World. In Katznelson, I. and Milner, H. V. (eds) *Political Science: state of the discipline*, Centennial Edition, W. W. Norton, 404–32.

Benhabib, S. (2015) Nobody Wants to be a Refugee, *Eurozine*, 7 October, www.eurozine.com/nobody-wants-to-be-a-refugee.

Berelson, B. (1970) Survival Through Apathy. In Kariel, H. S. (ed.) *Frontiers of Democratic Theory*, Random House, 68–77.

Blake, A. (2021) Ted Cruz Makes a Texas-Size Mess on Voter ID and Racism, *Washington Post*, 23 September, www.washingtonpost.com/politics/2021/09/23/ted-cruz-makes-texas-size-mess-voter-id-racism.

Blokker, P. (2018) Democracy and Democratization: theory and research. In Outhwaite, W. and Turner, S. P. (eds) *The Sage Handbook of Political Sociology*, Sage, 622–36.

Bouie, J. (2021) If It's Not Jim Crow, What Is It? *New York Times*, 6 April, www.nytimes.com/2021/04/06/opinion/georgia-voting-law.html.

Budd, J. M. (2013) Informational Education: creating an understanding of justice, *Education, Citizenship and Social Justice*, 8, 17–28.

Buschman, J. (2009) Information Literacy, 'New' Literacies and Literacy, *Library Quarterly*, 79, 95–118.

Buschman, J. (2012) *Libraries, Classrooms and the Interests of Democracy: marking the limits of neoliberalism*, Rowman & Littlefield/Scarecrow.

Buschman, J. (2018) On Democracy and Libraries, *Library Quarterly*, 88, 23–40.

Buschman, J. (2019) Good News, Bad News and Fake News, *Journal of Documentation*, 75, 213–28.

Buschman, J. (2022) Actually-Existing Democracy and Libraries: a mapping exercise. In Taylor, N. G., Kettnich, K., Gorham, U. and Jaeger, P. (eds) *Libraries and the Global Retreat of Democracy: confronting polarization, misinformation and suppression*, Emerald, 9–43.

Buschman, J. (forthcoming) Libraries, Democracy and Citizenship: twenty years after 9/11, *Library Quarterly*.

Callan, E. (2004) Citizenship and Education, *Annual Review of Political Science*, 7, 71–90.

Carmines, E. G. and Huckfeldt, R. (1996) Political Behavior: an overview. In Goodin, R. E. and Klingemann, H.-D. (eds) *A New Handbook of Political Science*, 223–54, Oxford University Press.

Chow, A. and Tian, Q. (2021) Public Libraries Positively Impact Quality of Life: a big data study, *Public Library Quarterly*, 40, 1–32.

Citrin, J. and Stoker, L. (2018) Political Trust in a Cynical Age, *Annual Review of Political Science*, 21, 49–70.

Clarke, K. and Koçak, K. (2019) Eight Years After Egypt's Revolution, Here's What We've Learned About Social Media and Protest, *Washington Post*, 25 January, www.washingtonpost.com/news/monkey-cage/wp/2019/01/25/eight-years-after-egypts-revolution-heres-what-weve-learned-about-social-media-and-protest.

Cloudesley, S. P. (2021) 'Informed', 'Active' and 'Engaged'? Understanding and enacting information literacy from a UK citizenship perspective, *Journal of Information Literacy*, 15 (3), 20–40.

Cohen, J. (1986) Review of *Spheres of Justice: a defense of pluralism and equality* by Michael Walzer, *Journal of Philosophy*, 83, 457–68.

Cooke, N. A. (2017) Posttruth, Truthiness and Alternative Facts: information behavior and critical information consumption for a new age, *Library Quarterly*, 87, 211–21.

Cooke, N. A. (2022) A Right to be Misinformed? Considering fake news as a form of information poverty. In Taylor, N. G., Kettnich, K., Gorham, U. and Jaeger, P. (eds) *Libraries and the Global Retreat of Democracy: confronting polarization, misinformation and suppression*, Emerald, 45–60.

Cope, R. L. (2001) Future Uncertain, *Australian Library Journal*, 50, 383.

Cottom, T. M. (2022) We're All 'Experts' Now. That's Not a Good Thing, *New York Times*, 10 January, www.nytimes.com/2022/01/10/opinion/scams-were-all-experts.html.

Crick, B. (2007) Citizenship: the political and the democratic, *British Journal of Educational Studies*, 55, 235–48.

Crowley, B. (2022) Facts (Almost) Never Change Minds: libraries and the management of democracy-supporting public perceptions. In Taylor, N. G., Kettnich, K., Gorham, U. and Jaeger, P. (eds) *Libraries and the Global Retreat of Democracy: confronting polarization, misinformation and suppression*, Emerald, 61–87.

Cunningham, F. (2002) *Theories of Democracy: a critical introduction*, Routledge.

Cyr, C. (2022) Container Collapse and Misinformation: why digitization creates challenges for democracy. In Taylor, N. G., Kettnich, K., Gorham, U. and Jaeger, P. (eds) *Libraries and the Global Retreat of Democracy: confronting polarization, misinformation and suppression*, Emerald, 91–108.

Dahlgren, P. (2006) Doing Citizenship: the cultural origin of civic agency in the public sphere, *European Journal of Cultural Studies*, 9, 267–86.

Dalton, R. J. (2006) The Two Faces of Citizenship, *Democracy & Society*, 3 (2), 21–3.

Derbaix, B. (2021) Rethinking School, Rebuilding Society, *Eurozine*, 8 November, www.eurozine.com/rethinking-school-rebuilding-society.

Dervin, B. (1994) Information Democracy: an examination of underlying assumptions, *Journal of the American Society for Information Science*, 45, 369–85.

Dittert, A. (2021) The Crisis That Must Not Be Named, *Eurozine*, 4 November, www.eurozine.com/brexit-the-crisis-that-must-not-be-named.

Ditzion, S. H. (1947) *Arsenals of a Democratic Culture: a social history of the American public library movement in New England and the Middle States from 1850–1900*, American Library Association.

Downey, A. (2016) *Critical Information Literacy: foundation, inspiration and ideas*, Litwin Books.

Dugan, R. E. (2001) *Libraries & Democracy* (Book Review), *Journal of Academic Librarianship*, 27, 485–6.

Dunn J. (2010) Tracking Democracy, *Political Theory*, 38, 106–10.

Edsall, T. B. (2021) 'The Capitol Insurrection Was as Christian Nationalist as It Gets', *New York Times*, 28 January, www.nytimes.com/2021/01/28/opinion/christian-nationalists-capitol-attack.html.

Edsall, T. B. (2022) Trump Poses a Test Democracy Is Failing, *New York Times*, 13 April, www.nytimes.com/2022/04/13/opinion/trump-democracy-decline-fall.html.

Fiels, K. M. (2011) A Library 'State of the State': trends, issues and myths. In Woodsworth, A. (ed.) *Librarianship in Times of Crisis*, Emerald, 3–17.

Fuchs, C. (2014) Social Media and the Public Sphere, *tripleC: Communication, Capitalism & Critique*, 12, 57–101.

Galston, W. A. (1993) Political Theory in the 1980s: perplexity amidst diversity. In Finifter, A. W. (ed.) *Political Science: the state of the discipline II*, American Political Science Association, 27–54.

Galston, W. A. (2001) Political Knowledge, Political Engagement and Civic Education, *Annual Review of Political Science*, 4, 217–34.

Galston, W. A. (2007) Civic Knowledge, Civic Education and Civic Engagement: a summary of recent research, *International Journal of Public Administration*, 30, 623–42.

Gey, S. G. (1993) The Unfortunate Revival of Civic Republicanism, *University of Pennsylvania Law Review*, 141, 801–98.

Gibson, J. L. (2008) Intolerance and Political Repression in the United States, *Democracy & Society*, 5 (2), 1, 13–20.

Goodin, R. E. (2003) Folie Républicaine, *Annual Review of Political Science*, 6, 55–76.

Goodwin, D. K. (2013) *The Bully Pulpit: Theodore Roosevelt, William Howard Taft and the golden age of journalism*, Simon & Schuster.

Gowen, A. (2022) Censorship Battles' New Frontier: your public library, *Washington Post*, 17 April, www.washingtonpost.com/nation/2022/04/17/public-libraries-books-censorship/?utm_source=rss&utm_medium=referral&utm_campaign=wp_homepage.

Gutmann, A. (1987) *Democratic Education*, Princeton University Press.

Gutmann, A. (1998) Undemocratic Education. In Hirst, P. H. and White, P. (eds) *Philosophy of Education: major themes in the analytic tradition*, Vol. 3, Routledge, 28–43.

Habermas, J. (2020) Year 30: Germany's second chance, *Eurozine*, 3 October, www.eurozine.com/year-30-germanys-second-chance.

Haigh, M., Haigh, T., Dorosh, M. and Matychak, T. (2022) Beyond Fake News: learning from information literacy programs in Ukraine. In Taylor, N. G., Kettnich, K., Gorham, U. and Jaeger, P. (eds) *Libraries and the Global Retreat of Democracy: confronting polarization, misinformation and suppression*, Emerald, 163–82.

Hajdarpasic, E. (2021) What Use is Fact-Checking Against Fact-Free Politics? *Eurozine*, 27 December, www.eurozine.com/what-use-is-fact-checking-against-fact-free-politics.

Halpern, S. (2018) Libraries Are Essential to Democracy, *Nation*, 306 (8), 20–5.

Hampton, J. (1997) *Political Philosophy*, Westview Press.

Harris, M. H. (1986) State, Class and Cultural Reproduction: toward a theory of library service in the United States, *Advances in Librarianship*, 14, 211–53.

Hart, R. P. (2018) *Civic Hope: how ordinary Americans keep democracy alive*, Cambridge University Press.

Held, D. (2006) *Models of Democracy*, 3rd edn, Stanford University Press.

Hogan, D. (2000) Autonomy and Civic Virtue: a republican educational fantasy, *Change: transformations in education*, 3, 17–34.

Honneth, A. (2020) Will the Pandemic Teach Us Democracy? *Eurozine*, 4 November, www.eurozine.com/will-the-pandemic-teach-us-democracy.

Honohan, I. (2007) Civic Republicanism and the Multicultural City. In Neill, W. and Schwedler, H.-U. (eds) *Migration and Cultural Inclusion in the European City*, Palgrave, 63–73.

Hove, T. (2009) The Filter, the Alarm System and the Sounding Board: critical and warning functions of the public sphere, *Communication & Critical/Cultural Studies*, 6, 19–38.

Howard, M. M. (2006a) American Civic Engagement in Comparative Perspective, *Democracy & Society*, 3 (2), 17–20.

Howard, M. M. (2006b) The Importance of National Citizenship, *Democracy & Society*, 4 (1), 6–8.

Huysmans, F. and Oomes, M. (2013) Measuring the Public Library's Societal Value, *IFLA Journal*, 39, 168–77.

Iati, M. (2021) What is Critical Race Theory and Why Do Republicans Want to Ban It in Schools? *Washington Post*, 29 May, www.washingtonpost.com/education/2021/05/29/critical-race-theory-bans-schools.

Ignatius, D. (2019) Why America is Losing the Information War to Russia, *Washington Post*, 3 September, www.washingtonpost.com/opinions/why-america-is-losing-the-information-war-to-russia/2019/09/03/951f8294-ce8e-11e9-b29b-a528dc82154a_story.html.

Ingraham, C. (2015) Libraries and Their Publics: rhetorics of the public library, *Rhetoric Review*, 34, 147–63.

Ingraham, C. (2018) An Awful Lot of People Use and Love Their Public Library, as an Economics Professor Discovered This Weekend, *Washington Post*, 23 July, www.washingtonpost.com/business/2018/07/23/an-awful-lot-people-use-love-their-public-library-an-economics-professor-discovered-this-weekend.

Jaeger, P. T. and Taylor, N. G. (2021) Arsenals of Lifelong Information Literacy: educating users to navigate political and current events information in world of ever-evolving misinformation, *Library Quarterly*, 91, 19–31.

Jaeger, P. T. and Taylor, N. G. (2022) Raking the Forests: information literacy, political polarization, fake news and the educational role of librarians. In Taylor, N. G., Kettnich, K., Gorham, U. and Jaeger, P. (eds) *Libraries and the Global Retreat of Democracy: confronting polarization, misinformation and suppression*, Emerald, 211–24.

Jaeger, P. T., Gorham, U., Sarin, L. C. and Bertot, J. C. (2013) Libraries, Policy and Politics in a Democracy: four historical epochs, *Library Quarterly*, **83**, 166–81.

Jaeger, P. T., Kettnich, K., Gorham, U. and Taylor, N. G. (2022) Afterword: reverse the retreat: countering disinformation and authoritarianism as the work of libraries. In Taylor, N. G., Kettnich, K., Gorham, U. and Jaeger, P. (eds) *Libraries and the Global Retreat of Democracy: confronting polarization, misinformation and suppression*, Emerald, 247–55.

Jaeger, P. T., Bertot, J. C., Kodama, C. M., Katz, S. M. and DeCoster, E. J. (2011) Describing and Measuring the Value of Public Libraries: the growth of the internet and the evolution of library value, *First Monday*, **16** (11), 1–14, https://firstmonday.org/ojs/index.php/fm/article/view/3765.

Jovanovic, S., Damasceno, C. S. and Schwartzman, R. (2021) Engaging Generation Z with Communication's Civic Commitments. In Robinson, R. (ed.) *Communication Instruction in the Generation Z Classroom*, Lexington Books, 129–47.

Kahane, D. (2000) Pluralism, Deliberation and Citizen Competence: recent developments in democratic theory, *Social Theory and Practice*, **26**, 509–25.

Katznelson, I. (2006) Affirmative Action in White and Black, *Democracy & Society*, **3** (2), 1, 6–8.

Katznelson, I. and Milner, H. V. (2002) American Political Science: the discipline's state and the state of the discipline. In Katznelson, I. and Milner, H. V. (eds) *Political Science: state of the discipline*, Centennial Edition, W. W. Norton, 1–32.

Keum, H., Devanathan, N., Deshpande, S., Nelson, M. R. and Shah, D. V. (2004) The Citizen-Consumer: media effects at the intersection of consumer and civic culture, *Political Communication*, **21**, 369–91.

Klein, E. (2020) *Why We're Polarized*, Avid Reader Press.

Koch, A. and Peden, W. (eds) (1944) *The Life and Selected Writings of Thomas Jefferson*, Modern Library.

Koposov, N. (2022) Nobody Knows What Russians Want. Not Even Russians Themselves, *Eurozine*, 22 March, www.eurozine.com/nobody-knows-what-russians-want-not-even-russians-themselves.

Kraft, P. W., Lodge, M. and Taber, C. S. (2015) Why People 'Don't Trust the Evidence': motivated reasoning and scientific beliefs, *Annals of the American Academy of Political and Social Science*, **658**, 121–33.

Kranich, N. (ed.) (2001) *Libraries & Democracy: the cornerstones of liberty*, American Library Association.

Kranich, N. (2020) Libraries and Democracy Revisited, *Library Quarterly*, **90**, 121–53.

Krugman, P. (2022) Another Dictator Is Having a Bad Year, *New York Times*, 17 March, www.nytimes.com/2022/03/17/opinion/china-russia-xi-jin-ping.html.

Kuklinski, J. H. and Peyton, B. (2007) Belief Systems and Political Decision Making. In Dalton, R. J. and Klingemann, H.-D. (eds) *Oxford Handbook of Political Behavior*, Oxford University Press, 45–64.

Kymlicka, W. (2002) *Contemporary Political Philosophy: an introduction*, 2nd edn, Oxford University Press.

Lenker, M. (2016) Motivated Reasoning, Political Information and Information Literacy Education, *portal: Libraries and the Academy*, 16, 511–28.

Lievrouw, L. A. and Farb, S. E. (2003) Information and Equity, *Annual Review of Information Science and Technology*, 37, 499–540.

Lilburn, J. (2017) Sociopolitical Barriers to Information and Community Well-Being: implications for librarian teaching practice, paper presented at the Canadian Association of Professional Academic Librarians (CAPAL) Conference, Ryerson University, Toronto, 31 May.

Lozada, C. (2021) 9/11 Was a Test. The Books of the Last Two Decades Show How America Failed, *Washington Post*, 3 September, www.washingtonpost.com/outlook/interactive/2021/911-books-american-values.

McCook, K. (2001) Poverty, Democracy and Public Libraries. In Kranich, N. (ed.) *Libraries & Democracy: the cornerstones of liberty*, American Library Association, 28–46.

McCook, K. and Bossaller, J. S. (2018) *Introduction to Public Librarianship*, 3rd edn, American Library Association/Neal-Schuman.

Maldonado, M. A. (2017) The Internet Against Democracy, *Eurozine*, 5 October, www.eurozine.com/the-internet-against-democracy.

Mansbridge, J. (2004) Representation Revisited: introduction to the case against electoral accountability, *Democracy & Society*, 2 (1), 1, 12–13.

Mansbridge, J., Bohman, J., Chambers, S., Christiano, T., Fung, A., Parkinson, J., Thompson, D. F. and Warren, M. E. (2012) A Systemic Approach to Deliberative Democracy. In Parkinson, J. and Mansbridge, J. (eds) *Deliberative Systems*, Cambridge University Press, 1–26.

Mara, G. M. (2008) *The Civic Conversations of Thucydides and Plato: classical political philosophy and the limits of democracy*, State University of New York Press.

Mara, G. M. (2015) Thucydides and the Problem of Citizenship. In Lee, C. and Morley, N. (eds) *A Handbook to the Reception of Thucydides*, John Wiley & Sons, 313–33.

Maret, S. (2013) Intellectual Freedom and U.S. Government Secrecy. In Alfino, M. and Koltutsky, L. (eds) *The Library Juice Press Handbook of Intellectual Freedom*, Library Juice Press, 247–81.

Mathiesen, K. (2015) Toward a Political Philosophy of Information, *Library Trends*, 63, 427–47.

Mehra, B. (2021) Enough Crocodile Tears! Libraries moving beyond performative antiracist politics, *Library Quarterly*, 91, 137–49.

Meyers, M. (ed.) (1973) *The Mind of the Founder: sources of the political thought of James Madison*, Bobbs-Merrill.

Milner, H. (2002) *Civic Literacy: how informed citizens make democracy work*, University Press of New England.

Moon, E. (2001) Book review: *Libraries & Democracy*, *Library Journal*, 126 (20), 183.

Mouffe, C. (1992) Democratic Citizenship and the Political Community. In Mouffe, C. (ed.) *Dimensions of Radical Democracy*, Verso, 225–39.

Mouffe, C. (2005) Some Reflections on an Agonistic Approach to the Public. In Latour, B. and Weibel, P. (eds) *Making Things Public: atmospheres of democracy*, MIT Press, 804–7.

Natanson, H. (2022) Parent-Activists, Seeking Control Over Education, Are Taking Over School Boards, *Washington Post*, 19 January, www.washingtonpost.com/education/2022/01/19/parents-school-boards-recall-takeover.

Panageotou, S. (2018) Corporate Power in the Twenty-First Century. In Outhwaite, W. and Turner, S. P. (eds) *The Sage Handbook of Political Sociology*, Sage, 999–1014.

Patterson, O. (1999) Liberty Against the Democratic State. In Warren, M. E. (ed.) *Democracy and Trust*, Cambridge University Press, 151–207.

Pawley, C. (2003) Information Literacy: a contradictory coupling, *Library Quarterly*, 73, 422–52.

Pennycook, G., Epstein, Z., Mosleh, M., Arechar, A. A., Eckles, D. and Rand, D. G. (2021) Shifting Attention to Accuracy Can Reduce Misinformation Online, *Nature*, 592 (7855), 590–5.

Peters, J. D. (1993) Distrust of Representation: Habermas on the public sphere, *Media, Culture & Society*, 15, 541–71.

Postman, N. (1988) The Contradictions of Freedom of Information. In Berman, S. and Danky, J. (eds) *Alternative Library Literature, 1986/1987*, McFarland, 37–49.

Powers, B. A. and Knapp, T. R. (2011) *Dictionary of Nursing Theory and Research*, 4th edn, Springer.

Przeworski, A. (2009) Self-Government in Our Times, *Annual Review of Political Science*, 12, 71–92.

Putnam, R. D. (2003) Democracy. In Dahl, R. A., Shapiro, I. and Cheibub, J. A. (eds) *The Democracy Sourcebook*, MIT Press, 157–67.

Putnam, R. D., Feldstein, L. M. and Cohen, D. (2003) *Better Together: restoring the American community*, Simon & Schuster.

Rivano Eckerdal, J. R. (2017) Libraries, Democracy, Information Literacy and Citizenship, *Journal of Documentation*, 73, 1010–33.

Robbin, A., Courtright, C. and Davis, L. (2004) ICTs and Political Life, *Annual Review of Information Science and Technology*, 38, 411–82.

Ryfe, D. M. (2005) Does Deliberative Democracy Work? *Annual Review of Political Science*, 8, 49–71.

Schlozman, K. L. (2002) Citizen Participation in America: What do we know? Why do we care? In Katznelson, I. and Milner, H. V. (eds) *Political Science: state of the discipline*, Centennial Edition, W. W. Norton, 433–61.

Schudson, M. (1998) *The Good Citizen: a history of American civic life*, Harvard University Press.

Schudson, M. (2006) The Troubling Equivalence of Citizen and Consumer, *Annals of the American Academy of Political and Social Science*, 608, 193–204.

Schudson, M. (2018) *Why Journalism Still Matters*, Polity Press.

Schumpeter, J. A. (2001) Selections from *Capitalism, Socialism and Democracy*. In Terchek, R. J. and Conte, T. C. (eds) *Theories of Democracy: a reader*, Rowman & Littlefield, 143–54.

Scott, J. C. (1999) Geographies of Trust, Geographies of Hierarchy. In Warren, M. E. (ed.) *Democracy and Trust*, Cambridge University Press, 273–89.

Scott, J. C. (2006) State Simplification. In Goodin, R. E. and Petit, P. (eds) *Contemporary Political Philosophy: an anthology*, 2nd edn, Blackwell, 26–54.

Shapiro, I. (2002) The State of Democratic Theory. In Katznelson, I. and Milner, H. V. (eds) *Political Science: state of the discipline*, Centennial Edition, W. W. Norton, 235–65.

Shera, J. H. (1949) *Foundations of the Public Library; the origins of the public library movement in New England, 1629–1855*, University of Chicago Press.

Shklar, J. (1990) American Citizenship: the quest for inclusion. In Peterson, G. B. (ed.) *The Tanner Lectures on Human Values*, vol. 11, University of Utah Press, 385–439.

Singh, R. and Brinster, K. N. (2022) Fighting Fake News: the cognitive factors impeding political information literacy. In Taylor, N. G., Kettnich, K., Gorham, U. and Jaeger, P. (eds) *Libraries and the Global Retreat of Democracy: confronting polarization, misinformation and suppression*, Emerald, 109–31.

Slačálek, O. (2021) The Horrifying Right to One's Own Context, *Eurozine*, 22 October, www.eurozine.com/the-horrifying-right-to-ones-own-context.

Smith, B. (2020) How Zeynep Tufekci Keeps Getting the Big Things Right, *New York Times*, 23 August, www.nytimes.com/2020/08/23/business/media/how-zeynep-tufekci-keeps-getting-the-big-things-right.html.

Snyder, T. (2017) *On Tyranny: twenty lessons from the twentieth century*, Tim Duggan Books.

Solnit, R. (2022) Why Republicans Keep Falling for Trump's Lies, *New York Times*, 5 January, www.nytimes.com/2022/01/05/opinion/republicans-trump-lies.html.

Sreedhar, A. and Gopal, A. (2021) Behind Low Vaccination Rates Lurks a More Profound Social Weakness, *New York Times*, 3 December, www.nytimes.com/2021/12/03/opinion/vaccine-hesitancy-covid.html.

Stauffer, B. (2022) What Are 21st Century Skills? *AES: Applied Educational Systems*, 10 January, www.aeseducation.com/blog/what-are-21st-century-skills.

Stenstrom, C., Cole, N. and Hanson, R. (2019) A Review Exploring the Facets of the Value of Public Libraries, *Library Management*, 40, 354–67.

Stevens, E. and Wood, G. H. (1995) *Justice, Ideology and Education: an introduction to the social foundations of education*, 3rd edn, McGraw-Hill.

Stolle, D. (2007) Social Capital. In Dalton, R. J. and Klingemann, H.-D. (eds) *Oxford Handbook of Political Behavior*, Oxford University Press, 655–74.

Sullivan, M. C. (2019a) Libraries and Fake News: What's the problem? What's the plan? *Communications in Information Literacy*, 13 (1), 91–113.

Sullivan, M. C. (2019b) Why Librarians Can't Fight Fake News, *Journal of Librarianship & Information Science*, 51, 1146–56.

Taylor, C. (2017) Some Conditions of a Viable Democracy, *Eurozine*, 14 August, www.eurozine.com/some-conditions-of-a-viable-democracy.

Taylor, N. G. and Jaeger, P. T. (2021) *Foundations of Information Literacy*, American Library Association.

Taylor, N. G., Kettnich, K., Gorham, U. and Jaeger, P. T. (2022) *Libraries and the Global Retreat of Democracy: confronting polarization, misinformation and suppression*, Emerald.

Urbinati, N. and Warren, M. E. (2008) The Concept of Representation in Contemporary Democratic Theory, *Annual Review of Political Science*, 11, 387–412.

Walker, J. L. (1970) Normative Consequences of 'Democratic' Theory. In Kariel, H. S. (ed.) *Frontiers of Democratic Theory*, Random House, 227–47.

Walt, S. M. (2002) The Enduring Relevance of the Realist Tradition. In Katznelson, I. and Milner, H. V. (eds) *Political Science: state of the discipline*, Centennial Edition, W. W. Norton, 197–230.

Walzer, M. (1970) *Obligations: essays on disobedience, war and citizenship*, Harvard University Press.

Warren, M. E. (1996) Deliberative Democracy and Authority, *American Political Science Review*, 90, 46–60.

Warren, M. E. (1999) Conclusion. In Warren, M. E. (ed.) *Democracy and Trust*, Cambridge University Press, 346–60.

Warren, M. E. (2002) What Can Democratic Participation Mean Today? *Political Theory*, 30, 677–701.

Warren, M. E. (2017) A Problem-based Approach to Democratic Theory, *American Political Science Review*, 111, 39–53.

Warren, M. E. and Castiglione, D. (2004) The Transformation of Democratic Representation, *Democracy & Society*, 2 (1), 5, 20–2.

Warren, M. E. and Gastil, J. (2015) Can Deliberative Minipublics Address the Cognitive Challenges of Democratic Citizenship? *Journal of Politics*, 77, 562–74.

Waters, R. L. (2001) Book review: *Libraries & Democracy*, *Public Library Quarterly*, 20 (2), 61.

Webster, F. (1999) Knowledgeability and Democracy in an Information Age, *Library Review*, 48, 373–83.

White, D. (2019) The Authoritarian's Worst Fear? A Book, *New York Times*, 3 October, www.nytimes.com/2019/10/03/opinion/books-censorship.html.

Wiegand, W. A. (1999) Tunnel Vision and Blind Spots: what the past tells us about the present; reflections on the twentieth-century history of American librarianship, *Library Quarterly*, 69, 1–32.

Wiegand, W. A. (2015) *Part of Our Lives: a people's history of the American public library*, Oxford University Press.

Wiegand, W. A. (2020) Sanitizing American Library History: reflections of a library historian, *Library Quarterly*, 90, 108–20.

Wolin, S. S. (1968) Paradigms and Political Theory. In King, P. T. and Parekh, B. C. (eds) *Politics and Experience*, Cambridge University Press, 160–91.

Wolin, S. S. (2004) *Politics and Vision: continuity and innovation in Western political thought*, Princeton University Press.

Young, I. M. (2001) Activist Challenges to Deliberative Democracy, *Political Theory*, 29, 670–90.

Zhou, X., Zafarani, R., Shu, K. and Liu, H. (2019) Fake News: fundamental theories, detection strategies and challenges. In *WSDM '19: Proceedings of the Twelfth ACM International Conference on Web Search and Data Mining*, https://doi.org/10.1145/3289600.3291382.

2
Information Literacy and the Social: Applying a Practice Theory View to Information Literacy

Annemaree Lloyd

Introduction

Multiple perspectives have been employed to conceptualise information literacy since the emergence of the concept in the 1970s. Each perspective (functional, skills-based and ideological) and its discourses articulate how information literacy is understood and practised (Lloyd, 2010). However, up until recently, few articles have sought to provide a deeper explanation of the inherent complexity of this social practice or how and in what ways information literacy and its internal and external practices emerge and travel.

This chapter is influenced by a suite of theories collectively described as practice theory, in particular the site ontology conception (Schatzki, 2002) and epistemological approaches, which locate the body as a central feature of *doing practice*. The power of the practice theory approach is that it opens up and draws attention to new analytical possibilities for thinking about and researching the connection and interplay between information literacy, sociality and materiality – the site where social life occurs (Schatzki, 2002, xi). It does this by emphasising the analytical role of context in shaping the discursive relationships between people, information and the materiality of practice (Lloyd, 2005).

It then locates practice theory ontologically and epistemologically in relation to the practice of information literacy and connects these theories to the concept of information landscapes, which forms the core of the theory of information literacy (ToIL) (Lloyd, 2017). The theory of information literacy (also described as the theory of information literacy landscapes (Lloyd, 2017), positions information literacy as a practice that is enacted within a social setting. It is composed of a suite and pattern of activities and skills and ways of communicating and understanding that reference structures and embodied knowledge and ways of knowing relevant to the context. Information literacy is a way of knowing (Lloyd, 2017, 2).

In the practice of information literacy, people connect not only with text but with the materialities linked to their settings; they draw from the social, epistemic and the physical/corporeal modalities of information and, through that connection, they form and shape their information landscapes.

The theory of information literacy (ToIL) (Lloyd, 2017) therefore advocates a broader understanding of information literacy as a social practice which, when enacted, connects people with information through the signs, symbols, materiality and embodiment associated with the sayings and doings of practising. Information literacy is a practice which is also a constituent part of other practices in everyday life.

Information literacy is described in this chapter as a complex situated practice that is embedded and enacted through the site of the social and therefore subject to the social and material conditions and arrangements that shape it. It involves the whole person being actively engaged in world making (Rapport, 2007) by accessing modalities of information, which have been identified and described by Lloyd (2006) as social, epistemic and corporeal, that are related to everyday practices (i.e. working, education, recreation, spiritual, sporting, leisure). Modalities reference the ways of knowing about collective forms of knowledge, i.e. ways of knowing are drawn from multiple information environments that compose and contribute to a person's lived experience and understanding of the world. Information environments refer to the larger stable knowledge environments created by collective contributions of people engaged in the same pursuit or projects (Lloyd, 2006).

World making is perspectival in that it references the intricate ontological and epistemological conditions that underpin engagement with information in the act of making and remaking realities (world views) and knowledge. In the process of establishing a world view, people interact with information environments (i.e. health, employment, financial, family, leisure, education) that are relevant to their situation. Based on their interaction, people's information landscapes are constructed, shaped and reshaped through the social, material and corporeal modalities that enable or constrain the practice.

Information landscapes emphasise the ongoing interaction of people with the sociocultural, historical, political and material economic conditions of their settings. Knowledge is drawn from information environments and is shaped and constructed to reflect shared ways of understanding and meaning making (Lloyd and Wilkinson, 2016). Consequently, landscapes represent knowledge spaces that have resonance with people who are involved in collective projects, endeavours or situations. A landscape can therefore be viewed as representing the sum of relations that exist between people who engage in similar performances and, through those performances, develop similar ways of knowing and meaning making (Lloyd, 2006; Lloyd and Wilkinson, 2016).

Information literacy therefore connects people-in-practice both intersubjectively and subjectively with sites of knowledge, sources of information and ways of knowing that contribute to enacting practice and becoming situated and emplaced. At an intersubjective level, practising information literacy positions people in relation to knowledge about the social and historical dimensions of the setting (what information is valued, legitimised and sanctioned). It also positions people in relation to how knowledge is operationalised materially, i.e. the agency of material, tools and source-related practice through which information is produced, reproduced, circulated, disseminated and archived. At a subjective level, the enactment of information literacy establishes information landscapes that allow actors to navigate and act within the site.

At both intersubjective and subjective levels, information literacy can therefore be described as having situational, relational, recursive, material and embodied dimensions that are drawn upon to make the experience of information and information practice meaningful (Lloyd, 2017, 2). This complex idea of information literacy extends from print to digital landscapes.

Practice theory landscape

This view of information literacy is informed by practice theory. The theoretical landscape of practice theory is varied, open and fluid and therefore eludes a single definition that captures its essence. However, commonalities do exist and most accounts reflect the 'prioritisations of practices' (Schatzki, 2001, 11) by providing accounts of the composition of practices, how practices happen, are mediated and communicated in the constitution of social life. According to Schatzki, all practices are social and rendered visible by doings and sayings with material arrangements that 'hang together, organised by practical understanding, a general understanding of rules and teleo-affective structures' (Schatzki, 2002, 2).

Practices are defined by Schatzki (2002, 2) as an organised nexus of human activities through which human intelligibility occurs. Social practices and their arrangements therefore become the starting point for theorising human affairs (Nicolini, 2012, 162; Schatzki, 2002) through which accounts of the social are made. In the enactment of practice, Shove, Pantzar and Watson (2012, 14) argue that people actively engage with meaning, materials and competences, although it can be argued that limiting this view to three elements (competences, meaning and material) simplifies the complexities of practice.

Practice theories, as a group of theories, are loosely united in a shared interest in the lifeworld and share a principal belief that practices are social and relational (Reckwitz, 2002, 244). These theories reject dualism, by acknowledging and centring the body and materiality in all social performances. Practice theories are viewed as 'processual' (Nicolini, 2012, 3) and pragmatic interrogation acknowledges the patterning of practices through routines of activities and shared understanding, with some strands of theories focusing on materials and materiality and the communication of practices through text and symbols.

While there is no definitional agreement about practice, there is common agreement about elements that are central to theories of practice. In general, there is a rejection of the mind/body/agency/structure dualism (Bourdieu and Wacquant, 1992; Feldman and Orlikowski, 2011; Nicolini, 2012). However, there is a common view of practices as temporally, spatially and materially composed, referencing the texture of everyday life and activity (Reckwitz, 2002; Schatzki, 2002; Lloyd, 2017, 25). Practices are viewed as being embodied in language as a discursive activity and realised corporeally and materially across the routinised aspects of everyday life activities. Emphasis is placed on the body, which is not merely described as an instrument that is required to act. Instead, action is inscribed upon the body as it is embodied within its setting (Reckwitz, 2002; Gherardi, 2009). There is agreement on the entwinement of corporeal and mental activities, materiality and background knowledge in the constitution of understanding and knowledge (Schatzki, 2002; Reckwitz, 2002; Shove, Pantzar and Watson, 2012).

Practice theorists also claim that practices represent organised assemblages of activity and understanding that are central to shaping everyday life and ordering in the world (Barnes, 2001, Schatzki, 2002). This view recognises and acknowledges agency and the affordances of materiality and communications as central to practice (Lloyd, 2010; Mahon et al., 2016). Finally, there is recognition that while sense-making has often been privileged as a mental process or symbolic exchange (Nicolini, 2012), a practice perspective locates agency discursively in the body, performance, activity, artefacts, habits and materiality that constitute everyday life.

While these are common features among the suite of theories, the landscape of practice is also unsettled (Feldman and Orlikowski, 2011). This is primarily because accounts of practice are situated within a diverse range of intellectual traditions (Nicolini, 2012), which tests the nature of the practice concept.

These commonalities are visible within the waves of practice theory that have influenced information literacy research (Lloyd, 2017). The first wave emerged from a primary interest in *how practice shapes everyday life*. The concept of practice was central to Bourdieu's understanding of the field, as a 'realm of activity in which people pursue certain stakes, drawing on capitals available to them, not just economic, but cultural and symbolic capitals' (Schatzki, 2005, 471). Bourdieu proposed that practice is organised through habitus, a stable system of dispositions and structures (Bourdieu, 1977). Another account is provided by Giddens (1984), who conceptualises practice as groups of actions, governed by rules and constituted through situated activities and interactions, which are influenced by the agency of other actors.

A second wave of theorists consider practice ontologically and epistemologically and include the philosophical theoretical work of Schatzki (1996; 2001; 2002); Reckwitz's (2002) use of cultural theory to frame practice, which identified the significance of shared collective symbolic knowledges to understand action and social order; and the development of a theory of practice architectures (Kemmis and Grootenboer, 2008). Epistemological approaches to practice theory have been adopted in the work of Lave and Wenger (1991) on situated learning, Nicolini (2012) and Gherardi's (2009) interrogation of organisational related practices and Shove, Pantzer and Watson's (2012) questioning of the relationship between social practice and conditions of change.

These waves of practice theory have been drawn upon and influenced research into information literacy by information practice researchers including Tuominen, Savolainen and Talja (2005); Gullbekk (2016); Hicks (2019); Lloyd and Olsson (2017; 2019); Pilerot, (2016), Rivera and Cox (2016); Schreiber (2013; 2014) – and Lloyd (2010; 2017), who has developed a Theory of Information Literacy Practice (ToIL). Writing from the library and information science field, Pilerot, Hammarfelt and Moring (2017) have attempted to highlight how practice is conceptualised in theoretical literature. The list of tenets states that practice theorists avoid dualisms and conceive practices as socially recognised and named sets of activities which encompass language as discursive activity; which are orientated towards ends, situated in time and space, and generative of rules and norms. Additionally, practices contribute to the ordering of the world, are reproductive of the social, comprise individual and collective agency and embrace bodies and materiality (Pilerot, Hammarfelt and Moring, 2017, n.p.). The practice-theoretical perspective locates information literacy in the enactment and negotiation between people who are engaged in joint projects and through site-specific intersubjective architectures that establish the social space, suggesting that information literacy is bound up in discourses that reflect discursive ways of knowing (Lloyd, 2005; 2010).

Theoretical questions

In general, a practice theory lens, when applied to the theoretical and methodological interrogation of information literacy, broadens researchers' understanding of how the practices emerge and the conditions that enable or constrain it. Before considering the ontological and epistemological questions that information literacy researchers might attend to, three conceptual themes that influence these questions are briefly described.

Site ontology

Emerging from practice theory is the concept of site ontology, which advances an analysis that all social life is constituted through a site (i.e. context or social field) as a place where co-existence happens through a mesh of entwined practices and arrangements (Schatzki, 2005, 471). The site of a practice is 'that realm or set of phenomena (if any) of which it is intrinsically a part' (Schatzki, 2003, 176) . A practice can be located within multiple sites or within multiple practices (Schatzki, 2002). For example, information literacy instructional practice can also be a site of assessment and evaluation practices (of instructional librarians or of students).

Context is composed of spatial, temporal and teleological features and to 'analyse sociality via a site is to hold *inter alia* that the nature and transformation of social life are inherently, as well as decisively, tied to the context in which it takes place' (Schatzki, 2000, 22). With this view, social life is an organised collective activity and constituted by the arrangements of people engaged in common purposes, emotions and corporeality through the 'nexus of action and teleological structures' that distinguish a given practice (Schatzki, 2000, 25).

Information and knowledge

The prevailing idea that information and knowledge are of more value when they are viewed objectively negates the multiple realities that constitute being in the world and continues to lead to a functional view of information literacy (Lloyd, 2003). Central to a practice view of information literacy, advocated by Lloyd (2010), is the idea from Bateson (1972, 315) that information is 'any difference which makes a difference in some later event'. When applied to the conception of information literacy, this definition suggests that *information* makes a difference to the construction of knowledge and to ways of knowing in either positive, negative or neutral terms (Lloyd, 2017). Knowledge represents stable discursive information environments (e.g. health, education, politics, religion) which are specific and normalised to a setting. Having been shaped when power is enacted, knowledge imposes homogenous categories and arrangements (what is enabled or contested knowledge) thus shaping the legitimisation of knowledge in specific social, political, economic and historical ways and creating sociopolitical orders and arrangements that include ways of knowing.

Creating information landscapes

People in practice (Lloyd, 2011) draw information from information environments to create information landscapes. Information landscapes are shaped by the modalities of information that represent the ways of knowing about collective forms of knowledge. The modalities also reflect the intersubjective meaning-making or the shared reference points between people engaged in mutual projects and ways of knowing that enable their subjective and intersubjective agency (ability to act individually or collectively) (Lloyd, 2021). The practice is therefore shaped and enacted in ways that reflect the sayings and doings of the setting. Examples of this proposed perspective can be seen in features of colonisation, where the imposition of specific ontological categories on groups of people impacted on their cultural practices and world making; or, closer to the library and information science field, the imposition of Anglo-centric/rational enactment of information literacy practices that constrain other ways of knowing and agentic practices, i.e. corporeal, orality and cultural. Finally, this can be extended to recognising the impact that algorithms (as culturally created and biased objects) have on agency and performativity (Lloyd, 2019).

Ontological questions

The idea that knowledge is a view from somewhere (Barad, 1996, 180) suggests an ontological basis for understanding the practice of information literacy. Ontology references accounts, beliefs, ideas that people hold about what exists in the world and contributes to their world making. Ontological assumptions held by people are shaped and reinforced in practice and interaction and reference the negotiation of different versions of truth and ways of knowing (see below). This view acknowledges the complexity of knowledge that constitutes and composes people being in and participating in the world and moves towards addressing a more critical perspective of information literacy, including how it is shaped, who it is for and who becomes silenced or marginalised when ontologies are neglected. It reinforces the idea that practices such as information literacy are the property of the social site rather than the individual. The social site comprises 'nexuses of practices and material arrangements' that hang and overlap (Schatzki, 2002).

When interrogating the practice of information literacy ontologically, questions are raised about the semantic spaces that shape participants' understanding of their site. Attention is paid to 'specific content and conduct of practice, its organisation in space and time, the arrangements that make it possible and hold it in place, its transformation and the sites in which it happens' (Mahon et al., 2017, 4). People's everyday lives are constructed by their engagement with the many information environments that intersect it and the multiple information landscapes that are constructed to make being in the world meaningful. It is therefore necessary to acknowledge the potential for *ontological multiplicity* (Blaser, 2014) and to demonstrate and acknowledge the intersecting information environments and power arrangements that influence the agency of lived experience and constitute being in the world.

Key questions that drive analytical ontological exploration focus on the nature of knowledge accepted within the setting; how language and the semantic community it creates acts to situate and position actors by enabling or constraining access to knowledges and ways of knowing; what counts as information, information source or a site of knowledge. An ontological perspective makes demands on researchers, requiring them to position themselves in relation to their own publics and the theories they employ.

Epistemologically

Epistemology focuses on the way we know what we know (Denzin and Lincoln, 2005) and what we count as knowledge. Advancing a practice view of information literacy from an epistemological position requires a broader understanding about the *doing* of practice or the rejection of dualist thinking by bringing the body into view (see Chapter 10, on embodiment, by Lloyd). The concept of ways of knowing *grounds knowledge into actions* (Ryle, 1949) and provides the epistemological anchor for understanding the doings of the practice relative to how the enactment of information literacy emerges as a situated and contextually relevant suite of activities and actions. These activities and actions connect participants with the sanctioned and legitimised knowledges of the setting. Ways of knowing are in themselves forms of skillful practical/pragmatic knowledge accessed *in situ* and linked to an acknowledgement of how the ontological features position the conditions of knowing. In becoming epistemologically open to the site, participants locate themselves and thus become open to the pragmatic, embodied and nuanced ways of knowing that enable information literacy practice (as a doing) to emerge.

Key questions when interrogating information literacy practice from an epistemological perspective relate to understanding how the performances connected to ways of knowing emerge, are *negotiated* and *enacted*. What kinds of (a) *information work* (work that connects people with the complex social structures of the workplace and the information modalities and ecologies that support them) and (b) *influence work* (how the community actively engages its members) are performed to inculcate new participants into the trajectory of information literacy and to maintain practices as information literacy evolves, transforms and grows within the setting (Lloyd, 2010, 173). How are the information modalities (social, epistemic, corporeal) coupled together in the composition of landscapes and then drawn upon by people in practice? (Lloyd, 2010). How do literacies of information, such as media, health, financial, etc. and ways of knowing (corporeal, social, epistemic) emerge? What emphasis is placed on specific literacies and which become silenced or marginalised? Finally, how is the practice of information literacy dispersed and how does it travel within the dimensions of a setting or across contextual boundaries?

Methodologically

From a methodological perspective, approaching information literacy from a practice perspective necessitates an acknowledgement of the power that influences and structures the complexity of the social setting. As a practice, information literacy is subject to the relations of power, which shape the context and organise, enable or constrain the arrangements that lead to accessing information and knowledge. Methodologically, information literacy needs to be interrogated both intersubjectively (to gain a sense of how the practice is shaped discursively and shared collectively) and subjectively to understand the subjective nature of the lived experience through which information landscapes are constructed.

The capturing of the *doing* of practices as they are experienced, pedagogically enacted or understood by others requires a deeper understanding of how people interact with intersubjective spaces in the process of constructing their information landscapes and the modalities of information that are coupled together to create the landscape. When the framework for analysis is a practice perspective, the methodological approach will focus on how the landscape of information literacy is enacted and negotiated relative to:

- *historical conditions* of the social space that relate to power, solidarity, which emerges intersubjectively through projects and ontological multiplicity
- *semantic space* as a reflection of the cultural discursive conditions of the setting, through language upon which the legitimacy of knowledges and ways of knowing are enabled or constrained
- *material economic space* creating the preconditions for the performance of information literacy practice.

When interrogating information literacy practice from a practice perspective and via these intersubjective dimensions, researchers acknowledge that information literacy practice reaches past what the 'individual enacting a practice brings to a site as a person (e.g. beliefs, physical attributes and abilities); it also encompasses arrangements found in or brought to the site, arrangements with which the individual interacts and without which the practice could not be realised (Mahon et al., 2017, 9).

Conclusion: how does practice theory explain information literacy?

The theory of information literacy presents information literacy as a situated practice, that is shaped by the conditions, materiality, arrangements and discourses of a social site rather than restricted to the skill-based enactments of text-based mediums (print or digital) (Lloyd, 2017). The use of practice theory promotes a deeper analysis and understanding of the role that context plays in the shaping of information literacy and the bundles of activities and arrangements through which it unfolds. Specifically, by framing information literacy through practice theory, we consider how the relationship between people and information and the sociocultural context is enabled and constrained (Lloyd, 2010). When a practice theory perspective is applied to information literacy it draws us deeper into the ontological and epistemological questions from where we can interrogate and unpack the practice and makes it evident that information literacy cannot be reduced to a competency-based view. Instead, practice theory helps us to recognise that the power of the practice lies in the realisation of its centrality to the lived experience of people as they engage in the sociality of everyday life.

References

Barad, K. (1996) *Meeting the Universe Halfway: quantum physics and the entanglement of matter and meaning*, Duke University Press.

Barnes, B. (2001) Practices as Collective Action. In Schatzki, T., Knorr Cetina, K. and von Savigny, E. (eds) *The Practice Turn*, Routledge, 17–27.

Bateson, G. (1972) *Steps to an Ecology of Mind*, Jason Aronson Inc.

Blaser, M. (2014) Ontology and Indigeneity: on the political ontology of heterogeneous assemblages, *Cultural Geographies*, 21, 49–58.

Bourdieu, P. (1977) *Outline of a Theory of Practice*, Cambridge University Press.

Bourdieu, P. and Wacquant, L. J. (1992) *An Invitation to Reflexive Sociology*, University of Chicago Press.

Denzin, N. K. and Lincoln, Y. (2005) *Handbook of Qualitative Research*, 3rd edn, Sage.

Feldman, M. S. and Orlikowski, W. J. (2011) Theorizing Practice and Practicing Theory, *Organizational Science*, 22 (5), 1240–53.

Gherardi, S. (2009) Knowing and Learning in Practice-based Studies: an introduction, *The Learning Organisation*, 16 (5), 352–9.

Giddens, A. (1984) *The Constitution of Society: outline of the theory of structuration*, Polity Press.

Gullbekk, E. (2016) Apt Information Literacy? A case of interdisciplinary scholarly communication, *Journal of Documentation*, 72 (4), 716–36.

Hicks, A. (2019) Mitigating Risk: mediating transition through the enactment of information literacy practices, *Journal of Documentation*, 75 (5), 1190–210.

Kemmis, S. and Grootenboer, P. (2008) Situating Practice. In Kemmis, S. and Smith T. J. (eds) *Enabling Praxis: challenges for education*, Sense Publishers, 37–62.

Lave, J. and Wenger, E. (1991) *Situated Learning: legitimate peripheral participation*, Cambridge University Press.

Lloyd, A. (2003) Information Literacy: the meta-competency of the knowledge economy? An exploratory paper, *Journal of Librarianship and Information Science*, 35 (2), 87–92.

Lloyd, A. (2005) Information Literacy: different contexts, different concepts, different truths?, *Journal of Librarianship and Information Science*, 37 (2), 82–8.

Lloyd, A. (2006) Information Literacy Landscapes: an emerging picture, *Journal of Documentation*, 62 (5), 570–83.

Lloyd, A. (2010) Framing Information Literacy as Information Practice: site ontology and practice theory, *Journal of Documentation*, 66 (2), 245–58.

Lloyd, A. (2011) Trapped between a Rock and a Hard Place: what counts as information literacy in the workplace and how is it conceptualized?, *Library Trends*, 60 (2), 277–96.

Lloyd, A. (2017) Information Literacy and Literacies of Information: a mid-range theory and model, *Journal of Information Literacy*, 11 (1), 95–105.

Lloyd, A. (2019) Chasing Frankenstein's Monster: information literacy in the black box society, *Journal of Documentation*, 75 (6), 1475–85.

Lloyd, A. (2021) *The Qualitative Landscape of Information Literacy Research: perspectives, methods and techniques*, Facet Publishing.

Lloyd, A. and Olsson, M. (2017) Losing the Art and Craft of Know-how: capturing vanishing embodied knowledge in the 21st century, *Information Research*, 22 (4), http://informationr.net/ir/22-4/rails/rails1617.html.

Lloyd, A. and Olsson, M. (2019) Untangling the Knot: the information practices of enthusiast car restorers, *Journal of the Association for Information Science and Technology*, 70 (12), 1311–23.

Lloyd, A. and Wilkinson, J. (2016) Knowing and Learning in Everyday Spaces (KALiEds): mapping the information landscape of refugee youth learning in everyday spaces, *Journal of Information Science*, 42 (3), 300–12.

Mahon, K., Kemmis, S., Francisco, S. and Lloyd, A. (2017) Introduction: Practice Theory and the Theory of Practice Architectures. In Mahon, K., Francisco, S. and Kemmis, S. (eds) *Exploring Education and Professional Practice: through the lens of practice architectures*, Springer, 1–30.

Nicolini, D. (2012) *Practice Theory, Work and Organization*, Oxford University Press.

Pilerot, O. (2016) A Practice-based Exploration of the Enactment of Information Literacy among PhD Students in an Interdisciplinary Research Field, *Journal of Documentation*, 72 (3), 414–34.

Pilerot, O., Hammarfelt, B. and Moring, C. (2017) The Many Faces of Practice Theory in Library and Information Studies, *Information Research*, 22 (1), CoLIS paper 1602, http://InformationR.net/ir/22-1/colis/colis1602.html.

Rapport, N. (2007) 'World-view' and 'Worldmaking'. In *Social and Cultural Anthropology: the key concepts*, Routledge, 427–41.

Reckwitz, A. (2002) Toward a Theory of Social Practices: a development in culturalist theorizing, *European Journal of Social Theory*, 5 (2), 243–63.

Rivera, G. and Cox, A. M. (2016) A Practice-Based Approach to Understanding Participation in Online Communities, *Journal of Computer-Mediated Communication*, 21 (1), 17–32.

Ryle, G. (1949) *The Concept of Mind*, Barnes & Noble.

Schatzki, T. R. (1996) *Social Practice: a Wittgensteinian approach to human activity and the social*, Cambridge University Press.

Schatzki, T. R. (2000) The Social Bearing of Nature, *Inquiry: An Interdisciplinary Journal of Philosophy*, 43 (1), 21–37.

Schatzki, T. R. (2001) Subject, Body, Place, *Annals of the American Association of Geographers*, 91 (4), 698–702.

Schatzki, T. R. (2002) *The Site of the Social: a philosophical account of the constitution of social life and change*, Pennsylvania State University Press.

Schatzki, T. R. (2003) A New Societist Social Ontology, *Philosophy of Social Sciences*, 33 (2), 174–202.

Schatzki, T. R. (2005) Peripheral Vision: the sites of organizations, *Organization Studies*, 26 (3), 465–84.

Schreiber, T. (2013) Questioning a Discourse of Information Literacy Practice in Web-Based Tutorials, *Information Research*, 18 (3), http://InformationR.net/ir/18-3/colis/paperC36.html.

Schreiber, T. (2014) Conceptualizing Students' Written Assignments in the Context of Information Literacy and Schatzki's Practice Theory, *Journal of Documentation*, 70 (3), 346–63.

Shove, E., Pantzar, M. and Watson, M. (2012) *The Dynamics of Social Practice: everyday life and how it changes*, Sage.

Tuominen, K., Savolainen, R. and Talja, S. (2005) Information Literacy as Sociotechnical Practice, *Library Quarterly*, 75 (3), 329–45.

3
Information Literacy in a Nexus of Practice: A Mediated Discourse Perspective

Noora Hirvonen

Introduction

Practice-theoretical information literacy research has conceptualised information literacy as a sociocultural (Lloyd, 2006) or sociotechnical (Tuominen, Savolainen and Talja, 2005) practice embedded in the activities of communities and domain specific practices rather than the 'behavior, action, motives and skills of monologic individuals' (Tuominen, Savolainen and Talja, 2005, 339). These understandings have opened a view on information literacy that acknowledges its complexity and the sociocultural features that enable the emergence of such practice in a specific site (Lloyd, 2010), explaining how information literacy happens (Lloyd, 2011). In this chapter, these understandings of information literacy are discussed from the viewpoint of mediated discourse theory (MDT), which can be characterised as a discursive theory of human action. Specifically, MDT can deepen the understanding of the relationship between discourse and action in information literacy practices and the way actions with information are mediated by a variety of material and symbolic tools in ways that are often unnoticeable to us. MDT as an approach can be useful in addressing the tensions between the individual and community-focused understandings of information literacy and the need to broaden the understanding of information literacy to better acknowledge the multimodality of information and information literacy practices. Furthermore, MDT not only provides analytical tools to understand information literacy but can also help identify actions 'with potential to become tactics to change' (Wohlwend, 2020, 14).

The core elements of mediated discourse theory

The central principles of MDT were introduced by linguist Ron Scollon (Scollon, R., 1998; 2001a; 2001b), who, with his colleagues, developed it mainly within the framework of mediated discourse analysis (MDA) and its methodologically oriented branch nexus analysis (NA) (see Scollon, S. W. and de Saint-Georges, 2013; Scollon, S. W., 2014). In their work,

Scollon and colleagues have brought together theorisation from several research areas, including sociolinguistics, critical discourse analysis, literacy studies, practice theories and sociocultural approaches to psychology, and combined them in a unique way with an attempt to understand and explain human *action*, specifically focusing on its relationship with *discourse*. Scollon's ideas specifically build upon the thinking of scholars such as Lev Vygotsky, James Wertsch, Ervin Goffman, Gunther Kress, Theo van Leeuwen, Norman Fairclough and James Paul Gee (see Larsen and Raudaskoski, 2019) and have been advanced further by a number of researchers, mainly within the fields of language studies and educational sciences and applied to research topics ranging from literacy practices and language pedagogy to climate change and immigration (see e.g. Norris and Jones, 2005; Scollon, S. W., 2014; Kuure, Riekki and Tumelius, 2018).

Essentially, MDT is a discursive theory of human action that focuses on discourse both as a kind of social action and as a component of that action (Scollon, R., 2001b). In MDT, the concept of *discourse* refers both to language-in-use and the large-scale 'ways of talking, listening . . . acting, interacting, believing, valuing and using tools and objects, in particular settings, at particular times, so as to display and recognize a particular social identity' (Gee, 1996, 128) that concern more than just language (Gee, 2015). Gee (2015) labelled these two levels as little 'd' discourses and big 'D' Discourses. While discourse is usually spelled uncapitalised in MDT, both levels are recognised: MDT attempts to explain how discourses reproduce and transform Discourses, or discourse systems (Scollon, R., 2001b), and, respectively, how Discourses enable action in a specific moment (Jones and Norris, 2005).

Importantly, in MDT, discourses are viewed from an instrumental standpoint (Scollon, R., 1998) in that they are not considered as such but in connection to *action*. The concept of *mediated action* highlights this instrumentality and the mutually mediating relationship between discourses and social practices (Scollon, R., 2001a; 2001b). Following the ideas of Vygotsky (1978) and Wertsch (1991; 1998), in MDT, all human action is viewed as inherently social and mediated by cultural tools; human action is carried out by social actors using cultural tools that can be material objects, such as a pen or a computer, or symbolic resources, such as a concept or a gesture (Scollon and Scollon, 2004). Regardless of their form, such tools embed a sociocultural history and enable particular actions and constrain other ones (Scollon, R., 2001a; 2001b). Yet, they take their shape only when being appropriated within a practice and as they are used by particular people in particular situations (Scollon, R., 1998; Jones, 2020). For example, a pen is likely to be used for writing or drawing, but can be used for other purposes too, as a toy weapon or a hair accessory, for instance. Therefore, cultural tools and actions carried out using them can only be understood as part of a practice (Scollon, R., 2001b). In MDT, cultural tools are referred to as *mediational means* to highlight their role in mediating action (Scollon and Scollon, 2004).

According to Suzie Scollon (Scollon, S. W., 2005), mediational means and the social actors in a situation embody discourses. Overall, mediated actions are viewed as inherently materially grounded, as they are always carried out using material objects in the world, including the materiality of the social actors' bodies and movements (Scollon, R., 2001b). Understood this way, any place in the world is a complex aggregate of discourses as they are manifested in various ways, in spoken language, in a passage of a book, or in an image on a computer screen, but also in a pen, a coffee cup, in the physical arrangement of a room (Scollon and Scollon, 2004) and as social action (Scollon, R., 2001b).

Mediated action, according to MDT, happens in *a site of engagement*, which is 'the real time moment when mediational means, social actors and the sociocultural environment intersect' (Norris and Jones, 2005, 5). This site is a unique historical moment and material space where social practices meet and open a window for a mediated action to happen (Scollon, R., 2001a). In other words, mediated action is the point of linkage of several social practices and, in fact, produces that linkage (Scollon, R., 2001b). When a site of engagement is regularly repeated, it can be considered to be a *nexus of practice* (Scollon and Scollon, 2004; Schatzki, 2002), not a unique event, but a type of social action as a constellation of humans, discourses and artefacts that together constitute that action (Larsen and Raudaskoski, 2019, 816). Following Schatzki's (2002) idea of the social order consisting of people, artefacts, organisms and things in different relations, a nexus of practice is a network of linked practices where the 'historical trajectories of people, places, discourse, ideas and objects come together to enable some action' (Scollon and Scollon, 2004, viii). These networks, according to Ron Scollon (2001b), position social actors in certain ways and are the basis of the identities and the social structures they (re)produce through their social actions.

In his book *Mediated Discourse: the nexus of practice*, Ron Scollon (2001a) sums up three principles that organise MDT, namely the principle of social action, the principle of communication and the principle of history. These are described in more detail below:

1 *The principle of social action* emphasises MDT's focus on social action rather than discourse as systems of thoughts or values (Scollon, R., 2001a). While MDT is a discursive theory of action (Scollon, R., 2001a), it does not concentrate on discourse *per se* but examines the relationship between social action and discourse (Scollon, S. W. and de Saint-Georges, 2013; Jones, 2020). Consequently, the interest is primarily in how action in society is taken and what role discourse plays in that action (Norris, 2011, 35). Following from this principle (a) the ecological unit of analysis is social action, (b) practice is considered as the milieu of social action, (c) individuals' accumulated social actions, their historical body (see Nishida, 1958), form the basis of social actions, (d) social actions happen within a nexus of practice which position participants in certain ways, (e) positions are aspects of group membership and connect to socialisation to a nexus of practice and, because of this, (f) also produce 'others' who are identified to not being part of the nexus of practice.
2 *The principle of communication* claims that the 'social' in social action implies a shared system of meaning (Scollon, R., 2001a). Following from this principle, (a) the production of shared meanings is considered as mediated by mediational means

which all carry their sociocultural histories and (b) the mediational means involved in a mediated action are related to each other in complex ways.
3 *The principle of history* entails that 'social' means historical, in that shared meanings derive from a common past (Scollon, R., 2001a). Social action in real time is simultaneously the production and re-production of social structures (Bourdieu, 1977), involving both the histories of the mediational means and the social actors (Norris, 2011, 35). Following from this principle, (a) all communication is positioned within multiple, overlapping and conflicting discourses, (b) all communication borrows from other discourses and is used in later discourses and (c) all communication responds to prior communication and anticipates future ones.

These principles have been explained and exemplified in the later developments of mediated discourse analysis and nexus analysis. Importantly, in this work, the central elements of social action are further defined. Social action is considered to happen in the intersection of three factors, namely:

1 *The historical bodies* of the participants referring to individuals' unique experiences and life histories. The historical body of an individual is the accumulation of their actions and habits that have become naturalised, often in a way that one's body carries out actions seemingly naturally. While building upon the concept of *habitus* (Bourdieu, 1977), Scollon and Scollon (2003; 2004) preferred the term *historical body*, referring to Nishida (1958), as it concretely places accumulated experiences in the corporeal body (Scollon, S. W., 2003). (See also Chapter 10 by Lloyd.)
2 *Discourses in place*, referring to the multimodal discourses circulating in a scene of action. All places in the world are viewed as complex aggregates (nexus) of discourses that circulate through them. Discourses can be slow (as in the material environment) or rapid (as in the topics of conversations) and can be used as mediational means in action (Scollon and Scollon, 2004).
3 *Interaction order*, referring to the mutually produced social arrangements between individuals. Making use of Goffman's (1983) term, this concept describes the social arrangements with which people form relationships and identities in social interaction. It points to the ways people's actions are dependent on who they are with and the roles and role expectations they have (Scollon and Scollon, 2004, 13). Whatever individuals do, they communicate something to others present in the physical space and time and take up social or psychological positions in relation to each other (Scollon and Scollon, 2003).

As Suzie Scollon (Scollon, S. W., 2005, 180) explained it, social action and, further, 'the nexus of practice' is 'composed of the historical body that takes social action, the discourses in place through which action is taken and the interaction order (Goffman, 1983) within which it is taken'. The examination of these interrelated aspects can help understand the complex ways in which 'actions are taken through discourse and the ways discourse works its way into actions' (Jones and Norris, 2005, 8). Moreover, these elements of social action highlight the central idea in MDT that even though an action would be taken by a specific person at a specific place at a specific moment, it is not independent of other persons, places, times and discourses (Scollon, S. W., 2005, 180). Accordingly, the agency of a social actor is not viewed merely as the property of an individual, but distributed among humans and mediational means and discourses circulating through them (Scollon, R., 2001a; Scollon, S. W., 2005; Jones and Norris, 2005).

Theoretical questions: information literacy from an MDT perspective

Theorisation on literacies, and specifically technologies of literacy as the mediational means involved in specific literacy practices, have been central for MDT (Scollon and Scollon, 1983; Scollon, R., 2001a, Wohlwend, 2020). Already in their early work, Scollon and Scollon (1979; 1981; 1983) examined literacy discourses and practices focusing on children. Especially important for the understanding of literacy are Ron Scollon's ideas of the *ontogenesis* of social practices, that is, the development of a practice and, as a related question, the aggregation of the historical body of an individual during their life course (Scollon, R., 2001a). Information literacy, however, has only rarely been examined with an MDT framework (see Multas and Hirvonen, 2019; Hirvonen and Palmgren-Neuvonen, 2019; Multas, 2022 for exceptions) and it is not entirely clear how we ought to understand information literacy from this perspective. However, to further our thinking in this area, in this section three central points are made (see the next three sections) as to how MDT may open up new perspectives on information literacy in the practice-theoretical, sociocultural and discourse-analytical branches of research with which the approach shares common ground (see Multas and Hirvonen, 2019).

Information literacy as a mediational means

First, MDT suggests that information literacy can be understood as a kind of mediational means that embeds a sociocultural history and enables particular actions while constraining other actions (Scollon, R., 2001a; 2001b). According to Jones and Norris (2005, 8), MDT shares the view with New Literacy Studies scholars that literacy is a 'mediational means through which people take actions in the world by which they show their identity and their membership in particular groups'. Understood this way, literacy is a matter of performing certain kinds of actions and reproducing social practices and power relations, not a matter of individuals' skills (Jones and Norris, 2005). Broadly speaking, this view is in alignment with the ways information literacy, or information literacies, has been described in sociocultural and practice-theoretical research (see Tuominen, Savolainen and Talja, 2005; Limberg, Sundin and Talja, 2012; Lloyd, 2017).

Ron Scollon (2001b, 119) explains that literacy can be understood as 'a mediational means which (1) is acquired over time through an interaction between the habitus [historical body] of the person and his or her actions in society, (2) affords or enables certain actions [...] over time, but also (3) constrains or reduces other actions or capacities'. Here he points to the discussion of literacy as a 'cultural amplifier' (see Bruner, 1966), meaning that literacy as a cultural tool can be considered to amplify the capacities of individuals in similar ways that a physical tool may amplify their physical capacities. For instance, a hammer can extend one's strength and literacy, in turn, one's memory or other cognitive skills (Scollon, R., 2001b). What the cultural amplifier metaphor misses, however, is the notion that the tools themselves are not neutral and transform their users. While a hammer may amplify strength, it can restrict sensation and similarly, amplification of one dimension of literacy comes with the cost of narrowing another one. Moreover, the habituated use of tools, like the hammer or certain literacy practices, bring about changes in the user of the tool; their historical bodies change as a result and not only in a physical or psychological sense, but also in sociopolitical and ideological ways (Scollon, R., 2001b). Additionally, as Wertsch and Rupert (1993) have formulated, against general assumptions, cultural tools that mediate human action do not always involve evolving for the better but can be detrimental to people. From this point of view, literacy, or information literacy for that matter, is not a cultural amplifier which increases an individual's capacity, nor a defining characteristic of the person, but a mediational means that enables certain actions and constricts other ones (Scollon, R., 2001b), along with the ways we can know about the world (Jones, 2020).

On its own, the concept of mediational means, particularly when broadly understood to refer to both complex things like literacy and concrete objects like a pen (Scollon, R., 2001b), is not especially useful in characterising information literacy. Indeed, in alignment with sociocultural theories, MDT implies that mediational means can only be understood as part of practices. Consequently, to understand information literacy as a mediational means, focus needs to be placed on (information literacy) practices and, as MDT specifically suggests, their linkages in a specific nexus of practice. Overall, according to Scollon (R., 2001b), a mediational means can be understood only as its historical existence intersects with its use in action. Following from this line of reasoning, if we were to understand information literacy as a mediational means, the important questions to ask would include: in what social practices, or linkages of practices, can it be understood as such?; and how is it constituted in the historical bodies of individuals engaged in such practices (see Scollon, R., 2001b)?

Information literacy in a nexus of practice

Second, MDT invites a focus on the nexus in which information literacy practices, people and the mediational means that are involved meet. MDT departs from many practice-theoretical information literacy studies (e.g. Lloyd, 2017) in the scale in which it conceptualises the term practice (Norris and Jones, 2005). Instead of understanding social practice in its abstract, singular form (see Chouliaraki and Fairclough, 1999) or to refer to broad practices such as information seeking (see McKenzie, 2003), MDT treats practice as a countable noun referring to concrete mediated actions that are linked to each other.

For example, Scollon (R., 2001a) has used handling, greeting and waiting in a queue as examples of practices. Larger-scale constellations of linked practices, in turn, are conceptualised as a nexus of practice (see Scollon, R., 2001b; Norris and Jones, 2005). According to Norris and Jones, this narrow approach to practice allows the identification of the actual, concrete occurrences of practices and their linkages in real time which, then, enables the examination of both micro and macro-sociological questions (see also Scollon, R., 2001a and the next sub-section).

For example, online searching could be understood as a nexus of practice – as an aggregate of multiple practices such as reading, typing, clicking on a link and so on and involving a variety of mediational means ranging from concepts to technological tools. Neither the individual practices nor the mediational means connected to online searching are restricted to this particular nexus but taken together, they, with specific people, constitute certain action (Scollon and Scollon, 2004, viii). According to Wohlwend (2020, 21), literacies too can be understood to be constituted from '[c]hains of small actions' that 'signal valued ways of making meanings and performing identities in a nexus of practice'. Importantly, MDT opens a view to understand how these actions are enabled and restricted by the discourses circulating in the scene of action, the historical bodies of people and the interaction order between individuals (Scollon and Scollon, 2004).

While MDT's central arguments in terms of mediational means are in accordance with the sociocultural view that 'people's use of information cannot be meaningfully separated from the tools that are an integral part of social practices' (Limberg, Sundin and Talja, 2012, 95), in MDT, social actions are not only considered to be mediated by cultural tools as commonly understood, but by 'the social-time-place' the actors are in (Norris, 2011, 37). The concept of *discourses in place* refer to the ways all places in the world are complex nexuses for discourses, which shape the actions of humans. These discourses can be slow, embodied in the built environment, the arrangement of a space, in a technological tool, or as text or rapid, visible in the way people talk and act, for example (Scollon, S. W., 2005; Scollon and Scollon, 2004). Wohlwend and colleagues (2017) point out that discourses are materialised in ways that can both enable and prevent people from doing certain things, including accessing and using particular resources such as information in different forms. As such they are the sociocultural affordances within a site (Lloyd, 2010) that enable and constrain actions with information.

However, the historical bodies of people and the interaction order between them, as two other central elements of social action, are viewed as equally important in understanding why specific action happens in the way it does. Interaction order, referring to the social arrangements with which people form relationships and identities in interaction, points to the roles and positions that are taken in different situations (see Chapter 5 by Hicks) and explains why people act in different ways in different groupings: alone, with friends, in a classroom and so on (Scollon and Scollon, 2004). Guided by tacit agreements about the rules of the interaction order, individuals tend to adhere to their culturally and historically shaped roles (Räisänen, 2015), but different people play the same role differently, driven by their own histories (Scollon and Scollon, 2004). People are considered to carry their unique corporeal experiences, learned practices and understandings in their historical body. In other words, historical body is the accumulation of prior mediated actions, which often have become so natural for the individual (Scollon and Scollon, 2004, 13; Scollon, S. W., 2003) that they are enacted without thinking (Wohlwend, 2020). These actions, at the same time, can be viewed as 'embodied cultural knowledge that has been learned by doing, while going about everyday routines in a particular place' (Wohlwend, 2020, 30).

These perspectives underline the notion that an individual's possibilities to act, including their possibilities to become 'information literate', are in many ways restricted. The agency of individuals is viewed as distributed among humans, mediational means and discourses circulating through them (Scollon, S. W., 2005; Jones and Norris, 2005). This view of agency highlights the idea that while social action is situated, it is also always connected to persons, places, times and discourses that are not immediately present in the moment of action (Scollon, S. W., 2005, 180). See also Chapter 13 by Pilerot.

The ontogenesis of information literacy practices

Third, a potentially important notion in terms of current understandings of information literacy is the way MDT frames the development of practices across overlapping communities of practice (Larsen and Raudaskoski, 2019; Jones, 2020) and within and through the historical bodies of people (Scollon, R., 2001a; 2003). In contrast to focusing on the information literacy practice(s) of fixed groups or communities (see Tuominen, Savolainen and Talja, 2005), MDT directs attention to the ways in which practices are linked in a specific nexus of practice where social action and social actors' identities are produced. In this way, MDT does not only enable focusing on the ways different communities or groups use conceptual, cultural and technical tools to access information and to evaluate and create knowledge (Tuominen, Savolainen and Talja, 2005) but zooms both in and out from the level of communities to examine how these practices or nexuses of practice are connected to broader discourse systems or Discourses (Scollon, R., 2001b) on the one hand and the historical body of an individual on the other (see Scollon, Scollon and Jones, 2012).

Scollon (R., 2001b) found it problematic to focus on communities or groups when examining social action or practices arguing that, first, as people are assigned to certain groups, these entities are themselves sociopolitical and ideological constructs and, second, people are easily equated with 'the reality set' of the group to which they belong. However, people express multiple and even conflicting memberships to different groups and can be viewed to possess several identities that they produce and act on (Scollon, R., 2001b). Scollon refers to the concept of *discourse system* to highlight the understanding that discourses and practices cross the boundaries of fixed groups. A discourse system, to Scollon (R., 2001a), involves a set of genres, registers or forms of discourse, practices of socialisation to that discourse system, an ideology and worldview and preferred practices of interpersonal relationships. Learning specific literacy practices can be understood as becoming a participant in a discourse system (Scollon, Scollon and Jones, 2012; see also Gee, 2015) and involves 'learning new patterns of discourse' (Scollon and Scollon, 1983, 42) which then come to symbolise identity and legitimate membership in the system (Scollon, Scollon and Jones 2012). This learning can happen through formal systems of socialisation like schooling and in informal ways in everyday interaction (Scollon, Scollon and Jones, 2012) and while it happens contextually, discourse systems can both extend beyond and meet within particular communities of practice (see Lave and Wenger, 1991; Scollon, Scollon and Jones, 2012).

Discourse-analytical information literacy research has uncovered socially and culturally shaped ways of understanding information literacy and associated practices (Limberg, Sundin and Talja, 2012) but has concentrated on discourses as such rather than the ways discourses and actions are connected. Practice-theoretical and sociocultural information literacy research, in turn, tends to focus on practices with little reference to discourse. This being said, Lloyd (2017, 94) for example, in her framing of information literacy as practice, seems to point to discourse systems with the concept of information environment, described as 'sites of stable knowledge (for example, health, education, politics, religion)', based on which, through different information modalities, information landscapes are constituted. From the perspective of MDT, discourse systems can be considered to shape actions and practices, but, importantly, discourses and actions also reproduce and transform the broader discourse systems (Scollon, R., 2001b; Jones and Norris, 2005). This transformation and the ontogenesis of new practices happens through the historical bodies of people (Scollon, S. W., 2003). To exemplify this idea, Suzie Scollon characterised historical body as a compost heap of social practices where individuals do not only store past practices but where new practices can also emerge (Scollon, S. W., 2003; Scollon, Scollon and Jones, 2012). Even the simplest practices submerged in the historical bodies of people have a history, linking them with particular forms of socialisation and, ultimately, particular ideologies (Scollon, Scollon and Jones, 2012). In this way, the concept of historical body refers to a relationship between an individual and discourse systems (Scollon, Scollon and Jones, 2012) and, ultimately, individual and society. For information literacy research, this view offers a way to consider the development of information literacy from a perspective that connects societal, interpersonal and individual perspectives (see also Lloyd, 2017).

Epistemological, ontological and methodological position

Scollon (R., 2003) has explained that the mediated discourse approach follows the ideas of critical realism (see Bhaskar, 1989), in that it couples a realist ontology with a constructivist epistemology. From this stance, it is accepted that there is a world that exists independently of our descriptions of it, but our knowledge of this world is inevitably discursively produced. The material world and discursive constructs are viewed to be in dialogical relationship and mutually constructed; what we can say about the world is conditioned by the 'real' material reality and at the same time our discursive constructs can bring about changes in this reality (Scollon, R., 2003; Soukup, 2010). Mutch (2002) has written about a critical realist stance to information literacy, saying that accounts of information literacy focus excessively on the construction of meaning and do not take into account the constraints of that construction. Such constraints relate to embodiment and the structural dimensions of practice, for example. Mutch (p. 1) argues that the exploration of the constraints requires paying attention to 'the temporal dimension of social analysis' and 'the inter-relationships between structure and agency', both of which are also in the core of MDT-based research strategies.

Larsen and Raudaskoski (2019, 819) in turn, have described MDT as a socioconstructive theory, as it concerns the ways in which individuals create things such as meaning and identity locally and render 'bodily and material options available to actors in the circumstances'. However, they noted that the approach has been applied to sociomaterial research too, as it considers the effects of local constructions from a sociohistorical perspective and addresses the ways they contribute to shaping the future. Moreover, the central ideas of MDT are aligned with site ontologies that view social life as constituted through a site (Schatzki, 2002) and that have informed previous practice-theoretical information literacy theorisation (Lloyd, 2010).

Jones (2020) has deliberated on *mediation* as ontology, epistemology and axiology from an MDT perspective. For him, ontology is a discursive process of 'capturing' reality and turning it into text, while epistemology is about making a phenomenon 'tangible' and 'knowable' by transforming it into a different semiotic mode (e.g. data). Consequently, the epistemological dimension of mediation is connected to the ways we can know about the world depending on the mediational means that we use to represent it. When people appropriate particular tools to take action, they connect themselves 'to communities associated with that tool and reproduce the interaction orders and forms of social organisation that that tool helps to make possible' (Jones, 2020, 211). With the axiological dimension of mediation, Jones refers to how the tools we use affect societies and how we think things 'ought to be'. While axiology usually refers to the ways value is assigned to different things, Jones views value as a matter of social relationships and agreements about 'what will be regarded as good and bad, right and wrong, normal and abnormal'. These notions do not only apply to the 'objects' of research but also to the researcher who makes use of particular mediational means, including computer programmes, analysis methods and genres of reporting, to take action.

Mediated discourse analysis (MDA) and nexus analysis are strategies for empirical research that are consistent with the ideas of MDT and offer practical guidelines for data collection and analysis, as well as for the positioning of the researcher. They are not strict methodologies but rather meta-methodologies (Hult, 2015) that allow the use of any kind of relevant and useful data or analytical tools for studying social action (Norris and Jones, 2005). MDA has been described as a blend of practice-theoretical research, critical discourse analysis and close linguistic analysis of social interaction (Scollon, R., 2001a). Nexus analysis, developed by Ron and Şuzie Scollon, is based on the central ideas introduced in MDT and MDA and develops them further to form an overarching research strategy for studying social action (Scollon and Scollon, 2004). It can be characterised as a combination of an ethnographic methodological approach and discourse analysis (Scollon and Scollon, 2004; Larsen and Raudaskoski, 2019) that addresses a specific social issue (Lane, 2014). The approaches share a common theoretical core and take social action, involving a social actor and mediational means, as the ecological unit of analysis (Norris, 2011, xii), but differ in their focus in certain ways. Here, nexus analysis as a later development is focused on.

Nexus analysis typically addresses a social issue (Scollon and Scollon, 2004) and is in this way rooted in the critical tradition of social sciences and humanities (Lane, 2014). According to Scollon and Scollon, the first and the final problem of nexus analysis is the discovery of the social action and social actors that are relevant for the identified social issue and, consequently, for the study. After identification of the central social issue, the next step, then, is to discover who the people relevant to that issue are and how the issue is manifested as concrete actions. The analysis initially focuses on mediated action as it happens *in situ* but moves into examining how that action was enabled by different trajectories of the participants' historical bodies, the discourses in place and interaction order (Scollon and Scollon, 2004). In this way nexus analysis combines the close analysis of action to historical analysis of the intersecting trajectories of practices, mediational means and participants. This approach differentiates nexus analysis from many ethnographic or practice-theoretical studies, including those focused on information literacy (see Chapter 13 by Pilerot), in that they typically take a fixed social group or a specific community as the starting point, whereas nexus analysis focuses first on social action (Scollon and Scollon, 2004; Scollon and Scollon, 2007). Scollon and Scollon (2004, 13) described nexus analysis as 'a form of ethnography that takes social action as the theoretical center of study, not any *a priori* social group, class, tribe, or culture'.

For conducting a comprehensive nexus analysis, Scollon and Scollon (2004) suggested three central tasks for a researcher:

1 *engaging* with the relevant scenes and actors, involving the identification of points in time and space where a selected social issue is manifested in action,
2 *navigating* the trajectories of the historical bodies of the participants, the interaction order and the discourses in place that together enabled the social action taking place as a nexus of practice, and
3 *changing* the nexus of practice, referring to the researcher becoming a part of the nexus of practice and thereby also influencing it (Scollon and Scollon, 2004; Lane, 2014).

These central tasks can involve several data collection and analysis methods that can range from close empirical analysis to broader historical approaches. Scollon and Scollon suggest combining different types of data including: (a) members' generalisations (what do participants say they do); (b) 'neutral' observations (what does a 'neutral' observer see); (c) individual experience (descriptions of participants' own experience); and (d) interactions with members (participants' account of the analysis).

With this approach, nexus analysis attempts to combine a microanalysis of social action and a broader sociopolitical-cultural analysis of matters influencing that action moving 'in a widening ethnographic circumference' (Scollon and Scollon, 2004, 9). According to de Saint-Georges (2005), the focus on trajectories is an important element of nexus analysis and it invites researchers to move from the analysis of single events and discourse patterns to address broader issues concerning our social reality. A characterising feature of nexus analysis is that the researcher is not considered as an objective observer but becomes part of the nexus of practice under study (Scollon and Scollon, 2004; Kuure, Riekki and Tumelius, 2018) and even transforms it (Scollon, S. W. and de Saint-Georges, 2013).

In empirical information literacy research, nexus analysis can be considered useful in critically examining and questioning taken-for-granted assumptions of the ways mediational means shape information literacy practices across different times and places – and the social consequences of these practices. Wohlwend (2020) emphasised the usefulness of nexus analysis in examining everyday life, saying that the approach is 'particularly apt in here-and-now settings where texts are moving and fluid or where spoken language is fragmented or developing' (p. ii). According to Wohlwend '[n]exus analysis is the critical analysis of literacies that move and matter' and 'opens paths for studying literacies in action and embodiment by tracing the interaction of bodies, materials and discourses in a here-and-now location' (p. 5). The close examination of social actions directs attention to the ways even the broadest social issues are grounded in mundane micro-actions which can be considered as a nexus through which large-scale cycles of social organisation and activity circulate (Scollon and Scollon, 2004, 9).

Wohlwend (2020, 6) argues that nexus analysis is not just deconstructive, but also reconstructive, as it 'not only uncovers the hidden assumptions behind an action, but it also identifies actions with potential to become tactics to change the nexus to better address equity and participants' concerns'. Somewhat similarly, Jones (2020, 203) describes the mediated discourse approach as a way to investigate 'how human social life is constituted and how it might be constituted differently through the exercise of human agency'. This agency, according to Jones (2020) can emerge from an awareness of the mediated nature of our experiences. Wohlwend and colleagues claim that especially in literacies research the mediated action approach is useful in revealing how routines and objects materialise discourses in ways that prevent some individuals from accessing certain modes and materials as resources. Recognition of these barriers can enable the creation of tactics to mitigate them and opportunities for participants to take up more empowered identities (Wohlwend et al., 2017). Indeed, there can be an overt activist element to nexus analysis, where the objective is not only to observe action but also to change the nexus of practice (Lane, 2014). However, Scollon and Scollon (2004) have emphasised that the researcher is not in a privileged position to change the nexus of practice and change can happen in many ways. Yet nexus analysis brings forth the notion that by doing research, researchers always make a difference in the world as they are acting in it, learning and asking important questions (Wortham, 2006).

Summary

The mediated discourse theory does not provide us with a unified approach to understanding information literacy, but it offers food for thought in considering how we might understand the complex relationships between discourse and action in information literacy practices. Three central theoretical notions, based on the key ideas of MDT, were considered especially relevant for further discussion: first, information literacy can be understood as a mediational means that embeds a sociocultural history and enables particular actions while constraining other actions (Scollon, R., 2001a; 2001b), also enabling and constraining 'what we can know and who we can be' (Jones, 2020, 203); secondly, information literacy and people's possibilities to become 'information literate' can be better understood if examined in a nexus of practice where people, places, discourse and objects and their historical trajectories meet (Scollon and Scollon, 2004, viii); and thirdly, the development of information literacy practices can be viewed as happening across overlapping communities of practice (Larsen and Raudaskoski, 2019; Jones, 2020) and within and through the historical bodies of people (Scollon, R., 2001a, 2003).

MDT as an approach can be useful in addressing the tensions between the individual and community-focused understandings of information literacy. Like sociocultural, practice-theoretical and discourse-analytical approaches (see Limberg, Sundin and Talja, 2012), from this theoretical perspective information literacy is not regarded only as individual-level skills to seek, evaluate and use information, but something that emerges through social and material practices (see Lloyd, 2017). However, MDT attempts to reflect, simultaneously, how actions and practices are both individual and collective and both historical and situated. With its approach, MDT enables the consideration of the social and personal nature of information literacy practices and their dialectic relationship. In this way, while viewing the actions of individuals as resulting from broad discursive trajectories, it also addresses the unique histories and agency of individuals, including the researcher who can take on the position of an agent of change.

MDT and its methodological extensions offer a way to take social action as the theoretical and empirical centre of the study while also considering the central role of discourses in that action. MDT's narrow view of practice directs attention to the occurrences of practices and their linkages (see Norris and Jones, 2005; Scollon, R., 2001a), the identification of which can increase understanding of what information literacy can mean in a concrete sense. The initial close examination of social actions opens a view to the ways even the broadest social issues are grounded in mundane micro-actions that can be considered as a nexus through which large-scale cycles of social organisation and activity circulate (Scollon and Scollon, 2004, 9). This perspective invites an information literacy researcher to look closer at the smaller-scale practices involved in seeking, evaluating, using and creating information, the mediated actions these practices are composed of and their constellations in a specific nexus of practice. With the 'widening ethnographic circumference' (Scollon and Scollon 2004, 9), nexus analysis can then move from a microanalysis of social action to broader sociopolitical-cultural analysis (Scollon and Scollon, 2004, 9). With this approach, MDT not only provides analytical tools to understand information literacy but can also help identify actions 'with potential to become tactics to change' (Wohlwend, 2020, 14).

MDT shares common ground with previous practice-theoretical, sociocultural and discourse-analytical information literacy research and may extend their perspectives. However, there is a need for further theoretical development in this area and especially in reflecting the relationships of the concepts of 'information', 'discourse' and 'literacy'. It should be noted that the central ideas of MDT have been developed during several decades and are described slightly differently in different texts from different times. As a result, it is likely that some of the ideas described here may have been developed further in Scollons' later work or by other scholars. Therefore, this description of MDT or its relationship with information literacy should not be taken as final, but as an invitation for further discussion.

References

Bhaskar, R. (1989) *Reclaiming Reality: a critical introduction to contemporary philosophy*, Verso.

Bourdieu, P. (1977) *Outline of a Theory of Practice*, (trans. Richard Nice), Cambridge University Press.

Bruner, J. S. (1966) On Cognitive Growth. In Bruner J. S., Olver, R. R. and Greenfield P. (eds) *Studies in Cognitive Growth*, Wiley.

Chouliaraki, L. and Fairclough, N. (1999) *Discourse in Late Modernity: rethinking critical discourse analysis*, Edinburgh University Press.

de Saint-Georges, I. (2005) From Anticipation to Performance: sites of engagement as process. In Jones, R. H. and Norris, S. (eds) *Discourse in Action: introducing mediated discourse analysis*, Routledge, 167–77.

Gee, J. P. (1991) What is Literacy? In Mitchell, C. and Weiler, K. (eds) Rewriting *Literacy: culture and the discourse of the other*, Bergin & Garvey, 159–212.

Gee, J. P. (1996) *Social Linguistics and Literacies: ideology in discourses*, Falmer.

Gee, J. P. (2015) *Social Linguistics and Literacies: ideology in discourses*, 5th edn, Routledge.

Goffman, E. (1983) The Interaction Order: American Sociological Association, 1982 Presidential Address, *American Sociological Review*, **48** (1), 1–17.

Hirvonen, N. and Palmgren-Neuvonen, L. (2019) Cognitive Authorities in Health Education Classrooms: a nexus analysis on group-based learning tasks, *Library and Information Science Research*, **41** (3), 100964.

Hult, F. M. (2015) Making Policy Connections across Scales Using Nexus Analysis. In Hult, F. M. and Johnson, D. C. (eds) *Research Methods in Language Policy and Planning*, https://doi.org/10.1002/9781118340349.ch19.

Jones, R. H. (2020) Mediated Discourse Analysis. In Adolphs, S. and Knight, D. (eds) *The Routledge Handbook of English Language and Digital Humanities*, Routledge, 202–19.

Jones, R. H. and Norris, S. (2005) Discourse as Action/Discourse in Action. In Norris, S. and Jones, R. H. (eds) *Discourse in Action: introducing mediated discourse analysis*, Routledge, 3–14.

Kuure, L., Riekki, M. and Tumelius, R. (2018) Nexus Analysis in the Study of the Changing Field of Language Learning, Language Pedagogy and Language Teacher Education, *AFinLA-e: Soveltavan kielitieteen tutkimuksia*, 11, 71–92.

Lane, P. (2014) Nexus Analysis. In Östman, J.-O. and Verschueren, J. (eds) *Handbook of Pragmatics*, 2014 Instalment, John Benjamins, 1–18.

Larsen, M. C. and Raudaskoski, P. (2019) Nexus Analysis as a Framework for Internet Studies. In Hunsinger, J., Klastrup, L. and Allen, M. (eds) *Second International Handbook of Internet Research*, Springer, 1–20.

Lave, J. and Wenger, E. (1991) *Situated Learning: legitimate peripheral participation*, Cambridge University Press.

Limberg, L., Sundin, O. and Talja, S. (2012) Three Theoretical Perspectives on Information Literacy, *Human IT: journal for information technology studies as a human science*, 11 (2), 93–130.

Lloyd, A. (2006) Information Literacy Landscapes: an emerging picture, *Journal of Documentation*, 62 (5), 570–83.

Lloyd, A. (2010) Framing Information Literacy as Information Practice: site ontology and practice theory, *Journal of Documentation*, 66 (2), 245–8.

Lloyd, A. (2011) Trapped Between a Rock and a Hard Place: what counts as information literacy in the workplace and how is it conceptualized? *Library Trends*, 60 (2), 277–96.

Lloyd, A. (2017) Information Literacy and Literacies of Information: a mid-range theory and model, *Journal of Information Literacy*, 11 (1).

McKenzie, P. (2003) A Model of Information Practices in Accounts of Everyday-Life Information Seeking, *Journal of Documentation*, 59, 19–40.

Multas, A.-M. (2022) New Health Information Literacies: a nexus analytical study, University of Oulu, dissn, http://urn.fi/urn:isbn:9789526232157.

Multas, A.-M. and Hirvonen, N. (2019) Employing Nexus Analysis in Investigating Information Literacy. In Proceedings of the Tenth International Conference on Conceptions of Library and Information Science, Ljubljana, Slovenia, 16–19 June, *Information Research*, 24 (4), paper colis1944, http://InformationR.net/ir/24-4/colis/colis1944.html.

Mutch, A. (2002) Critical Realism, Managers and Information, *British Journal of Management*, 10 (4), 323–33.

Nishida, K. (1958) *Intelligibility and the Philosophy of Nothingness*, Maruzen.

Norris, S. (2011) *Identity in (Inter)action: introducing multimodal (inter)action analysis*, De Gruyter.

Norris, S. and Jones, R. H. (2005) Introducing Mediated Action. Jones, R. H. and Norris, S. (eds) *Discourse in Action: introducing mediated discourse analysis*, Routledge, 17–19.

Räisänen, S. (2015) Changing Literacy Practices: a becoming of a new teacher agency, University of Oulu, dissn, http://jultika.oulu.fi/files/isbn9789526208480.pdf.

Schatzki, T. R. (2002) *The Site of the Social: a philosophical account of the constitution of social life and change*, Pennsylvania State University Press.

Scollon, R. (1998) *Mediated Discourse as Social Interaction*, Taylor & Francis.

Scollon, R. (2001a) Action and Text: toward an integrated understanding of the place of text in social (inter)action, in Wodak, R. and Meyer, M. (eds) *Methods of Critical Discourse Analysis*, Sage, 139–82.

Scollon, R. (2001b) *Mediated Discourse: the nexus of practice*, Routledge.

Scollon R. (2003) The Dialogist in a Positivist World: theory in the social sciences and the humanities at the end of the twentieth century, *Social Semiotics*, **13** (1), 71–88.

Scollon, R. and Scollon, S. W. (1979) *Linguistic Convergence: an ethnography of speaking at Fort Chipewyan, Alberta*, Academic Press.

Scollon, R. and Scollon S. W. (1981) *Narrative, Literacy and Face in Interethnic Communication*, Ablex Publishing Corporation.

Scollon R. and Scollon, S. W. (1983) Face in Interethnic Communication. In Richards, J. and Schmidt, R. (eds) *Language and Communication*, Longman, 156–88.

Scollon, R. and Scollon, S. W. (2003) *Discourses in Place: language in the material world*, Routledge.

Scollon, R. and Scollon, S. W. (2004) Nexus Analysis: discourse and the emerging internet, Routledge.

Scollon, R. and Scollon, S. W. (2007) Nexus Analysis: refocusing ethnography on action, *Journal of Sociolinguistics*, **11** (5), 608–25.

Scollon, R., Scollon, S. W. and Jones, R. H. (2012) *Intercultural Communication: a discourse approach*, 3rd edn, Wiley & Blackwell.

Scollon, S. W. (2003) Political and Somatic Alignment: habitus, ideology and social practice. In Wodak, R. and Weiss, G. (eds) *Critical Discourse Analysis: theory and interdisciplinarity*, Palgrave Macmillan.

Scollon, S. W. (2005) Agency Distributed through Time, Space and Tools: Bentham, Babbage and the census. In Norris, S. and Jones, R. H. (eds) *Discourse in Action: introducing mediated discourse analysis*, Routledge, 172–82.

Scollon, S. W. (2014) From Mediated Discourse and Nexus Analysis to Geosemiotics: a personal account. In Sigrid Norris and Carmen Daniela Maier (eds) *Interactions, Images and Texts*, De Gruyter Mouton, 7–12.

Scollon, S. W. and de Saint-Georges, I. (2013) Mediated Discourse Analysis. In *The Routledge Handbook of Discourse Analysis*, Routledge, 66–78.

Soukup, B. (2010) Navigating Maps: review and personal commentary on Ron Scollon's (2003) *The Dialogist in a Positivist World*, *eVox*, **4** (1), Special Issue in Honor of Ron Scollon.

Street, B. (1995) *Social Literacies*, Longman.

Tuominen, K., Savolainen, R. and Talja, S. (2005) Information Literacy as a Sociotechnical Practice, *Library Quarterly*, **75** (3), 329–45.

Vygotsky, L. S. (1978) *Mind in Society: the development of higher psychological processes*, Harvard University Press.

Wertsch, J. V. (1991) *Voices of the Mind: a sociocultural approach to mediated action*, Harvard University Press.
Wertsch, J. V. (1998) *Mind as Action*, Oxford University Press.
Wertsch, J. V. and Rupert, L. J. (1993) The Authority of Cultural Tools in a Sociocultural Approach to Mediated Agency, *Cognition and Instruction*, 11 (3/4), 227–39.
Wohlwend, K. (2020) *Literacies that Move and Matter: nexus analysis for contemporary childhoods*, Routledge.
Wohlwend, K. E., Peppler, K. A., Keune, A. and Thompson, N. (2017) Making Sense and Nonsense: comparing mediated discourse and agential realist approaches to materiality in a preschool makerspace, *Journal of Early Childhood Literacy*, 17 (3), 444–62.
Wortham, S. (2006) Review of Ron Scollon and Suzie Wong Scollon, *Nexus Analysis: Discourse and the Emerging Internet*, *Journal of Sociolinguistics*, 10 (1), 127–31.

Acknowledgements

I would like to thank University Lecturer Emerita Leena Kuure and Professor Ola Pilerot for their constructive comments for this chapter.

4
The Radical and the Radioactive: Grasping the Roots of Theoretically Informed Praxis in Brazilian Studies on Critical Information Literacy

Arthur Coelho Bezerra and Marco Schneider

> If humankind produces social reality (which in the 'inversion of the praxis' turns back upon them and conditions them), then transforming that reality is an historical task, a task for humanity.
>
> (Paulo Freire, *Pedagogy of the Oppressed*)

> The coincidence of the changing of circumstances and of human activity or self-changing can be conceived and rationally understood only as revolutionary practice [*revolutionäre Praxis*].
>
> (Karl Marx, *Theses on Feuerbach*)

Introduction

Unlike the term *information literacy*, whose literary debut took place in the midst of the cold prescriptive format of institutional reports (Zurkowski, 1974), the concept of *critical information literacy* was forged in the heat of the academic environment – more specifically, in articles published in scientific journals from the North American field of library and information science, right at the dawn of the 21st century.

These first studies on critical information literacy (CIL) brought a teleological turn in the essence of information literacy (IL) goals as they were presented not only in Zurkowski's Related Paper, but also in the two documents of the American Library Association (1989; 2000) that became an international reference for IL researchers in the area of library and information science (LIS), including the Brazilian field (Dudziak, 2016). Once directed towards efficiency in the search and use of information for personal growth, information literacy, in its critical frame, does not aim at the achievements of singular individuals, but at the emancipation of society as a whole.

In order to achieve emancipation and equality, an objective that traces back to the Aristotelian ethics of the common good, it is necessary to stimulate and encourage the development of a *social consciousness* about existing inequalities and forms of oppression. This social consciousness is what should guide individuals in their actions – something that CIL North American researcher James Elmborg (2006) summarises as *theoretically informed praxis*. The idea of praxis that permeates Elmborg's writings has its origins in the critical pedagogy of the Brazilian philosopher and educator Paulo Freire (2005), a fundamental reference for Elmborg and other CIL pioneers from the USA such as Michelle Simmons (2005), Heidi Jacobs (2008), John J. Doherty and Kevin Ketchner (2005).

In Brazil, when we first published our theoretical reflections on CIL (Bezerra, 2015; Bezerra, Schneider and Brisola, 2017), our goal was to seek inspiration from our contemporary sources in the North. It was also to grasp the critical theory of society that inspired Freire's own thinking, back in the middle of the 20th century, by immersing ourselves within the waters of his critical pedagogy. Freire's *Pedagogy of the Oppressed*, one of the most cited books in the social sciences worldwide, was published in 1967.

Going even deeper into the sea of critical thinking, our theoretical dive reveals that both critical pedagogy *and* critical theory are anchored in Marx's philosophical legacy. Marx, in his famous *Theses on Feuerbach* (Marx, 2007, 534), states that 'all mysteries which lead theory to mysticism find their rational solution in human practice and in the comprehension of this practice', and, therefore, 'the coincidence of changing circumstances and of human activity or self-changing can be conceived and rationally understood only as revolutionary practice (*revolutionäre Praxis*)'. These theses, written in the middle of the 19th century, remind us of Freire's (1980; 2005) invitation to the task of humanity: to change the world through practical actions mediated by critical consciousness, an invitation that represents the basis for our recent CIL definition: 'the emancipatory praxis acting in informational practices mediated by critical consciousness' (Bezerra and Schneider, 2022, 268).

To grasp the roots of theoretically informed praxis, which is the stated objective of this text, we shall start by clarifying, in the next section, what we mean by 'criticism'. This effort is made to deepen the understanding of a word that is often used loosely in expressions such as 'critical thinking', 'critical evaluation' and so on. The two following sections describe the path of our research in CIL in recent years, which will allow the reader to become familiar with CIL as an analytical approach employed in Brazil and the authors that served as reference for our first studies. After that, we will deal with the 'radical' and the 'radioactive' elements of our studies, which are represented, respectively, by philosophers Paulo Freire (1921–97) and Karl Marx (1818–83). We shall then explain why these intellectuals are associated with such adjectives. To conclude this chapter, we bring the prospect of using the 'radioactivity' of radical studies to inject energy into the instability of everyday social life.

The critical perspective

Both in philosophy and in scientific research, criticism is an essential element to make judgements about the potentialities and limits of human knowledge and to evaluate the pretensions of a theory to speculate on the world and create mental schemes to demonstrate the truth.

Criticism is especially important to the Brazilian field of information science, whose history is usually told through changing perspectives, paradigms and dominant theories in the area. Such changes – from a 'syntactic theory' (Rendón-Rojas, 1996) or 'physicalist epistemology' (Capurro, 2003) to a cognitive perspective, as well as from a cognitive paradigm to a social or pragmatic one (Araújo, 2018) are representative of the search to overcome the limits observed in the previous dominant view: after all, what is the cognitive turn if not a critique of the limits of the mathematical studies of information by Shannon and Weaver (1964, 31), representatives of the physicalist epistemology previously referred to, for which 'semantic aspects of communication are irrelevant'? And what would the social paradigm be if not a critique of the cognitive point of view that, according to Bernd Frohmann (in Capurro, 2003), 'relegates the social processes of production, distribution, exchange and consumption of information to a noumenal level, indicated only by its effects on the representations of atomized image generators', to becoming a factor that excludes 'the social construction of informative processes . . . from the theory of librarianship and information science'?

> The limits of the cognitive paradigm rest precisely on the metaphor, or *pars pro toto*, of considering information either as something separate from the user located in a noumenal world, or of seeing the user, if not exclusively as a knowing subject, first of all as such, leaving aside the social and material conditionings of human existence. It is this reductionist view that is criticized by Bernd Frohmann, who considers the cognitive paradigm not only idealistic but also asocial.
>
> (Capurro, 2003)

If critical thinking is so fundamental in the epistemic historiography of information science, it is not reasonable to imagine that a term such as information literacy – taken from a report on information resource management for the North American industry and afterwards elevated to the status of institutional guidelines for professional standardisation, with a view towards neoliberal goals such as competitiveness, effectiveness, efficiency and profit – would remain untouched by critical scrutiny. Like Shannon's mathematical theory, which underlies the physicalist character of information science in the USA in the mid-20th century, the concept of information literacy dates back to a war context – in this case, the Cold War between the USA and the USSR, with its hot developments, as in Vietnam and Afghanistan. The need for an industrial apparatus to support warfare creates an environment in which the management of information resources becomes strategic. It is symptomatic, in this context, that the term 'information literacy' appears first in a US government report and not in an academic article.

The famous 1974 document of the United States National Commission on Libraries and Information Science, signed by its then President, Paul Zurkowski, suggests implementing a nationwide information literacy programme 'to facilitate the recognition and maintenance of the mutually supported roles of industry and libraries' (Zurkowski, 1974, 2). In accordance with such interests, the 'information literate' are 'people trained in the application of information resources to their work', capable of 'molding information solutions to their problems'; those who can read and write, but do not have such 'ability to mold information to their needs' (p. 6), should be considered information-incompetent or information-illiterate. It is not surprising that a government report with such objectives does not propose any discussion on critical evaluation and ethical use of information.

Although the above document is from the 1970s, it was only in the late 1980s, with the free market economic policy on the rise in the USA, that the American Library Association (ALA) published the report that would become the basis of the dissemination of information literacy as a worldwide movement, bringing the term closer to a more postmodern, post-structural and notably neoliberal framework (Seale, 2013; Dudziak, 2016). Released to the public in the same year as the fall of the Berlin Wall, in 1989, the final report of the ALA Presidential Committee proposes a definition for the term information literacy and advises schools and universities to integrate it into their learning programmes, 'to take advantage of the opportunities inherent within the information society' (American Library Association, 1989). Among the pillars of IL, the effective and efficient use of information for problem solving, decision making, productivity maximisation and insertion in the labour market stand out, with a proposal of lifelong learning that, in the context of the values to the ideology implicit in the document, translates into a need for eternal updating to maintain the competitiveness of the workforce.

> Out of the super-abundance of available information, people need to be able to obtain specific information to meet a wide range of personal and business needs. These needs are largely driven either by the desire for personal growth and advancement or by the rapidly changing social, political and economic environments of American society. What is true today is often outdated tomorrow. A good job today may be obsolete next year. To promote economic independence and quality of existence, there is a lifelong need for being informed and up-to-date.
>
> (ALA, 1989)

The scarce references to expressions such as 'critical thinking' and 'critical evaluation' of information, which appear in the aforementioned document alongside terms such as 'business needs', 'economic environment' and a 'nation's ability to compete internationally', defy any attempt to integrate critical theory, critical philosophy or critical pedagogy. In this sense, it could be admitted today that employees of big-tech multinationals that create mechanisms to transform social media into addictive environments are 'information literates', since the critical thinking of these individuals is successfully oriented to shape information to their needs (and, for that matter, the profit needs of the companies they work for). The same could be said of IBM's information literacy during World War 2, if we consider the company's ability to shape information in Eastern European concentration camps to the needs of its contractors – which included the Nazi regime (Black, 2001). Although IBM was not directly involved in the Holocaust, Black explains that its technology for storing data on punched cards allowed the Third Reich to automate its persecution of Jews, gypsies, homosexuals and other groups oppressed by the Nazi regime through the generation of lists of groups of people who were to be sent to concentration camps.

Such rhetorical arguments reveal how the idea attributed to the notion of 'criticism' is closely related to its ethical-political horizon, which leads us to a teleological question: what is the purpose of criticism that underlies information literacy? The 'critical' meaning of the aforementioned 1989 ALA report appears unchanged in the document on Information Literacy Standards for Higher Education, published in 2000 by the Association of College & Research Libraries (ACRL, a division of the ALA), which consolidates the technicist, neoliberal and uncritical contours of IL.

> The criticism proposed to the idea of 'competence' that underlies the concept of information literacy is mainly aimed at its eminently instrumental character, which converts the learning related to the acquisition of such literacy into something machinic, not very reflective, very operational and, finally, subordinated to the market.
>
> (Bezerra, Schneider and Saldanha, 2019, 14)

It is against this instrumental conception of criticism of the ALA documents on IL that the researchers who adopted the term 'critical information literacy' position themselves – which includes authors from the Brazilian field of LIS, as we will see below.

CIL in Brazil: approaches

Research carried out in different databases on scientific publications (Bezerra and Beloni, 2019) indicates that the first mention of critical information literacy in the field of Brazilian library and information science was in an article by Vitorino and Piantola. The statement that 'many of these studies are based on the strand of critical theory, which postulates emancipatory education and the formative experience' (Vitorino and Piantola, 2009, 136), was decisive in provoking our interest when we started our research on the subject, back in 2012.

The first Brazilian paper dedicated to a discussion of critical information literacy addressed the philosophical framework of the concept with the purpose of bringing theoretically mediated praxis to the informational environment of digital networks (Bezerra, 2015). This paper highlighted the approximations between North American CIL and Marxist thought, as well as in its revisions and adaptations made by theorists of the so-called Frankfurt School – 'although the North American authors don't spell it out directly' (Bezerra, 2015, 8). These critical Marxist perspectives share with our notion of CIL:

i) the perception of historical reality as constructed through class struggles; ii) the sensitivity to observe the social inequalities that shape the social structure in dominant and dominated groups; and iii) the recognition that the dominant ideas in all epochs and societies are the ideas of the dominant class, that is, the one that owns the means of material production.

(Bezerra, 2015, 8–9)

In 2017, the first article on CIL in a Brazilian academic journal was published (Bezerra, Schneider and Brisola, 2017), followed by a number of papers presented at academic conferences and other forms of scientific communication in Brazil. In 2019, the book *iKritika: critical information studies* brought together the main points of our research on CIL, in dialogue with a critical information theory inspired by the critical theory developed by Marxist philosophers from Frankfurt (Bezerra, 2019) and with praxis in the fight against post-truth. In this title, Schneider (2019) developed a particular notion of critical information literacy in seven articulated levels or dimensions (CIL/7):

1 *Concentration or suspension of everyday life*, which is based on Agnes Heller's (1984) notion that the transition from common sense to critical thinking means the suspension of everyday life, with concentration being the first movement.
2 *Instrumental:* in order to have critical information literacy, one cannot do without the knowledge of sources of information (both analogue and digital), the systematics of its use, the ability to handle certain technical equipment or search systems, etc.
3 *Taste:* the notion of 'informational taste' has a double function: to question the essentialist character of the very notion of informational need and to propose a debate about what types of 'needs' should or should not be stimulated, from the perspective of social emancipation. We employ the notion of taste as a sociohistorically mediated need to emphasise precisely that so-called individual needs are socially determined. Therefore, it is advocated that CIL should problematise the notion of informational need, always questioning the social determinations that form the so-called individual needs. 'Informational taste' is a concept that dialectically articulates the most universal notion of necessity with those related to particular cultures and singular experiences. Making an analogy with food: the need to eat is universal, but the set of foods available varies according to regional particularities, social class, etc. And the preferences among the available options are singular, individual, but not independent of the (universal) need for food, nor of the particular limits and possibilities of access to food according to the regions of the world, cultural traditions, social class, etc.
4 *Relevance:* how are information relevance hierarchies established, by search systems, by individuals who seek information, by information mediators such as newspaper editors, librarians, teachers and others responsible for preparing curricula and bibliographies, etc.? What are their criteria and foundations? How and to what

extent, in each case, are these hierarchies and criteria influenced by political and economic powers, nationally and internationally?
5 *Credibility:* what makes one or another source more credible? How are cognitive authorities produced and destroyed? This doubt highlights the need to question the credibility of the information source as well as the criteria for assigning credibility to this source; one should also keep in mind that the credibility of the speaker is not enough to ensure the correctness of the statement.
6 *Ethics:* we must remember that legal and ethical use of information are not the same thing (Bezerra and Sanches, 2018) – although they seem to be in the ALA's notion of information literacy (American Library Association, 1989; Association of College & Research Libraries, 2000; 2016). Ethics is a vital field of praxis, which has interconnected epistemological, political and aesthetic or existential dimensions. We must take seriously the ethical principles and uses of information as a vital field of reflection, because truth and lie, freedom and oppression, happiness and unhappiness are not decorative questions.
7 *Criticism:* CIL requires accurate knowledge of critical social theories and critical theories of information.

Later, Bastos (2020; Schneider and Bastos, 2021) suggested an eighth level: (8) *critical engagement*, which assumes that an effective fair use of information requires commitment to social justice, involving attachment of the subject with emancipatory praxis, 'to overcome the individuals' everyday and phenomenal relationship with each other and the world through the mediation of socio-technical networks, in a reified way' (Bastos, 2020, 206). Finally, Brisola (2021) suggested a ninth and a tenth level: (9) *gender* and (10) *ethnic-racial relations*.

In parallel to the establishment of these levels, our studies focused on addressing the ideology of competence that, according to the Brazilian philosopher Marilena Chauí, 'conceals the social division of classes by stating that the social division takes place between the competent (the specialists who have scientific and technological knowledge) and the incompetent (those who perform the tasks commanded by the specialists)' (Chauí, 2003, 105). Such an ideology, promoted as part of neoliberal rhetoric in the sense of linking the need for subjects' perpetual adaptation to market fluctuations, can lead to the understanding that if a person cannot get a well-paid job, it is because they have not pursued information literacy hard enough (Seale, 2013, 49). This proposition clearly illustrates how 'dominant notions of information literacy reinforce and reproduce neoliberal ideology, which is invested in consolidating wealth and power within the upper class through the dispossession and oppression of non-elites' (Seale, 2013, 40).

CIL in Brazil: influences
Among the CIL authors who served as references for our first criticism of the standard notion of IL were Simmons (2005), Doherty and Ketchner (2005), Elmborg (2006; 2012),

Jacobs (2008) and Tewell (2015). All of them carried out their research in North America, either in the library or in the classroom, and all were influenced not only by Freire's critique of the 'banking' education model (that would somehow be the default IL model), but also for his pedagogical perspective of praxis, which can be summarised as the dialectical relation between critical consciousness and action upon the world in order to transform it.

Elmborg (2012, 90) states that, for Freire, 'in order to learn to read and write, these learners needed to develop a consciousness, a literate awareness of the power of having a mind, of having thoughts of one's own. They needed to move beyond thinking of the world as existing in a reified reality that they could experience but not change.' Paraphrasing Marx's well-known (and poorly understood) analogy between opium and religion, he says:

> For Freire, consciousness is central to literacy. In articulating a concept like the 'banking concept,' Freire wants to challenge the idea that we can deposit knowledge in people's minds while leaving them relatively unchanged in terms of how they see themselves in the world. For Freire, this 'depositing' represents the ultimate fraud, a sort of parlor trick that separates real human growth from the accumulation of knowledge as thing. This trick is necessary to keep learners from asking fundamental questions about where they stand in this world and how it might be different. Viewed this way, 'banking education' (rather than religion) is the opiate of the people.
> (Elmborg, 2012, 90)

'By developing critical consciousness', Elmborg (2006, 193) writes, 'students learn to take control of their lives and their own learning to become active agents, asking and answering questions that matter to them and to the world around them'. As Doherty and Ketchner (2005, 1) remind us, 'Freire's critical form of educational theory suggests that educators (and we include librarians here) need to first engage their students in the contexts of the students' experiences'. In this sense, 'the real task for libraries in treating information literacy seriously lies not in defining it or describing it, but in developing a critical practice of librarianship – a theoretically informed praxis' (Elmborg, 2006, 198).

On the same note, Tewell (2015, 33) says that 'significant overlap exists in the critical information literacy literature in regard to theory and practice and appropriately so, as critical pedagogy calls for the continual reciprocity of both theory and practice to form praxis'. These arguments are in line with CIL premises of not only pointing out the problems related to the concept of IL, but also considering the ways to 'encourage students to engage with and act upon the power structures underpinning information's production and dissemination' (p. 25).

The conceptual framework on which the idea of praxis is built in the work of Paulo Freire is the same that underlies the critical theory of the so-called Frankfurt School: the historical materialism of Marx and Engels. The concept of praxis is of fundamental importance for the construction of the Marxist philosophical system, as we can see not only in the aforementioned *Theses on Feuerbach*, in which the references to praxis are explicit (and summarised in the idea of philosophers transforming the world, in the famous Thesis Eleven), but in practically all Marxian work, from his youth (Marx was 26–27 years old when he wrote the theses) to his last writings.

Nevertheless, although Freire's critical pedagogy is assumed as a theoretical reference for North American studies of CIL and it is possible to identify, in some of these authors, approximations between CIL and critical theory (such as in Doherty and Ketchner, 2005), there are practically no mentions of the Marxist philosophers who established such a theory as a school of thought. One rare exception is Elmborg's mention that 'Freire's pedagogy also derives from his Christian perspective, which boosted his concern for the poor and which he allied to a Marxist philosophy of class and power' (Elmborg, 2012, 89).

In fact, the critical legacy present in the thoughts of Karl Marx, Friedrich Engels, György Lukács, Rosa Luxemburg, Antonio Gramsci and other Marxist thinkers, including the Frankfurtian philosophers of critical theory (Max Horkheimer, Theodor W. Adorno, Herbert Marcuse and others), seems to go unnoticed, or just appear through Freirian echoes. For Donaldo Macedo, prefacer of the North American edition that celebrates 30 years since the first publication of *Pedagogy of the Oppressed* in that continent, one of the main places in which he sees a 'misinterpretation of Freire's philosophical and revolutionary pedagogical proposals' lies in the 'disarticulation of Freire's thinking from his enormous debt to a philosophical tradition that included Marx, Gramsci, Hegel and Sartre among others' (in Freire, 2005, 25).

It is precisely at this point that studies on CIL developed in Brazil differ from the North American ones: by recognising that Freire's praxis (which criticises oppressive 'banking' education and aims at the emancipation of individuals through a libertarian education) has its method and theoretical-epistemological perspectives rooted in the revolutionary praxis of Marx and Engels' historical materialism (as illustrated by the comparison between the epigraphs by Freire and Marx chosen for this chapter), we are able to return to the studies of these German philosophers – and those who later developed critical theory inspired by their writings – to converge in new modalities of praxis that embrace the critical appropriation and ethical use of information.

This differentiation between Brazilian and North American CIL approaches, however, does not constitute a departure. On the contrary, it points to greater possibilities for intellectual exchange between the North American and the Brazilian schools of studies in CIL, in a critical perspective – as it should be. In fact, such a dialogue was held recently, as we will see below.

The radical and the radioactive

Critical Literacy Information: theory, conscience and praxis (Bezerra and Schneider, 2022) is the title of the first book that presents a compilation of studies on CIL in Brazil. This collective work brings together chapters signed by over 15 researchers from north to south of the country, in addition to in-depth interviews with the aforementioned CIL researchers Michelle Simmons, Eamon Tewell and James Elmborg.

In these interviews with our peers from the north (which were conducted in partnership with PhD student Ana Lúcia Borges in 2021), we were able to address several issues, such as access to information, (absence of) pedagogical neutrality, the importance of libraries in the formation of critical thinking, surveillance and disinformation in current digital networks, radical democracy, social justice and the influence of Marxism on Freirean thought – and, consequently, the theoretical framework of CIL, which is the subject we are interested in approaching here.

Among the issues listed above, we put the same question to our three interviewees: 'What do you think would be the reasons for Marxist critical thought to remain invisible in CIL studies, which seem to share the same philosophical and ethical-political principles?' Interestingly, despite giving us an interesting interview with thoughtful responses, Simmons kindly chose not to answer this particular question. Elmborg and Tewell, on the other hand, gave us strong answers, which we reproduce here in summary.

Assuming that we, the interviewers, are 'absolutely correct both in recognizing that Marx has largely been excluded from the applied critical discussion in the U.S.', Elmborg (2022, 238) lists a series of reasons he believes are more related to 'a pragmatic rhetorical decision by writers and their relationship to audience and effect' and the very 'nature of higher education in the U.S.'. He does so through an energetic metaphor:

> First, to put it bluntly, Marx is radioactive in the culture of the United States. John Lennon famously sang the words: 'If you go carrying pictures of Chairman Mao, You ain't going to make it with anyone anyhow.' For fifty years, the U.S. was locked in cold war with communism. For that time, American attitudes toward Marx and Marxism were conflated into a propaganda framework that proposed that capitalism and democracy were intimately and productively linked in the American character and that individual liberty was threatened by the collectivity and 'welfare' state of Marxism/Communism. To bring Marx directly to bear on the discussion of Critical Pedagogy generally and Critical Information Literacy specifically results in an immediate rejection of the position among a very large percentage of the audience, particularly those who oversee it or fund it. This is especially true in the large rural areas of the country where rugged individualism and self-sufficiency is baked into the cultural identity.
>
> (Elmborg, 2022, 238)

On the one hand, Elmborg states that, in the intellectual environment of the North American academy, 'Marx finds a ready place in the scholarship of pure disciplines like Philosophy, Political Science and Economics.' Conversely, 'Marx is much more problematic in applied fields like Social Work, Education and Library Science where we train people to go out and work with the public in active and positioned ways' (Elmborg, 2022, 238). This would be one of the main reasons why 'we can read Paulo Freire, but it's best to tread carefully around his debt to Marx' (Elmborg, 2022, 239).

Also in a pragmatic piece of analysis, Tewell states:

> . . . the general inclination among librarians in North America to avoid discussing politics explicitly, in their work and scholarship, as well as an emphasis overall on immediate applicability and practicality of one's research, undoubtedly contribute to this. Major journals in North American Library & Information Science rarely respond favorably to studies that are not empirical or quantitative, so critical theory in general does not often appear in scholarly conversations there.
>
> (Tewell, 2022, 256)

Furthermore, the authors point out that 'the world of academic Marxism is a tough place. Marx was such a voluminous and complex thinker and his commentators and adherents have been prolific as well. It is extremely difficult to become an 'expert' in Marx' (Elmborg, 2022, 239); thus, 'many researchers contributing to the literature are librarians who may or may not have a formal educational background in this area, so they may feel unequipped to comment on or effectively incorporate these theorists into their work' (Tewell, 2022, 258).

What we believe is that, precisely because Marx is an author whose philosophical, sociological, economic and political contribution is as vast as it is complex, his study should be valued by academic programmes that have the 'awakening of critical consciousness' as an ethical-political horizon. Fortunately, Elmborg tells us, 'as older generations die off, the cold war mentality fades and today many public figures in the U.S. are willing to declare themselves Marxists or at least that they have been influenced by Marx', remembering the self-declared Democratic Socialist Bernie Sanders.

> In Canada in particular, an increasing number of researchers are examining the political economy of libraries and information and are drawing upon Marxism in particular to do so. Being explicit about these connections and where influences are drawn from is important and as the field progresses I expect there will be more explicit acknowledgement of Marxist thought as well as other important thinkers, particularly in critical race theory, who have much to offer in expanding the current bounds of CIL.
>
> (Tewell, 2022, 256)

Tewell believes that *radical democracy theory*, defined by him as 'one approach among many for moving towards social justice', is 'one possibility for arriving at a more socially just world', recognising that 'there is value in building democracy around dissent, so that the oppressive power relations that liberal democracy upholds can be challenged' (Tewell, 2022, 251).

Nevertheless, it is worth pointing out that Freire, who is often cited as the major influence of CIL in the US model, is considered a radical thinker. And what does it mean to be radical? In accordance with Marx (2005), 'to be radical is to grasp the matter at the root. But for man the root is man himself'. Once again, Freire's own words seem to be in line with Marx: 'radicalization, which implies the rooting that man makes in the choice he has made, is positive, because it is predominantly critical. Because it is critical and loving, is humble and communicative' (Freire, 1980, 50). It is this shared comprehension of radical thinking in the defence of social emancipation from the prevailing forms of oppression that has guided our research on CIL in the last decade.

Conclusion

From the testimonies of our peers from the north, we see that, outside the islands of purely philosophical and merely theoretical thought of the universities, associating the radical Freire with the radioactive Marx can bring problems, compromise research funding, alienate interlocutors and even put jobs at risk. This would be, in addition to the theoretical difficulty inherent to the dense Marxist critical thought, a possible reason why North American studies on critical information literacy do not put themselves in direct contact with such epistemology.

Just as the term 'critical theory' was used as a kind of euphemism for the Marxist Frankfurt theorists Horkheimer and Adorno when they were in exile in the USA due to the Nazi rise in Germany during World War 2, the term 'philosophy of praxis' was employed by the Italian philosopher Antonio Gramsci to camouflage his writings on historical materialism of Marx during his imprisonment by the fascist regime of Benito Mussolini.

Recently in Brazil, we were almost falling into a similar situation after four years of a militarised government that several times flirted with the possibility of returning to dictatorship (under which Brazil was governed between 1964 and 1985), a tragic destiny fortunately interrupted by the victory, in the presidential elections of October 2022, of the Workers' Party candidate Luiz Inácio Lula da Silva – who had already been president of Brazil for two consecutive terms (from 2003 to 2010). Right now, however, while we finish the writing of this chapter (January 2023), neofascists and their disinformation army, who act in an increasingly similar way to hallucinating sects, tried to forge a *coup d'état* that the elected government, alongside researchers, teachers and activists in critical media and information literacy, among other light and radical democrats, are fighting to dismantle.

This dangerous moment reminds us why literacy and competence that is manifested in the most diverse informational practices cannot be glimpsed in its merely technical dimension, being necessarily linked to the critical consciousness that guides the ethical-political action. In this sense, we insist on stating that effective practices and efficient information strategies that are oriented to the interests of valuing political or economic capital, in clear lack of engagement and commitment to the fight against inequalities and oppression, are not an expression, but a target of criticism of CIL studies.

References

American Library Association (ALA) (1989) Presidential Committee on Information Literacy:
    Final Report, www.ala.org/acrl/publications/whitepapers/presidential.
American Library Association (ALA) (2000) *Information Literacy Competency Standards for Higher*
    Education, https://alair.ala.org/handle/11213/7668.

Araújo, C. A. A. (2018) *O que é ciência da informação*, KMA.

Association of College & Research Libraries (ACRL) (2000) *Information Literacy Competency Standards for Higher Education*.

Association of College & Research Libraries (ACRL) (2016) *Framework for Information Literacy for Higher Education*.

Bastos, P. N. (2020) Dialectics of Engagement: a critical contribution to the concept, *Matrizes*, 14 (1), 193–220.

Bezerra, A. C. (2015) Vigilância e Filtragem de Conteúdo nas Redes Digitais: desafios para a competência crítica em informação. In *Anais do XVI ENANCIB – Encontro Nacional de Pesquisa em Ciência da Informação*, ANCIB.

Bezerra, A. C. (2019) Teoria Crítica da Informação: proposta de integração entre os conceitos de regime de informação e competência crítica em informação. In Bezerra, A. C., Schneider, M., Pimenta, R. M. and Saldanha, G. S. (eds) *iKritika: estudos críticos em informação*, 1st edn, Garamond.

Bezerra, A. C. and Beloni, A. (2019) Os Sentidos da 'Crítica' nos Estudos de Competência em Informação, *Em Questão*, 25 (2), 208–28.

Bezerra, A. C. and Sanches, T. (2018) Copyright Infringement: between ethical use and legal use of information. In *Proceedings of the Fifteenth International ISKO Conference*, 9–11 July, Porto, Portugal, https://doi.org/10.5771/9783956504211-762.

Bezerra, A. C. and Schneider, M. (2022) *Competência Crítica em Informação: teoria, consciência e práxis*, Garamond.

Bezerra, A. C., Schneider, M. and Brisola, A. (2017) Pensamento Reflexivo e Gosto Informacional: disposições para competência crítica em informação, Informação & sociedade: estudos, 27 (1), 7–16.

Bezerra, A. C., Schneider, M. and Saldanha, G. S. (2019) Competência crítica em informação como crítica à competência em informação, *Informação & Sociedade: Estudos*, João pessoa, 29 (3), https://periodicos.ufpb.br/ojs/index.php/ies/article/view/47337.

Black, E. (2001) *IBM and the Holocaust: the strategic alliance between Nazi Germany and America's most powerful corporation*, Random House.

Brisola, A. C. C. de A. S. (2021) Competência Crítica em Informação como Resistência à Sociedade da Desinformação sob um Olhar Freiriano: diagnósticos, epistemologia e caminhos ante as distopias informacionais contemporâneas. Orientador: Prof. Dr. Marco André Feldman Schneider. Tese (Doutorado em Ciência da Informação) – Escola de Comunicação, Universidade Federal do Rio de Janeiro; Instituto Brasileiro de Informação em Ciência e Tecnologia.

Capurro, R. (2003) Epistemologia e Ciência da Informação. In *Anais do V ENANCIB – Encontro Nacional de Pesquisa em Ciência da Informação*, ANCIB, www.capurro.de/enancib_p.htm.

Chauí, M. (2003) Ideologia da competência. In *O Que é Ideologia*, Brasiliense.

Doherty, J. J. and Ketchner, K. (2005) Empowering the Intentional Learner: a critical theory for information literacy instruction, *Library Philosophy and Practice*, Nebraska, 8 (1).

Dudziak, E. A. (2016) Políticas de Competência em Informação: leitura sobre os primórdios e a visão dos pioneiros da information literacy. In Alves, F. M. M., Corrêa, E. C. D. and Lucas, E. R. O. (eds) *Competência em Informação: políticas públicas, teoria e prática*, EDUFBA.

Elmborg, J. (2006) Critical Information Literacy: implications for instructional practice, *Journal of Academic Librarianship*, 32 (2), 192–9.

Elmborg, J. (2012) Critical Information Literacy: definitions and challenges. In Wilkinson, C. W. and Bruch, C. (eds) *Transforming Information Literacy Programs: intersecting frontiers of self, library culture and campus community*, Association of College & Research Libraries.

Elmborg, J. (2022) Interview. In Bezerra, A. C. and Schneider, M. (eds) *Competência Crítica em Informação: teoria, consciência e práxis*, Garamond.

Freire, P. (2005) *Pedagogy of the Oppressed* (trans. Myra Bergman Ramos; introduction by Donaldo Macedo), 30th anniversary edn, The Continuum International Publishing Group Inc.

Heller, A. (1984) *Everyday Life*, Routledge & Kegan Paul, 1984.

Jacobs, H. L. M. (2008) Information Literacy and Reflective Pedagogical Praxis, *Journal of Academic Librarianship*, 34 (3), 256–62.

Marx, K. (2005) *Crítica à Filosofia de Direito de Hegel*, Boitempo.

Marx, K. (2007) Teses sobre Feuerbach. In Marx, K. and Engels, F., *A Ideologia Alemã*, Boitempo.

Marx, K. (2013) *O Capital: crítica da economia política*, Livro I, Boitempo.

Rendón-Rojas, M. A. (1996) Hacia un Nuevo Paradigma en bibliotecologia, *Transinformação*, 8 (3), 17–31.

Schneider, M. (2019) CCI / 7: competência crítica em informação (em 7 níveis) como dispositivo de combate à pós-verdade. In Bezerra, A. C., Schneider, M., Pimenta, R. M. and Saldanha, G. S. (eds) *iKritika. Estudos críticos em informação*, 1st edn, Garamond.

Schneider, M. and Bastos, P. (2021) Critical Information Literacy. In Coetzee Bester, C., Britz, J., Capurro, R. and Fischer, R. (eds) *Nelson Mandela: a reader on information ethics*, International Center for Information Ethics.

Seale, M. (2013) The Neoliberal Library. In Gregory, L. and Higgins, S. (eds) *Information Literacy and Social Justice: radical professional praxis*, Library Juice Press, 39–61.

Shannon, C. and Weaver, W. (1964) *The Mathematical Theory of Communication*, University of Illinois Press.

Simmons, M. H. (2005) Librarians as Disciplinary Discourse Mediators: using genre theory to move toward critical information literacy, *Libraries and the Academy*, 5 (3), 297–311.

Tewell, E. (2015) A Decade of Critical Information Literacy: a review of the literature, *Communications in Information Literacy*, 9 (1), 24–43.

Tewell, E. (2022) Interview. In Bezerra, A. C. and Schneider, M. (eds) *Competência Crítica em Informação: teoria, consciência e práxis*, Garamond.

Vitorino, E. V. and Piantola, D. (2009) Competência Informacional – bases históricas e conceituais: construindo significados, *Ciência da Informação*, 38 (3), 130–41.

Zurkowski, P. (1974) Information Services Environment Relationships and Priorities. Related paper, No. 5, National Commission on Libraries and Information Science.

5
Locating Information Literacy within Discursive Encounters: A Conversation with Positioning Theory

Alison Hicks

Positioning theory

Positioning theory provides a framework through which the fine-grained dynamics of social episodes can be studied. At the heart of this work lies the position, a sociological concept that has been used to refer to a person's status or constellation within a community (Bjerre, 2021, 266). However, beginning in the 1990s, position took on a new meaning as Rom Harré and other constructionist and post-structuralist theorists started to reconceptualise positions and related acts of positioning in terms of the distribution of rights and duties within a particular interaction. Drawing attention to how people locate themselves (and others) within conversation, this development also introduced a more overt focus on the ways in which the position obliges and limits the potential to act. Positioning theory was labelled as a theory in 1999 (Van Langenhove and Wise, 2019). Still relatively unchanged since then, it constitutes a multi-layered framework through which the impact of living in 'an ocean of language' (Harré, 2008, 32) can be analysed, including how people construct themselves – and have their opportunities and worlds constructed – through social encounters.

For information literacy, positioning theory presents an opportunity to consider the role that granular, social interactions play in shaping information landscapes (Lloyd, 2006). Involving a shift from thinking about information literacy itself to the 'flow of talking and writing' within which information literacy actions are set (cf. Moghaddam, Harré and Lee, 2007, 4), a focus on position-positioning relationships draws attention to language use and interaction, whether this is written, spoken or material. It also extends research examining the social sites of information practice (e.g. Tuominen, Savolainen and Talja, 2005; Lloyd, 2005) by interrogating the conditions that shape information environments, including the impact that discursive constructions have upon what kinds of knowledge are valued, who can access learning opportunities and claims about how information literacy should happen. In focusing on social encounters, this chapter follows Davies and Harré (1990, 45) to define discourse as an 'institutionalised use of language and language-like sign systems' that both constitutes and forms a resource through which speakers and hearers negotiate social practice (Davies and Harré, 1990, 62).

Overview of positioning theory

At its heart, positioning theory centres on how people make sense of reality in a discursively constructed world. Establishing meaning as the basis of social action (Harré and Van Langenhove, 1999, 3), the emphasis on discourse locates social interactions as the mechanism through which these 'meanings are progressively and dynamically achieved' (Davies and Harré, 1990, 46). Individual subjectivity is consequently understood as constituted through the discursive practices in which people participate. At the same time, opportunities to interact within these discursive spaces are not always evenly distributed; discourses are seen to make specific positions available for people to take up (Hollway, 1984, 236). Positioning theory, with its focus on how the attribution of positions locates people within social structures, consequently provides the means to explore the constitutive force of discourse in more detail, including the impact that the adoption or the rejection of discursive practices has upon everyday life. In this sense, positioning theory draws attention to what enables or constrains a person's actions within an encounter – rather than what people do, as in the behaviourist tradition, or what people can do, as in a cognitive approach (Harré et al., 2009, 9).

The central concept that gives shape to this theoretical work is the position, which is employed as both a noun and a verb. As a noun, positions are theorised as the distribution of a loose set of rights and duties to perform certain acts (Harré and Moghaddam, 2003, 5–6), an idea that goes beyond a simple metaphor to encompass the normative frames and boundaries of everyday practice. As a verb, positioning refers to the acquisition or assignment of this structure of rights to oneself and others, which recognises individual agency as well as the social shape of discourse. Traced to a variety of influences, including military and marketing strategy as well as Hollway's (1984) work examining gender differences (Harré and Van Langenhove, 1999, 16), these definitions acknowledge how social acts are made determinate through discursive processes. In further emphasising that moral orders create 'ever-shifting patterns' of obligational characteristics (Harré and Van Langenhove, 1999, 1), the concept of a position also emerges in direct contrast to a role, which is seen to focus on predetermined 'fixed, often formally defined and long-lasting' states (Harré, 2008, 30) rather than the more ephemeral ways in which speech and action play out.

Foundational positioning theory work further establishes different modes of positioning, including the designation of performative or first-order positioning, which refers to how people locate themselves and others within a conversation; accoutive or second- and third-order positioning, which refers to the negotiation of first-order positioning during and after an encounter; and moral and personal positioning, which link expectations to either a person's role or their individual attributes. Positioning is additionally understood to be either tacit or intentional (Harré and Van Langenhove, 1991, 396–9). Elaborating some of the potential ways in which positioning unfolds, these analytical distinctions establish that positions are contestable, in that people can acquiesce in a positioning as well as challenge and subvert it (Davies and Harré, 1990, 2). They also affirm that positions are relational, in that the positioning of a person or group also positions the person or group doing the positioning (Harré and Van Langenhove, 1999, 1). These ideas imply that social life must be seen as actively shaped, both through the recognition that conversation unfolds through joint forms of action and through the labelling of people as 'choosing subjects' who bring a lived history to narratives (Davies and Harré, 1990, 52).

Origins of positioning theory

Positioning theory emerged in the 1990s at a time when traditional, causal models of human behaviour were becoming increasingly critiqued; experimental research methods and the manipulation of variables was thought to over-emphasise isolated individuals in static situations (Harré and Moghaddam, 2003, 2). In contrast, the emergence of what has been labelled as a second 'dynamic paradigm' of psychology (Harré and Moghaddam, 2003, 3) refocused attention on the dynamics of social interaction or the meanings that people accord to social phenomena and the rules and customs that govern these understandings. However, social psychologist Rom Harré argued that there was still one significant omission from this work, namely the recognition that the ability to act or contribute to social episodes was not 'uniformly distributed through the group in question' (Harré and Moghaddam, 2003, 4). Positioning theory was developed to account for this oversight and to draw attention to the impact of socially possible actions.

The basis of foundational positioning theory work consequently lies in social constructionist psychology; social acts are taken 'as the "matter" of social reality' (Harré and Van Langenhove, 1991, 394) while discourse is seen to be the process through which 'meanings are progressively and dynamically achieved' (Davies and Harré, 1990, 46). Other noted influences include the work of Vygotsky (1978), whose impact can be traced through the emphasis that positioning theory places upon the individual appropriation of social language use. The focus on rights and duties also implies a theoretical debt to Wittgenstein's (1953) philosophy of psychology, including how language is sustained through social rules. Since then, Harré's foundational positioning theory work has continued to be developed through co-authorship with Bronwyn Davies, Luc Van Langenhove and Fathali Moghaddam, amongst others, all of whom have introduced different emphases into the overarching guiding framework. These divergences have led scholars to represent positioning theory as constituted by loosely related subfields, including post-structuralist, social ontological and cultural positions (Bjerre, 2021, 252), rather than forming a shared tree trunk with distinct but related branches (e.g. McVee et al., 2019).

Positioning theory consequently enjoys a broad set of 'intellectual underpinnings' (Howie and Peters, 1996, 51); Harré's work with Davies, for example, demonstrates that post-structuralist influences have also played an important role within positioning theory since its creation (McVee et al., 2019, 386). Analysis into the origins of positioning theory also spotlights theoretical inconsistencies, including whether Davies and Harré's emphasis on post-structuralist notions of the subject align with the humanistic, ego-centred traditions that have been traced within other foundational positioning theory work (Peters and Appel, 1996). These issues are further complicated through the pinpointing of cognitivist elements in Harré's original theorisation, which raises questions about the underlying claims that positioning theory makes about 'mind, world and discourse' (Korobov, 2010, 263; Gergen, 2019). While this critical reflection speaks to the enduring possibilities that positioning theory offers for the study of social action, it also has implications for the use of this theoretical work within information literacy research, particularly related to our understandings of agency and social order.

Positioning theory within library and information science

Positioning theory has had a small but significant impact within library and information science (LIS) research. Employed within a flurry of Canadian studies in the early 2000s (e.g. McKenzie and Carey, 2000; Given, 2002; Julien and Given, 2003; McKenzie, 2004), positioning theory emerged at a time when LIS research was engaging more concretely with sociocultural and everyday phenomena. The use of positioning theory was consequently used to extend these new theoretical shifts through drawing attention to the impact of discursive constructions upon information practice (McKenzie, 2004). However, research that has employed positioning theory to date has tended to centre on information seeking and needs rather than other aspects of human information activity (e.g. Genuis, 2013; Given, 2002; McKenzie, 2003; 2004; Villanueva, 2021). It has also predominantly centred on healthcare settings, perhaps due to the noted potential for the unequal distribution of power within medical encounters (e.g. McKenzie, 2003; 2004; Genuis, 2013; Villanueva, 2021). Within the field of information literacy, the use of positioning theory has been less widespread, being initially limited to an examination of teaching librarian roles (Julien and Given, 2003). However, Rivano Eckerdal's (2011) exploration of decision making within contraceptive clinics opened the field up to the possibility of using positioning theory to examine the contextual shape of information literacy, including how information evaluation is negotiated within professional encounters. Since then, Lloyd and Hicks (2021) and Hicks and Lloyd (2021; 2022b) have built on these ideas through their examination of positioning within the COVID-19 information environment and higher education discourse respectively. Noting that information literacy is shaped through the ways in which people are discursively positioned within a specific context, Lloyd and Hicks' research also draws attention to the interplay of discursive spaces, or the complex arrangements that both constrain and enable the enactment of information literacy practice (Lloyd, 2010a).

Positioning theory and information literacy

Having provided an overview of positioning theory, the chapter will now focus in more detail on examining its conceptual framework in relation to information literacy, an important goal given the scarcity of literature in the field. Positioning theory was originally employed within LIS to extend the 'social constructionist turn', which shifted research towards linguistically oriented social analysis (McKenzie, 2004). In emphasising social activity, positioning theory also reinforced the even earlier 'user turn', which unsettled the previously dominant systems focus (Talja and Hartel, 2007). Twenty years on, what does positioning theory offer for information literacy research and practice? More explicitly, what claims does positioning theory make and how do these ideas open up (and close off) information literacy research? These questions will be the subject of the second part of this chapter.

How does positioning theory enable or open up understandings of information literacy?

The origins and theoretical heritage of positioning theory mean that it has the potential to have a significant impact on the shape of information literacy, including opening it up to certain ideas while closing it off to others. An examination of these influences will help to unpack the value of positioning theory as well as to consider the preconceptions that it introduces.

One of the first understandings that positioning theory opens information literacy up to is the ways in which social conditions shape the construction of information landscapes or how information activities are enabled and constrained within the context of a specific setting. Drawing upon the idea that discourse enables or constrains what is possible – and that positioning unfolds through discursive practice – positioning can be seen as shaping action through establishing what is logically and socially possible (Harré and Moghaddam, 2003, 5). Thus, information literacy is enabled through the ways in which midwives position young women within Rivano Eckerdal's study of contraceptive counselling; in providing information about contraceptive choice, midwives are using their moral positioning to give agency or offer opportunities to young women to take responsibility for their sexuality (Rivano Eckerdal, 2011). A similar function is performed by the UK government in Lloyd and Hicks' (2021) study of the COVID-19 pandemic, where the positioning of people in relation to risk catalyses their transition into new information environments. In effect, information literacy is enabled through the creation of discursive spaces that position a person's actions and performances. Taking place on three different levels, including on institutional, semantic and operational levels, these discourses make information literacy happen by establishing the 'preconditions' for agency (Lloyd and Hicks, 2021), including in relation to rules as well as how we talk about and operationalise understandings in our everyday activities.

At the same time, discursive spaces can also constrain the construction of information landscapes through limiting the range of actions that people can perform; unlike other sociocultural theories (e.g. Wenger, 1998), positioning theory recognises that rights to allocate or contest presuppositions within society are often unevenly distributed (Harré and Moghaddam, 2003, 4). Thus, the assignment of a position, with its attendant agentic responsibilities and possibilities, constrains information literacy practice through determining opportunities to access information resources (Collett, 2020, 527) as well as an ability to act. During the COVID-19 pandemic, for example, being positioned as vulnerable or as furloughed exposed people to very different forms of social and governmental messaging (Lloyd and Hicks, 2021). Positioning also impacts a person's opportunity to access information-rich spaces, as Given (2002, 138) found in her study examining how the negative positioning of mature students led to their withdrawal from 'information-seeking venues', such as office hours. Positioning consequently does not just constrain information literacy by curbing opportunities to engage with community knowledge structures. Instead, it also constricts practice by delegitimising a person's information needs and agency or delimiting who can come to know and develop a subject position within an information landscape and move towards full participation in a setting.

Barriers to practice are further reinforced through the relational nature of positioning, which establishes that positioning also positions the person or group doing the positioning (Harré and Van Langenhove, 1999, 1). Enabling groups or individuals to claim hegemony for themselves, relational processes constrain information literacy practice through configuring and regulating appropriate activity, including what is considered to constitute a proper form of knowledge. Thus, textbook and popular handbook representations of pregnant women as compliant patients reinforce biomedical knowledge structures by entrenching the physician's authority as both information source and director of healthcare processes (McKenzie and Carey, 2000). Limiting opportunities to engage in certain additional information activities, such as asking questions, this positioning additionally delegitimises other forms of knowledge (and subjectivity) through denying a woman the ability to 'direct her medical team, to resist their superordinate positions, or even to act as the ultimate authority on the status of her own body' (McKenzie and Carey, 2000). Similar control of the narrative is noted in an analysis of information literacy models, where the positioning of learners as uncritical plagiarisers establishes librarians as moral and social authorities of information literacy activity (Hicks and Lloyd, 2021). Drawing attention to what counts as knowledge and how it is constituted, these discursive practices open information literacy up to a consideration of how practice is constrained through local manifestations of power, including normative understandings about how the construction of information landscapes should happen.

Beyond the shape of practice, positioning theory opens information literacy up to a broader appreciation of the various – often hidden and unacknowledged – information activities that shape the construction of knowing within a specific setting. One of the key tenets of positioning theory is that people are 'choosing subjects' (Davies and Harré, 1990, 52) who have the opportunity to 'acquiesce, contest or subvert' how they are positioned within everyday interactions (Harré and Van Langenhove, 1999, 2). Differentiating positioning theory from role theory, the emphasis on reframing subject positions draws attention to the strategies or workarounds that people employ to contest categorisation and meet their broader information needs. Women in McKenzie's (2001, 207) study of pregnancy, for example, employed a wide range of counter-information strategies to resist their positioning as external to the healthcare process, such as by making pre-emptive lists of questions for medical appointments. Legitimising their information needs and concerns, a refusal to accept positioning also supported these women's intersubjective constructions by repositioning them in relation to the healthcare system. People may also meet their information needs through engaging in information activities that distance themselves from the ways in which they are positioned, including through avoiding being in the company of the stigmatised group (Hicks, 2018, 105; Sabat, 2003, 92). Illustrating the reflexivity of (re)positioning, the attempt to legitimise a position that will allow a person to be 'effective and powerful as a speaker' (Tan and Moghaddam, 1999, 188) draws attention to how legitimate means for participation within a community (Wenger, 1998) must be negotiated rather than happening automatically.

Positioning theory can consequently be seen as opening information literacy up to a range of new understandings, including related to the shape of practice as well as how practice is enabled and constrained. These understandings are, in turn, enabled by claims that are ingrained within positioning theory's guiding apparatus, including related to knowledge, context, people and learning. The understanding that information literacy is shaped in relation to social conditions, for example, is made possible by claims that positioning theory makes about the nature of knowledge, namely that knowledge is produced through 'interactions between people and the social environment in which they operate' (Harré and Van Langenhove, 1999, 5). A social constructionist perspective that centres linguistic rather than mental processes, these ideas draw attention to what counts as knowledge as well as how it is legitimated (Harré and Van Langenhove, 1999, 3). From an information literacy perspective, the positioning of knowledge as socially shaped supports an emphasis on the construction of meaning or how people build intersubjective understanding through shared information interactions. These ideas are further extended by the claims that positioning theory makes about context, including that meanings of language do not remain stable and that human action is culturally and historically shaped (Harré and Van Langenhove, 1999, 4). Highlighting the situated shape of discourse, these claims further support the positioning of information literacy as constructed in practice or made visible through 'the contextualised sayings and doings of a social setting' (Lloyd, 2021, 26).

The emphasis that positioning theory places upon social action means that understandings about information literacy are also predicated upon claims about people and groups. Insight into the hidden or unacknowledged information activities that people are forced to engage in because of how they are positioned, for example, is enabled by the way in which positioning establishes people as active or intentional users of symbolic systems rather than passive subjects (Harré and Van Langenhove, 1999, 4). Linked to

Wittgenstein's theorising on meaning and language and emerging from a deliberate rejection of positivist psychological paradigms, this claim also draws attention to individual agency by establishing people rather than role as the determining basis of social action (Harré and Van Langenhove, 1999, 3). From an information literacy perspective, the positioning of individuals as 'capable of exercising choice' (Davies and Harré, 1990, 46) emphasises how people participate in the construction of their information landscapes, such as through the realisation of subjectivity and the subversion of social structures that limit the capacity to act. Understandings about information literacy are further shaped through claims that positioning theory makes about learning, including how the development of knowing is determined by 'having rights and duties in relation to local corpus of sayings and doings' rather than individual competence (Harré et al., 2009, 6). While consideration of learning does not play a prominent role within positioning theory (Howie and Peters, 1996, 61) these ideas draw attention to how the practice of information literacy unfolds and is made possible within the social site.

How does positioning theory close off understandings of information literacy?

The previous section has demonstrated how positioning theory opens up information literacy to a consideration of granular social interactions, a unique focus that has enormous potential to extend research in the field. However, positioning theory's theoretical heritage means that it must also (necessarily) neglect other elements of information literacy practice. This section consequently seeks to acknowledge these tensions while remaining highly committed to the use of positioning theory within information literacy research.

One important aspect of information literacy that is neglected by using a positioning theory lens is the body or the role that 'multimodal data' (McVee et al., 2021, 198) and other non-linguistic discourse plays within co-constructed talk. As Chapter 10 by Lloyd demonstrates, corporeal experience plays a central role within information literacy practice, both as a source of embodied knowing and as 'the visible enactment of knowing and situatedness' (Lloyd, 2010b). However, the emphasis that positioning theory places on speech, writing and other 'verbocentric communication' (McVee et al., 2021, 192) means that the body is absent from foundational positioning theory work and is rarely explicitly considered within even contemporary positioning analysis (see McVee et al., 2021 for an exception). From an information literacy perspective, this is problematic, because it impedes a broader examination of the ways in which corporeal positioning both catalyses and stigmatises the enactment of information literacy, as McKenzie and Carey's (2000) examination of pregnancy and lupus suggests (also see Gibson, Hughes-Hassell and Bowen, 2021). Similarly, a focus on words also neglects to account for the ways in which people's bodies are positioned through space and physical movement, an idea that is particularly meaningful given the important role that observing plays within information literacy practice (e.g. Lloyd et al., 2013; Lloyd and Hicks, 2021).

Another aspect of information literacy that is bypassed through positioning theory's centring of linguistic systems of meaning is the material dimension of practice, including the role that artefacts and structures play within the construction of information landscapes. Sidelined through the same privileging of words, the material is further neglected through the emphasis that foundational positioning theory places upon conversation, which situates positioning within the present moment or the here and now rather than in past or future situations (Davies and Harré, 1990, 55). Introducing a temporal dimension into positioning theory, this 'presentist' ontological framing emerges from the wish to differentiate positioning from the immutability of pre-existing roles (Davies and Harré, 1990, 33). However, as Bjerre (2021, 259) points out, the positioning of the present as the only basis of social reality also has the effect of sidelining structural conditions, including how institutions and frameworks shape and reproduce social order. The reduction of social reality to speech acts further diminishes cultural and historical context or the background for activity (Bjerre, 2021, 262). From an information literacy perspective, these oversights are problematic, because they neglect to account for the important role that material artefacts play in ascribing meaning onto bodies, as categorisations of mask-wearers during the early days of the COVID-19 pandemic demonstrates (Lloyd and Hicks, 2021; McVee at al., 2021). They also risk sidelining the power that discourse holds within information literacy practice, including in positioning key actors, concepts and activities, as Hicks and Lloyd (2021; 2022a) found in their study of foundational information literacy documents.

Lastly, a positioning theory conceptual framework obstructs the development of critically reflective approaches to information literacy, including that which is invited by constructionist dialogue and the action-oriented conceptualisations of practice that inform critical information literacy (cf. Drabinski and Tewell, 2019). As Gergen (2019, 79) points out, there is a 'conservative undertone to much positioning theory work' wherein power relationships are recognised but not questioned or challenged, including how rights and duties are distributed and why this distribution 'so often favors those in power', something that could also be said about information literacy. In addition, there is little space for reflection on ideology or researchers' own positions despite the debt that foundational positioning theory owes to feminist post-structuralist theory (e.g. Hollway, 1984). From an information literacy perspective, these limitations are troublesome, given the close connections between information practice and questions of social justice, including the ways in which power structures shape the circulation of information (Drabinski and Tewell, 2019). Issues are further compounded by positioning theory's fixation on the mechanics of interaction; there is no guarantee that a resolution will follow from even the most insightful analysis of social positioning (Moghaddam, Harré and Lee, 2007, 18). While a focus on complexity rather than practical solutions extends information literacy research, particularly given 'ever-narrowing conceptions' of what counts as legitimate educational scholarship (cf. McVee, 2011, 11), it also sidelines information literacy's anti-oppressive activist precepts, including the development of critically conscious instructional practice.

Limitations on understandings of information literacy are consequently linked to positioning theory's constructionist theoretical shape and heritage, which directs attention towards and away from certain aspects of practice. However, this conceptual framework is further complicated by theoretical inconsistencies that impact the claims upon which positioning theory is predicated. Claims about the person form a useful first example of these difficulties. The previous section demonstrated that information literacy is opened up through the emphasis that positioning theory places upon individual agency. Yet, Harré's commitment to the person has also been critiqued for traces of humanism, most specifically through the significance he places on a unified, rational subject who brings the world into being. As Peters and Appel (1996, 127) point out, 'in the end, positioning theory is a theory of the ego and its actions', an idea that clashes with the overarching post-structuralist emphasis on the discursive production of the self. From an information literacy perspective, a lingering espousal of humanism risks reinforcing the Cartesian subject (cf. Peters and Appel, 1996, 138) wherein the construction of information landscapes forms a rational and conscious individual endeavour rather than a messy and embodied social practice. It also risks sidelining understanding about the constitutive role that discourse plays within information literacy practice, including its ideological formations and the power that it bears.

Another tension relates to the claims that positioning theory makes about the nature of knowledge. The previous section illustrates how positioning theory's orientation towards constructionism opens information literacy up to a focus on social conditions as well as the production of intersubjective understanding. However, while foundational positioning theory work resonates with many constructionist ideas, its representation of the rules that govern rights and duties as somehow essential means that it has been critiqued for treating phenomena as existing independently in the world rather than as shaped through collective constructions of reality (Gergen, 2019, 73; Korobov, 2010, 266). As Gergen (2019, 74) points out, 'Harré approaches these issues largely as a realist', an idea that changes the focus of positioning theory from discursive conventions to the accurate representation of truth. This confusion also creates issues for an understanding of information literacy, particularly on an ontological level. The claim that positioning theory provides insight into independently existing phenomena, for example, risks (re)conceptualising information literacy as anchored upon a fixed 'storehouse of social knowledge' (Korobov, 2010, 266) as opposed to social negotiation. It also reframes information literacy instruction in terms of the skills needed to perform these implicit norms and rules rather than the enactment of situated knowledge activities. The emphasis on 'insight' into representations of truth further helps to explain how positioning theory hampers the development of critically reflective approaches to information literacy; scientific explanation needs objective observers who are 'free of political, moral or personal biases' (Gergen, 2019, 78) rather than a constructionist reflection on partiality. This includes refraining from advocating a particular form of action as well as questioning unjust or limited ways of knowing.

Information literacy is also constrained through the lack of focus that positioning theory pays to learning. This oversight is even more surprising given the strong influence of

Vygotsky on foundational theoretical work (Harré and Van Langenhove, 1999). Howie and Peters (1996, 61) rightly point out that in many senses, learning is the central goal of positioning theory due to the importance that is placed upon the dynamics of change. However, for all these underlying objectives, positioning theory makes little reference to how people become 'socialised' within a new context, or how they might reconcile previous subject positions with new categorisations, two important ideas for learning. Similarly, there is only a token reference to how people become 'choosing subjects' (Davies and Harré, 1990, 52) and even less interest in positive positioning, with its implications for strengths-based educational programming (although see Howie, 1999). Even the field of education, which had carried out 130 positioning theory studies by 2013 (McVee et al., 2019, 392), has tended to use positioning theory to focus on how teachers present themselves within the classroom rather than to examine the impact on learning. A lack of focus on learning curtails information literacy through failing to account for how positioning influences participation in discursive practices, including developing a positioning (and positioned) identity. More problematically, it diminishes information literacy by introducing simplistic ideas into practice, such as the rendering of positions as both bipolar and irrevocably linked to conflict (cf. Howie and Peters, 1996, 61). This understanding of a position, which is linked to early examples of positioning processes (e.g. Davies and Harré's 1990 analysis of a medical encounter) and positioning theory's military and business heritage (Harré and Van Langenhove, 1991, 395), focuses attention away from key aspects of learning, including related to care, emotion and the fluidity of mediating activity.

How does positioning theory shape methodological choices for information literacy research?

Finally, positioning theory influences methodological decision making, which, in turn, shapes what understandings about information literacy are brought into view. However, these ideas are complicated by positioning theory's difficult relationship with methods and methodological choices. From the outset, Harré and other foundational theorists made it clear that experimental and lab-based methods were not suitable for use with positioning theory, given the focus on active people and everyday language (Harré and Van Langenhove, 1999, 3). Since then, though, there has been a distinct lack of attention paid to questions of methods within positioning theoretical texts, with Gergen (2019, 75) pointing out that it is, ironically, extremely hard to find any attempt to test positioning theory's claims at all. Others have critiqued the tendency for positioning theory to rely on 'contrived' or 'illustrative' examples rather than real-world data (McVee et al., 2021, 197). Decisions about the most appropriate methodological choices for information literacy research are consequently shaped in relation to a lack of empirical justification as much as the rejection of positivist procedures. One key consideration that emerges for information literacy research methods is the emphasis that positioning theory places on naturalistic data, a requirement that materialises through Davies and Harré's (1991, 48) assertion that 'selves are located in conversations as observably and subjectively coherent participants'.

Focusing attention on participant observation methods, the emphasis on mundane, everyday lives also lends itself to the employment of ethnographic enquiry to introduce background knowledge into positioning research as well as recurring aspects of practice. The importance that positioning theory accords to practical use (Harré and Moghaddam, 2003, 10) also opens the door to action-oriented approaches to research, including reflexive and participatory methods of inquiry.

However, it is the central role that conversation plays within positioning theory that has the biggest impact on methodological choices for information literacy research; the ability to pay fine-grained attention to participants' interactions means that discourse analysis has frequently been seen as the natural partner for positioning research. Used to examine spoken settings and written documents, discourse analysis builds understanding about the mechanics of positioning, including tracing how people draw up and make subject positions intelligible (Tirado and Gálvez, 2008, 230) and how discursive constructions are organised. From an information literacy perspective, research that examines how agency is shaped within everyday spaces illustrates how discourse analysis methods draw out the dynamic shape of positioning, including interrogating how these discourses are talked into practice (Hicks and Lloyd, 2021; Lloyd and Hicks, 2021). McKenzie's (2004) examination of authoritative knowledge during pregnancy provides a similar illustration of how a focus on discourse questions both the purpose and the process of evaluative accounts within information literacy practice, including related to the establishment of evidence. Lastly, the identification of third-order positioning, or positioning that takes place in later conversations, means that discourse analysis foregrounds the role of privilege and preconception within information literacy research by highlighting the important role that the non-neutral interviewer plays within analytical procedures. Conversely, discourse analysis also limits information literacy research by focusing on words rather than embodied and artefactual practice. The ephemeral shape of positioning activity (Harré, 2008, 30) consequently calls for the introduction of methods that centre an emic analysis of information literacy practice, including visual and other projective processes.

How does positioning theory interpret and explain information literacy?

The previous two sections have explored how information literacy is both opened up and closed off through the use of positioning theory. While this approach has highlighted a small number of shortcomings, positioning theory is still considered to form a valuable addition to theoretical information literacy work. This third section will draw these ideas together to present a balanced understanding of how positioning theory explains information literacy before examining its connections to other theoretical perspectives.

To summarise, positioning theory draws upon the sociological concept of a position to establish a 'conceptual apparatus' (Harré and Van Langenhove, 1999, 2) for the analysis of conversation and possibilities of action. The principles and claims of this framework mean that when positioning theory is used as a conceptual lens, information literacy is viewed as discursively produced, or as constructed within social practice and referencing dynamic local values and norms. These ideas position the construction of information landscapes as linguistically shaped or as taking place against the backdrop of discourses that 'categorise the world and bring phenomena into view' (Talja, Tuominen and Savolainen, 2005, 89). Beyond language processes, the overarching emphasis that positioning theory places upon categorising and being categorised means that information literacy is further positioned as an agentic information practice that is shaped by local power structures. Power is only touched upon lightly within positioning theory, but the emphasis on possibilities of action means that it is hard to ignore. From an information literacy perspective, these ideas see the construction of information landscapes as vested in the manifestations of power that configure and are built into a social site or setting. They further situate information literacy as riddled with inequities, including who does and does not have the power to sanction the forms of knowledge that are valued within a specific setting and the unequal basis on which the power to define this competence is allocated. At the same time, the emphasis on 'choosing subjects' (Davies and Harré, 1990, 52) means that positioning theory also frames the construction of information landscapes as rooted in everyday human agency, or through purposive engagement within information, people and artefacts.

This conceptual apparatus consequently creates an interesting conundrum, wherein information literacy becomes caught up in positioning theory's theoretical inconsistencies. Epistemologically, positioning theory categorises information literacy as realised through the ways in which people take up and situate themselves in relation to meanings that a discourse makes available (cf. Hollway, 1984, 236). These ideas situate a positioning theoretical-informed approach to information literacy within the field's sociocultural turn (Tuominen, Savolainen and Talja, 2005; Lloyd, 2005). The ontological basis of positioning theory, however, is far more complex, with various critiques suggesting that Harré's focus on the existence of pre-existing positions belies a cognitive ontology rather than one that is based in the social construction of reality (e.g. Korobov, 2010; Gergen, 2019). Consequently, information literacy is simultaneously positioned as shaped through interaction, by the emphasis that positioning theory places on 'anti-nativist' positions (Harré and Van Langenhove, 1999, 2) and as existing objectively, through the focus on pre-existing and implicit positioning norms (Harré and Moghaddam, 2003, 4). Any use of positioning theory within information literacy must consequently be aware of these ontological dualisms if positioning theory is to contribute to the advancement of theoretical research.

Positioning theory can consequently be seen to constitute a flawed theory. However, in the spirit of Gergen (2019, 76), who combined respect for Harré with reservations about his theoretical underpinnings, assessment of positioning theory should examine what difference it makes to information literacy, rather than remaining bogged down in protracted 'metatheoretical conflict'. In this light, positioning theory is useful for information literacy research because it draws attention to the multiple ways in which language defines, limits and enables information activity; as Gergen (2019, 76) points out, 'it enables us to "see" how the significance of a given utterance is not exhausted by an analysis of its content'. Extending understanding of the situated shape of information literacy, the emphasis on the pragmatics of language use further sharpens awareness of the delicately complex roles that relationships play within practice, something that is lost when we merely focus on roles. The value of positioning theory to information literacy further lies in the work that it does to extend the field's sociocultural turn, not least by continuing to challenge individual conceptions of practice and stimulate naturalistic research methods. Positioning theory's potential to dispute how positioning rights and duties are distributed in society also illustrates how its significance lies in its 'generative properties' (cf. Gergen, 2019, 77) or its ability to galvanise future meaningful interrogations of practice.

How might the employment of positioning theory be enhanced by other theories?

Very finally, this chapter posits that positioning theory can be enhanced by a variety of other perspectives. Emerging in the 1990s within the field of psychology, positioning theory's heritage means that it is removed from more recent considerations of social life, as well as continuing theoretical debates and critiques. However, its constructionist roots as well as its focus on granular, local dynamics means that there are several ways in which positioning theory could connect with ongoing theoretical information literacy research.

One of the major ways in which positioning theory could be enhanced is through connection to theoretical work that centres the purpose of interaction rather than just its mechanics. Communities of practice (Wenger, 1998), which form one of the more recognisable theoretical approaches within information literacy research (e.g. Harris, 2008; McCluskey-Dean, 2020; Moring, 2012), is a prime example. An analytical tool that is centred on meaning and identity, community of practice theory establishes that information literacy is shaped through changing participation in shared group activities (Wenger, 1998), an idea that is shared by other sociocultural theories commonly employed within the field (e.g. Lave and Wenger, 1991; Vygotsky, 1978). However, as commentators have pointed out, these theories often present a limited or idealistic view of community participation by overlooking power dynamics, permeable community boundaries and non-linear trajectories of movement (e.g. Engeström, 2013). Positioning theory's focus on the negotiation of shared interactions provides the means to extend community of practice work, including by presenting a richer account of the ways in which interaction supports and impedes participation. From an information literacy perspective, the coupling of these two theoretical approaches could interrogate the impact of contested information environments upon the enactment of practice, including in relation to knowledge gatekeeping, institutional readiness to afford learning opportunities and the achievement of legitimate means of participation. A focus on positioning might further extend understanding about how conflict shapes the development of identity, e.g. through forcing people to respond to and locate themselves within an information environment (cf. Tirado and Gálvez, 2008, 244).

At the same time, issues noted within this chapter indicate that positioning theory might also be enhanced through engagement with theoretical work that extends positioning metaphors. One example is affordance theory, which refers to opportunities that an environment offers for interaction. Foregrounded through Gibson's (1979) ecological work and developed through Norman's (1988) design studies, affordances have been understood within information studies as 'invitational qualities' (Billett, 2001, 212) or the participatory opportunities that a setting provides (e.g. Lloyd, 2005). Constituting a broader conception of how possibilities of action are enabled and constrained within a specific context, affordance theory also brings a more overt focus on materiality to positioning theory, including how access to tacit forms of information or the 'know-how' of performance (Lloyd, 2010a, 169) is shaped by the positioning of bodies, artefacts and tools. These ideas could be further enhanced through a consideration of how positioning constitutes and is constituted by material arrangements amongst which practice unfolds (Schatzki, 2002). A second example of theoretical work that could enhance positioning theory is social capital theory, which has been defined by Bourdieu (1986) as relating to the networks and resources that make actions possible. Within this framing, information literacy facilitates the construction of social capital by shaping access to the nuanced and tacit forms of information that will allow people to (re)construct information landscapes (Lloyd, Pilerot and Hultgren, 2017). Drawing attention to how social capital is unevenly distributed in society, social capital theory could bring a more nuanced examination of how the power to position others is constructed, including the basis upon which the power is distributed and maintained.

Conclusion

Positioning theory is a powerful concept that opens information literacy research up to a broader consideration of how social dynamics shape the construction of information landscapes. The emphasis on what is logically or socially possible draws attention to the ways in which positioning impedes and enables opportunities to engage with local knowledge structures, while the relational shape of positioning highlights how appropriate activity is configured. A recognition that people can both concur with and contest how they are positioned means that positioning theory also spotlights the unacknowledged information activities that people engage in to mediate structural barriers. Positioning theory is not without its flaws; a focus on conversation neglects the role that the body and material artefacts play within co-constructed talk while sidelining a critically reflexive approach to practice. These issues are further compounded by the conceptual inconsistencies that underscore foundational theoretical work. However, positioning theory is beneficial for both information literacy research and broader society through the work it does to extend understanding about the situated shape of practice. For these reasons, it is to be hoped that positioning theory will become more prominently 'positioned' within information literacy's theoretical toolbox.

References

Billett, S. (2001) Learning Through Work: workplace affordances and individual engagement, *Journal of Workplace Learning*, 13 (5), 209–13.

Bjerre, J. (2021) The Development of Positioning Theory as a Process of Theoretical Positioning, *Journal for the Theory of Social Behaviour*, 51 (2), 249–72.

Bourdieu, P. (1986) The Forms of Capital. In Richardson, J. E. (ed.) *The Handbook of Theory and Research for the Sociology Of Education*, Greenwood Press, 241–58.

Collett, J. (2020) Researching the Complex Nature of Identity and Learning: positioning, agency and context in learners' identities, *International Journal of Qualitative Studies in Education*, 33 (5), 524–48.

Davies, B. and Harré, R. (1990) Positioning: the discursive production of selves, *Journal for the Theory of Social Behaviour*, 20 (1), 43–63.

Drabinski, E. and Tewell, E. (2019) Critical Information Literacy. In Hobbs, R. and Mihailidis, P. (eds) *The International Encyclopedia of Media Literacy*, John Wiley and Sons, 1–4.

Engeström, Y. (2013) From Communities of Practice to Mycorrhizae. In Hughes, J., Jewson, N. and Unwin, L. (eds) *Communities of Practice: critical perspectives*, Routledge, 51–64.

Genuis, S. K. (2013) Social Positioning Theory as a Lens for Exploring Health Information Seeking and Decision Making, *Qualitative Health Research*, 23 (4), 555–67.

Gergen, K. J. (2019) A Constructionist Conversation with Positioning Theory. In Christensen, B. A. (ed.) *The Second Cognitive Revolution: a tribute to Rom Harré*, Springer, 73–80.

Gibson, A. N., Hughes-Hassell, S. and Bowen, K. (2021) Navigating 'Danger Zones': social geographies of risk and safety in teens and tweens of color information seeking, *Information, Communication & Society*, 26 (8), 1513–30.

Gibson, J. (1979) *The Ecological Approach to Visual Perception*, Houghton Mifflin.

Given, L. M. (2002) Discursive Constructions in the University Context: social positioning theory and mature undergraduates' information behaviours, *The New Review of Information Behaviour Research*, 3, 127–42.

Harré, R. (2008) Positioning Theory, *Self-Care, Dependent Care & Nursing*, 16 (1), 28–32.

Harré, R. and Moghaddam, F. (2003) Introduction: the self and others in traditional psychology and in positioning theory. In Harré, R. and Moghaddam, F. (eds) *The Self and Others*, Praeger, 1–11.

Harré, R. and Van Langenhove, L. (1991) Varieties of Positioning, *Journal for the Theory of Social Behaviour*, 21 (4), 393–407.

Harré, R. and Van Langenhove, L. (1999) *Positioning Theory: moral contexts of intentional action*, Blackwell Publishers.

Harré, R., Moghaddam, F., Cairnie, T., Rothbart, D. and Sabat, S. (2009) Recent Advances in Positioning Theory, *Theory & Psychology*, 19 (1), 5–31.

Harris, B. (2008) Communities as Necessity in Information Literacy Development: challenging the standards, *Journal of Academic Librarianship*, 34 (3), 248–55.

Hicks, A. (2018) The Theory of Mitigating Risk: information literacy and language-learning in transition, Doctoral dissn, Högskolan i Borås, Sweden.

Hicks, A. and Lloyd, A. (2021) Deconstructing Information Literacy Discourse: peeling back the layers in higher education, *Journal of Library and Information Science*, 53 (4), 559–71.

Hicks, A. and Lloyd, A. (2022a) Reaching into the Basket of Doom: learning outcomes, discourse and information literacy, *Journal of Librarianship and Information Science*, https://doi.org/10.1177/09610006211067216.

Hicks, A. and Lloyd, A. (2022b) Relegating Expertise: the outward and inward positioning of librarians in information literacy education, *Journal of Library and Information Science*, https://doi.org/10.1177/09610006211020104.

Hollway, W. (1984) Gender Difference and the Production of Subjectivity. In Henriques, J., Hollway, W., Irwin, C., Venn, L. and Walkerdine, V. (eds) *Changing the Subject: social regulation and subjectivity*, Methuen, 223–61.

Howie, D. (1999) Preparing for Positive Positioning. In Harré, R. and Van Langenhove, L. (eds) *Positioning Theory: moral contexts of intentional action*, Blackwell, 53–9.

Howie, D. and Peters, M. (1996) Positioning Theory: Vygotsky, Wittgenstein and social constructionist psychology, *Journal for the Theory of Social Behaviour*, 26 (1), 51–64.

Julien, H. and Given, L. M. (2003) Faculty-Librarian Relationships in the Information Literacy Context: a content analysis of librarians' expressed attitudes and experiences. In *Proceedings of the Annual Conference Of CAIS/Actes Du Congrès Annuel De L'ACSI*, https://doi.org/10.29173/cais526.

Korobov, N. (2010) A Discursive Psychological Approach to Positioning, *Qualitative Research in Psychology*, 7 (3), 263–77.

Lave, J. and Wenger, E. (1991) *Situated Learning: legitimate peripheral participation*, Cambridge University Press.

Lloyd, A. (2005) Information Literacy: different contexts, different concepts, different truths?, *Journal of Librarianship and Information Science*, 37 (2), 82–8.

Lloyd, A. (2006) Information Literacy Landscapes: an emerging picture, *Journal of Documentation*, 62 (5), 570–83.

Lloyd, A. (2010a) *Information Literacy Landscapes: information literacy in education, workplace and everyday contexts*, Chandos.

Lloyd, A. (2010b) Corporeality and Practice Theory: exploring emerging research agendas for information literacy, *Information Research*, 15 (3), http://informationr.net/ir/15-3/colis7/colis704.html.

Lloyd, A. (2021) *The Qualitative Landscape of Information Literacy Research*, Facet Publishing.

Lloyd, A. and Hicks, A. (2021) Contextualising Risk: the unfolding information work and practices of people during the Covid-19 pandemic, *Journal of Documentation*, 77 (3), 1052–72.

Lloyd, A., Pilerot, O. and Hultgren, F. (2017) The Remaking of Fractured Landscapes: supporting refugees in transition (SpiRiT), *Information Research*, 22 (3), http://informationr.net/ir/22-3/paper764.html.

Lloyd, A., Kennan, M. A., Thompson, K. M. and Qayyum, A. (2013) Connecting with New Information Landscapes: information literacy practices of refugees, *Journal of Documentation*, 69 (1), 121–44.

McCluskey-Dean, C. (2020) *Identifying and Facilitating a Community of Practice in Information Literacy in Higher Education*, Doctoral dissn, Robert Gordon University, Scotland.

McKenzie, P. J. (2001) Negotiating Authoritative Knowledge: information practices across a life transition, Doctoral dissn, University of Western Ontario, Canada.

McKenzie, P. J. (2003) Justifying Cognitive Authority Decisions: discursive strategies of information seekers, *Library Quarterly*, 73 (3), 261–88.

McKenzie, P. J. (2004) Positioning Theory and the Negotiation of Information Needs in a Clinical Midwifery Setting, *Journal of the American Society for Information Science and Technology*, 55 (8), 685–94.

McKenzie, P. J. and Carey, R. F. (2000) 'What's Wrong with that Woman?'– Positioning Theory and Information-Seeking Behaviour. In *Proceedings of the Annual Conference Of CAIS/Actes Du Congrès Annuel De L'ACSI*, https://doi.org/10.29173/cais20.

McVee, M. B. (2011) Positioning Theory and Sociocultural Perspectives. In Brock, C. and McVee, M. (eds) *Sociocultural Positioning in Literacy: exploring culture, discourse, narrative, power in diverse educational contexts*, Hampton Press, 1–22.

McVee, M., Silvestri, K., Barrett, N. and Haq, K. (2019) Positioning Theory. In Alvermann, D., Unrau, N., Sailors, M. and Ruddell, R. (eds) *Theoretical Models and Processes of Literacy*, Routledge, 381–400.

McVee, M. B., Silvestri, K., Schucker, K. A. and Cun, A. (2021) Positioning Theory, Embodiment and the Moral Orders of Objects in Social Dynamics: how positioning theory has neglected the body and artifactual knowing, *Journal for the Theory of Social Behaviour*, 51 (2), 192–214.

Moghaddam, F., Harré, R. and Lee, N. (2007) Positioning and Conflict: an introduction. In Moghaddam, F., Harré, R. and Lee, N. (eds) *Global Conflict Resolution through Positioning Analysis,* Springer Science and Business Media, 3–20.

Moring, C. (2012) Newcomer Information Practice: negotiations on information seeking in and across communities of practice, *Human IT: journal for information technology studies as a human science*, 11 (2), https://humanit.hb.se/article/view/66.

Norman, D. (1988) *The Psychology of Everyday Things*, Basic Books.

Peters, M. and Appel, S. (1996) Positioning Theory: discourse, the subject and the problem of desire, *Social Analysis*, 40, 120–41.

Rivano Eckerdal, J. (2011) To Jointly Negotiate a Personal Decision: a qualitative study on information literacy practices in midwifery counselling about contraceptives at youth centres in southern Sweden, *Information Research*, 16 (1), http://informationr.net/ir/16-1/paper466.html.

Sabat, S. (2003) Malignant Positioning and the Predicament of People with Alzheimer's Disease. In Harré, R. and Moghaddam, F. (eds) *The Self and Others*, Praeger, 85–98.

Schatzki, T. (2002) *The Site of The Social: a philosophical account of the constitution of social life and change*, Pennsylvania State University Press.

Talja S. and Hartel, J. (2007) Revisiting the User-Centred Turn in Information Science Research: an intellectual history perspective, *Information Research*, 12 (4), www.informationr.net/ir/12-4/colis/colis04.html.

Talja, S., Tuominen, K. and Savolainen, R. (2005) 'Isms' in Information Science: constructivism, collectivism and constructionism, *Journal of Documentation*, 61 (1), 79–101.

Tan, S.-I. and Moghaddam, F. (1999) Positioning in Intergroup Relations. In Harré, R. and Van Langenhove, L. (eds) *Positioning Theory: moral contexts of intentional action*, Blackwell, 178–94.

Tirado, F. and Gálvez, A. (2008) Positioning Theory and Discourse Analysis: some tools for social interaction analysis, *Historical Social Research/Historische Sozialforschung*, 33 (1), 224–51.

Tuominen, K., Savolainen, R. and Talja, S. (2005) Information Literacy as a Sociotechnical Practice, *Library Quarterly*, 75 (3), 329–45.

Van Langenhove, L. and Wise, D. (2019) Introduction: the relation between social representation theory and positioning theory, *Papers on Social Representations*, 28 (1).

Villanueva, E. (2021) The Body as Information: an emergent theory of social positioning and information behaviours in a virtual diet community, MA thesis, University of Alberta, Canada.

Vygotsky, L. S. (1978) *Mind in Society: the development of higher psychological processes*, Harvard University Press.

Wenger, E. (1998) *Communities of Practice: learning, meaning and identity*, Cambridge University Press.

Wittgenstein, L. (1953) *Philosophical Investigations*, (trans. G. E. M. Anscombe), Blackwell.

6
Plural Agonistics

Johanna Rivano Eckerdal

Introduction
This chapter presents Chantal Mouffe's theory of plural agonistics with a focus on its relevance to information literacy research. Plural agonistics is positioned on the radical strand of democratic theories (see also Chapter 1 by Buschman). But, contrary to other radical theories, it does support the representative liberal form of democratic rule (Mouffe, 2013, xiii).[1] The theory builds on the collaborative work of Ernesto Laclau and Mouffe (2014), in which they set out to inquire into why left politics was unable to take account of social movements not based on class. They suggested a radicalisation of democracy as a response to the essentialist view of class they identified as dominating the left: 'What we stressed was the need for a left politics to articulate the struggles about different forms of subordination without attributing any *a priori* centrality to any of them' (Mouffe, 2018, 3).

It has been pointed out that both information literacy practice and research suffer from a lack of theoretical awareness when connecting the concept to democracy (see also Chapter 1 by Buschman). James Elmborg has stated (2006, 196) that '[m]uch of the conflict inherent in information literacy as a critical project can be traced to contested definitions of "democracy"'. Plural agonistics is here suggested as a democracy theory that can help us to elaborate the possible connection between information literacy and democracy. However, neither information literacy nor libraries are specifically mentioned by Mouffe. Before moving on to why and how this theory is proposed for understanding information literacy, it can be helpful to present the basic tenets of the theory.

Outline of the chapter
Next, antagonism and hegemony will be introduced, two important concepts that Laclau and Mouffe developed and from which Mouffe's theory of plural agonistics was built. The democratic paradox will then be presented, followed by the role institutions have when addressing the democratic paradox. A second part follows with a focus on plural agonistics and information literacy. Passionate decisions and democratic institutions constitute the first topic, followed by a discussion of an agonistic view on consensus and compromises,

how politics and ethics should be understood and the impossibility of neutrality when advocating democracy. A closer look at an agonistic view of identity and a description of how chains of equivalences should be formed follows before suggesting what an agonistic take on information literacy research would entail. The chapter ends with a short, but very important note on the limitations of plural agonism and a conclusion. Throughout the chapter several quotes from Mouffe's writing are included, inviting the reader to be acquainted with her political theory also in her own words.

Part one: Core elements of the theory of plural agonistics
Antagonism
Plural agonistics starts off by stating that there are conflicts for which there will not ever be any rational solution. This ontological statement is called *radical negativity* or *antagonism*. The phrase *the ineradicability of antagonism* firmly underscores that antagonism will never be overcome. Plural agonistics is Mouffe's suggestion of a productive way to advocate democracy while taking this reality into account. Recognising severe problems in the present form of rule, plural agonistics proposes a roadmap for continuous development of democracy to enhance social equality. Hence democracy is construed not as an endpoint a society can arrive at and feel safe at, but as a process. The ineradicability of antagonism will make this process fraught with conflicts and an aim of the agonistic take on a democratic form of rule is to offer ways for those conflicts to unfold without violence.

As individuals we belong to several groups, all important for how we shape our identities. For making this point Mouffe draws on Carl Schmitt's work,[2] while at the same time clearly pointing out how they completely disagree about their conclusions (Mouffe, 2005, 10–16; 2013, 137–9). Groups are first and foremost formed by making a distinction of what they do not include: by drawing a clear line, a demarcation is made between them and us, what Mouffe calls the we/they distinction. The establishing of group identities is therefore always potentially the root to a conflict, an antagonism:

> . . . the we/they distinction, which is the condition of possibility of formation of political identities, can always become the locus of an antagonism. Since all forms of political identities entail a we/they distinction, this means that the possibility of emergence of antagonism can never be eliminated. It is therefore an illusion to believe in the advent of a society from which antagonism would have been eradicated.
>
> (Mouffe, 2005, 16)

In order to discern the ontological reality of antagonism from the present shape of democracy, Mouffe establishes a difference between *politics* and *the political* by proposing to call: ' . . . this ineradicable dimension of antagonism "the political" in order to distinguish it from "politics", which refers to the manifold practices aiming at organizing human coexistence' (Mouffe, 2013, 130–1).

Politics includes all the arrangements and institutions that are developed in society for the political processes. In the western democracies as we know them it is considered crucial that these include free elections, a parliament, a free press and an independent judiciary system. Mouffe points out that all these arrangements are the outcome of specific historical and social conditions. The political, on the other hand, forms the precondition for the social life of humans. In other words, politics are various ways developed over time to address the political condition for human social life.

At present politics in the western world has a representative liberal form. There are several possible forms of rule, from autocracies to democracy. Democracy can be envisaged in diverse ways (for example as liberal, republican, deliberative or radical). Plural agonistics advocates radical democracy but, contrary to other theories endorsing radical democracy, plural agonistics supports the present form of rule but with an agenda to reform and improve it.

The majority of political theories have focused on offering solutions to problems faced by society, solutions that indicate a possible future without conflicts. From a plural agonistic perspective, these are utopian theories, whereas plural agonistics is anchored in reality, recognising conflicts as inherent elements of the human condition and society. Indeed, Mouffe argues that an idealised view of humans as inherently good is dangerous:

> It is my contention that envisaging the aim of democratic politics in terms of consensus and reconciliation is not only conceptually mistaken, it is also fraught with political dangers. The aspiration to a world where the we/they discrimination would have been overcome is based on flawed premises and those who share such a vision are bound to miss the real task facing democratic politics.
>
> To be sure this blindness to antagonism is not new. Democratic theory has long been informed by the belief that the inner goodness and original innocence of human beings was a necessary condition for asserting the viability of democracy. An idealized view of human sociability, as being essentially moved by empathy and reciprocity, has generally provided the basis of modern democratic political thinking. Violence and hostility are seen as an archaic phenomenon, to be eliminated thanks to the progress of exchange and the establishment, through a social contract, of a transparent communication among rational participants. Those who challenged this optimistic view were automatically perceived as enemies of democracy. Few attempts have been made to elaborate the democratic project on an anthropology which acknowledges the ambivalent character of human sociability and the fact that reciprocity and hostility cannot be dissociated.
>
> (Mouffe, 2005, 2–3)

Instead of offering solutions that lead to a future without conflicts, it is emphasised that the always-present risk of antagonisms needs to be addressed when drawing up a theory for a democratic society. Plural agonistics therefore offers a way forward to understand how social change can happen without conflicts building up to violence. This is achieved by taming conflicts between enemies into debates between adversaries. Mouffe states that:

> I will reveal how the consensual approach, instead of creating the conditions for a reconciled society, leads to the emergence of antagonisms that an agonistic perspective, by providing those conflicts with a legitimate form of expression, would have managed to avoid. In that way I hope to demonstrate that acknowledging the ineradicability of the conflictual dimension in social life, far from undermining the democratic project, is the necessary condition for grasping the challenge to which democratic politics is confronted.
>
> (Mouffe, 2005, 4)

Hegemony

The possibility of new antagonisms occurring points to the temporal aspect of democracy as suggested from a plural agonistic perspective: democracy is not an end point to be reached by a society, but an unending process (Mouffe, 2013, 132).

As social life goes on, new groups are formed, facing new challenges that need to be addressed in order to reach a political solution. Distinguishing groups from one another involves separating them by describing and pointing out what they are not. Furthermore, groups that experience any need to ameliorate their situation also recognise how the present order is putting them in disadvantage. Expressing this and suggesting a change often infringes on other groups' possibilities and situations. All these processes are shaped by our understanding them and expressing them as *the way things are* and the concept of hegemony helps to grasp how fundamental this characteristic of social life is.

> Next to antagonism, the concept of hegemony is the key notion for addressing the question of 'the political'. To take account of 'the political' as the ever present possibility of antagonism requires coming to terms with the lack of a final ground and acknowledging the dimension of undecidability which pervades every order. It requires in other words recognizing the hegemonic nature of every kind of social order and the fact that every society is the product of a series of practices attempting to establish order in a context of contingency.
>
> (Mouffe, 2005, 17)

This entails that every order is shaped not by how things ought to be but how they have come to be. By acknowledging the contingency of any social order, the possibility to change the present is opened up. Important for making social change happen is to formulate and create alternatives, to engage in *counter-hegemonic practices*.

The struggle between different hegemonies and the fact that this struggle is a never-ending story implies that power is always an issue.

> But if we accept that relations of power are constitutive of the social, then the main question for democratic politics is not how to eliminate power but how to constitute forms of power more compatible with democratic values.
>
> (Mouffe, 2000, 100)

It is not certain that the counter-hegemonies that are created are more democratic than the present order. In fact, Mouffe has explicitly issued a warning. Politics is endangered first because criticism against the democratic form of rule as we know it is not given room within the democratic institutions and second because the content of this criticism is not advocating a strengthening of democracy (Mouffe, 2005, 21).

Much of the criticism arises as people express that they are left out of politics and report discontent with the prevailing neoliberal hegemony that has focus on freedom at the expense of equality. The tension between these two concepts is addressed by Mouffe as a fundamental paradox of democracy.

The democratic paradox

A common meaning when talking about the democratic paradox is that within democracy, opponents of the democratic form of rule must be given a voice. Mouffe, instead, deploys the democratic paradox for describing the tension between two beacons of democracy: equality and freedom. '. . . it is vital for democratic politics to understand that liberal democracy results from the articulation of two logics which are incompatible in the last instance and that there is no way in which they could be perfectly reconciled' (Mouffe, 2000, 5). It is difficult to give them equal weight.

> It is therefore crucial to realize that, with modern democracy, we are dealing with a new political form of society whose specificity comes from the articulation between two different traditions. On one side we have the liberal tradition constituted by the rule of law, the defence of human rights and the respect of individual liberty; on the other the democratic tradition whose main ideas are those of equality, identity between governing and governed and popular sovereignty. There is no necessary relation between those two distinct traditions but only a contingent historical articulation.
>
> (Mouffe, 2000, 2–3)

That many people criticise the political system is not because the form of rule is outdated but as a reaction to the neoliberal hegemony shaping its present design, leaving many voices out. Plural agonistics is offered as a solution to the current problematic state of democracy by presenting how more people can be included and heard within the democratic institutions.

Neoliberal hegemony positioned the opposition between left and right as obsolete and 'political questions were reduced to mere technological issues to be dealt with by experts' (Mouffe, 2018, 4). Mouffe did not welcome this post-political situation but warned that it would lead to people being less interested in the political institutions and to a rise of right-wing populism (Mouffe, 2018, 4). In line with these predictions, democracy is declining globally. The Varieties of Democracy Institute stated in their 2023 annual report that for the first time in more than 20 years the world has more closed autocracies than liberal democracies (Papada et al., 2023, 6). More people express a lack of support for democracy and are reluctant to vote in public elections (Foa and Mounk, 2017). In a recent book Mouffe provides a prescription for remedying this tendency. Acknowledging the need to deepen democracy while advocating the plurality of our societies she proposes a left populism (Mouffe, 2018).

> In the next few years, I argue, the central axis of the political conflict will be between right-wing populism and left-wing populism. And as a result, it is through the construction of a 'people', a collective will that results from the mobilization of common affects in defence of equality and social justice, that it will be possible to combat the xenophobic policies promoted by right-wing populism.
>
> (Mouffe, 2018, 6)

The democratic paradox and institutions

Democratic institutions are vital for society, but they are never safe from harm. Therefore, they are in constant need of support and defence.

> Liberal-democratic institutions should not be taken for granted: it is always necessary to fortify and defend them. This requires grasping their specific dynamics and acknowledging the tension deriving from the workings of their different logics. Only by coming to terms with the democratic paradox can one envisage how to deal with it.
>
> (Mouffe, 2000, 4)

The name of the theory, plural agonistics, captures the importance of the heterogeneity in society. In order to address the current democratic deficit, institutions need to recognise and include more people. To reform politics to become more democratic requires emphasising that the *demos* – people – are not one but many groups, a plurality. Therefore, not one but plural hegemonies need to be created and heard within the democratic institutions (Mouffe, 2013, xiii).

Mouffe's solution to the democratic paradox is the agonistic struggle. When a conflict between groups arises, an important role is played by democratic institutions as places where the conflict can be given room. Otherwise, the conflict might lead to violence. Therefore, institutions must offer a way for the opponents in a conflict to meet and debate in order to reach an acceptable solution. In order to do so, opponents must transform their view of each other from enemies to adversaries. As adversaries the opponents recognise each other's rights and the agonistic struggle can take place, aiming for a solution to the issue at hand, bearing in mind that the outcome will most certainly mean concessions from both parts. The underlying we/they conflict is not erased but a solution is reached in practice.

> If we want to acknowledge on one side the permanence of the antagonistic dimension of the conflict, while on the other side allowing for the possibility of its 'taming', we need to envisage a third type of relation. This is the type of relation which I have proposed to call 'agonism'. . . . While antagonism is a we/they relation in which the two sides are enemies who do not share

> any common ground, agonism is a we/they relation where the conflicting parties, although acknowledging that there is no rational solution to their conflict, nevertheless recognize the legitimacy of their opponents. They are 'adversaries' not enemies. This means that, while in conflict, they see themselves as belonging to the same political association, as sharing a common symbolic space within which the conflict takes place. We could say that the task of democracy is to transform antagonism into agonism.
>
> (Mouffe, 2005, 20)

The ineradicability of antagonism is an unchangeable reality. What can be done is to find ways to handle this situation. That is what the theory entails; it offers a solution to how antagonism can be changed into agonism. It also points out as a 'central task of democratic politics to provide the institutions which will permit conflicts to take an agonistic form' (Mouffe, 2013, xii). The democratic institutions therefore play a crucial role as places where the agonistic struggle may unfold.

> What is at stake in the agonistic struggle, on the contrary, is the very configuration of power relations around which a given society is structured: it is a struggle between opposing hegemonic projects which can never be reconciled rationally. The antagonistic dimension is always present, it is a real confrontation but one which is played out under conditions regulated by a set of democratic procedures accepted by the adversaries.
>
> (Mouffe, 2005, 21)

Part two: Plural agonistics and information literacy

Information literacy is not a concept discussed by Mouffe; nevertheless, the theory can contribute to our understanding of the concept in productive ways. Some aspects of plural agonistics with significant bearing on information literacy will therefore be discussed.

Plural agonistics can be helpful, as it firmly positions information literacy as a political concept. Information literacy is repeatedly presented as one main requisite for people to exert their civic rights and duties (for example ALA, 1989; IFLA, 2005; Wilson et al., 2011). Agonistics states that democracy includes solving social conflicts and, when doing so, decisions need to be made. As Mouffe (2005, 10) argues, 'properly political questions always involve decisions which require us to make a choice between conflicting alternatives'.

Making choices between conflicting alternatives involves considering various types of information. Choices relate to the formation of collective identities and therefore choices imply the involvement of affects. Accordingly, the important role played by decisions in plural agonistics invites us to attend to information literacy aspects of these recurring decisions. Information literacy research can contribute to plural agonistics by opening up and problematising what is happening in relation to these decisions. It would help both to understand in detail the activities that surround and involve decisions as these are made and to provide analytical tools for developing such activities with awareness of the political dimensions of information literacy.

Before moving on, the view of information literacy that is proposed here must be established. Information literacy can refer to many things. It can be a way to describe, for example, activities that concern finding and using information for a school assignment, a work task or for forming an opinion before everyday life choices are made. It can also refer to the content of activities that aim to train and prepare people for such engagements with information, often at libraries or educational institutions. Furthermore, information literacy can refer to rhetorical arguments for such activities, to research exploring those and also, as in this volume, to theories for grasping how the concept may be understood. A contextual, sociomaterial understanding of the concept is advocated here. It is also crucial to be aware of the fact that information literacy in itself is a perspective that can be used for describing aspects of activities as people engage with information in various ways (Rivano Eckerdal, 2017, 1025–7). It is a description made by someone about something being observed. Such descriptions are done by librarians or teachers and further developed and analysed by researchers. Information literacy research can therefore offer a vocabulary for describing information literacy aspects of activities.

Passionate decisions and democratic institutions

I now want to zoom in on decisions. When decisions are made, activities that can be described with information literacy vocabulary take place. Schematically put, people are likely to base decisions on prior knowledge, look for further information and advice, consider options available and arrive at deciding upon one of them, at least for the time being. In these activities people use, choose and evaluate information and make decisions.

Many decisions are made easily and effortlessly. However, there are decisions, like political decisions, that can be more demanding. Political questions concern conflicts between groups with different claims regarding the issue at hand. Decisions need to be made over and over again as issues and conflicts must be solved.

Political decisions are likely to have consequences for the identities of the people involved in making them, as the result will have impact on how the involved people understand both themselves and each other. Since our identities are fundamentally important for us, decisions that relate to them are not just rational but also emotional ones. Due to the passions involved when making political decisions, it is important to emphasise that a radical view of democracy is that of democracy as a conflictual process.

Every identity is relational (Mouffe 2005, 15). Crucial for the formation of groups are the collective identities that they establish by defining what they are not. To understand how these collective identities are moulded Mouffe turns to psychoanalysis:

> According to Freud, the evolution of civilization is characterized by a struggle between two basic types of libidinal instincts. Eros the instinct of life and Death the instinct of aggressiveness and destructiveness.
>
> (Mouffe, 2005, 26)

It is a role of the hegemonic practices to solve the issues at hand, although it is known that the underlying conflict will not be solved. Acknowledging the opponents' right to express their view means that the adversaries' solution to the current issue is recognised as legitimate. It is not the solution chosen by the opposing party in the debate, but it is deemed as equally relevant to one's own group's solution. This means that the adversaries' solution is not understood as a wrong one but as belonging and being relevant to a different political position.

> The agonistic confrontation is different from the antagonistic one, not because it allows for a possible consensus, but because the opponent is not considered an enemy to be destroyed but an adversary whose existence is perceived as legitimate. Her ideas will be fought with vigour but her right to defend them will never be questioned.
>
> (Mouffe, 2018, 91)

People want to be part of groups they feel that they belong to. This is foundational for society to emerge. In Freud's vocabulary the libidinal instinct of love is fuelling this process (Mouffe 2005, 26). But the ever-present possibility of aggression needs to be addressed. Mouffe proposes that 'democratic institutions can contribute to this disarming of the libidinal forces leading towards hostility which are always present in human societies' to solve this issue (Mouffe, 2005, 26). The democratic institutions are important places where the democratic process fraught with conflicts can be tamed to become an agonistic struggle. Besides the institutions that are part of the formal political arrangements – the politics – there are other institutions, also a part of a viable democratic society. For the democratic outcome it is necessary to involve many institutions. 'Democratic individuals can only be made possible by multiplying the institutions, the discourses, the forms of life that foster identification with democratic values' (Mouffe, 2000, 96).

Libraries as democratic institutions for information literacy activities

Libraries are not explicitly identified by Mouffe as democratic institutions but are described as democratic institutions by library and information science scholars (Hansson, 2010, 255; Rivano Eckerdal, 2017, 1016). It is important that people have the possibility of forming their own opinion on topics of their interest. Libraries, including librarians, are important as providers of knowledge required to make informed decisions between alternatives. They can offer support and scaffolding for counter-hegemonic practices. This is one way that libraries as institutions contribute to the democratic process by enabling formulation of counter-hegemonic articulations important to perform the agonistic debates. Libraries and librarians form part of the democratic institutions. This can be argued from the theory even though libraries or librarians are never explicitly mentioned. What the theory lacks is a more precise view of how such knowledge can be created.

Information literacy has gained attention over the years. As a consequence, activities aiming to strengthen and enhance information literacy – more recently media and information literacy – are part of contemporary library practices. Such activities could be developed as opportunities for agonistic debates to unfold. The agonistic debate is an activity in which it is possible to pay attention to the information literacy aspects of the activity. As the debate unfolds the parties draw on what they know and relate their arguments to each other. How the parties react to each other and the knowledge claims that are made can be analysed as enactments of information literacy.

As mentioned above, information literacy research provides a vocabulary to describe activities that include how people engage with information to make some kind of use of it: how they enact information literacy. By using this vocabulary, we can make descriptions of activities taking place in specific situations, descriptions that are made in relation to a set of norms (Rivano Eckerdal, 2017, 1025–7). Information literacy research has mainly focused on situations within school settings or related to work tasks. The teacher or the librarian are usually the ones making the description in school settings, the norms being found in the curricula. Information literacy is relevant in many other situations and an agonistic view on information literacy requires the identification of the actors involved in situations where information literacy is discussed. The descriptions of how the actors are engaging with information become meaningful once the involved parties are identified.

From a plural agonistic perspective, activities at libraries that support democracy in an empowering way are beneficial. Such measures can also be beneficial for information literacy enactments by preparing people for engaging in dialogues and debates. Understanding the agonistic struggle requires training and libraries and librarians can be part of the institutions that provide it. This is another way that libraries and librarians can contribute to the democratic process by offering not only the resources but also the opportunities for people to engage with information in an empowering way.

It has been pointed out that the approach to activities aiming at promoting or training information literacy will differ depending on what kind of democracy is drawn upon, implicitly or explicitly (Rivano Eckerdal, 2017). The critical analysis of activities with information literacy as a goal allows us to identify the set of norms that are guiding them and thus which view of democracy is supported. Information literacy research can contribute with important knowledge about the norms, including the views on democracy, that are used in information literacy practices (Rivano Eckerdal, 2017).

Consensus and compromises

Mouffe opposes deliberative democratic views. One major objection is the view on consensus that diverges from the one elaborated by Mouffe. Radical negativity entails an understanding of consensus as both an ontological impossibility and a necessity in the process of solving conflicts during agonistic debates.

> A democratic society requires a debate about possible alternatives and it must provide political forms of collective identification around clearly differentiated democratic positions. Consensus is no doubt necessary, but it must be accompanied by dissent.
>
> (Mouffe, 2005, 31)

Mouffe also mentions the use of compromises as a possibility; in practice 'they are part and parcel of politics; but they should be seen as temporary respites in an ongoing confrontation' (Mouffe 2000, 102).

In both a deliberative and a radical take on democracy the debates are crucial, issues being often solved with consensus reached through compromise. However, for Mouffe this is only a solution in practice. Consensus will never solve the underlying conflict. In other words: usually a consensual solution will mean that one party gains more at the other's expense. Power is not in perfect balance, giving advantage to one party. It is a solution that is accepted for the issue at hand. But it can always become fuel for future conflicts.

The criticism of consensus is of relevance in relation to the understanding of information literacy. Christine Bruce's groundbreaking thesis, *The Seven Faces of Information Literacy* (Bruce, 1997), is an early, important work aiming at conceptually framing the concept. She presents her study in opposition to previous work about information literacy and Christina Doyle's work (Doyle, 1992), in particular. One major criticism raised by Bruce relates to Doyle's (1992) application of the Delphi technique method, which aims at producing a consensus definition. Bruce, on the other hand, argued for the varying ways that a complex concept is understood within a group. Bruce used phenomenography to arrive at her relational definition of the concept, which instead presents the understanding of information literacy as a variation of seven aspects (also see Chapter 11 by Maybee). Bruce's critique of a consensus view and its problematic consequences echoes the critique of consensus as a goal for politics within plural agonistics, albeit from a different theoretical outlook.

Politics, ethics and information literacy

The notion of radical negativity does not fit with deliberative democratic views, precisely because the latter aim at consensus and also to describe debates as rational. Mouffe, instead points out that passions have an important role in politics (Mouffe, 2005, 24).

In 2000 Mouffe reacted to the contemporary political debate as increasingly ascribing political alternatives with a moral register:

> What is happening is that nowadays the political is played out in the *moral register*. In other words, it still consists in a we/they discrimination, but the we/they, instead of being defined with political categories, is now established in moral terms. In place of a struggle between 'right and left' we are faced with a struggle between 'right and wrong'.
>
> (Mouffe, 2005, 5)

Due to the democratic paradox – that equality and freedom can never be seamlessly successfully reconciled – such associations are wrong and even potentially a threat to the democratic institutions. At the time of writing this in 2023, democratic institutions have suffered from attacks of various sorts in a number of countries, making the democratic form of rule diminish globally (Lührmann and Lindberg, 2019; Papada et al., 2023). From a theoretical point of view, Mouffe foresaw such a development.

Recognising the fragility of democratic institutions is of utmost importance. Instead of describing the opponent as wrong it is important to bear in mind that the solution they advocate is of relevance for their group. The recognition of the opponent as an adversary and not as an enemy is not just an initial statement before starting an agonistic debate. On the contrary, it is something that needs to colour the whole process. Showing respect for the solution suggested by an adversary is one way in which this recognition is achieved. If a decision is not in line with their demands, it means that they are entitled to be disappointed. The opponents can continue to formulate their demands for future political debates – a production of counter-hegemonic articulations that is important for the democratic process.

> To summarize this point: every order is political and based on some form of exclusion. There are always other possibilities that have been repressed and that can be reactivated. The articulatory practices through which a certain order is established and the meaning of social institutions is fixed are 'hegemonic practices'. Every hegemonic order is susceptible of being challenged by counter-hegemonic practices, i.e. practices which will attempt to disarticulate the existing order so as to install another form of hegemony.
>
> (Mouffe, 2005, 18)

For information literacy the connection between decisions and ethics has important implications. With a plural agonistic perspective on decisions, it is not possible to shy away from the consequences that decisions have for the parties making it and those affected by it. Instead of combining morality and politics Mouffe points out that all decisions have ethical consequences and should be interrogated by the ethical. If one group's wishes are set aside by a decision that favours another group, questions need to be asked whether the consequences are ethically acceptable.

> Refusing to reduce the necessary hiatus between ethics and politics and acknowledging the irreducible tension between equality and liberty, between the ethics of human rights and the political logic which entails the establishments of frontiers with the violence that they imply, this is to recognize that the field of the political is not reducible to a rational moral calculus and always requires decisions. To discard the illusion of a possible reconciliation of ethics and politics and to come to terms with the never-ending interrogation of the political by the ethical, this is indeed the only way of acknowledging the democratic paradox.
>
> (Mouffe, 2000, 140)

Neutrality

Agonistic debates are activities in which people engage with information in ways that can be described with information literacy vocabulary. One consequence of the importance libraries can have as one of the institutions that scaffolds the agonistic debates is the impossibility of libraries to be neutral. Democracy, regardless of which shape it adopts, always brings with it a certain view about how society should be: it offers a set of norms. These are not neutral. Taking a stand for equality and freedom is never neutral.

In the radical view, democracy is understood as a process fraught with conflicts that requires making decisions with concrete consequences for people. How these consequences can give the best possible balance between freedom and equality is emphasised, but – recognising that a perfect balance is unattainable – equality is favoured.

One rationale for libraries is that they are places where people can freely develop their opinion and therefore, libraries need to be neutral. A plural agonistic view on democracy points out that this is impossible, insofar that neutral equals being passive. In order to remain relevant to as many as possible it is important that library staff uphold a professional role welcoming and supporting a plurality of voices. That the idea of objectivity and neutrality can be addressed in diverse ways by librarians, has been shown in empirical research (Rivano Eckerdal and Carlsson, 2022).

To further the theoretical understanding of information literacy and its practical consequences for libraries it is helpful to draw on Nora Schmidt's typology of different views of a neutral library and the consequences they have for librarianship (Schmidt, 2020, 274–84). She discerns between passive, active and culturally humble neutrality. The last-named is described in the following way:

> The library observes that power relations in society privilege certain voices, so they produce a biased . . . 'central' communication accompanied by respective information resources. In consequence, the library works towards balancing the observed bias, hence furthering social justice.
>
> (Schmidt, 2020, 282)

Schmidt's typology was developed for discussing libraries' collection development. It is also useful for discussing a plural agonistic take on information literacy. The humble view of neutrality fits well with a plural agonistic approach in its support for social justice. As stated above, information literacy is positioned as a political concept with an agonistic view. Both libraries and librarians have a vital role to play in society, a role that can be strengthened and developed further. When doing that it is important to bear in mind that one's understanding of neutrality is always political.

Identity

Decisions form an important part of activities that can be described as information literacy enactments and they can have consequences for people's identity. Mouffe rejects the idea of the existence of an essential identity, instead she talks about 'forms of identification' (Mouffe, 2013, 45). Zooming in from the statement of radical negativity, plural agonistics understands individuals as being part of different groups with varying claims. The formation of these groups is shaped by what Mouffe calls the *constitutive outside*: what unites people is awareness of what they are not. For both group and individual identities, it is important to discern what group one is not belonging to.

> The aim is to highlight the fact that the creation of an identity implies the establishment of a difference which is often constructed on the basis of a hierarchy, for example between form and matter, black and white, man and woman, etc.
>
> (Mouffe, 2005, 15)

As individuals belong to several groups, they are heterogenous internally but form a unity externally. As the basis for the collective identity is what the group is not, attention is paid to other groups outside their own and a relation is created built on difference (Mouffe, 2005, 15). When collective identities are formed, a *we* is created as opposed to a *they* – the constitutive outside. This can be unproblematic but may give rise to conflicts.

> In the field of collective identities, we are always dealing with the creation of a 'we' which can exist only by the demarcation of a 'they'. This does not mean of course that such a relation is necessarily one of friend/enemy, i.e. an antagonistic one. But we should acknowledge that, in certain conditions, there is always the possibility that this we/they relation can become antagonistic, i.e. that it can turn into a relation of friend/enemy. This happens when the 'they' is perceived as putting into question the identity of the 'we' and as threatening its existence.
>
> (Mouffe, 2005, 15–16)

In situations where a conflict occurs between different groups what happens is that in one way or another the collective identity of each group is questioned. Given how important our identities are to us – albeit not in an essential understanding but as how we relate to each other – such situations evoke emotions. Therefore, Mouffe argues, the political is not only rational but also by necessity includes emotions.

To acknowledge and give room to passion within politics is important for well-functioning democracies. Mouffe derives the crisis of democracy from politics not realising and acknowledging this.

> A well functioning democracy calls for a clash of legitimate democratic political positions. This is what the confrontation between left and right needs to be about. Such a confrontation should provide collective forms of identification strong enough to mobilize political passions.
>
> (Mouffe, 2005, 30)

Wayne Wiegand, exploring the role US public libraries play in people's everyday life, found the stories to which they provide access to be very significant for people. Library users have witnessed how reading stories provided at a public library help them make sense of the world and how, in many cases, it is a transformative experience (Wiegand, 2015). Wiegand refers to this significant role in terms of literacy but not information literacy. He concludes that from users' perspectives, libraries do not live up to the library and information science's rhetoric about being vital for democracy. Wiegand's conclusion draws from a specific interpretation of the democratic role: it should manifest itself in people's knowledge about political processes and democratic theory (Wiegand, 2015, 362). However, from a plural agonistic view on democracy, the role that public libraries play in people's lives as places in which people's identities can develop is a democratic role. Envisioning how things could be different should also include ideas about how things could be better. Choosing between political alternatives that present a way to proceed for making the change happen is not only a rational process:

> There is an important affective dimension in voting and what is at stake there is a question of identification. In order to act politically people need to be able to identify with a collective identity which provides an idea of themselves they can valorize. Political discourse has to offer not only policies but also identities which can help people make sense of what they are experiencing as well as giving them hope for the future.
>
> (Mouffe, 2005, 25)

Carol Kuhlthau's (2004) inclusion of feelings alongside thoughts and actions in her model of the information-seeking process is an example of how emotions previously have been brought to attention as relevant for information seeking within library and information science. In plural agonistics, emotions are related to collective, not to individual, identities. What is shared is the holistic approach to how people interact with information, in which the rational and emotional are intertwined.

> An important difference with the model of 'deliberative democracy' is that for 'agonistic pluralism', the prime task of democratic politics is not to eliminate passions from the sphere of the public, in order to render a rational consensus possible, but to mobilize those passions towards democratic designs.
>
> (Mouffe, 2000, 103)

People react to the situations they are involved in and emotions influence their reactions. Therefore, emotions must be brought into politics. For information literacy this realisation implies that interactions with information need to be understood as holistic experiences with possible consequences for people's identities (also see Chapter 10 by Lloyd).

Forming chains of equivalences

There are many social movements and these have various goals and diverse political interests. In order to make social change happen, alliances between groups that share similar claims must be established. Laclau and Mouffe mention this as the formation of *chains of equivalents*.

> In the face of the project for the reconstruction of a hierarchic society, the alternative of the Left should consist of locating itself fully in the field of the democratic revolution and expanding the chains of equivalents between the different struggles against oppression. *The task of the Left therefore cannot be to renounce liberal-democratic ideology, but on the contrary, to deepen and expand it in the direction of a radical and plural democracy.* [italics in original]
> (Laclau and Mouffe, 2014, 160)

Mouffe later uses the term *chain of equivalence* (Mouffe, 2005, 54; 2013, 14). Focus is then on accepting differences between groups but forming temporary alliances. This allows for more voices to be heard. The formation of chains of equivalences is a way to move towards a more equal society. Given the current discussion and division within the left, plural agonistics proposes a way of reconciling different social movements and offers a way for them to work together in order to achieve social change.

Groups can make change happen through the formulation of counter-hegemonic practices. When formulating these practices, it is possible that they cause opposition from one or more groups due to their other claims. This is the moment when the different groups must recognise each other as legitimate opponents and engage in an agonistic debate. Libraries with their resources and staff are providing the infrastructure to develop the knowledge needed for these debates. They can also be the places where the debates can unfold. This constitutes examples of activities that can be analysed as enactments of information literacy.

Researching information literacy with an agonistic view

When considering adopting an agonistic theory in research it is important to bear in mind, as already mentioned, that information literacy is not something that exists in any objective or observable way. Instead, it is a description of certain activities that involve information. Therefore, in order to study information literacy from an agonistic perspective, attention must be paid to situations involving such activities, which makes ethnographic methods suitable for the task. To gain insights not only into what is happening but also into how the parties understand what is happening, a combination of observations and conversations, either in the form of interviews or more informal, is suitable (Rivano Eckerdal, 2013).

Combining plural agonistics with other theoretical approaches contributes a theoretical lens that positions information literacy as a political concept and also takes a stand for a radical view of democracy, striving to enhance social equality. Suggestions for theories that could fit well with it are practice theories and theories with a sociomaterial focus (see Chapter 9 by Haider and Sundin and Chapter 10 by Lloyd). The strong ontological emphasis in plural agonistics opens an opportunity for a combination with post-humanist theories. One such example is a combination of plural agonistics with ideas developed by Gilles Deleuze and Félix Guattari that formed the theoretical basis for suggesting an understanding of libraries not as a noun but as a verb (Rivano Eckerdal, 2018).

Limitations

Agonistic debates are only possible for parties that recognise each other as legitimate opponents. Thus, the theory does not answer the problem of how to solve conflicts in situations when this is not the case.

> A democratic society cannot treat those who put its basic institutions into question as legitimate adversaries. The agonistic approach does not pretend to encompass all differences and to overcome all forms of exclusions. But exclusions are envisaged in political and not in moral terms. Some demands are excluded, not because they are declared to be 'evil', but because they challenge the institutions constitutive of the democratic political association.
>
> (Mouffe, 2005, 120–1)

This reservation could be pointed out as a major flaw of the theory, but it can also be argued to be a call for the imperative to reform democratic institutions to avoid (further) violence. This reservation also has consequences for library practices when they are understood as institutions that have a role as providers of knowledge and space for agonistic debates. There will be situations when a conflict arises in which one or both parties do not recognise their opponent as legitimate or question the legitimacy of the institution. Then the door to a proper agonistic debate is closed. Discerning if an agonistic debate is at all possible is therefore an important and difficult task that is bestowed upon librarians, a task that requires ethical awareness.

Concluding remarks

Plural agonistics is here proposed as a valuable contribution to information literacy research and practice, as it accentuates information literacy as a political concept. As shown, it is a theory that productively can help us to understand the link between information literacy and democracy. Democracy is never neutral and the plural agonistic democratic theoretical perspective is positioned in the realm of radical democracy. But, contrary to other radical democratic theories, plural agonistics supports the liberal form of democratic rule.

The ineradicable dimension of antagonism is a perspective that does not strive to formulate a utopian ultimate goal towards which it is important to strive regardless of cost, an endeavour most likely involving brutal repression of resistance. This ontological statement is beneficial not because it is optimistic but because it starts with the realisation that power always corrupts. Furthermore, it does not fall into the trap of prescribing for itself a way forward where a peaceful future is foreseen for everyone if agonism came into power. At the same time, it is constructive because it does not stop at stating that power always corrupts but formulates a way forward to work towards a more democratic –

understood as more egalitarian – society. The approach is to change the focus of aspirations, from focus on future goals to focus on the situation here and now and how the situation can change.

Plural agonistics highlights how institutions are crucial for democracy by being sites for agonistic debate; it is within the democratic institutions that enemies are shaped into adversaries that are able to debate issues related to dissimilar views on situations.

Mouffe prescribes a way to change the prevailing hegemony by producing counter-hegemonies and strives to prevent the erosion of existing institutions from within. Libraries are important institutions both as places in which people can learn, from both fiction and non-fiction, envision and articulate possible counter-hegemonies and debate them. These are information activities that here are construed as including information literacy aspects. Institutions need to be defended and, in every decision made, political solutions must be questioned ethically in terms of whether they offer better terms for most people. New articulations should aim to include those that are excluded today.

The increased polarisation that we are witnessing is understood, from a plural agonistic point of view, not as caused by the debate but by the failure to politically shape conflicts within democratic institutions. Conflicts are always potentially occurring due to the ineradicability of antagonism. The democratic institutions in society, including libraries, have a crucial mission to help shape and tame those conflicts – antagonisms – into debates, agonism.

With the help of plural agonism, mundane everyday activities are connected with their social role, importance and impact. Such mundane activities include, for example, activities in which people interact with information in ways that are possible to describe as enactments of information literacy. If we understand those situations better, we become better equipped for developing and defending our institutions, including libraries, as well-functioning institutions in a pluralist democratic society.

> On the contrary, it is by finally acknowledging the contradictory tendencies set to work by social exchange and the fragility of the democratic order that we will be able to grasp what I have argued is the task confronting democracy: how to transform the potential antagonism existing in human relations into an agonism.
>
> (Mouffe, 2000, 135)

Notes

1 Democracy is a form of rule where the people – *demos* in Greek – hold the power. It has evolved over time and there exists a number of varieties of how it can be executed. The representative liberal form of democratic rule is then one way to realise a democratic regime in practice. Important in such a regime are the democratic institutions that are separated to ensure a division of power. Such institutions include free elections, a parliament, a free press and an independent judiciary system. When we talk about democracy it can refer to these institutions,

what Mouffe calls 'the symbolic framework within which democracy is exercised'. (Mouffe, 2000, 2) See also Rivano Eckerdal, 2017, 1012–13.
2 Carl Schmitt (1888–1985), a German political philosopher, presented a critique of liberalism that Mouffe draws upon in her theory. Schmitt is controversial, as he was a member of, and intellectually supported, the Nazi party (www.britannica.com/biography/Carl-Schmitt). Mouffe acknowledges that he is a real challenge for her but that she found his analysis of the antagonistic dimension of the political useful. However, she draws an opposite conclusion of its effects, what she calls to 'think with Schmitt against Schmitt' (Mouffe, 2013, 138; see also Mouffe, 2000, 57, n. 2).

References

ALA (American Library Association) (1989) Presidential Committee on Information Literacy: final report, www.ala.org/acrl/publications/whitepapers/presidential.

Bruce, C. (1997) *The Seven Faces of Information Literacy*, Auslib Press.

Doyle, C. S. (1992) *Outcome Measures for Information Literacy Within the National Education Goals of 1990*, Final report to the National Forum on Information Literacy, summary of findings, ED351033, ERIC Clearinghouse on Information Resources.

Elmborg, J. (2006) Critical Information Literacy: implications for instructional practice, *Journal of Academic Librarianship*, 32 (2), 192–9.

Foa, R. S. and Mounk, Y. (2017) The Signs of Deconsolidation, *Journal of Democracy*, 28 (1), 5–15.

Hansson, J. (2010) Chantal Mouffe's Theory of Agonistic Pluralism and its Relevance for Library and Information Science Research. In Leckie, G. J., Given, L. M. and Buschman, J. E. (eds) *Critical Theory for Information Science: exploring the social from across the disciplines*, Libraries Unlimited, 249–57.

IFLA (International Federation of Library Associations and Institutions) (2005) *Beacons of the Information Society: the Alexandria proclamation on information literacy and lifelong learning*, www.ifla.org/publications/beacons-of-the-information-society-the-alexandria-proclamation-on-information-literacy-and-lifelong-learning.

Kuhlthau, C. C. (2004) *Seeking Meaning: a process approach to library and information services*, Libraries Unlimited.

Laclau, E. and Mouffe, C. (2014) *Hegemony and Socialist Strategy: towards a radical democratic politics*, 2nd edn (first published 1985), Verso.

Lührmann, A. and Lindberg, S. I. (2019) A Third Wave of Autocratization is Here: what is new about it?, *Democratization*, 26 (7), 1095–113.

Mouffe, C. (2000) *The Democratic Paradox*, Verso.

Mouffe, C. (2005) *On the Political*, Routledge.

Mouffe, C. (2013) *Agonistics: thinking the world politically*, Verso.

Mouffe, C. (2018) *For a Left Populism*, Verso.

Papada, E., Altman, D., Angiolillo, F., Gastaldi, L., Köhler, T., Lundstedt, M., Natsika, N., Nord, M., Sato, Y., Wiebrecht, F. and Lindberg, S. I. (2023) *Defiance in the Face of Autocratization:*

Democracy Report 2023, University of Gothenburg: Varieties of Democracy Institute (V-Dem Institute), https://v-dem.net/documents/29/V-dem_democracyreport2023_lowres.pdf.

Rivano Eckerdal, J. (2013) Empowering Interviews: narrative interviews in the study of information literacy in everyday life settings, *Information Research*, 18, paper C10.

Rivano Eckerdal, J. (2017) Libraries, Democracy, Information: literacy and citizenship: an agonistic reading of central library and information studies' concepts, *Journal of Documentation*, 73, 1010–33.

Rivano Eckerdal, J. (2018) Equipped for Resistance: an agonistic conceptualisation of the public library as a verb, *Journal of the Association for Information Science and Technology*, 69, 1405–13.

Rivano Eckerdal, J. and Carlsson, H. (2022) Plastic Policies: contemporary opportunities and challenges in public libraries' enactment of cultural policy, *Nordic Journal of Library and Information Studies*, 3 (1), 1–25.

Schmidt, N. (2020) The Privilege to Select: global research system, European academic library collections and decolonisation, dissn, Lund University.

Wiegand, W. (2015) 'Tunnel Vision and Blind Spots' Reconsidered: part of our lives (2015) as a test case, *Library Quarterly*, 85 (4), 347–70.

Wilson, C., Grizzle, A., Tuazon, R., Akyempong, K. and Cheung, C. K. (2011) *Media and Information Literacy Curriculum for Teachers*, UNESCO, http://unesdoc.unesco.org/images/0019/001929/192971e.pdf.

7
Critical Literacy and Critical Design

Veronica Johansson

Introduction

Information and information systems are designed in many ways and on many levels, including the choice of content included or excluded; graphical layouts and linguistic choices; the crafting of internal structures, links and metadata; and the contextual embedding of units and systems into networks of others. Much current research and development in information design-related areas emphasise 'solutionist' approaches, whereby design is intended to resolve externally defined 'problems', while simultaneously striving to achieve user experiences that are as 'seamless', 'intuitive', 'transparent' and 'immersive' as possible. The argument here, in contrast, emphasises critical literacy-motivated needs and possibilities of *designing for the opposite*; of designing in ways that highlight and problematise the limited and biased character of information representations – and that make visible and inspire reflection and dialogue on critically informed future improved alternatives. This argument is achieved by way of introducing concepts and theories associated with the field of *critical design* to elaborate theoretical and empirical understandings of and approaches to *critical literacy*.

A primary motivation for this combination is the recognition of a foundational 'problem of representation' affecting conditions for and consequences of all forms of information construction, use and exchange, with related power imbalances. This position postulates two particularly important things: (a) for objects, entities, experiences, events and actions to become *information*, they have to be *represented* somehow; and (b) that this representational requirement is not only unavoidable but problematic. Representation in the sense implied here is what gives potentially informative resources and entities a form, structure and context with subjective and social meaning potential (cf. Blackwell, 2013; Buckland and Ramos, 2010; Johansson, 2012; Johansson and Stenlund, 2021). Whether sorted in mental categories, expressed through spoken discourse, visualised as data points on a map, enacted by a bodily gesture or processed and published as a written academic publication, representational tools in the form of concepts, classifications, grammar, visual forms, colour schemes and even body language are necessary verbal and non-verbal representation schemes ('structuring devices', Buckland and Ramos, 2010) for the construction of information that is meaningful and communicable across bodies, minds, places and times.

The problem, in this view, is that all representational tools are situated constructs and, as such, malleable to social and material limitations, bias and variations across times, cultures and contexts (cf. Beaulieu, 2002; Blackwell, 2013; Drucker, 2014; 2020). This means on the one hand that the more conventional and well-established a certain representational form is, the more efficiently it can be assumed to function as a tool for interpretation and communication (Blackwell, 2013). But on the other hand, forces and interests of convention, norm, efficiency, profit and power also work to naturalise and black-box representational forms, obscuring their artificial, limited and biased characters and consequences (Beaulieu, 2002; Bowker and Star, 1999; van Dijck, 2005).

To purposefully identify, use and interact with the (by necessity representationally mediated) information of relevance to ourselves and others in various situations, more or less complex *information literacy* practices are required and will emerge. But as the reader will have noted, this chapter primarily deals with *critical literacy*, a specific and related approach, described in Lupton and Bruce's (2010) GeST model as a 'window' on information literacy emphasising subjective and societal transformation. At its core, critical literacy is always concerned with power and liberation/transformation, most often associated with specific political and 'standpoint' epistemological and ontological orientations. Prominent among these are the historical/dialectical materialism of Marx, the normative rationality of critical theory/the Frankfurt School and the liberatory agenda of Freirean critical pedagogy (e.g. Bezerra and Schneider, Chapter 4 in this volume; Elmborg, 2006; Luke, 2019; Marinopoulou, 2019; Tewell, 2015). A related but less common and therefore less explored philosophical orientation connects instead with post-structuralist and sociomaterial – predominantly sociotechnical – theories (e.g. Johansson, 2012; Kapitzke, 2003a; 2003b; Simmons, 2005; Tuominen, Savolainen and Talja, 2005). It is impossible – and not desirable – to completely separate these traditions, but focus in the following is on the latter.

Unless otherwise specified, thus, a post-structuralist and sociomaterially based definition of critical literacy as dimension of, or perspective on, information literacy is used in what follows. This approach conceptualises critical literacy as pertaining to *the identification, contestation and transformation of representational limitations and bias affecting power relations in information construction, use and exchange* (cf. Johansson, 2012, 204). The synthesis of critical literacy and critical design presented here has two implications in particular. First, it shifts focus away from critical literacy as object and result of formal learning activities and pedagogies, pointing instead to an understanding of critical literacy as orientation and process, as 'ways of being and doing' (cf. Markham, 2020; Vasquez, 2012; Vasquez, Janks and Comber, 2019). Empirical studies are hereby directed towards the situated intersections of information design and social interaction through which the construction and mediation of values and power can be surfaced. Secondly and following from the first, it prompts researchers, information designers and professionals towards normative-ethical considerations of what could and should be asked for and striven to be accomplished, in the design of alternative information and information systems. The approach offers suggestions for reflexive, critical design practices in support of critical literacy awareness and enactment possibilities among individual users and society at large. However, before delving deeper into such theoretical and methodological implications for critical literacy, a presentation of the roots and central ideas of critical design is offered.

Critical design: origins and overview

Critical design (CD) – sometimes also described as critical and speculative design (CSD) – is a field rather than a coherent theory in itself, and a young one at that. It is mainly distinguishable from the late 1990s onwards, although roots of similarly inclined design-oriented lineages reach back to the 1960s (Jakobsone, 2017), including the Italian Radical Design movement, the hypothetical avant-garde architecture of the British Archigram group and later Scandinavian participatory design (Elsden et al., 2017; Gregory, 2003; Wong and Mulligan, 2019). The family tree also includes developments in human–computer interaction (HCI) and interaction design (IxD) (Malpass, 2013; Wong and Mulligan, 2019). The concept itself, however, is mainly associated with scholars in design and social inquiry Anthony Dunne and Fiona Raby, through their seminal publications *Hertzian Tales: electronic products, aesthetic experience and critical design* (Dunne, 1999) and *Design Noir: the secret life of electronic objects* (Dunne and Raby, 2001).

Although disciplinarily diverse, the critical design field emerged as, and continues to be united by, a reaction against assumptions that design is 'somehow neutral, clean and pure', whereas on the contrary, '. . . all design is ideological, the design process is informed by values based on a specific world view, or way of seeing and understanding reality' (Dunne and Raby, 2001, 58). At its core, critical design problematises and opposes those instrumental goals and functions of design that frame and establish design as purposeful plans for fulfilling user 'needs'; for the maximisation of profit interests; or as uncritical enactments of technical determinist imperatives and social norms in the design of products in general (Jakobsone, 2017; Malpass, 2013) and of information systems in particular (Cecez-Kecmanovic, Klein and Brooke, 2008).

The scope and applicability of critical design are broad, able to encompass all human constructs and the factors contributing to shaping them, an orientation which in Gonsher's view represents '. . . a critique of the context and culture in which the designed object exists'. In this way, it is, he argues '. . . closer to what is traditionally thought of as art in so far as it functions as a critique of culture' (Gonsher, n.d.). The analogy between critical design and art is interesting, since it is as common as it is controversial: refuted by originators (Dunne and Raby, n.d.; 2001); identified as a hindrance to widespread 'real-world' application and effects by others (e.g. Malazita, 2018; Malpass, 2015); and requested as a necessary disciplinary crossover and a creative synergy factor in comprehensive critical approaches to research and society by still others (e.g. Markham, 2020; Oxman, 2016; Wong and Mulligan, 2019).

Inconsistencies aside, the critical design field undoubtedly provides '... its own culture of inquiry and action' (Nelson and Stolterman, 2014). It is generative, performative (Wong and Mulligan, 2019), activist, transformative and *re*constructivist (Woodhouse et al., 2002), carrying an agenda with theories and goals of its own, expressing intellectual, philosophical and ethical imperatives of disciplinary and professional reflexivity, responsibility and agency, as illustrated in the following section.

Central concepts in critical design

According to Dunne and Raby, all design inevitably falls into one of two categories: *affirmative (problem-solving)* or *critical (problem-finding)* (Dunne and Raby, 2001; Gonsher, n.d.). The first perpetuates the status quo, and repeats and reinforces social norms and dominant power relations. The second takes as an ethical obligation the intention to design in ways that strive to make bias and power imbalances visible. Problem-finding design, and critical literacy as well, is often found overlaid with Marxist theory. Jakobsone, for example, makes this connection in describing the problem-finding approach as a reaction to: '... everything that the western society takes for given and unalterable, as part of the governing ideology – from seemingly irrelevant everyday routines, to the social roles and the whole capitalistic system' (Jakobsone, 2017, 4260). But these are not the only problems highlighted in critical design and, as has been declared, in the interpretation advanced here we step back from specific political theories and draw instead on post-structuralist and sociotechnical problems of representation.

Central criteria of critical design include the affordance of *perspective-changing accounts* of a given phenomenon; a *problematising* ('*speculative*') rather than *declarative* ('*truth-claiming*') approach; a reflection of *dialogical methodology*; the improvement of *cultural competence* on behalf of users; and *reflexive awareness* of the design process itself (Bardzell and Bardzell, 2013; Dunne and Raby, 2001). Beyond this, other authors have provided additions to elaborate on this theoretical 'core' of the field. Malpass, the first to have attempted a comprehensive introduction of critical design as a field, including accounting for its history, influences and theories, identifies three main categories of critical design theory and practice. The categories are defined according to their domain, scope, visual narrative and topic and are described as *associative design*, *speculative design* and *critical design* (Malpass, 2013; 2017).

Associative design is design that aims to subvert users' and the public's expectations of the ordinary and the everyday. Such design draws on practices that rely on communicative, representational, design conventions and create effects by subverting some of the expected conventional elements of objects, contexts and use practices. Common methods to accomplish this subversion effect comprise *cut-up*, *context-transfer*, *hybridity* and *bricolage*, primarily operating through 'ambiguity and context', or 'correspondence and context'. The objects in this category tend to be 'more rational' and mundane than those in speculative and critical design (Malpass, 2013, 336–7).

Speculative design is primarily concerned with the future, used for critical investigation of advances in science and technology. Presentational formats include *scenarios* of products, their use and contexts within society and the role that design plays in this delivery. The main objective is to 'encourage the user to reconsider how the present is futuring and how we might potentially have the chance to reconfigure the future' (Malpass, 2013, 340). Speculative design occupies a central place in the 'original', or 'prototypical' critical design fields (i.e. the creative, arts-oriented), mirrored not least in the common addendum of 'S' for speculative in certain versions of the field name as CSD (critical and speculative design) and in Dunne's and Raby's (2013) *Speculative Everything: design, fiction and social dreaming*.

Critical design, finally, is characterised by its focus on 'present social, cultural and ethical *implications* of design objects and practice' (Malpass, 2013, 341). It is influenced by critical social theory and its 'intention is to engage the audience's imagination and intellect to convey message' (Malpass, 2013, 341). Through mechanisms of *defamiliarisation* and *estrangement*, designers extend the *critical distance* between the object and the user, producing comment on current sociotechnical, economic, political, cultural and psychological concerns. The designs often employ familiar shapes, colours and forms, but '. . . suspend the user uncomfortably between reality and fiction. They seem real but there is something not quite right; barriers are introduced or exaggerated in a way that is defamiliarizing, engaging the audience's imagination and intellect' (Malpass, 2013, 341).

Thus, in Malpass' framework of categories, critical design denotes both the field as such and a particular subset focusing on implications of design. The categories, in other words, are not mutually exclusive. Perhaps we may more readily conceive of them as fleeting positions on intersecting or parallel scales. One scale ranging from *associative* (mundane) to *speculative* (abstract) characteristics and another, denoting temporal directionality from *present* to *future*, as examples in the following section will show.

Theoretical questions

In this section, we move on to discuss central theoretical and methodological assumptions in critical literacy and critical design and their compatibilities. The first sub-section addresses underlying ontological and epistemological orientations of the two; the second discusses what understandings about critical literacy critical design opens us to and what it closes us to; and the third explicates methodological implications of this critical design approach to critical literacy.

On being and knowledge

Neither critical literacy nor critical design are unified schools of thought or theories with explicit philosophy of science positions. Beyond sharing the actual word 'critical', however, works in these traditions do display similar ontological and epistemological orientations – i.e. ways of conceiving of 'being', 'the world' and entities and relations in it and of how we can come to 'know' about these things. As previously mentioned, much work in both critical literacy and critical design are clearly inspired by the critical theory traditions of Marxism and the Frankfurt School (Bezerra and Schneider, this volume; Gonsher, n.d.;

Jakobsone, 2017; Johansson and Limberg, 2017; Luke, 2019; Malpass, 2013; 2017; Vasquez, 2012). But today, as illustrated by Wigger and Horn (2017), the connotation of 'critical' has widened to pertain to postpositivist stances in general and a host of approaches including '. . . feminist, reflexive, postcolonial, postmodern or poststructuralist'. The theoretical elaboration presented here is part of these latter developments – specifically the sociotechnical sub-branch of the post-structuralist framework.

Let us therefore start by addressing a common objection to post-structuralism: that it leads to relativism or even nihilism, renouncing possibilities of any value judgements or indeed of any meaning at all and as leaving, e.g. the field of critical pedagogy to '. . . work in a relativist universe of competing significations with no fixed epistemological grounds . . .' (Luke, 2019, 349). Although likely to be refuted by discourse theorists in general, this objection is even less tenable in relation to specific sociomaterial and sociotechnical sub-branches. Connected to the so-called 'ontological turn' in social theory in general and within post-structuralism in particular, these branches incorporate and attend to material ontology and downplay the previously strong epistemological emphasis on language and discourse (Woolgar and Lezaun, 2013; 2015). Notable scholars in the tradition include Latour and his 'matters of concern', Deleuze and Guattari's 'assemblages' and Barad's 'posthumanist materialist performativity' (Feely, 2016; valentine and Seear, 2020; Woodward, Dixon and Jones III, 2009). Variations on these ideas inform sociotechnical approaches in both critical literacy and critical design (e.g. Johansson, 2012; Johansson and Stenlund, 2021; Malazita, 2018; Tuominen, Savolainen and Talja, 2005).

The ontological turn implies that sociotechnical approaches are ontologically rather than epistemologically inclined. What becomes perceived as reality is 'made-in-practice' (valentine and Seear, 2020), enacted in situated interactions involving both the social and material. 'Scientific knowledge' itself is understood as constituted in sociomaterial processes; it is partial, biased, shaped by and in turn shaping perceptions of the world and of things and relations in it. Building upon and incorporating such provisional knowledge, the instruments of science themselves demand similar critical attention as the primary objects of study. But this is not to say that the results of sociotechnical and sociomaterial studies can have no social and political relevance and application-use value – on the contrary, numerous arguments and examples illustrate the opposite.

Post-structuralist and sociomaterial approaches, just like critical design and critical literacy (see above), are often proclaimed as political stances, in which 'claims and arguments are developed in the name of political commitments to progressive change', even though what should count as 'progressive' often remains 'open to discussion and debate' (Bacchi, 2021, n.p.). Bacchi's argument ties into valentine and Seear's, who claim that rather than vaguely suggesting 'multiple realities' of little usefulness, sociotechnical analysis should be seen as '. . . a political response to *particular* realities, those that produce and reproduce social injustices' (valentine and Seear, 2020, 2). The authors then move on to illustrate the considerable value and applicability of sociotechnical research to the field of medical policy development.

Even a hint of normative aspirations, however, may bring up a second, common, objection, also borrowed from Luke (2019). With reference to *a priori*, normative, political concepts and theories (whether Marxist, Freirean, feminist, etc.) he points to risks of (re)-introducing equally limiting and oppressive ideological standpoints as the very ones that critical literacy activities intend to contest and transform. How, he asks, should '. . . interpretive communities resolve issues of which cultural representations; which versions of truth and objectivity, political ideologies and ethical positions [that] will be made to count. . . ' (Luke, 2019, 356). This objection, notably, can be posed to any number of theories that at least imply certain normative political and ideological ideas. In comparison to most of these, sociotechnical approaches may be in one of the lowest-risk zones for such imposition, as they (often) halt at a primary interest in power relations without more specific *a priori* determined analytical focal points. This more undetermined focus on power reduces the risk of prematurely foreclosing the analytical focus. Rather, it supports interrogations that consider a broad spectrum of conceivably relevant explanations.

Nevertheless, there are also other, more outspokenly application-oriented, normative and ethical, approaches in sociotechnical and science and technology studies (STS), that may seem closer to critical design intents and stances. Woodhouse and colleagues distinguish a longstanding division between on the one hand 'academic' and on the other hand 'activist' or 'reconstructivist' orientations. The latter, they claim, '. . . assumes that technoscience is contingent and socially negotiated – and goes on to tackle the problems of how to *reconstruct* technoscience to promote a more democratic, environmentally sustainable, socially just, or otherwise preferable civilization' (Woodhouse et al., 2002, 297–8). Sociotechnical approaches of this sort provide an opening for normative, prescriptive and ethical agendas and objectives that echo the similarly normative, ethical and interventionist-transformational dimensions of both critical literacy and critical design. Such a stance in critical design is made explicit, e.g. by Malazita, who states that:

> . . . as science and technology studies (STS) scholars have long argued, every designed artifact, system and process is enmeshed within larger structures of political power and thus participates in the political world. In practice, every stage of various design processes furthers normative, ethical and ontological arguments – implicit and explicit claims about how the world is, how the world should be, for what purpose and for whom and what.
>
> (Malazita, 2018, 98)

This openness to normative views makes it possible to conceive of additions to sociomaterial and sociotechnical approaches in terms of more specific standpoint or ideological constructs. Although some would argue that Marxism/critical theory and post-structuralism are incompatible, others claim that the latter's '. . . critical stance toward simplistic forms of truth, representation, materiality and politics have become points of engagement . . .' between it and other critical theories of feminism, race, body and postcolonialism (Woodward, Dixon and Jones III, 2009, 297). We may conclude, therefore, that a wide variety of theoretical and philosophical combinations are both deducible from and applicable within a critical design-inspired approach to critical literacy: loosely united by a material ontology, constructionist epistemology and transformative, ethical, normative-political goals and concerns. Related consequences in terms of perspectives are discussed in the following section.

In and out of focus

Elaborating critical literacy through the lens of critical design foregrounds certain aspects while downplaying and renouncing others. Not least, this construct differs from the more common Marxist and critical theory versions by its more general critical and material ontology approach to power relations as situated enactments of meaning. This approach assumes more generally that any instance of information construction, use and exchange will be embedded in and incorporate (more or less of) values, interests and conflicts that are biased and biasing, affecting and effecting power imbalances. More specifically, *what* values, interests and actors and *how* this is accomplished are empirical questions that need to be explored in context. As mentioned, however, this approach still retains possibilities to be combined with more specific political, ideological and standpoint theories if a research problem or interest calls for this.

Further, it follows from this approach that what is found in one empirical setting, with one particular research approach, has little validity outside the context in question and only even provisionally so within it. Results of inquiries, whether by researchers or designers, are evaluated on the basis of *usefulness* rather than truth and on the basis of *strength of connection* between induction and empirical basis. The only thing we will know for sure with this approach – a recognition shared with numerous other recent theoretical developments of information literacy – is that this understanding of critical literacy is incompatible with any form of generic, objective, 'check-list' approach detailing specific problems and concerns, design solutions, and/or user skills and competences out of context (e.g. Johansson, 2012; Johansson and Limberg, 2017; Kapitzke, 2003a; 2003b; Tuominen, Savolainen and Talja, 2005; Wong and Mulligan, 2019).

What, then, *do* we in fact gain from this synthesis of critical literacy with critical design? Primarily, the sociotechnically grounded critical design perspectives bring to critical literacy an interest in and emphasis on the value-laden, power- and politics-enacting, situated and mutually shaping, sociomaterial construction of ideas, meanings, social relations, artefacts and tools. Specifically in our context, it brings to the fore ways in which the construction, use and exchange of information and information systems incorporate, mediate, shape and are shaped by limitations and bias in the form of values, interests, power and politics. And we can add to this, the way that critical design concepts and ideas highlight and focus means to explore and attend to representational problems in the present and mundane, as well as in the future and abstract.

What also happens with this approach, is that focus shifts from placing main responsibility for 'being critical' in information contexts away from users, to instead and more markedly defer this to the designers, producers and other authorities with influence over information and information system construction, use and exchange. In Gonsher's words, critical design describes:

> ... a creative strategy that establishes design as a medium for making visible that which is usually obscured in our daily interactions with the quotidian objects of our material culture ... [it] creates affordances for awareness, framing how we understand, question and critique the society and culture around us.
>
> (Gonsher, n.d.)

In order to respond to the responsibility and strive for critical rather than affirmative design, designers need to actively research and learn from users' experiences and interactions with the designed objects in question. There is an obligation to consider what old problems that remain or what new ones that arise and how these can be addressed and counteracted through (re)design. It also includes 'thinking ahead' and proactively pushing and introducing possible but not yet realised information tools and systems through the use of participatory and critically reflective platforms for exchange with potential to influence and improve future conditions and trajectories. With this view, neither information professionals nor researchers can contentedly stand on the sideline and present critical literacy guides and workshops on the limitations and bias of search engines and databases, smartphone apps and social media news services. They are explicitly implicated as responsible actors in sociomaterial processes of design and redesigns.

Finally, and as foreshadowed above, this view also shifts emphasis from the common literacy focus (both in information and critical literacy) on competences and goals, towards a focus on *processes* and in particular in the design department. Critical design draws attention to the ways in which material qualities of sociomaterial entities such as information and information systems can and should be used for continuous and active engagement, dialogue and exchange on issues of value, meaning, power and politics between designers, users, other stakeholders and researchers.

Methodological consequences

The theoretical elaboration of critical literacy with critical design offers a prism through which the elements of design, research and conceptualisation continuously shift and recombine depending on views and aims. Overall, the approach leads us to explore what there is 'to be critical of' in existing or anticipated information-related sociotechnical contexts and how this could be researched and addressed. Empirical studies should yield implications for design, research and critical conceptualisation ranging from ideas on how to redesign objects to incorporate and mediate more fair, just, representative, inclusive or similar normative-ethical values; how to better understand the concepts of critical literacy and critical design themselves; and how critical literacy research can be (further) combined with critical design to explore and address issues of critical concern. On an overarching level of methodology, we may however begin by distinguishing between two main approaches, in simple terms described as 'research-for-design' and 'design-for-research'.

The methods of critical design range from traditional social science methods to field-specific methodology, alone or in combination. Traditional methods are more common in the aforementioned category of 'mundane and present'-oriented studies, whereas specific critical design methods dominate at the other end of the scales, aiming towards 'abstract' and 'future-oriented' approaches. Wong and Mulligan (2019) describe a division of critical design research methods as connected to two main types of studies: one aiming *to explore people and situations*; and another aiming *to critique, speculate, or present critical alternatives*. The first, more mundane and 'present-oriented' types of studies are primarily conducted within existing sociomaterial contexts and may make use of both research-for-design and design-for-research, whereas the abstract and future-oriented types of studies are more exclusively associated with design-for-research methods. We will start with the category of mundane, present-time-oriented studies and discuss how traditional, interdisciplinary research methods serve these purposes. After this, we move on to specific critical design methodology and how this can be used for both the mundane here-and-now and abstract future-oriented approaches. In practice, it is likely that many projects display a variety of combinations of critical design methods with traditional methodology. In all of these, dialectic and reflexive approaches are understood as integral.

The mundane and 'research-for-design'-oriented focus of studies aiming *'to explore people and situations'* comprises methodological approaches that seek to capture user interactions with and experiences of design that evoke perceptions of and responses to bias and power imbalances and why and how this occurs. This includes, e.g. feelings or tangible effects of inclusion and exclusion, oppression, marginalisation and discrimination. The results provide insights into what there is to be critical of in specific situations and from specific perspectives and the insights provide implications for critical (re)design. Even purportedly thought-through designs can have limited and misguided use effects, which situated interaction and empirical study can uncover. An example of the kind is exemplified by Wong and Mulligan's account of the US Department of Homeland Security's privacy impact assessment (PIA) of airport body scanners. Using the common conception of privacy as 'control of personal data', they cleared the use of unique body imaging since faces were blurred and images quickly deleted. Nevertheless, widespread objections from the public, policy makers and interest organisations illustrated a different cause of perceived privacy invasion, one that '. . . arose from TSA agents viewing images of naked bodies, not from identifying people in the images'. Consequently, a critically informed redesign based on empirical insights led to the use of a generic body outline rather than specific body images (Wong and Mulligan, 2019, 2).

For critical literacy research in this category, naturalistic field studies provide an opportunity for close examination of interactions with information and information systems, describing situated enactments of meanings and appropriations, as illustrated by the use of contextual inquiry and critical ethnography in Johansson (2012). However, any type and combination of observations (including subject–object interactions) and interviews, possibly incorporating elicitation material/prompts and think-aloud, is conceivable. Wong and Mulligan also specifically mention combined qualitative and quantitative strategies and the values in studying: '. . . specific populations, such as older adults, children, or medical practitioners; locations such as workplace organizations; or specific technologies, such as social media and online communities' (Wong and Mulligan, 2019, 5).

The other version of the mundane-present *'to explore people and situations'* type of studies takes the reverse 'design-for-research' orientation. This approach opens up the design process itself through versions of participatory design as method of inquiry, engaging stakeholders in discussion and development of concepts, concerns, values, products and services. Design-for-research in the other, abstract and future-oriented, type of studies includes the use of specific conceptual technology probes ('diagetic prototypes', or 'counterfactual artifacts' (Elsden et al., 2017) intentionally introduced in daily activities or controlled research settings to elicit responses on the objects and issues of concern. Here, design is used with conceptual overtones to create spaces in which people can discuss the future and 'futuring' of artefacts, technology, values and ethics. Focus is not primarily on exploring the world as it is, but how it could be. It '. . . creates conceptual designs and design artifacts that subvert expectations, provoke, or exaggerate existing trends in order to surface, critique and discuss values issues and utilizes different evaluation criteria than performance, efficiency, or usability' (Wong and Mulligan, 2019, 6). Ideally, according to Malazita (2018), these methodologies enable conversations that question the social and epistemological – and therefore political – status quo. They are, in other words, *performative*.

Specific future-oriented 'design-for-research' methods in an increasingly critically oriented HCI design tradition include Design Fiction, Experiential Futures, User Enactments (UE), Anticipatory Ethnography, Blast Theory/Mixed Reality Lab (MRL), Near Future Laboratory, material speculation and Speculative Enactments (Elsden et al., 2017). Empirical examples of design-for-research at different positions along the scales of mundane-abstract- and present-future-oriented include the polyvocality and participatory opportunities in deaf heritage futures projects in Scotland (Jamieson and Discepoli, 2021); the design of a game critiquing 'ableism', the privileging of able-bodied people over persons with diverse body states (Malazita, 2018); and the Quantified Wedding speculative enactment of future practices for 'remembering with data' (Elsden et al., 2017).

The 'design-for-research' orientation encourages researchers and design practitioners alike to experiment with 'design for debate' (Dunne, 2008; Dunne and Raby, 2013) through products and spaces designed to spur critical reflection, dialogue and discourse among users, audiences and participants. However, as shown, the methods also apply to mundane 'associative' studies with more concrete (less conceptual) critical design methods and techniques such as cut-up, context-transfer, hybridity, bricolage, juxtaposition and interactivity, operating through 'ambiguity and context' or 'correspondence and context' (Malpass, 2013; cf. also Johansson and Stenlund, 2021). Adding to this the fully mundane and present-oriented studies with traditional social science methods yields a very broad methodological palette. In the final discussion, potentials and challenges associated with critical literacy applications and concerns are summarised.

Discussion and conclusions

In the last section of this chapter, we turn attention more concretely to the ways in which critical design perspectives elaborate our theoretical and empirical understanding of and approach to critical literacy.

Critical literacy through critical design

The definition presented here describes critical literacy as pertaining to the identification, contestation and transformation of representational limitations and bias affecting power relations in information construction, use and exchange. Viewing critical literacy in this understanding through the lens of critical design has very specific consequences. One of these consequences is that representations that restrict or privilege certain viewpoints, interests and actors over others are cast not merely as inevitable 'condition', but emerge as ethical responsibility of information system designers and critical literacy researchers to make visible, challenge and transform. It draws attention to explorations of what critical literacy viewed from this perspective entails, for whom, under what circumstances and how this may be supported and cultivated through design. As minimum, a well-rounded elaboration of critical literacy through critical design requires alignment with central concerns relating to: identification of the taken-for-granted and seemingly natural; an integrated attention to the mutual enactment of social and material factors; contestation of limitations, bias and power imbalances embedded in and emanating from these enactments; a transformative/interventionist approach; and a reflexive stance on behalf of central actors, including researchers and designers.

In a larger societal perspective, critical literacy through critical design also highlights more overarching consequences of problems of representation; of how we relate – or more often do *not* relate – to them in daily interactions with information and information systems. Public and scientific communities alike seek and prioritise increasingly stronger and harder knowledge and facts and understandably so – there are diseases to cure, an environment to save, financial markets and personal investments to keep in check. And of course there is progress in these and other fields, but even so, the knowledge acquired remains provisional. If failing to communicate the limitations of science and otherwise authoritative knowledge claims openly and transparently in the way information is represented, there is also failure to adhere to critical literacy concerns and awareness in the ways defined here. Such failure may add stone on stone on a veritable Babel's tower of misunderstandings, misguided expectations and wrongful conclusions, causing general mistrust. Markham provides a warning example from the 2016 US election prognoses that – erroneously – forecasted Hillary Clinton as winner. When Clinton instead was defeated, '. . . shock about this unforeseen turn of predicted outcomes shifted to anger;

social media exploded into heated arguments about who or what was to blame for such miscalculations in the expected results. . . . One might ask: why was everyone so shocked?' (Markham, 2018, 512). The answer points to mismatches between what we *actually* can know and do with data and what people *think* we can know: '"Data" is not a bad term in itself, but because its value in this decade of big data is overstated, many faulty logics and premises about data, truth, and algorithmic computation can end up influencing how we make sense of the world around us' (Markham, 2018, 512). A critical design perspective applied to the post-structuralist, sociomaterial understanding of critical literacy advanced here would, in an ethical-normative vein, seek to address and reduce such mismatches, shifting focus in relevant representational forms from the affirmative to the critical.

It seems, perhaps, easier to think of examples of this sort in relation to increasingly digital data and AI-oriented information and information systems – but representational choices *matter* in analogue and less 'datafied' information contexts as well. Looking closer at existing research and design projects in a wider spectrum of information-related areas (critical literacy, information practices, algorithm auditing, data literacy and library events) reveals numerous examples of critical design application, potential and implications, even though not necessarily framed as such. A few examples are included in the following to demonstrate the potential of a critical design-elaborated critical literacy approach within overall contexts of information construction, use and exchange.

Using a critical design-inspired categorisation, information science studies of a mundane, 'research-for-design', character include Johansson's (2012) study of user interactions with data visualisations, illustrating tacit and informal user appropriations of errors and mismatches as meaningful guidance to critical interaction. Haider and Sundin's (2021) study, demonstrating ways in which teenagers consciously perform 'lo-tech hacking' of algorithmic logics in media streaming services to avoid unwanted consequences, also fits this category. Results of such everyday user studies tell us about the existence and characteristics of 'critical' aspects associated with various types and conditions of information and information systems, insights that also can be interpreted as implications for critical redesign.

In the other category of 'design-for-research' and somewhat more future-oriented, we may consider several interesting prototypes and suggestions of critical search interface (re)design. Epstein and Robertson (2015) suggest an equivalent to the 'equal time rule', translating to providing political candidates equal weight and place in search engine results pages. Hyman and Franklyn (2015) propose as a further architectural design measure presentation and emphasis of links to rivalling specialised search services. Khulshrestha et al. (2019) suggest that results pages should aspire to balance relevance, popularity and currency with consideration of diversification. Additional design solutions for supporting and increasing users' awareness of bias in search results include incorporation of 'warning flags' that describe how the order of search results may reflect bias (Epstein and Robertson, 2015; Khulshrestha et al., 2019) and clearer labelling remedies for Google's specialised search results (ads, snippets, etc.) (Hyman and Franklyn, 2015). There is also attention to general aspirations to 'open up' the black box of search engine technology through graphical information aiming to explain why search results look the way they do; of making visible the existence and functions of algorithms and ranking logics (Sandvig et al., 2014).

Examples that would fit the category of more abstract, critical and speculative, future and/or conceptually oriented research and projects, finally, may include Markham's interesting series of public arts-based experiments that '. . . build critical curiosity and develop data literacy via self-reflexive public interventions . . . Reflexivity, bricolage and critical pedagogy are emphasised as approaches for responding to changing needs in the public sphere' (Markham, 2020, 227). The experiments are designed to elicit or provoke critical reflection on subjective positions and experiences in social circumstances of increasingly data- and AI-driven decision making. Library projects, too, can serve similar purposes, whether intentionally designed for critical reflection on information representation or not. We might, for example, reflect on the potentially disruptive and transformative effects of reframing library users as 'guests' and replacing print books with 'living books' in the form of activists and survivors sharing personal experiences of discrimination, inequality and violence in intimate interpersonal oral meetings, as arranged by the Human Library event in Bangkok in 2019 (Mitchell, 2019). Possible effects of such library arrangements include possibilities of providing new perspectives on 'real', subjective and local/close events and experiences otherwise at risk of being routinely and unconsciously perceived as fictional, impersonal, and distant when mediated in standardised form as written stories in books.

The examples above illustrate not only the potential, applicability and relevance of critical design for critical literacy, but also its potential scope, variation and novelty. Nevertheless, any critical design approach aiming to open up the black box of information and information systems design and representation will also incarnate, to some extent, the famous statement by Bowker and Star (1999) that infrastructures only become visible to us upon breakdown. As the argument goes, when the always imperfect and value-laden classifications and similar information representations become commonplace, they also become naturalised and invisible, thereby exerting more powerful influence over social values, perceptions, actions and interactions. Instances of breakdown, when the representational systems malfunction – i.e. do not work, or do not work as intended – can therefore crucially *re*-mind us of (bring back to our conscious attention) their existence in beneficial ways. Critical design in the service of critical literacy, as understood and argued here, can be considered an organised and intentional agenda for elaborating and incorporating artificial features of information representation breakdown in various ways, aiming to support revelatory effects. Making visible and making aware of possible bias and shortcomings in information and information systems also make these biases and shortcomings actionable – for critique, resistance and transformation (redesign) – in iterative and interlinking loops for designers, users and researchers.

Further elaborations

An elaboration of critical literacy through the lens of critical design as offered in this chapter has not previously been undertaken. What is hoped to have been accomplished here, therefore, is to introduce and illustrate a partly new perspective on critical literacy with theoretical, empirical and professional significance, in line with critical (design) developments in other fields (e.g. Elsden et al., 2017; Markham, 2020; Oxman, 2016; Wong and Mulligan, 2019; Woodward, Dixon and Jones III, 2009). In moving on and looking forward, a few aspects in particular demand attention.

First, significant work remains to be done on how a post-structuralist and sociomaterial critical design elaboration of critical literacy fits or can be pieced together with other branches of critical literacy, as well as with information literacy in general. Conceptual relations *are* important, even though this has not been in focus for the present discussion. The conclusions here at least point to good opportunities for combinations with more specific normative, ethical and political ideas and theories frequently invoked in more 'traditional' critical literacy approaches, including Marxist and Freirean conceptions of critical literacy (e.g. Bezerra and Schneider in Chapter 4 of this volume).

Secondly, the theoretical construct also opens up the possibility of innovative disciplinary crossovers. The design processes and characteristics central to critical literacy as presented here should fruitfully benefit from the bridging of disciplinary boundaries between art–science, nature–culture and applied–non-applied, as argued e.g. by Oxman (2016) in her position article Age of Entanglement, as well as in Markham (2020), Wong and Mulligan (2019) and Johansson and Stenlund (2021). Such inter- and intradisciplinary synergy potentials have not previously attracted much interest in critical and information literacy, but judging from the review and discussions here, developments of this sort seem promising for boosting both creativity and exploration.

Thirdly, critical design as a tool for critical literacy needs extensive theoretical and empirical attention within contexts of information construction, use and exchange in particular. The general critical design field is replete with methods and techniques but what, more specifically, would the toolbox of bricolage, context-transfer, cut-up, suspense, speculation and dialectics imply for research and theorising on critical dimensions of information literacy in practice? We need an increased body of information-relevant conceptual and empirical contributions to elaborate what information-specific critical design 'repertoires' exist and may be conceived of in various contexts. Johansson and Stenlund (2021) take a related approach as foundation for a conceptual '4C-model' of critical data visualisation analysis and design, but additional theoretical work is needed.

Finally, theoretical and conceptual studies also need to be balanced and followed up by empirical studies of how such theories and models of critical design 'work' in information practices: how they become interpreted, appropriated, transformed, or resisted – by users as well as by developers, intermediaries and other relevant stakeholders and actors. For example, are critical design measures at risk of 'fatigue-effects' similar to those observed in Privacy by Design (PbD) (e.g. Agozie and Kaya, 2021) and how do functions and effects vary across different design categories, contexts of use and user groups, as well as over time (cf. Epstein and Robertson, 2015; Hyman and Franklyn, 2015; Khulshrestha et al., 2019; Sandvig et al., 2014)? What the theoretical critical design elaboration first and foremost brings is a view of critical literacy not as a hurdle to overcome, a battle to win, or a goal to attain, but as a continuous social process of critically attuned exchanges between and through design, interaction and response/redesign with considerable relevance and urgency to information research and practice alike.

References

Agozie, D. Q. and Kaya, T. (2021) Discerning the Effect of Privacy Information Transparency on Privacy Fatigue in e-Government, *Government Information Quarterly*, **38** (4), 101601, https://doi.org/10.1016/j.giq.2021.101601.

Bacchi, C. (2021) Poststructuralism and Critical Realism: revisited, *Carol Bacchi*, Blog post, 28 February, https://carolbacchi.com/2021/02/28/poststructuralism-and-critical-realism-revisited.

Bardzell, J. and Bardzell, S. (2013) What is 'Critical' about Critical Design?, *Proceedings of the SIGCHI Conference on Human Factors in Computing Systems, April 27–May 2, 2013, Paris*, 3297–306. https://doi.org/10.1145/2470654.2466451.

Beaulieu, A. (2002) Images Are Not the (Only) Truth: brain mapping, visual knowledge and iconoclasm, *Science, Technology & Human Values*, **27** (1), 53–86.

Blackwell, A. F. (2013) Visual Representation. In Soegaard, M. and Dam, R. F. (eds) *The Encyclopedia of Human-Computer Interaction*, 2nd edn, The Interaction Design Foundation. www.interaction-design.org/encyclopedia/visual_representation.html.

Bowker, G. and Star, S. L. (1999) *Sorting Things Out: classification and its consequences*, MIT Press.

Buckland, M. K. and Ramos, M. R. (2010) Events as a Structuring Device in Biographical Mark-up and Metadata, *Bulletin of the American Society for Information Science and Technology*, **36** (2), 26–9.

Cecez-Kecmanovic, D., Klein, H. K. and Brooke, C. (2008) Exploring the Critical Agenda in Information Systems Research (Editorial), *Information Systems Journal*, **18**, 123–35, https://doi.org/10.1111/j.1365-2575.2008.00295.x.

Drucker, J. (2014) *Graphesis: visual forms of knowledge production*, Harvard University Press.

Drucker, J. (2020) *Visualization and Interpretation: humanistic approaches to display*, MIT Press.

Dunne, A. (1999) *Hertzian Tales – Electronic Products, Aesthetic Experience and Critical Design*, RCA/CRD Research Publications, Royal College of Art, London.

Dunne, A. (2008) Design for Debate, *Architectural Design*, **78**, (6), 90–3.

Dunne, A. and Raby, F. (n.d.) *Critical Design FAQ*, https://dunneandraby.co.uk/content/bydandr/13/0.

Dunne, A. and Raby, F. (2001) *Design Noir: the secret life of electronic objects*, Birkhauser.

Dunne, A. and Raby, F. (2013) *Speculative Everything: design, fiction and social dreaming*, MIT Press.

Elmborg, J. (2006) Critical Information Literacy: implications for instructional practice, *Journal of Academic Librarianship*, **32** (2), 192–9.

Elsden, C., Chatting, D., Durrant, A. C., Garbett, A., Nissen, B., Vines, J. and Kirk, D. S. (2017) On Speculative Enactments. In *Proceedings of the 2017 CHI Conference on Human Factors in*

Computing Systems (CHI '17), Association for Computing Machinery, 5386–99, https://doi.org/10.1145/3025453.3025503.

Epstein, R. and Robertson, R. E. (2015) The Search Engine Manipulation Effect (SEME) and its Possible Impact on the Outcomes of Elections, *Proceedings of the National Academy of Sciences – PNAS*, 112 (33), E4512–E4521, https://doi.org/10.1073/pnas.1419828112.

Feely, M. (2016) Disability Studies after the Ontological Turn: a return to the material world and material bodies without a return to essentialism, *Disability & Society*, 31 (7), 863–83, https://doi.org/10.1080/09687599.2016.1208603.

Gonsher, I. (n.d.) Beyond Design Thinking: an incomplete design taxonomy, *Critical Design – Critical Futures*, www.cd-cf.org/articles/beyond-design-thinking.

Gregory, J. (2003) Scandinavian Approaches to Participatory Design, *International Journal of Engineering Education*, 19 (1), 62–74.

Haider, J. and Sundin, O. (2021) Information Literacy as a Site for Anticipation: temporal tactics for infrastructural meaning-making and algo-rhythm awareness, *Journal of Documentation*, 78 (1), 129–43, https://doi.org/10.1108/JD-11-2020-0204.

Hyman, D. A. and Franklyn, D. J. (2015) Search Bias and the Limits of Antitrust: an empirical perspective on remedies, *Jurimetrics*, 55 (3), 339–79.

Jakobsone, L. (2017) Critical Design as Approach to Next Thinking, *The Design Journal*, 20, 4253–62, https://doi.org/10.1080/14606925.2017.1352923.

Jamieson, K. and Discepoli, M. (2021) Exploring Deaf Heritage Futures through Critical Design and 'Public Things', *International Journal of Heritage Studies*, 27 (2), 117–33, https://doi.org/10.1080/13527258.2020.1771750.

Johansson, V. (2012) *A Time and Place for Everything? Social visualisation tools and critical literacies*, University of Borås, http://urn.kb.se/resolve?urn=urn:nbn:se:hb:diva-3638.

Johansson, V. and Limberg, L. (2017) Seeking Critical Literacies in Information Practices: reconceptualising critical literacy as situated and tool-mediated enactments of meaning, *Information Research*, 22 (1), http://urn.kb.se/resolve?urn=urn:nbn:se:hb:diva-12549.

Johansson, V. and Stenlund, J. (2021) Making Time/Breaking Time: critical literacy and politics of time in data visualisation, *Journal of Documentation*, 78 (1), 60–82, https://doi.org/10.1108/JD-12-2020-0210.

Kapitzke, C. (2003a) Information Literacy: a positivist epistemology and a politics of *out*formation, *Educational Theory*, 53 (1), 37–53.

Kapitzke, C. (2003b) Information Literacy: a review and poststructural critique, *Australian Journal of Language and Literacy*, 26 (1), 53–66.

Khulshrestha, J., Eslami, M., Messias, J., Zafar, M. B., Ghosh, S., Gummadi, K. P. and Karahalios, K. (2019) Search Bias Quantification: investigating political bias in social media and web search, *Information Retrieval (Boston)*, 22 (1–2), 188–227, https://doi.org/10.1007/s10791-018-9341-2.

Luke, A. (2019) Regrounding Critical Literacy: representation, facts and reality. In Alvermann, D. E., Unrau, N. J., Sailors, M. and Ruddell, R. B. (eds) *Theoretical Models and Processes of Literacy*, 7th edn, Routledge, Ch. 17.

Lupton, M. and Bruce, C. (2010) Windows on Information Literacy Worlds: generic, situated and transformative perspectives. In Lloyd, A. and Talja, S. (eds) *Practising Information Literacy*, Chandos Publishing, 3–27.

Malazita, J. W. (2018) Translating Critical Design: agonism in engineering education, *Design Issues*, 34 (4), 96–109.

Malpass, M. (2013) Between Wit and Reason: defining associative, speculative and critical design in practice, *Design and Culture*, 5 (3), 333–56, https://doi.org/10.2752/175470813X13705953612200.

Malpass, M. (2015) Criticism and Function in Critical Design Practice, *Design Issues*, 31 (2), 59–71.

Malpass, M. (2017) *Critical Design in Context: history, theory and practice*, Bloomsbury.

Marinopoulou, A. (2019) Critical Theory: epistemological content and method. In Liamputtong, P. (ed.) *Handbook of Research Methods in Health Social Sciences*, Springer, https://doi.org/10.1007/978-981-10-5251-4_58.

Markham, A. (2018) Troubling the Concept of Data in Qualitative Digital Research. In Flick, U. (ed.) *The Sage Handbook of Qualitative Data Collection*, Sage, 511–23.

Markham, A. (2020) Taking Data Literacy to the Streets: critical pedagogy in the public sphere, *Qualitative Inquiry*, 26 (2), 227–37.

Mitchell, A. (2019) Turning the Page on Stereotypes at the Human Library Event, *UN Women/Asia and the Pacific,* blog post, 6 December, https://asiapacific.unwomen.org/en/news-and-events/stories/2019/12/turning-the-page-on-stereotypes-at-the-human-library-event.

Nelson, H. G. and Stolterman, E. (2014) *The Design Way: intentional change in an unpredictable world*, 2nd edn, MIT Press.

Oxman, N. (2016) Age of Entanglement, *Journal of Design and Science*, https://doi.org/10.21428/7e0583ad.

Sandvig, C., Hamilton, K., Karahalios, K. and Langbort, C. (2014) Auditing Algorithms: research methods for detecting discrimination on internet platforms, *64th Annual Meeting of the International Communication Association, May 22, 2014*.

Simmons, M. (2005) Librarians as Disciplinary Discourse Mediators: using genre theory to move toward critical information literacy, *portal: Libraries and the Academy*, 5 (3), 297–311.

Tewell, E. (2015) A Decade of Critical Information Literacy: a review of the literature, *Communications in Information Literacy*, 9 (1), 24–43, https://doi.org/10.15760/comminfolit.2015.9.1.174.

Tuominen, K., Savolainen, R. and Talja, S. (2005) Information Literacy as a Sociotechnical Practice, *Library Quarterly*, 75 (3), 329–45.

valentine, k. and Seear, K. (2020) Commentary on Alex Stevens (2020) 'Critical Realism and the "Ontological Politics of Drug Policy"', *International Journal of Drug Policy*, 84, 102879.

van Dijck, J. (2005) *The Transparent Body: a cultural analysis of medical imaging*, University of Washington Press.

Vasquez, V. M. (2012) Critical Literacy. In Banks, J. A. (ed.) *Encyclopedia of Diversity in Education*, Sage, 467–9.

Vasquez, V. M., Janks, H. and Comber, B. (2019) Critical Literacy as a Way of Being and Doing, *Language Arts*, 96 (5), 300–11.

Wigger, A. and Horn, L. (2017) Taking Critical Ontology Seriously: implications for political science methodology. In Keman, H. and Woldendorp, J. (eds) *Handbook of Research Methods and Applications in Political Science,* Edward Elgar Publishing, 38–53, https://doi.org/10.4337/9781784710828.00010.

Wong, R. Y. and Mulligan, D. K. (2019) Bringing Design to the Privacy Table: broadening 'design' in 'privacy by design' through the lens of HCI. In *Proceedings of the 2019 CHI Conference on Human Factors in Computing Systems (CHI '19)*, Association for Computing Machinery, Paper 262, 1–17, https://doi.org/10.1145/3290605.3300492.

Woodhouse, E., Hess, D., Breyman, S. and Martin, B. (2002) Science Studies and Activism: possibilities and problems for reconstructivist agendas, *Social Studies of Science*, **32** (2), 297–319, https://doi.org/10.1177/0306312702032002004.

Woodward, K., Dixon, D. P. and Jones III, J. P. (2009) Poststructuralism/Poststructuralist Geographies. In Kitchin, R. and Thrift, N. (eds) *International Encyclopedia of Human Geography*, 8, Elsevier, 396–407.

Woolgar, S. and Lezaun, J. (2013) The Wrong Bin Bag: a turn to ontology in science and technology studies?, *Social Studies of Science*, 43 (3), 321–40, www.jstor.org/stable/48646311.

Woolgar, S. and Lezaun, J. (2015) Missing the (Question) Mark? What is a turn to ontology?, *Social Studies of Science*, 45 (3), 462–7, www.jstor.org/stable/43829036.

8
Information Literacy Through an Equity Mindset

Amanda L. Folk

Introduction

This chapter focuses on Dr Estela Mara Bensimon's concept of equity mindedness and its application to information literacy scholarship, both theoretical and empirical. Equity mindedness is an orientation to our scholarship that influences the decisions we make about how we approach information literacy-related research, including the theories and methodologies we draw upon to shape our explorations. I argue that an equity mindset requires us to interrogate how information literacy is understood and valued in various contexts, including communities, organisations or institutions, as well as how individuals access critical information about expectations for the development and enactment of information literacy within those contexts, by drawing upon existing theories related to sense-making (Dervin, 1983; 1998) and critical social theories (Bourdieu, 1986; 1993; Coleman, 1988; Lave and Wenger, 1991). Communities, organisations and institutions, including learning environments, are not neutral spaces and an individual's identity characteristics are likely to influence how they navigate a particular community and how they are perceived by others in the community. Equity mindedness extends the existing scholarly discourse about the sociocultural nature of information literacy by exploring the role of power dynamics and how information literacy could be used to marginalise or empower.

In the content that follows, I will first define and describe an equity mindset, as it has been developed by Bensimon (2005). A critical aspect of equity mindedness is the use of data to explore inequities within particular contexts, as well as applying an equity mindset to the analysis and interpretation of data. When an equity mindset is used to interrogate the cause of inequities, it requires one to consider systemic causes of inequities at the community, organisational or institutional level(s). Then I will outline three critical assumptions that we must make about the nature of information literacy to apply an equity mindset to our research and scholarship. These include the acknowledgement that information literacy is shaped by and situated within communities that have their own value systems; that information literacy is characterised by complex ways of thinking, knowing and communicating and is not simply a discrete set of skills that is durable across communities or contexts; and that power, privilege, oppression and exclusion are part of the contexts or communities in which information literacy is situated. Based on these assumptions, I argue that our traditional approaches to information literacy research and scholarship, in which we seek to assess or measure individuals' information literacy, often ignoring potentially relevant identity characteristics, must be re-examined to identify potential barriers or inequities to the development of information literacy within a context. In the final section, I discuss the theoretical and methodological implications of applying equity mindedness to our information literacy research and scholarship. I believe the application of an equity mindset to our research and scholarship will result in a more nuanced and realistic understanding of information literacy development and enactment, as it has the potential to transform the questions that drive our inquiries, the voices we include and the lenses we use to analyse and interpret the data we collect.

Defining equity mindedness

Bensimon (2005) first introduced the idea of an equity mindset in an article exploring the application of organisational learning theory to persistent racial equity gaps in higher education in the USA. In this article, Bensimon problematises how higher education practitioners and research have approached racial (in)equities in student outcomes. Prior to this article, these practitioners primarily relied on student development theories, such as Chickering and Reisser's (1993) theory of identity development or Baxter Magolda's (2001) theory of self-authorship. Because these theories focus primarily on the student, they did not provide opportunities to explore (in)equity from an organisational, institutional or systemic perspective, which is critical to identifying the barriers to racial equity in any organisational or cultural context. While Bensimon is clear that the issue of inequitable outcomes needs to be addressed at the organisational level, she highlights the importance of individual actors' mindsets in enabling systemic change. She writes 'The problem of unequal outcomes resides within individuals, in the cognitive frames that govern their attitudes, beliefs, values and actions' (Bensimon, 2005, 101). The equity mindset that Bensimon proposes is based on the concept of cognitive frames (Argyris, 1991; Bensimon, 1989), which are the mental moves an individual makes to interpret their environment or a situation. Bensimon highlights the important role that cognitive frames play in how we approach our work, stating that they 'determine what questions may be asked, what information is collected, how problems are defined and what action should be taken' (Bensimon, 2005, 101).

Bensimon proposes three different mindsets based on the foundation of cognitive frames – deficit, diversity and equity. Before I discuss how Bensimon describes and defines the equity mindset, I will provide a brief overview of the deficit and diversity mindsets. In the *deficit mindset*, inequitable outcomes are viewed as a problem of the individual or the population that is affected by the inequities (Bensimon, 2005). In higher education in the USA, for example, African-American students, in general, are less likely to graduate from a four-year postsecondary institution. (Throughout this chapter, I draw heavily upon the higher education context in the USA to provide specific examples, because this is the context with which I am most familiar as both a scholar and a practitioner.) A deficit mindset would attempt to fix these students, which might include remedial or developmental education courses (which often do not count towards degree requirements) or other programmes that attempt to change the students so that they acculturate to the institutional environment. While proponents of these kinds of solutions might have good intentions (i.e. a sincere desire to increase the graduation rates of African-American students), undue burden is placed squarely on the student to participate in additional programming or coursework to succeed. This is not a sustainable or fair solution to addressing inequity. In other cases, some deficit-minded individuals attribute inequitable outcomes to factors beyond the institution's control and accept the inevitability of inequity rather than seeking to narrow or close outcomes gaps (Bensimon, 2005).

In the *diversity mindset*, differences between various groups of individuals are recognised and even celebrated. At the organisational level, the focus is on increasing diversity, as well as providing learning opportunities to help diverse individuals to work together successfully (i.e. developing cultural competence; Bensimon, 2005). While all of this can be positive, the diversity mindset focuses primarily on representation and less on the creation of inclusive, welcoming and equitable environments for all members of the community to thrive regardless of their identities. If we return to our example about African-American students, the diversity frame might highlight the need to increase the proportion of this population in student enrolments without considering the inequitable outcomes that these students might face and the institutional factors that might present barriers to degree completion, such as poor campus racial climate or a lack of African-American faculty. While attention to representational diversity is not inherently negative, this narrow focus on representation does not automatically result in equitable outcomes among diverse groups.

Equity-minded individuals not only acknowledge the inequities among diverse groups, they recognise that these inequities are produced by cultural beliefs in which some groups have privilege and others do not. They recognise that these inequities are rooted in larger historical or societal patterns of inequity and also take responsibility for making change within their own organisational contexts. According to Bensimon (2005), equity-minded individuals reflect on their role in reproducing persistent inequities and identify ways in which they can change their practices at the individual and collective levels. Bensimon draws upon single- and double-loop learning (Argyris, 1991) to explain the differences between individuals who adopt an equity mindset and individuals who adopt a deficit or diversity mindset. In single-loop learning, which is related to a deficit or diversity mindset, individuals 'externalize the problem', which results in failing 'to see how changes in their own attitudes, beliefs and practices could reverse unequal outcomes' (Bensimon, 2005, 104). Double-loop learning, however, results in systemic or cultural change, as it 'focuses attention on the root causes of a problem and the changes that need to be made in the attitudes, values, beliefs and practices' of an individual and organisation (Bensimon, 2005, 104). Returning to the example with African-American students, an equity-minded instructor would analyse course-level data about how different racial groups perform to identify possible inequities and would advocate that their department also regularly analyse student outcomes by race or ethnicity to determine if the department is adequately supporting this student population. If equity gaps are identified, teaching practices would be reviewed and the instructor might implement inclusive or culturally relevant teaching practices, arrange professional development on the topic for their colleagues to discuss and implement inclusive teaching strategies consistently across the curriculum.

While individual and collective practices that initiate cultural or organisational change are essential for addressing inequities, Bensimon highlights the critical role of inquiry and data in individual and collective learning. Data-driven inquiry can uncover inequitable patterns in outcomes for groups within an organisation, thus creating individual and collective awareness of inequities that can be used to initiate change. Disaggregation of the data is imperative for uncovering these patterns. Bensimon and her colleagues focus specifically on racial equity gaps and they argue that granular disaggregation of data into specific racial or ethnic categories is critical, as opposed to data analysis that disaggregates broadly between white and non-white individuals, which is likely to continue to obscure specific inequities (McNair, Bensimon and Malcom-Piqueux, 2020).

However, basic data analysis is not enough to constitute an equity mindset; rather, 'equity-minded sense-making' is necessary. Equity-minded sense-making 'involves interpreting equity gaps as a signal that practices are not working as intended and asking equity-minded questions about how and why current practices are failing to serve students experiencing inequities' (McNair, Bensimon and Malcom-Piqueux, 2020, 61). In other words, equity-minded sense-making requires us to look at the institutional or systemic causes of inequities, rather than seeking solutions that focus on fixing students. Equity-minded sense-making aligns with Dervin's (1983) theory of sense-making, which has a long history of application in the library and information science literature. Not only does Dervin's theory of sense-making attend to gaps, it also accounts for power dynamics that are involved in the collective sense-making process. Dervin (1998, 41) writes, 'More difficult to handle, however, are the forces of power in society and in organizations, forces that prescribe acceptable answers and make disagreeing with them, even in the face of evidence of one's own experience, a scary and risky thing to do. Even more difficult is when the forces of power flow through an organization or system hidden and undisclosed.' Equity-minded sense-making requires one to surface those forces of power (particularly those based on identity characteristics that result in privilege or marginalisation) that remain hidden and to counter these forces intentionally as one makes sense of data to identify inequities and propose solutions. If the sense-makers have identity characteristics that hold power and privilege, it is necessary for those sense-makers to develop an awareness of their power and privilege and how they might manifest in making sense of the data, especially considering the harm they might do to marginalised populations in proposing solutions. As one begins to apply equity-minded sense-making, it can be natural for some to fall back into a deficit mindset during the sense-making process, such as blaming the students' background characteristics or larger societal issues for inequities, due to one's discomfort with issues like racism and classism. Individuals must be cautious to centre the ways in which institutional or organisational processes and practices must change to resolve inequities, rather than attempting to remediate or fix the students.

Critical assumptions about the nature of information literacy

An equity-minded approach to our research and scholarship begins with three critical assumptions that are interrelated. First, an equity-minded approach requires us to view information literacy within specific sociocultural contexts, such as professions, organisations, disciplines and other kinds of communities. Second, we must view information literacy not as a discrete set of skills that neatly transfer from one context to another, but as complex ways of thinking, knowing and acting that will be shaped by the values and expectations of a particular community (Lloyd, 2005; 2006; 2010; 2017). For example, the characteristics of authoritative sources (i.e. how authority is constructed and determined) will differ between stockbrokers, carpenters, art historians and evolutionary biologists and these differences will influence the processes that individuals in these professions use to obtain, evaluate and use information sources. Because of this, many individuals will need to learn what constitutes authority and appropriate ways of finding and evaluating information within a particular context as they become members of that community, profession or organisation. Some of what they have learned in previous cultural contexts might transfer, but they must be willing to view authority from a different perspective to participate successfully in that new community. In the following paragraphs, I discuss scholarship highlighting the situated nature of information literacy (Lloyd, 2010) and then discuss the relatively recent shift away from conceptualising information literacy as a discrete skill set.

Two decades of scholarship have advocated and provided evidence for the importance of sociocultural contexts for understanding information literacy development and associated behaviours, so this first critical assumption is neither novel nor groundbreaking. Over 20 years ago, Bruce discovered that 'social collaboration or interdependence between colleagues' was a salient characteristic of how individuals experience information literacy within their workplace (Bruce, 1999, 35). Just a few years later, Marcum argued for the importance of the social and contextual nature of learning, noting that these characteristics had not been adequately explored in relationship to information literacy. Marcum called on librarians to consider 'the social determinants of learning effectiveness' (Marcum, 2002, 20) in future information literacy scholarship, though he stopped short of fully articulating what those determinants might include. Neely (2002) did consider the social determinants of learning effectiveness in her study that explored both the individual (i.e. psychological) and sociocultural (i.e. sociological) factors that contribute to both undergraduate and graduate students' development of information literacy and research skills. She hypothesised that the students' relationships with their faculty would be a determinant of the development of information literacy. Neely concluded that faculty were not modelling information literacy or library usage for their students and that future research exploring this relationship is essential.

Tuominen, Savolainen and Talja continued to build on these calls to action, arguing that information literacy to that point had been conceived primarily as a set of 'individual-centered generic skills' (Tuominen, Savolainen and Talja, 2005, 333), highlighting the failure of the library and information science (LIS) profession to take seriously the social, cultural and contextual elements that shape information literacy both as a concept and as an impetus for action. To address this, they introduced two key ideas – information literacy as a practice and the placement of information literacy within epistemic communities/communities of practice, both of which rely on sociocultural theories. Wang, Bruce and Hughes draw upon Vygotsky (1978) in their characterisation of sociocultural theories as theories that 'describe learning and development as being embedded within social events and occurring as a learner interacts with other people, objects and events in a collaborative environment' (Wang, Bruce and Hughes, 2011, 297). With this in mind, viewing information literacy as a practice shifts the emphasis from the behaviours of an individual actor and considers how individuals operate within a group or organisational context (Tuominen, Savolainen and Talja, 2005) (see Chapter 2 by Lloyd for an extended examination of the use of practice theory within information literacy). To explore this argument further, Tuominen, Savolainen and Talja (2005) draw on the work of Knorr Cetina (1999) to introduce the concept of epistemic communities. Epistemic communities 'provide their members with the background and approaches for seeking, analyzing, using and evaluating knowledge' (Tuominen, Savolainen and Talja, 2005, 339). Communities of practice, a concept introduced by Lave and Wenger (1991) which will be discussed in more depth in the final section of this chapter, are the smaller contexts in which an individual enacts information literacy and are 'the sites where people learn and share insights and form and negotiate meanings, values and objectives' (Tuominen, Savolainen and Talja, 2005, 340). By drawing on sociocultural theories, Tuominen, Savolainen and Talja provided the conceptual foundations for exploring the role of sociocultural context in the development and enactment of information literacy.

Concurrently, Lloyd was also exploring the sociocultural and situated nature of information literacy and published a culminating book of her work in the first decade of the 21st century that provided an in-depth treatment of these concepts, with chapters dedicated to information literacy within different contexts, such as the workplace or public libraries (Lloyd, 2010). Furthermore, Lloyd introduced a definition of information literacy that highlights the critical importance of the sociocultural context, which she has refined over the subsequent years: information literacy is 'a practice that is enacted in a social setting. It is composed of a suite of activities and skills that reference structured and embodied knowledge and ways of knowing relevant to the context. Information literacy is a way of knowing' (Lloyd, 2021, 2). Cope and Sanabria's 2014 research provides evidence that supports Lloyd's definition. They interviewed faculty at two colleges and found that faculty mostly perceived that information literacy could not be divorced from disciplinary practices. The faculty believed that information literacy 'should result in the internalization of new behaviors and adaptive strategies that allow individual students to learn within the context of a specific discipline . . .' (Cope and Sanabria, 2014, 489). This finding reinforces the importance of the contextual situation to the development and enactment of information literacy.

Given the centrality of the sociocultural context to an equity-minded approach to information literacy research and scholarship, the second critical assumption is that the evolution of information literacy from a set of 'individual-centered generic skills' to ways of thinking, knowing and acting within particular contexts is appropriate. This evolution has been particularly apparent in the North American context, with the shift from the *Information Literacy Competency Standards for Higher Education* (Association of College & Research Libraries, 2000) to the *Framework for Information Literacy for Higher Education* (Association of College & Research Libraries, 2016) (see Chapter 12 by Budd for further reflections on the ACRL Framework). Initial conceptualisations of information literacy, such as those represented in the *Standards* document, listed skills and tasks that an information-literate person could accomplish and suggested that there could be both information-literate and information-illiterate individuals. For example, either a person knew how to search for information effectively and efficiently or they did not. Because of this, assessment or measurement of individuals' information literacy skills became popular (Lloyd, 2021; Tuominen, Savolainen and Talja, 2005) and these examinations were often divorced from a sociocultural context or from an authentic information-seeking and usage scenario. This reinforced the belief that these skills could be readily transferred from one context to another.

A more recent conceptualisation of information literacy, such as that represented in the *Framework* document, seems to be more mindful of the role of sociocultural context and articulates nuanced characteristics that are related to ways of knowing, thinking and acting within higher education, rather than simply enumerating skills that are important for general information seeking and usage. That is not to say that skills are no longer important, but that skills will change based on the scenario and will be determined by how well an individual understands the values and expectations of a particular sociocultural context. The *Framework* document draws heavily on threshold concepts (Meyer and Land, 2006) to identify key elements of information literacy as well as associated dispositions (i.e. attitudes or ways of thinking) and knowledge practices (i.e. behaviours or ways of acting). Meyer and Land liken threshold concepts to conceptual portals that learners pass through and experience a 'transformed way of understanding, or interpreting, or viewing', which can result in a 'transformed internal view of subject matter, subject landscape, or even world view' (Meyer and Land, 2006, 3). To cross these conceptual thresholds, learners must rely on insider knowledge they bring to that context or rely on peers or more established members to transparently communicate acceptable ways of participating within a sociocultural context.

The third and defining critical assumption for approaching information literacy research and scholarship with an equity mindset is the assumption that power dynamics exist in the sociocultural contexts in which individuals are developing and enacting their information literacy and this can create inequities. While specific inequities will differ between different cultural and/or national contexts, the existence of marginalised and oppressed groups is present globally. Despite this, the LIS profession has often attempted to position libraries and information literacy as being neutral (Rapchak, 2019) and this simply is not appropriate if we are to take an equity-minded approach to information literacy research and scholarship. Equity mindedness requires us to consider the historical and contemporary inequities of a sociocultural context and how the legacies of those inequities shape the development of an individual's development of information literacy and their ability to thrive within a particular community, profession, or organisation through the enactment of their information literacy.

With this in mind, there are two factors that must be considered when thinking about information literacy research. First, privileged identities within the context will determine and dominate the ways of knowing and communicating that are considered the 'correct' or legitimate ways of participating in the context with other members. For individuals whose identities have historically been or are currently marginalised in that context, information literacy might become a *contact zone*. Mary Louise Pratt applies the concept of a contact zone to educational spaces and describes contact zones as 'social spaces where cultures meet, clash and grapple with each other, often in contexts of highly asymmetrical relations of power' (Pratt, 1991, 4). James Elmborg (2006) builds on this to argue that libraries are also contact zones for learners with marginalised identities. However, activities in which individuals enact information literacy could also create a contact zone for these same learners as they attempt to negotiate an environment that values different ways of thinking, knowing and acting than other cultural contexts in which they have participated. Some learners might find that elements of information literacy that they have developed in other cultural contexts might clash with elements of information literacy in their new cultural context. For example, indigenous cultural traditions in North America construct authority differently than Western academia (Chong, 2022). For North American indigenous students studying at tertiary institutions founded on Western values, this could create doubt about whether or not they belong, or these students might feel discomfort or even anxiety as they attempt to reconcile competing constructions of authority. Because of this, students might think that they must alter their identities, reject previous ways of thinking, knowing, acting and adopt those of the new context, or develop strategies to codeswitch (i.e. alternating between the values or discourse practices of the two different contexts) to successfully navigate and participate in both contexts. Both of these outcomes can be difficult, painful and exhausting for these students. Furthermore, these students might decide that they do not belong and ultimately decide to depart their institution prior to receiving a degree.

We also must consider the role of bias in the ability to participate within a particular sociocultural context. Meyer and Land (2006) acknowledge that threshold concepts can represent a 'privileged or dominant view', which can be problematic for learners with identities that are marginalised within a specific learning context (i.e. discipline, profession, organisation or institution) and this could create a hidden curriculum for students who do not possess insider knowledge of the context or do not have strong social networks with other members who have this insider knowledge (Folk, 2019). In either case, an individual's relationships are important for uncovering this potentially hidden curriculum. This can be problematic because implicit and explicit biases of established or powerful members of the context might prevent individuals with marginalised identities from accessing the information they need to successfully participate within the context. For example, research has indicated that implicit biases of teachers might influence their perceptions of students' abilities to learn or succeed (Fish, 2017; Gershenson, Holt and Papageorge, 2016; Irizarry and Cohen, 2019). If this kind of a bias exists, it will likely shape how much time and effort a teacher is willing to invest in a particular student, favouring other students who they believe will have better outcomes. This can lead to feelings of disenfranchisement and exclusion for learners with marginalised identities, thus making it virtually impossible to accumulate and construct knowledge about acceptable ways of thinking, knowing and acting within that context. Learning spaces, educational institutions, places of employment and professions are not neutral and this must be acknowledged when exploring information literacy. Because of this, we cannot ignore the real implications that a learner's background and identity characteristics potentially have in developing and demonstrating their information literacy within various sociocultural contexts.

If we believe the first three critical assumptions to be true – that information literacy encompasses ways of thinking, knowing, communicating and participating within sociocultural contexts that are imbued with power dynamics that either privilege or marginalise certain groups – then we must rethink dominant approaches to information literacy. As mentioned above, early explorations of information literacy focused primarily on measuring individuals' information literacy skills and most of these explorations were context-independent. Within higher education in the USA, these skill assessments could be used to advocate the expanded inclusion of library expertise within the curriculum. Common approaches to librarian inclusion in the curriculum might include one-shot instruction sessions, online tutorials or guides or standalone workshops. Once additional interventions had been put in place, additional assessment could be conducted to determine the efficacy of those interventions on students' information literacy skills. Documents like the *Standards* supported both the focus on individual-level assessment and these common interventions, as that document laid out competencies in such a way that they could easily be developed into measurable learning outcomes. While the goals of these interventions and assessments were to enhance students' skills, these practices tended to be quite librarian-focused. In other words, these practices seemed to prioritise the librarians' role in enhancing students' skills, rather than encouraging a holistic engagement with all of the factors that might enable or constrain student learning with respect to information literacy, such as the social determinants that Marcum (2002) called for. In addition, they had a tendency to approach students with a deficit mindset, in that they often sought to surface inadequacies and then find solutions to remediate these inadequacies, rather than examining larger institutional or systemic issues that might be at play, such as a curriculum that completely neglects the development of the skills based on the erroneous assumptions that all students will have been exposed to and mastered these skills equally in their secondary schools.

However, more recent conceptualisations of information literacy do not lend themselves as easily to the development of skill assessments or standalone interventions, for which these documents have received much criticism (Bombaro, 2016). The very nature of threshold concepts, as well as the development of dispositions, is not something that can easily be addressed in a single instruction session, nor can these changes in thinking and knowing be easily captured with a standardised, context-independent assessment tool. For this reason, we must move away from simply examining whether an individual is information literate or not to more nuanced explorations of the ways in which individuals develop their information literacy within a particular context and how they navigate and participate in these contexts with respect to information literacy. This would include exploring how individuals gain access to critical information about the values and expectations of information usage and knowledge creation within a specific sociocultural context, what barriers individuals might face in learning the values and expectations of that context and how individuals use this information to inform their participation within that context. All of these explorations are likely to be dependent on social relationships, either with established, authoritative, or powerful individuals within a context or with an individual's peers who are also learning to navigate a particular context but might have some insider cultural knowledge. In this case, librarians become one of many key individuals in supporting the development of individuals' information literacy within a particular context. In other words, we need to shift from assessing individuals' skills to understanding learning processes that enable or constrain individuals' development of the ways of thinking, knowing and acting associated with information literacy within a particular context.

Theoretical and methodological considerations

As our conceptualisations of information literacy evolve and become more sophisticated, we need to give thoughtful consideration to the theories and methodologies that underpin and guide our research and scholarship. Despite almost two decades of scholarship highlighting the sociocultural nature of information literacy and the potential power of sociocultural learning theories for exploring information literacy, we still have not achieved 'an understanding of [sociocultural learning theories'] implications for the nature and scope of information literacy' (Hicks, 2018, 70). As such, additional empirical explorations that are firmly grounded in sociocultural theories are warranted. Bensimon reminds us that 'cognitive frames represent conceptual maps and determine what questions may be asked, what information is collected, how problems are defined and what action should be taken' (Bensimon, 2005, 101). Given that there are historical and contemporary inequities in each of our cultural, national, institutional and organisational contexts, an equity-minded approach is imperative if we are to develop (to the extent that is possible) a holistic understanding of information literacy, including how it is developed and enacted. While equity mindedness is not a theoretical approach *per se*, it guides the selection of the theoretical and methodological foundations we use for our explorations. In the sections that follow, I highlight theories and methodologies that I believe are consistent with an equity-minded approach to information literacy research. While equity-minded sense-making is not necessarily inherent in these theories and methodologies, I believe they set a solid foundation for resisting deficit approaches in our scholarship.

Theories

The use of equity mindedness requires us to holistically examine information literacy within certain sociocultural contexts. This means shifting our focus from summative assessments of individuals' information literacy skills, as has been common over the past couple of decades, to explorations of how information literacy is constructed within specific contexts; how individuals accumulate information and construct knowledge about information literacy within a context; how they make decisions about enacting their information literacy; and how other members, particularly those with power, make judgements about individuals' enactment of information literacy. To address this shift, more reliance on theories related to sociality and socialisation will be critical. By this I mean that we need to continue to explore the ways in which communities construct information literacy, including how information literacy evolves over time, as well as how individuals learn about a community's conceptualisation of information literacy and then participate in the community according to their understanding.

Though these explorations have not been common, some work (Folk, 2021; 2022; Lloyd, 2010, for example) has been done that draws upon Jean Lave and Etienne Wenger's (1991) communities of practice concept. Communities of practice allows for an examination of how new members of a community learn about appropriate ways of participating in the community, including the values, preferences and expectations of that community. In this theory, both established members and peers (i.e. other new members) can serve as important sources of information and new members primarily develop their understanding of the community's values through active participation and engagement in the community. In other words, learning about the community's values, as well as expectations for participation, is embedded within relationships and is a social activity. The value of socialisation theories like communities of practice is that they identify several relationships that should be considered in the way individuals develop their information literacy within a particular context, including relationships with powerful, established members and those with their peer group. Furthermore, theories like this one reject the idea of meritocracy, as hard work alone might not be enough to develop one's information literacy – the ability to develop productive relationships with others is critical.

Equity mindedness also requires us to think about power dynamics and how implicit or explicit biases might shape individuals' willingness to share valuable information about appropriate participation within a context with respect to information use. To adequately account for these power dynamics, we must also consider the use of critical theories (see also Chapter 7 by Johansson and Chapter 4 by Bezerra and Schneider for a further exploration of critical theory). Critical theories, such as critical race theory, or cultural capital, are helpful for exploring why certain inequities are produced and persistently reproduced in particular contexts. For example, in higher education in the USA, there are persistent equity gaps for certain groups of students, including students of colour, students with disabilities and students whose parents have not attained a college degree. These gaps include lower rates of enrolment and degree completion. On the one hand, these gaps are not surprising when they are viewed in their historical context. Higher education in the USA was designed for wealthy, white men and was not meant to be inclusive of other identities. On the other hand, higher education institutions, particularly in the USA, repeatedly indicate that they value inclusivity and equity but continue to reproduce these equity gaps (Bensimon, 2005; McNair, Bensimon and Malcom-Piqueux, 2020). Critical theories can help to identify why these gaps are continually reproduced (i.e. continue to exist in the contemporary context) and how individuals who are affected by them either cope with or resist a community that marginalises them or how they make decisions about leaving that community.

Critical theories provide the opportunity for us to explore how broader social inequities might manifest in specific sociocultural contexts and affect individuals' development of information literacy. Theories like social capital (Bourdieu, 1986; Coleman, 1988) and cultural capital (Bourdieu, 1993) can be useful in exploring the development of information literacy and the existence of power dynamics within particular sociocultural contexts. Within educational contexts, both Bourdieu (1986) and Coleman (1988) highlight the importance of relationships for accessing essential information about how to succeed in school (i.e. social capital). Differences in relationships, including relationships with people who have that essential knowledge, help to explain why students might have different levels of achievement within the same educational setting, even when other variables are held constant. Bourdieu, in particular, highlights the importance of status competition to the sharing or hoarding of essential information about a community's values and preferences, such that privileged identity groups seek to retain their privilege and reproduce social stratification across generations. Cultural capital (Bourdieu, 1993) helps to explain the type of information that might be transmitted through the accumulation of social capital. When one accumulates social capital with privileged or powerful members of a community, one has access to cultural capital, or the values, expectations, discourses and preferences for communication and behaviour of a particular community or culture that might remain invisible or hidden to outsiders. Scholars have argued that information literacy is a form of cultural capital within the academic context (Folk, 2019; Lloyd, 2010), as faculty expect that students will apply critical thinking to finding, evaluating and using information sources in their academic work. However, if a student has not accumulated social capital, they might not be aware of this or of information literacy's disciplinary nuances and faculty might make erroneous judgements about the student's ability to succeed within the discipline or higher education more generally.

In addition, the use of critical theories requires us to consider whose voices have been absent from information literacy research and scholarship. For example, information literacy research in the USA has mostly avoided any discussion of race or disaggregation of data based on race, despite the prevalence of persistent racial equity gaps within educational spaces and society more broadly. Because of this, we must assume that the findings of much of our research focusing on information literacy in higher education in the USA is representative of white students, who are the majority racial demographic in most US higher education institutions. A critical race theory approach to information literacy research would require us to think about centring the voices and experiences of students of colour to understand how they develop their information literacy throughout their academic journeys, including the role(s) that relationships and biases (both explicit and implicit) play, the assets they bring with them from other facets of their lives (i.e. funds of knowledge) and the barriers that they encounter in being successful. There have been robust critical theories developed around particularly identities, including critical race theory (Bell, 1995; Bonilla-Silva, 2018; Crenshaw, 1991; Yosso, 2005), queer theory (Foucault, 1978; Sedgwick, 2008; Warner, 1993), disability theory (Davis, 1999; Linton, 1998) and feminist theory (Butler, 1990; hooks, 1987). These theories allow us to develop a more nuanced understanding of how individuals with marginalised identities develop and enact their information literacy within particular sociocultural contexts, including factors that might enable or constrain this development and enactment, while also centring and honouring their voices and lived experiences. These theories can also help to determine if and how marginalised identities bring to bear aspects of information literacy in other parts of their lives in a particular sociocultural context or if they decide to resist socialisation or acculturation into a particular sociocultural context. Inequities can only be addressed once they have been made visible and recognisable.

Methodologies

There are a host of methodologies that could align with an equity-minded approach to information literacy research and scholarship. The types of research questions we develop drive various aspects of our studies, including the theoretical underpinnings, intentionality about our samples and how we approach the interpretation and analysis of the data, and those activities are critical in terms of taking an equity-minded approach to information literacy. Decisions that we make will also be determined by the overarching paradigm of the methodology we select. A paradigm 'represents a philosophy or basic set of beliefs and values, which influence the way we see and make sense of the world' (Lloyd, 2021, 12).

Of the overarching paradigms for methodologies, there are two that are particularly well suited for equity-minded information literacy research – constructivist and transformative.

In the *constructivism* paradigm, 'researchers should attempt to understand the complex world of lived experience from the point of view of those who live it' (Mertens, 2010, 16). Often this kind of research aligns well with qualitative methodologies, such as phenomenology or grounded theory, as researchers attempt to gather deep, rich and nuanced data to explore, interpret and make sense of how individuals might experience a certain phenomenon or navigate particular sociocultural contexts. While a constraint of these methodologies is that samples are often quite small, researchers have the opportunity to define a narrow population to sample (and seek maximum variation within that sample) and are able to elevate the voices and lived experiences of that population. For example, I used phenomenology to explore first-generation college students' experiences with research assignments to understand the opportunities and barriers they faced in developing their information literacy, since their parents were likely not able to be sources of social capital in their collegiate academic experiences (Folk, 2018; 2021). (In the USA, first-generation college students are students whose parents have not attained a four-year college degree, often referred to as a bachelor's degree.) In this study, these students identified opportunities and barriers, but I was able to apply my own expert perspective to the interpretation of their experiences to highlight barriers or opportunities that might not have been visible to the students.

The *transformative* paradigm takes constructivism one step further and is intentional about exploring power dynamics that might affect individuals' lived experiences and create social change such that equity and justice are primary goals of the research (Mertens, 2010). Transformative research intentionally includes and centres 'traditionally silenced voices' (Mertens, 2010, 33) and often takes the form of participatory research, in which the research participants are also integral to various aspects of the research process, including the development of research questions, interpretation of the data and recommendations for the future. While the transformative paradigm is perhaps the most aligned with an equity-minded approach to information literacy research, I argue that the LIS profession is not quite ready to undertake that work. Information literacy research, particularly within the higher education context, has not taken a sophisticated or nuanced stance to exploring the intersections of demographics (i.e. gender, race or ethnicity, religion, social class or socioeconomic status, disability status, etc.), learning and information literacy, despite calls to do this kind of work for 20 years. McNair, Bensimon and Malcom-Piqueux (2020) highlight that the granular disaggregation of data is critical to creating equitable environments. This kind of disaggregation can be an important diagnostic tool in identifying where inequities exist within particular communities, including at our own institutions, professions, or organisations.

However, we must approach this kind of work with caution and intentionality, including the way we frame research questions, how we recruit participants and collect data, how we interpret the data that we collect, the recommendations we make and changes or interventions that result from our research (McNair, Bensimon, Malcom-Piqueux, 2020). To do this, McNair, Bensimon and Malcom-Piqueux argue that we must engage in equity-minded sense-making. They define equity-minded sense-making as going beyond simply identifying equity gaps, but 'interpreting equity gaps as a signal that practices are not working as intended and asking equity-minded questions about how and why current practices are failing to serve students experiencing inequities' (McNair, Bensimon and Malcom-Piqueux, 2020, 61). Many of us who conduct information literacy research likely have privileged identities and could easily fall into deficit-mindedness at any stage of the research process. In equity-minded research, we do not seek to identify ways in which to 'fix' or remediate individuals who are marginalised – they are not broken. Rather, we seek to determine what kind of barriers or obstacles might exist within a sociocultural context that prevent individuals from thriving and identify ways to make meaningful change. In undertaking this work, we need to centre a strong desire to make sociocultural contexts more inclusive and equitable, so that individuals with diverse identities have opportunities to succeed and thrive.

References

Argyris, C. (1991) Teaching Smart People How to Learn, *Reflections*, 4, 4–15.

Association of College & Research Libraries (2000) *Information Literacy Competency Standards for Higher Education*, https://alair.ala.org/handle/11213/7668.

Association of College & Research Libraries (2016) *Framework for Information Literacy for Higher Education*, www.ala.org/acrl/standards/ilframework.

Baxter Magolda, M. B. (2001) *Making Their Own Way: narratives for transforming higher education to promote self-development*, Stylus Publishing.

Bell, D. A. (1995) Who's Afraid of Critical Race Theory? *University of Illinois Law Review*, 1995, 893–910.

Bensimon, E. M. (1989) The Meaning of 'Good Presidential Leadership': a frame, *Review of Higher Education*, 12, 107–23.

Bensimon, E. M. (2005) Closing the Achievement Gap in Higher Education: an organizational learning perspective, *New Directions for Higher Education*, 131, 99–111.

Bombaro, C. (2016) The Framework Is Elitist, *Reference Services Review*, 44, 552–63.

Bonilla-Silva, E. (2018) *Racism without Racists: colorblind racism and the persistence of racial inequality in America*, Rowman & Littlefield.

Bourdieu, P. (1986) The Forms of Capital. In Richardson, J. D. (ed.) *Handbook of Theory and Research for the Sociology of Education*, Greenwood Press, 241–58.

Bourdieu, P. (1993) *The Field of Cultural Production: essays on art and literature*, Polity Press.

Bruce, C. S. (1999) Workplace Experiences of Information Literacy, *International Journal of Information Management*, 19, 33–47.

Butler, J. (1990) *Gender Trouble: feminism and the subversion of identity*, Routledge.

Chickering, A. W. and Reisser, L. (1993) *Education and Identity*, 2nd edn, Jossey-Bass.

Chong, R. (2022) *Indigenous Information Literacy*, Kwantlen Polytechnic University.

Coleman, J. S. (1988) Social Capital in the Creation of Human Capital, *American Journal of Sociology*, 94, S95–S120.

Cope, J. and Sanabria, J. (2014) Do We Speak the Same Language? A study of faculty perceptions of information literacy, *portal: Libraries & the Academy*, 14, 475–501.

Crenshaw, K. (1991) Mapping the Margins: intersectionality, identity politics and violence against women of color, *Stanford Law Review*, 43, 1241–99.

Davis, L. J. (1999) Crips Strike Back: the rise of disability studies, *American Literary History*, 11, 500–12.

Dervin, B. (1983) An Overview of Sense-making Research: concepts, methods and results, paper presented at the annual meeting of the International Communication Association, Dallas, TX.

Dervin, B. (1998) Sense-making Theory and Practice: an overview of user interests in knowledge seeking and use, *Journal of Knowledge Management*, 2, 36–46.

Elmborg, J. (2006) Libraries in the Contact Zone: on the creation of educational space, *Reference & User Services Quarterly*, 46, 56–64.

Fish, R. E. (2017) The Racialized Construction of Exceptionality: experimental evidence of race/ethnicity effects on teachers' interventions, *Social Science Research*, 62, 317–34.

Folk, A. L. (2018) Drawing on Students' Funds of Knowledge: using identity and lived experience to join the conversation in research assignments, *Journal of Information Literacy*, 12, 44–59.

Folk, A. L. (2019) Reframing Information Literacy as Academic Cultural Capital: a critical and equity-based foundation for practice, assessment and scholarship, *College & Research Libraries*, 80, 658–73.

Folk, A. L. (2021) Exploring the Development of Undergraduate Students' Information Literacy through Their Experiences with Research Assignments, *College & Research Libraries*, 82, 1035–55.

Folk, A. L. (2022) Conceptualizing the Sociocultural Nature of the Development of Information Literacy in Undergraduate Education. In Schlak, T., Corrall, S. and Bracke, P. (eds) *The Social Future of Academic Libraries: new perspectives on communities, networks and engagement*, Facet Publishing, 181–95.

Foucault, M. (1978) The *History of Sexuality*, Pantheon Books.

Gershenson, S., Holt, S. B. and Papageorge, N. W. (2016) Who Believes in Me? The effect of student-teacher demographic match on teacher expectations, *Economics of Education Review*, 52, 209–24.

Hicks, A. (2018) Making the Case for a Sociocultural Perspective on Information Literacy. In Nicholson, K. P. and Seale, M. (eds) *The Politics of Theory and the Practice of Critical Librarianship*, Litwin Books, 69–85.

hooks, b. (1987) *Ain't I a Woman: black women and feminism*, Pluto Press.

Irizarry, Y. and Cohen, E. D. (2019) Of Promise and Penalties: how student racial-cultural markers shape teacher perceptions, *Race and Social Problems*, 11, 93–111.

Knorr Cetina, K. (1999) *Epistemic Cultures: how the sciences make knowledge*, Harvard University Press.

Lave, J. and Wenger, E. (1991) *Situated Learning: legitimate peripheral participation*, Cambridge University Press.

Linton, S. (1998) *Claiming Disability: knowledge and identity*, NYU Press.

Lloyd, A. (2005) Information Literacy: different contexts, different concepts, different truths?, *Journal of Library and Information Science*, 37, 82–8.

Lloyd, A. (2006) Information Literacy Landscapes, *Journal of Documentation*, 62, 570–83.

Lloyd, A. (2010) *Information Literacy Landscapes: information literacy in education, workplace and everyday contexts*, Chandos Publishing.

Lloyd, A. (2017) Information Literacy and Literacies of Information: a mid-range theory and model, *Journal of Information Literacy*, 11, 91–105.

Lloyd, A. (2021) *The Qualitative Landscape of Information Literacy Research: perspectives, methods and techniques*, Facet Publishing.

McNair, T. B., Bensimon, E. M. and Malcom-Piqueux, L. (2020) *From Equity Talk to Equity Walk: expanding practitioner knowledge for racial justice in higher education*, Jossey-Bass.

Marcum, J. W. (2002) Rethinking Information Literacy, *Library Quarterly*, 72, 1–26.

Mertens, D. M. (2010) *Research and Evaluation in Education and Psychology*, 3rd edn, Sage.

Meyer, J. H. F. and Land, R. (eds) (2006) *Overcoming Barriers to Student Understanding: threshold concepts and troublesome knowledge*, Routledge.

Neely, T. Y. (2002) *Sociological and Psychological Aspects of Information Literacy in Higher Education*, Scarecrow Press.

Pratt, M. L. (1991) Arts of the Contact Zone. In Wolff, J. M. (ed.) *Professing in the Contact Zone: bringing theory and practice together*, National Council of Teachers of English, 1–18.

Rapchak, M. (2019) That Which Cannot Be Named: the absence of race in the framework for information literacy for higher education, *Journal of Radical Librarianship*, 5, 173–96.

Sedgwick, E. K. (2008) *Epistemology of the Closet*, University of California Press.

Tuominen, K., Savolainen, R. and Talja, S. (2005) Information Literacy as a Sociotechnical Practice, *Library Quarterly*, 75, 329–45.

Vygotsky, L. S. (1978) *Mind in Society: the development of higher psychological processes*, Harvard University Press.

Wang, L., Bruce, C. and Hughes, H. (2011) Sociocultural Theories and Their Application in Information Literacy Research and Education, *Australian Academic & Research Libraries*, 42, 296–308.

Warner, M. (1993) *Fear of a Queer Planet: queer politics and social theory*, University of Minnesota Press.

Yosso, T. J. (2005) Whose Culture Has Capital? A critical race theory discussion of community cultural wealth, *Race Ethnicity and Education*, 8, 69–91.

9
Sociomateriality

Jutta Haider and Olof Sundin

Introduction

Sociomateriality as a theoretical perspective has its roots in science and technology studies (STS), organisation studies and feminist research. It is one of many traditions within a broader framework of practice-based research. Sociomateriality is a broad theoretical church and as such it encompasses a variety of different interpretations and terminologies. Nevertheless, several assumptions are commonly shared by the different thinkers and schools of thought united under the umbrella of sociomateriality, although there are nuances that are also reflected in terminological variations. In this chapter, we explain these assumptions, introduce a selection of commonly used notions and discuss how they can be applied in information literacy research.

The chapter mainly refers to sociomateriality as it was developed in the works of Karen Barad (2003; 2007), Silvia Gherardi (2017), Lucas Introna (2013; Introna and Hayes, 2011), Wanda Orlikowski (2007) together with Susan Scott (Orlikowski and Scott, 2015; Scott and Orlikowski, 2014) and Lucy Suchman (2014). In addition, we follow the reasoning of Paul Dourish (2017, 4), whose work is specifically concerned with information, when he writes: '. . . the material arrangement of information – how it is represented and how that shapes how it can be put to work – matters significantly for our experience of information and information systems'. Based on these works, we would like to present a dynamic understanding of sociomateriality that supports the analysis of information literacies within the specific infrastructural settings of contemporary society and is open to further development.

We should emphasise at the outset that the theoretical framework presented in this chapter is not just for developing an understanding of information literacy in terms of today's commercial, digital information infrastructure. There is nothing digital built into it, so to speak. That being said, it is based on certain assumptions that we think become particularly clear when we shed light on the enormous challenges that society currently faces concerning information seeking and the evaluation of information sources in an algorithmic information infrastructure in which machine learning challenges traditional notions of, for example, trust, agency, intentions and even knowledge.

The chapter begins by contextualising sociomateriality, introducing some of the current challenges in information literacy research and explaining how sociomateriality can help us. It introduces some important questions that sociomateriality can help information literacy research to answer. This is followed by an overview of some key notions and central tenets of sociomateriality. We then turn to theoretical issues and assumptions, how they are folded into information literacy research, how sociomateriality relates to other information literacy research and what methodological considerations arise from sociomateriality. The chapter concludes with a call to accept a certain degree of definitional and conceptual ambiguity.

Sociomateriality and a rapidly changing information infrastructure

In recent decades, the relationship between society, people and information has changed in profound ways. Whereas it used to be assumed that people actively find the information they are looking for, today it is increasingly the other way around: information finds people, often without them knowing how and sometimes without them knowing why. Commercial platforms such as search engines, social media and various algorithmic recommendation systems form the backbone of a rapidly changing market for curating, publishing, communicating, searching and evaluating information. In previous writing, we have discussed the various challenges associated with this as a crisis of information that is interlaced with a variety of other contemporary crises, including a crisis of democracy and the climate crisis (Haider and Sundin, 2022).

This crisis of information entails an increasing fragmentation, individualisation and emotionalisation of information (see also Davies, 2018). What people find in their various feeds on social media, via search engines, chatbots or recommendation systems often depends on the algorithms of commercial platforms and generative language models trained on often undisclosed data. End-users, but also legislators and even content producers, have limited insight into how these algorithms work or the data they collect, interpret and are trained on. This is a situation with obvious implications for how information literacy can be conceptualised. The fragmentation of information is evident in the way short messages, decontextualised film clips, heavily edited or even completely made-up but still realistic images, memes or status updates converge on the same devices. Every person's feed is different and it is increasingly difficult to know how and in what combinations others will come across information. Content is created, distributed, made visible and reassembled in new configurations across platforms. Often this happens in ways designed to trigger emotional responses to increase traffic and engagement by end-users.

At the same time, even in many formerly stable democracies, we can observe a decline in trust in societal institutions (Kavanagh and Rich, 2018), where groups in society tend to trust, for example, formal experts, scientific institutions, professional journalism, etc. less. During the COVID pandemic, this decline in trust became fatal in many countries (Gisondi et al., 2022). The COVID pandemic has made some information inequalities visible. These include unequal access to content behind paywalls, inequality of opportunity or the education gap, all of which are linked to increasing economic inequality along race, class and gender lines. Such inequalities are certainly nothing new, but as always, they are typical of the times and at the same time shaped by historical developments. Today's information infrastructure brings together different spheres of life in new constellations. Public debates intertwine with private conversations and professional or educational concerns within the specific commercial logic of multisided platforms. Moreover, the activities of people within the information infrastructure are themselves constitutive of the infrastructural arrangements that emerge. This also highlights some of the challenges of AI-based services in general, namely the increasing absence of direct control by (human) end-users, accompanied by an invisible form of agential control by technology.

With regard to information literacy, a number of questions come to the fore. For instance, how can an understanding of an ever-changing information infrastructure, invisibly folded into the practices and discourses of everyday life, be achieved and supported? How can we envision information literacies that support critical engagement with information and include an understanding of the mechanisms that sustain the institutions that produce information as trust in those institutions diminishes? What theoretical tools are needed to develop and support the analysis of information literacies in a situation where pervasive and dominant information systems are largely beyond society's control? These are not questions that can be answered once and for all with an empirical study, certainly not in this chapter. Rather, they are questions that shape the way we as researchers understand and conceptualise information literacy. In this chapter, we propose sociomateriality as an approach that enables such an understanding.

Key notions and core elements of sociomateriality

A cornerstone of sociomateriality is anti-anthropocentrism. That is, it stems from a critique of traditional views that place humans at the centre of the world. Instead, sociomateriality assumes that nonhuman entities, such as technologies and other tools, also have agency that enables them to play a role in shaping the social and material world. From a sociomaterial perspective, humans and nonhumans are seen as actors in the shaping of the world and the focus is on understanding the various ways in which they are entwined. For this reason, sociomateriality is referred to as an example of *posthumanism* (Gherardi, 2017). This entails a critique of many traditional approaches in the humanities and social sciences that assign an overriding role to humans, their sense-making, agency and unique intentions. Instead, sociomateriality strives to extend analytical interest to include various nonhuman entities as actors.

In line with anti-anthropocentrism, sociomateriality, as the name suggests, starts from 'the materialities of bodies, technologies, discourses, meanings and material-institutional contexts of interconnected practices' (Gherardi, 2017, 50). In other words, it pays particular attention to things, artefacts and other entities and their becoming in the world. Importantly, in sociomateriality, material is not equivalent with tangible (Dourish, 2017,

47), but also includes the materiality of the digital as well as that of the discursive, not just that of physical artefacts. For instance, the code, algorithms, data and software that enable digital technologies are considered material entities that shape and are shaped by social practices. Information too can be cast in such a way.

To establish a foundation, we first present a set of key notions in sociomateriality, focusing on some that we consider particularly useful for information literacy research. We then return to how materiality is conceived, providing additional nuance to the notion. Sociomateriality is a field that is notoriously cluttered with figurative and often suggestive concepts, including some neologisms that attempt to capture terminological, analytical or other forms of nuance. In the following, we introduce a selection of these and use them to outline some of the fundamental assumptions in sociomateriality. It should be noted that there are numerous other notions that we cannot discuss here. The notions discussed in this section are entanglement and co-constitution, intra-action and agential cut, becomings, performativity, configurations and, lastly, infrastructure. Some of these notions are foundational to sociomateriality, others overlap, or their use extends across different takes on sociomateriality, while some are strongly associated with a particular thinker.

Entanglement and co-constitution

A central assumption of sociomateriality is that the social and the material are entangled and mutually constituted. Rather than viewing the social and the material as distinct levels in an analysis, sociomateriality emphasises their inseparability. Since they are mutually constituted, we cannot understand what is happening in the world if we draw a line between a social and a material side of things. From a sociomaterial perspective that remains true to its anti-anthropocentric position, the notion of materiality as separate from something called 'the social' or society makes no sense. Instead, the approach assumes that the world is sociomaterial and is constantly being recreated and reshaped in various arrangements and practices of co-constitution.

Intra-action and agential cut

Karen Barad (2003; 2007) has developed a number of influential concepts making up what she calls material-discursive theory or agential realism, but which we include in a broader church of sociomateriality. In particular, the notions of intra-action and agential cut are useful in clarifying some aspects of the ideas of entanglement and co-constitution presented above. To explain, intra-action differs from the notion of interaction, which presupposes that entities first come into being and then enter into relation with each other. In contrast, intra-action emphasises that social, including discursive and material, entities are not fixed with clear boundaries, but are constantly being created and shaped. Intra-action is a means of describing how phenomena are never just there, but they are constantly being produced and acquire meanings through different and changing connections. Barad (2007, 333) explains that 'phenomena are the ontological inseparability of intra-acting "agencies"'. In this sense, everything is to some extent dependent on everything else, but in continuously shifting constellations. At the same time, it is important to note that she still considers phenomena in certain situations as stable enough to be studied. Barad calls this local stabilisation an 'agential cut', which not least provides researchers with an analytical tool to decide what to include and what to exclude in a given study. In other words, it is a momentarily stable configuration that can be examined and that is achieved through temporal, spatial and relational severances, or cuts. We will return to this idea in the context of methodological considerations later in this chapter.

Becomings

Another concept that originates in the work of Barad is that of becomings. She describes the relationship between phenomena in the world as 'not a static relationality but a doing' (2003, 803). This idea of *doing* is closely connected to the notion of becomings, which is an important idea in sociomateriality that refers to the constant change and development of things and their relations. Sociomaterial research often speaks of actors, bodies, or entities as emergent. This implies that tangible and intangible material entities are conceived of as being in constant states of becoming in which their meaning is established and re-established. Such a focus on constant becoming necessarily presupposes that nothing is essential. Drawing on the work of Judith Butler, Barad (2003, 821) describes 'matter as a process of materialization'.

Performativity

The notion of performativity refers to the idea that things and entities are not passive, but actively participate in creating and shaping the sociomaterial world and also historically and culturally contingent. In other words, things do not simply exist but their meaning is emergent and they are actively involved in producing meaning and shaping the world. In the words of Karen Barad (2007, 141), 'agency is not an attribute but the ongoing reconfiguring of the world'. As such, performativity occupies a central position in sociomaterial thinking. It is often invoked to describe how various qualities, such as agency, take place in practices, i.e. how they are performed. Related theoretical examples can be found in the work of Michel Foucault (e.g. 1980), who shows how knowledge, bodies and power do not simply exist, but are continuously produced in relation to each other and in that of feminist scholar Judith Butler (2010), who laid the foundation for understanding gender as performatively produced (Introna, 2013, 336).

Configurations

In addition to the notion of entanglement, terms such as assemblage, apparatus or configuration are common in sociomateriality. These and similar expressions are used to describe the fluctuating ways in which people and nonhuman actors or other kinds of elements join up and how material and discursive entities and practices come together to shape the world and each other. In particular, the idea of configuration is discussed by Lucy Suchman (2007; 2014), who understands the configuration as 'a device for studying technologies with particular attention to the materialities and imaginaries that they *join together*' (Suchman, 2014, 48, italics in original). One aspect, in particular, is relevant here, namely how thinking in terms of configurations helps to draw boundaries that are culturally and temporally specific, which is a prerequisite for articulating and delimiting objects of study. In other words, similar to the notion of the agential cut (Barad, 2007), configuration is primarily an analytical device.

Infrastructure

Another key concept of sociomateriality is infrastructure, which refers to the background systems and structures that support and shape practices, amongst other things. It can include physical infrastructures such as roads, buildings or fibre-optic cables, but also intangible infrastructures such as the intangible part of the internet or various software systems. Importantly, infrastructures incorporate standards, build on layers of older infrastructures, and they go unnoticed until they break down (Star, 1999). Understanding the role of infrastructure is important for understanding how different entities and practices are shaped, enabled and constrained by the systems and technologies that support them. The notion of information infrastructure then describes the sociomaterial relations implicated in configuring the entities and practices associated with how information (in its material form and as an imaginary) is produced, organised and accessed. This means that information infrastructure is never completely stable, but neither is it completely formless. Therefore, if we think in sociomaterial terms, information infrastructures should rather be understood as entanglements that emerge in and through specific (sociomaterial) practices (Bowker and Star, 1999; Star and Bowker, 2010; Bowker et al., 2009; see also Orlikowski, 2007; Orlikowski and Scott, 2008). In our research on information literacies, we build on the work of Susan Leigh Star and Geoffrey Bowker to develop an understanding of information literacies that accounts for the particularities of the corporate information infrastructure that pervades contemporary society. We suggest that infrastructural meaning-making should permeate conceptualisations of information literacies (e.g. Haider and Sundin, 2019; 2022) (see also Chapter 7 by Johansson for further discussion of infrastructure).

Materiality

After this introduction of a selection of central notions and elements of sociomateriality, we can now return to the issue of materiality. Here, despite the fundamental importance of materiality, there are also ever-so-slight variations in the way different thinkers elaborate the notion in their respective works. Karen Barad (2007, 350), for example, insists: 'Matter is . . . not to be understood as a property of things but, like discursive practices, must be understood in more dynamic and productive terms . . .' and also speaks of matter as 'not a thing but a doing' (Barad, 2007, 351). Paul Dourish (2017), on the other hand, offers a slightly different perspective, bringing in aspects from media archaeology and software studies. Writing in the same tradition, he also emphasises the interdependence between the social and the material (or the cultural and the digital) and their emergent character, but he describes the materialities of information in terms of 'properties of representations and formats that constrain, enable, limit and shape the ways in which those representations can be created, transmitted, stored, manipulated and put to use – properties like their heft, size, fragility and transparency' (Dourish, 2017, 6). This is indicative of a terminological ambiguity that is characteristic of sociomateriality. However, it is also seductive and, importantly for information literacy research, dynamic and productive, in that it allows for a rich and detailed consideration of information technologies while avoiding technological determinism.

In summary, the terms, concepts and definitions presented here are, as already mentioned, only a selection of those available. Taken together, however, they provide a good picture of the core tenets of sociomateriality, particularly for the study of information literacies. It is important to bear in mind that some of the terms overlap, some might even contradict each other or are ambiguous in how they relate to each other. It goes without saying that it is not advisable to use all of the above terms in the same study.

Theoretical questions

In what follows, sociomateriality is anchored in the information literacy tradition by discussing its potential contribution in relation to other traditions. To begin with, the question of materiality is re-examined in relation to intention and agency.

Materiality in information literacy research

Sociomateriality helps research on information literacy to recognise the role of technology as co-constitutive and in this way makes it analytically perceptible and relevant. It represents a departure from the anthropocentric assumptions that have dominated most previous information literacy research, in which humans are, as a matter of course, the sole focus of enquiry, while information literacy technologies are assigned a subordinate role (see also the discussion in Chapter 5 by Hicks). In contrast, sociomateriality does not separate technologies and information literacies, but sees them as interdependent. An early proponent of the need to focus on the interdependence of literacy and technology is Bertram Bruce. As early as 1997, he wrote: 'the technologies of literacy are not optional add-ons, but are part of the definition of every form of literacy' (Bruce, 1997, 304).

As mentioned earlier, sociomateriality and practice theory (e.g. Cox, 2012; Lloyd, 2010; Pilerot, Hammarfelt and Moring, 2017) share several starting points in terms of framing information literacy (see also Chapter 2 on practice theory by Lloyd). In particular, they share a critique of general models of information literacy. A focus on practices rather than individual intentions and behaviours brings to the fore that information literacies need to be understood in the plural to capture how literacies are necessarily always dependent on the actual practices of which they are part. Nevertheless, the specific interest in materiality that underlies sociomateriality and that enables concrete technologies to come into view, is usually absent from other practice-theoretical research on information literacy. On occasion, a practice-theoretical approach to understand practices of information seeking and information literacy may even contribute to obscure the technologies, as the approach deliberately – and often for good reason – emphasises practices over information systems (Cox, 2012). However, this may also hinder the emergence of a deeper understanding of the co-constitutive relationship between information systems and practices and of the creation of social meaning through these configurations (Haider and Sundin, 2019, 36).

There is certainly research on information literacy that develops a theoretical notion of information technology. In their highly cited article *Information Literacy as a Sociotechnical Practice*, Kimmo Tuominen, Reijo Savolainen and Sanna Talja (2005) creatively combine a focus on practices and materiality to examine information literacy that is in some ways similar to that supported by sociomateriality. However, it is important to note that they do not explicitly refer to sociomateriality and several significant distinctions can be made out. Strictly speaking, they consider the interaction between technology and practices rather than how their relations are co-constitutive and configured in sociomaterial practice. In other words, the analytical focus is on the getting together of distinct phenomena with distinct meanings that exist separately. A sociomaterial approach to information literacy, on the other hand, would emphasise how all actors involved are always in processes of becoming, how relationality happens and meaning arises through this performance.

Although it is not the most common approach in information literacy research or information studies more broadly, there are numerous interesting examples of more or less rigorous applications of sociomateriality (e.g. Bates et al., 2019; Ekström, 2021; Haider and Sundin, 2019; Huvila, 2018; McCoy and Rosenbaum, 2019; Rivano Eckerdal and Sundin, 2015; Rivano Eckerdal, 2012; Veinot and Pierce, 2019). These examples – along with others that could not be listed – should give ideas on how to go about researching information literacy and related information issues with a sociomaterial framing.

Understandings of information literacy

Research on information literacy traditionally starts from the doings and sayings of students, workers or other groups of people and from there on investigates their knowledge (or rather lack of it) about and experiences from using certain information systems in schools, at workplaces and in other spheres of everyday life. Often this research tends to have a detached relationship to materiality. In Carol Kuhlthau's (1991) famous research on information seeking in schools, the focus is on the experience of students' feelings, thoughts and actions, while the material aspects of information seeking are almost invisible. The result of Kuhlthau's groundbreaking research is formulated as a generalised model of a typical information-seeking process. Her research deliberately distanced itself from what she referred to as a *source approach*, in which the focus of the research was on learning how to use different information sources or the order in which those sources ought to be used (Kuhlthau, 1987). Kuhlthau's research was developed during the end of the 1980s and early 1990s, at a time when there was a growing interest in cognitive and constructivist research on information seeking and information literacy. A title of a chapter by Brenda

Dervin (1992) illustrates how at the time information systems tended to be viewed: 'From the mind's eye of the user'. Ever since, a so-called user perspective has been strong in information literacy and information literacy research.

There is, of course, much research on information literacy and in particular on information literacy as a professional practice that deals with search engines, bibliographic databases and the evaluation of information sources. However, this research (and professional practice) tends to lack theoretical depth. Information literacy technologies are mostly viewed as neutral tools that people interact with or are ignored altogether in the analysis. Read with a sociomaterial lens, it might be argued that such a way of conceptualising information literacy neglects the materialities involved, as it forgets to consider how information literacies are integrated with literacy technologies (cf. Bruce, 1997). Sociomateriality is, in a sense, a re-appropriation of information sources and retrieval technology into information literacy research and professional practice; not as something outside literacy, but as a part of literacy practices as such. Furthermore, sociomateriality, at least potentially, opens up for a critical understanding of why people meet the kind of information they do on social media, via chatbots, in recommendation systems, search engines and so forth. From a perspective of learning and literacy, these platforms can be referred to as information literacy technologies. In such a way, information literacy can contribute to *infrastructural meaning-making* and vice versa (e.g. Haider and Sundin, 2019). With an interest in infrastructural meaning-making, we can ask questions such as: Why do we meet what we meet on information systems?; or How are information systems related to each other? What are the implications of these material relations for the emergence of meaning?

As an example, let us take a closer look at Google Search – an information literacy technology that has often been strangely ignored or considered only as a neutral tool in much information literacy research. When we approach Google Search from a sociomaterial perspective on information literacy, particular aspects are brought into relief. First, the role of materiality (including intangible, digital materiality) comes into view; materiality not as something that stands alongside the social, but as enacted with it in sociomaterial practices of co-constitution or, to use Barad's concept, intra-actions.

Secondly, compared to many other theories of information literacy (e.g. cognitive and phenomenographical notions), a sociomaterial approach directs attention to configurations and entanglements and to how performance occurs, not in general, but situated, with an agential cut, at a specific moment. An enormous number of components are involved and can be considered in a Google search: for example, there are algorithms, a huge index, bots, websites, language models and not least the data that people provide to the search engine. There is also physical technology such as devices, cables, data centres, hard drives and their cooling units. In addition, it involves a large number of people: programmers, raters and data labellers, advertisers, legislators, content producers and providers, end-users in their practices and so on. Each time someone searches for something in whatever way (using voice control, images, written queries, or by following a suggestion offered by the system), these and many other components come into play. And they come into play together with their politics, values and ideologies and – it could be said – every time this happens an instance of information literacy is performed. This way, information literacy relates to the emergent, or the *becoming*, character of dominant information systems. Yet, when subject to analysis, it is also situated in one specific configuration of commercial platforms, algorithms, the flow of data, practices, actual demands, constraints and lived experiences and particular implications for people's lives, bodies and relations.

Thirdly, another aspect of information literacy that has received much attention is the evaluation of information sources. The need for such evaluation is often justified by the increased awareness of the conditions of contemporary digital culture with regard to various types of false or harmful information (e.g. misinformation, disinformation, malinformation). To apply a sociomaterial perspective to information literacy is to place the evaluation of information sources in the realm of the (digital) infrastructure in which they intra-act, and, thus, to recognise that this infrastructure is constantly in the making. The vetting of information and meaning-making more broadly can then be related to the emergent character of the infrastructure and also to values, interests or limitations that arise from the practices of which they are a part. After all, all evaluation of information sources is situated. This means it takes place in practices and these practices are constitutive components of infrastructures and vice versa.

Information literacies configure sociomaterialities in different ways (and the other way around). This implies that the co-constitutive relationships of people, platforms, institutional requirements, social expectations, laws and regulations, technical devices, cultural and educational resources and so on play out differently each time. But, and this is important, not arbitrarily different. Since they are also practices, these relationships are stable enough to be recognised as such and related to each other. When evaluating search results, for example, their meaning must be established in relation to the infrastructure that generated them and this infrastructure includes, not least, the action of whoever performed the search in the first place. In other words, infrastructural meaning-making clearly matters. However, infrastructural meaning-making can only take place if one understands not only that, but also how, practices are sociomaterial. Concerning the example of Google Search, then, understanding the sociomaterial entanglement of search and its performance is a prerequisite for critically evaluating information and information sources. That is, we cannot focus only on a source *per se* without understanding how the source is interwoven with other components in the various sociomaterial arrangements that make it possible in the first place. Finally, Orlikowski (2007, 1440) makes the point that when you search with general-purpose commercial search engines like Google, you are not looking for reality as represented by that search engine. From a sociomaterial theoretical point of view, reality emerges during the search, or as Orlikowski and Scott (2014, 8739) write: 'reality is enacted through performance'.

To reiterate, sociomateriality opens up the possibility of taking the material aspects of information literacy seriously, in a way that allows for a better understanding of how practices, technologies and information literacies are jointly constituted. Today, a rapidly evolving digital information infrastructure, with its dominance by a few global, multisided platforms, co-produces the practice of finding information, of evaluating its credibility and of much of public debate.

Reflections on methodological choices

In research on information literacy, the empirical focus has often been on the study of different user groups. The individuals who make up these groups have usually been taken for granted as the focus of interest – either through questionnaires, interviews or observation. Oftentimes, researchers studying information literacy have assumed a norm of how to evaluate or search for information and their study has then measured the extent to which a particular group of people meets that norm. However, frequently, this kind of research lacks adequate reflection on its own norms (see e.g. Haider and Sundin, 2022, Chapter 3, for a discussion). Highlighting this blind spot does not necessarily imply a critique of a normative information literacy agenda as such. However, a sociomaterial approach gives us a certain methodological direction. The most obvious of these is the valorisation of nonhuman actors in research. Also, with sociomateriality, the focus is not on either people or nonhuman actors, but on how they are configured in certain practices. Obviously, such an approach also poses challenges. For example, how do we get close enough to the specific sociomaterial practices? How can we get at what data and algorithms are doing when platform companies in most cases restrict access to their trade secrets? Today, research usually has to make do with the results of the configurations that people remember, because the specific sociomaterial arrangement at any given time is difficult to observe. Research has to take what we can get, with a 'good enough' attitude. This attitude is also rooted in defiance of the corporate takeover of large parts of society's basic and necessary information infrastructures, politely referred to as *platformisation* (Plantin et al., 2018). Most importantly this attitude makes it possible to see value in working with presets, defaults and approximations and indeed with failures, glitches and breakdowns. After all, these are the *agential cuts* where the materiality of infrastructural arrangements comes into being most of the time and where the historical, cultural and even political layering that constitutes them becomes most palpable.

Much of sociomaterial research begins with the assertion that nonhuman actors should play as important a role in the analysis as human ones. This theoretical assumption is also present in most practice theory (Pilerot, Hammarfelt and Moring, 2017). At the same time, traditional methods of data creation – questionnaires, interviews and observations – are still favoured and materiality is 'invited' (Hultin, 2019) through these. When nonhuman actors are included in the analysis, it is usually through the senses of the people being studied. This critique of a lot of work on sociomaterial information literacy, including our own, can be and has also been made of empirical information literacy studies in other theoretical traditions, most notably practice theory. In reply to this, two points can be raised. First, it is important to note that a sociomaterial approach does not mean that all well-established qualitative research methods for data creation, such as observations, interviews or focus groups, should be abandoned. Rather, it can be argued, what is important is *how* one approaches interviews, observations, focus groups or similar methods. Materiality needs to be invited, so to speak, as Lotta Hultin puts it when she points out how she has shifted the focus in observations 'from the sayings, doings and interactions of primarily human actors to how the temporal flow of practice enacted conditions of possibility to speak, act and interact in certain ways' (Hultin, 2019, 98). A second important consideration can be found in the compound material-discursive. This term is often used to describe not least Karen Barad's theoretical work and it reflects even more clearly than the notion of sociomateriality itself how the discursive is material and the material is discursive. That said, discourse or the discursive are not synonymous with language. As Barad (2007, 146) so neatly summarises Foucault in this regard: 'Discourse is not what is said; it is that which constrains and enables what can be said. Discursive practices define what counts as meaningful statements.' These statements include language-based ones, among and in conjunctions with other things.

Another concern of methodological significance arises from the specific understanding of materialities, which may seem overwhelming. If everything is material, yet at the same time, matter does not exist as such, but only takes on meaning in processes of co-constitution, then how exactly can the role of materiality come into view and how can co-constitution become noticeable to the researcher? Here it helps to think of sociomateriality as a theoretically informed sensitising concept, as David Ribes (2019, 58) suggests for the study of materiality in STS more broadly: 'A materialist approach should not be a dogma – a drive for materialist purity – rather it is a sensitizing tool of the analyst, allowing us to hone in and make sense of the central aspects of the study at hand.' Moreover, research is itself a practice that studies another. The phenomenon at hand thus consists of two practices that are distinguished from each other by the way in which they are intra-actively performed, to use sociomaterial language. Such a perspective, which situates research in relation to the configuration being researched, also supports an understanding of how seemingly identical materialities are performed differently in and through different practices.

Summary and conclusion: embracing definitional ambiguity and a punk approach to sociomateriality

This chapter is written for a theory book on information literacy. Of course, we hope that the chapter will encourage readers to approach information literacy research from the point of view of sociomateriality. Nevertheless, we would like to emphasise that the chapter is not a recipe for analysis. Indeed, we oppose any form of theoretical literalism that ends in a categorical distinction between right and wrong. Theories are always in motion and not meant to be rigid templates; they are always being adapted and further developed in the research process. Just as it emphasises the constant becoming and performance of the world, sociomateriality itself is not a fixed and stable theoretical position. Rather, it is an approach or a way of thinking, made up of allied analytical moves grouped around a set of central ontological assumptions and concepts that share a particular interest in materialities and the social as situated, co-constituted and emergent. We are not advocates of a purist understanding of sociomateriality. Instead, the terminological creativity and ambiguity that characterise the field can be understood as an invitation to adopt an eclectic approach to sociomateriality. Such an approach, in our view, might also be necessary to engage analytically with the ever-evolving and fast-moving messiness of society's infrastructural arrangements without getting lost in discussions about terminological precision or conceptual consistency. That being said, an eclectic approach to sociomateriality, while allowing for terminological plasticity, must nevertheless adhere to some central tenets of sociomateriality to ensure theoretical coherence and not fall into the trap of technical determinism. Moreover, an eclectic interpretation of sociomateriality allows for a degree of definitional ambiguity and is open to methodological inventiveness (Lury and Wakeford, 2012). This, we argue, is a prerequisite for examining information literacies in relation to the corporate and platformised information infrastructure that increasingly defines and pervades much of contemporary society. Furthermore, it is a way to facilitate the inclusion of other theories that may be better suited to understanding, for example, power, democracy, economic or political structures, history, etc. in an investigation.

We argue for an approach we have earlier in this chapter described as 'good enough', which aims to create an understanding based on playful – and sometimes angry or defiant – relations with configurations of commercial information infrastructures. A fitting term to describe this approach would be a punk approach to sociomateriality. This includes an interest in things like autosuggestions, default settings or the repurposing of marketing tools for situated data creation and it allows the researcher to constantly perform sociomateriality through their own actions. Such a punk approach entails a critical, yet dynamic stance and responsiveness to the messiness of the world, but also a deeply rooted social justice ethos and a do-it-yourself (DiY) attitude (Smith, Dines and Parkinson, 2017; Stewart and Way, 2023). Instead of aiming for perfection and frictionless conceptual consistency, we propose to get to work creating the data, respecting people's limits and ethical, personal and other boundaries. However, we must not be intimidated by the limits set by the corporate information infrastructure or fetishising technology and technological progress in a way that shrouds the various systems we live by in such mystery that studying and controlling what they do and refusing them becomes the privilege of a minority.

When we point out in the introduction to this chapter that information in contemporary society tends to find people rather than people finding the information, this is a statement that is made from such a position. Thus, a response informed by sociomateriality would emphasise that we need to understand more precisely how the agency of the information infrastructures is performed in and through sociomaterial practices. A punk approach to sociomateriality then would add that since there is only so much we can – or are allowed to – know and what we can know is always already past, the fastest and loudest path to creating the data is to create it from the people who want to tell us and from the systems we can access in the way we can access them. Analytically, on the other hand, such a sociomaterial approach implies most of all employing materiality as a sensitising concept (Ribes, 2019) throughout when approaching the data and letting this tie the different parts of the analysis together.

The ongoing datafication fundamentally challenges the conditions for knowledge, ignorance and doubt in society. It also changes the conditions for the deliberate spread of misinformation and the online mobilisation of people for various causes. The creation, dissemination and amplification of harmful information can be and has been automated. From a sociomaterial perspective, we should also ask ourselves critical questions such as: 'To what extent can and has information literacy been automated and how?' 'What would it mean if information literacy were delegated to AI systems?' 'What about information literacy can be and what ought not to be automated?' 'Can a bot ever teach information literacy in a way that is beneficial and for what?' A punk approach to sociomateriality based on such inquiries asks: what is the price – in terms of suffering or harm – of training an AI model for such a purpose, who will pay that price and who will profit? And above all: how can we refuse and what theoretical and analytical allies do we need to bring on board to do so?

References

Barad, K. (2003) Posthumanist Performativity: toward an understanding of how matter comes to matter, *Signs: Journal of Women in Culture and Society*, 28, 801–31.

Barad, K. (2007) *Meeting the Universe Halfway: quantum physics and the entanglement of matter and meaning*, Duke University Press.

Bates, J., Goodale, P., Lin, Y. and Andrews, P. (2019) Assembling an Infrastructure for Historic Climate Data Recovery: data friction in practice, *Journal of Documentation*, 75, 791–806.

Bowker, G. C. and Star, S. L. (1999) *Sorting Things Out: classification and its consequences*, MIT Press.

Bowker, G. C., Baker, K., Millerand, F. and Ribes, D. (2009) Toward Information Infrastructure Studies: ways of knowing in a networked environment. In *International Handbook of Internet Research*, Springer, 97–117.

Bruce, B. C. (1997) Critical Issues Literacy Technologies: what stance should we take?, *Journal of Literacy Research*, 29, 289–309.

Butler, J. (2010) Performative Agency, *Journal of Cultural Economy*, 3, 147–61.

Cox, A. M. (2012) An Exploration of the Practice Approach and its Place in Information Science, *Journal of Information Science*, 38, 176–88.

Davies, W. (2018) *Nervous States: how feeling took over the world*, Jonathan Cape.

Dervin, B. (1992) From the Mind's Eye of the User: the sense-making qualitative-quantitative methodology. In Glazier, J. D. and Powell, R. R. (eds) *Qualitative Research in Information Management*, Libraries Unlimited, 61–84.

Dourish, P. (2017) *The Stuff of Bits: an essay on the materialities of information*, MIT Press.

Ekström, B. (2021) Trace Data Visualisation Enquiry: a methodological coupling for studying information practices in relation to information systems, *Journal of Documentation*, 78, 141–59.

Foucault, M. (1980) *Power/knowledge: selected interviews and other writings 1972–1977* (edited by Colin Gordon), Pearson Education.

Gisondi, M. A., Barber, R., Faust, J. S., Raja, A., Strehlow, M. C., Westafer, L. M. and Gottlieb, M. (2022) A Deadly Infodemic: social media and the power of COVID-19 misinformation, *Journal of Medical Internet Research*, 24, e35552.

Gherardi, S. (2017) Sociomateriality in Posthuman Practice Theory. In Hui, A., Schatzki, T. and Shove, E. (eds) *The Nexus of Practices: connections, constellations, practitioners*, Routledge, 38–51.

Haider, J. and Sundin, O. (2019) *Invisible Search and Online Search Engines: the ubiquity of search in everyday life*, Routledge.

Haider, J. and Sundin, O. (2022) *Paradoxes of Media and Information Literacy: the crisis of information*, Routledge.

Hultin, L. (2019) On Becoming a Sociomaterial Researcher: exploring epistemological practices grounded in a relational, performative ontology, *Information and Organization*, 29, 91–104.

Huvila, I. (2018) Putting to (Information) Work: a Stengersian perspective on how information technologies and people influence information practices, *The Information Society*, 34, 229–43.

Introna, L. D. (2013) Epilogue: performativity and the becoming of sociomaterial assemblages. In Vaujany, F.-X. and Mitev, N. (eds) *Materiality and Space: organizations, artefacts and practices*, Palgrave Macmillan, 330–42.

Introna, L. D. and Hayes, N. (2011) On Sociomaterial Imbrications: what plagiarism detection systems reveal and why it matters, *Information and Organization*, 21, 107–22.

Kavanagh, J. and Rich, M. D. (2018) *Truth Decay: an initial exploration of the diminishing role of facts and analysis in American public life*, Rand Corporation.

Kuhlthau, C. C. (1987) Information Skills: tools for learning, *School Library Media Quarterly*, 16, 22–8.

Kuhlthau, C. C. (1991) Inside the Search Process: information seeking from the user's perspective, *Journal of the American Society for Information Science*, 42, 361–71.

Lloyd, A. (2010) Framing Information Literacy as Information Practice: site ontology and practice theory, *Journal of Documentation*, 66, 245–58.

Lury, C. and Wakeford, N. (eds) (2012) *Inventive Methods: the happening of the social*, Routledge.

McCoy, C. and Rosenbaum, H. (2019) Uncovering Unintended and Shadow Practices of Users of Decision Support System Dashboards in Higher Education Institutions, *Journal of the Association for Information Science and Technology*, 70, 370–84.

Orlikowski, W. J. (2007) Sociomaterial Practices: exploring technology at work, *Organization Studies*, 28, 1435–48.

Orlikowski, W. J. and Scott, S. V. (2008) 10 Sociomateriality: challenging the separation of technology, work and organization, *Academy of Management Annals*, 2, 433–74.

Orlikowski, W. J. and Scott, S. V. (2014) What Happens when Evaluation Goes Online? Exploring apparatuses of valuation in the travel sector, *Organization Science*, 25, 868–91.

Orlikowski, W. J. and Scott, S. V. (2015) The Algorithm and the Crowd, *MIS Quarterly*, 39, 201–16.

Pilerot, O., Hammarfelt, B. and Moring, C. (2017) The Many Faces of Practice Theory in Library and Information Studies, *Information Research*, 22, CoLIS paper 1602, http://InformationR.net/ir/22-1/colis/colis1602.html.

Plantin, J. C., Lagoze, C., Edwards, P. N. and Sandvig, C. (2018) Infrastructure Studies Meet Platform Studies in the Age of Google and Facebook, *New Media and Society*, 20, 293–310.

Ribes, D. (2019) Materiality Methodology and some Tricks of the Trade in the Study of Data and Specimens. In Vertesi, J. and Ribes, D. (eds) *digitalSTS: a field guide for science & technology studies*, Princeton University Press, 43–60.

Rivano Eckerdal, J. (2012) Information Sources at Play: the apparatus of knowledge production in contraceptive counselling, *Journal of Documentation*, 68, 278–98.

Rivano Eckerdal, J. and Sundin, O. (2015) Relocating the Owl of Wisdom: encyclopaedias in a life-historical perspective, *Nordisk Tidsskrift for Informationsvidenskab og Kulturformidling*, 4, 21–34.

Scott, S. V. and Orlikowski, W. J. (2014) Entanglements in Practice, *MIS Quarterly*, 38, 873–94.

Smith, G. D., Dines, M. and Parkinson, T. (2017) Presenting Punk Pedagogies in Practice. In Smith, G. D., Dines, M. and Parkinson, T. (eds) *Punk Pedagogies: music, culture and learning*, Routledge, 1–9.

Star, S. L. (1999) The Ethnography of Infrastructure, *American Behavioral Scientist*, 43, 377–91.

Star, S. L. and Bowker, G. C. (2010) How to Infrastructure. In Lievrouw, L. A. and Livingstone, S. (eds) *Handbook of New Media: social shaping and social consequences of ICTs*, Sage, 230–45.

Stewart, F. and Way, L. (eds) (2023) *Punk Pedagogies in Practice: disruptions and connections*, Intellect Books.

Suchman, L. (2007) *Human-Machine Reconfigurations: plans and situated actions*, 2nd edn, Cambridge University Press.

Suchman, L. (2014) Configuration. In Lury, C. and Wakeford, N. (eds) *Inventive Methods*, Routledge, 48–60.

Tuominen, K., Savolainen, R. and Talja, S. (2005) Information Literacy as a Sociotechnical Practice, *Library Quarterly*, 75, 329–45.

Veinot, T. C. and Pierce, C. S. (2019) Materiality in Information Environments: objects, spaces and bodies in three outpatient hemodialysis facilities, *Journal of the Association for Information Science and Technology*, 70, 1324–39.

10
Surfacing the Body: Embodiment, Site and Source

Annemaree Lloyd

Introduction

What happens when bodies are foregrounded as information sources and brought into thinking about information literacy? In what ways do theories of embodiment and of the body disrupt current discourses and practices about information literacy and help to shape a deeper understanding of the complexity of the practice? What do we gain when we bring the body into view?

Embodiment represents knowledge that is acquired by doing and by subjecting or being subject to experiences with knowledges (our own and others) derived from enculturation, encoding or embedded performance (Blackler, 1995). Embodied knowledge is only partially explicit but nonetheless important, as it references our tangible interactions and developing experiences with practices, performances and others over time and space. Embodiment represents the enmeshment of the corporeal, emotional, sensory and sentient dimensions of the lived experience. Upon this view embodiment is a construction that is subject to the various discourses that construct, deconstruct, emplace and disrupt the body in-practice and as-it-practises. To put this in another way, embodiment *is* informational.

The centrality of the body to our everyday practice should not, therefore, be relegated or reduced to secondary knowledge in the library and information science (LIS) field. Our bodies act as site and source for our inward reflection and reflexivity and outwardly as site and source for others. As we reflect upon and 'read' embodied performances, we access the trajectories and history of the lived experience. The increasing enmeshment of our information culture with digital platforms and technologies further means that theories of embodiment and corporeality are required to ensure the centrality of the body as site and source is foregrounded and not silenced or relegated to secondary knowledge.

An argument for the body

A claim for the inclusion of the body and embodiment in information literacy research and, more broadly, in LIS, is woven through this chapter. Primarily this claim proposes that disassociating information literacy from the corporeal and embodied experience will lead to an incomplete understanding of the complexity of the practice. This, in turn, diminishes the field's understanding of the central role that information, in all its manifestations, plays in practice.

In the field of LIS, the body as an information source/site and embodiment or the corporeality of experience remains a contested ground, particularly (and ironically) in human information behaviour, where there is still a tendency to funnel the concepts of corporeality and embodiment through a cognitive lens. Researchers such as Hartel (2018) have recently questioned whether the LIS field would be diminished if it failed to enter the domain of corporeal/embodiment research and instead, remained focused on the unanswered questions related to documentary practice and established LIS themes. Hartel asserts that research that moves into areas of embodiment and corporeality would place LIS researchers at a disadvantage and could be unproductive because of the established and mature research being conducted in other disciplines. Hartel has gone as far as to suggest that a corporeal/embodied line of enquiry is largely unnecessary in a field that has an established research tradition focusing on documents. This is a short-sighted position given that the LIS field is generally devoid of a breadth of theories which explain how people operate with information.

Hartel's position neglects the pivotal and obvious point that we are our bodies and our bodies are awash with knowledge and information that documents and informs our own internal reflexive practices and externally, informs the practices of others (Bates, 2018; Lloyd, 2007a; Lueg, 2015; 2020). The histories and trajectories of our lived experiences are inscribed onto our bodies and reference our access not only to privilege, but also to information and knowledges that have been denied (rights, education, health) resulting in an unequal politics of knowledge and terrain of struggle. When we read the body as source and site, we are reading histories, trajectories and terrains of embodiment.

It is axiomatic to say that bodies are centrally positioned in any information experience. This includes recorded/documentary practices, which in themselves emerge because of the performances of the body. While not all documentary focused research silences the body (see for example Lindh, 2015; Pilerot and Söderholm, 2019), positions which have traditionally adopted a cognitive focus or which solely focus on text as the primary thing can often negate the broader understanding that what constitutes information as any 'difference which makes a difference in some later event' (Bateson, 1972, 315) is situated and dependent on contextual fields for understanding and operationalisation. It also continues the practice of privileging certain types and forms of information and knowledge over others (e.g. epistemic/written knowledges over displayed or oral knowledges). The dualism of this privileging disenfranchises and excludes the ways of knowing that are fundamental to non-western cultures.

As information culture transitions towards becoming predominately digital, theories of embodiment are required to reinsert the body back into LIS as a significant source and site of knowledge and one that is central to becoming informed.

This chapter draws from several established fields (sociology, anthropology, psychology, philosophy) for its theoretical and analytical depth. It is within those fields that we find a deeper and established tradition of corporeal research and embodiment thinking that can be employed to frame and enrich our understandings of how people interact with information.

An argument is presented for the importance of corporeality and embodiment in LIS. The underlying premise being that continued emphasis on text impoverishes the field by failing to acknowledge the rich and complex layering of information on and through the body, which, in turn, enriches our information landscapes. This continues previous analysis and theorising (Lloyd, 2010a; 2010b; 2014; 2017) about the centrality of the body and embodiment. It will contend that including the body and related theories enriches and deepens our understanding of interaction with information and knowledge which, in turn, deepens our understanding of the sociology of information literacy practice and how it happens. Themes central to the thesis of information literacy and embodiment – the body as absent presence, as inscribed, as unfinished state and the body that matters – will be considered. Ontological and epistemological points of departure that influence methodological choices, position, enable or constrain the body (as site, source and performative object) are interrogated. A focus on the body disrupts documentalist advocacy for LIS (Hartel, 2018) and the reductionist discourse of dualism by surfacing the body as an information source that matters and is pivotal to meaning-making that is essential in all forms of human existence.

In the following section the theory of information literacy is briefly described, followed by a succinct but incomplete overview of corporeality and embodiment in social theory. The second section will discuss and consider how the theories of the body and embodiment operate ontologically, epistemologically and methodologically. Both sections consider the ways in which theories of embodiment or corporeality enable or constrain our understanding of information literacy. What aspects or dimensions are highlighted; what aspects are ignored? How does the theory we use shape our methodological choices?

Theory of information literacy

Central to this chapter is the thesis that humans are located at the centre of a swirling maelstrom of information environments and constructed landscapes in which our bodies play a central role. Information environments represent larger sites of stable instrumental/rational knowledge (Lloyd, 2006; 2017; 2021). Information landscapes are constructions that emerge from interaction with information environments and are shaped by the modalities of information that represent ways of knowing about collective forms of knowledge. The modalities of information may be social, epistemic, or corporeal. Coupled together, these modalities shape the enactment of information literacy practice specific to that setting (Lloyd, 2017; 2021).

To buy into and become positioned as an insider within a landscape requires access to information that is relevant to people engaged in joint enterprise within that space. To have the capacity to navigate the paths, nodes and edges of a landscape (Lloyd, 2003) requires an ability to enter and understand the discourses, narratives and performances – to be able to act and interact and to read the inscriptions of the landscape upon the body or the doings and nuances of practice. In this respect, it is necessary to acknowledge and interrogate the corporeal experience that leads to embodiment. To fail to do so means that the body remains disassociated from the information experience, which, in turn, means that understanding of this experience remains incomplete (Lloyd, 2010a).

The theory of information literacy (ToIL) (Lloyd, 2017) states that:

> Information literacy is a practice that is enacted in a social setting. It is composed of a suite of activities and skills that reference structured and embodied knowledges and ways of knowing relevant to the context. Information literacy is a way of knowing.

Lived bodies, embodiment and embodied knowledge play a pivotal role in this theory of information literacy. Centring the body as a significant site and source of information counterbalances the established Cartesian dualism that silences the body by asserting that information and knowledge are something that simply resides in the head. In making this point, Gherardi argues that:

> Knowledge is not what resides in a person's head or in the books or in databanks. To know is to be capable of participating with the requisite knowledge competence in the complex web of relationships among people, material artefacts and activities.
>
> (Gherardi, 2008, 517)

In the practice of information literacy, requisite knowledge about ways of knowing and how these knowledges are enacted is central to practice and practising. Research (Lloyd, 2006) has demonstrated that information literacy is a multimodal practice, comprising textual, social and epistemic modalities, and is shaped by and through interaction with cultural discursive, material economic and historic preconditions (social/political) through which power and social conditions of the lifeworld are established (Habermas, 1987; Lloyd, 2011).

Bringing the body into view: themes and theories of embodiment

Recent theorising of the body has produced a suite of themes that have surfaced and privileged analysis of the body, corporeality and embodiment. These themes advance a critical view of the body, while at the same time working to reduce the dualist reductionism that relegates the body to a secondary site and source of knowledge.

Absenting the body: privileging the mind in early theory

Descartes' prioritisation of rational thought and the privileging of mind over body is articulated in the dictum that I am only a vessel that thinks – *Cogito ergo sum* ('I think therefore I am' – Descartes, 1634, 105, 156). Similarly, the Enlightenment thinker, Kant (1785), raised rational epistemic thought above that of the sentient body and desire. The impact of these early philosophical thinkers was to evaluate and create 'opposition positions between cognitive thought over the material body' (Shilling, 2009, 451) or a conceptual hegemony that has remained unchallenged until recently. In social theory, this early thinking led to an avalanche of literature that privileged rationalisation, normativity and the mind over the body, drawing on the assumption that the social world operates upon us 'intellectually and consensually rather than directly upon our bodies' (O'Neill, 1985, 48).

In social theory, early theorists continued to prioritise the mind over the body. The early work of Parsons (1937), a structural functionalist, downgraded the body and emphasised the importance of culture and information-rich values in steering human behaviour, which did little to emphasise or reclaim the body (Shilling, 2009, 440). Weber (1968) argued that all action was based on rational human thought while Durkheim (1938) contended that social and moral 'facts' were beyond the physical embodied individual. The sociology of Berger and Luckman (1966), often cited in LIS research, continued to reinforce the mind/body duality and sequestered the body by suggesting that society was only meaningful when viewed in terms of cognitive process. Similarly in the influential structuration theory of Giddens (1986), there is an absence of the productive role for the body in mediating the formation of social structure (Shilling, 2009).

Bringing the body into view

In more recent history, a challenge was made to the downgrading and devaluing of the body as a minor player in rational thought. Social theorists and philosophers began to question this entrenched view and focus on the central role the body plays in 'becoming and being'. Four major factors noted by Shilling (2021) led to several distinct lines of enquiry. These are defined by Shilling as (a) consumer culture, which drew attention to the body as a performative self and symbol, (b) feminism's interrogation of the sex/gender divide, which focuses attention on the female body and corporeality, (c) control of the body via changes in governmentality, which attempted to create normative performance via rules and regulations, (d) doubt about the reality of the body (i.e. what is a body) in the light of the development of constructionist theoretical enquiry.

In a general sense all theories of embodiment (the emplaced corporeal body) recognise and acknowledge that the body has become decoupled and disassociated in interpretations and representations of everyday life. Embodiment theories draw from a constellation of social and cultural perspectives and all centrally position the body and bodily experience in the construction of understanding. How the term and its theories are understood is contingent on discipline (philosophy, psychology, or sociology). In general, the concept references the body via its interactive processes and relationships with the physical experience. This interdependency emphasises meaning-making activities through bodily experience, such as gaze, gesture, posture, expression and movement, which shapes interaction with the environment. The central gaze therefore turns to concepts such as the lived body, power, identity, position, signification and references to action and community.

Key theorists

While there is no unified social theory of embodiment, several key theorists have been influential in their rejection of dualism and centre the lived experience of the body, corporeality and embodiment as sites for research. In this section, several themes that have contributed to theorisation in LIS are identified.

The lived body: Merleau-Ponty

Merleau-Ponty (1962) rejected dualism and asserted that the mind and body were not discrete entities. This position challenged the Cartesian idea of *res extensa* (body as an extended thing) and established a phenomenological view of the body, embodiment and corporeality, which contributes to the ontological idea of the lived body as a locus of experience (Leder, 1991) and the self as integrated being. According to Merleau-Ponty, the body is both lived from within and an object of the external gaze. It has two sides – the sentient (it sees) and the sensible (it is seen), which Crossley (1995, 47) argues positions it in relation to the world. The concern of phenomenology is the essence of the thing and our perception of the world situates us through our bodies and affords opportunities to act and become. In early accounts of the lived body, Merleau-Ponty argued that all human perception is embodied and knowledge is rooted in experience that is always embodied (Lloyd, 2010a). Bodies therefore act as an experiential conduit through which we exist in the world, interacting with other body subjects and materials temporally and spatially (Crossley, 2001; Nettleton and Watson, 1998; Shilling, 2001; Wacquant, 2004; Howson and Inglis, 2001). This view of the lived body and experience challenges the notion of objectivity and rationality by advancing the idea that the body is situated in the world with the capacity to enable the interpretation of events to occur in multiple ways.

Bodies as inscribed by culture: Foucault, Goffman

The plasticity of the body and role of power constituted a major theme in the work of Foucault, who viewed the body (ontologically and epistemologically) as a discursive product constructed by social factors. According to Foucault, the body represents the inscribed surface of events:

> The body is the inscribed surface of events (traced by language and by ideas), the locus of a disassociated self (adopting the illusion of a substantial unity) and a volume in perpetual disintegration.
>
> (Foucault, 1984, 83)

In relation to power, Foucault asserted that:

> The body is . . . directly involved in a political field; power relations have an immediate hold upon it; they invest it, mark it, train it, torture it, force it to carry out tasks, to perform ceremonies, to emit signs . . . power is not exercised simply as an obligation or prohibition on those who 'do not have it'; it invests them, is transmitted by them and through them; it exerts pressure upon them, just as they themselves, in their struggle against it, resist the grip it has on them.
>
> (Foucault, 1977, 25)

The interest, for Foucault, rests on understanding how power becomes inscribed upon the body. The socially inscribed body, according to Foucault, references power relations of gender and cultural discourses. This view has led feminist authors such as Davies (2000, 55) to argue that the body is always spoken into existence within the terms of the available discourse. An epistemological view of the body is not without challenges and has led to claims of discursive reductionism, where the body is no longer present as 'lived experience' but disappears as a 'material and phenomenological entity' and its existence and experience vanishes behinds the grids of meaning that are imposed upon it by discourse (Butler, 1990, 195).

Goffman (1983) emphasises the body in social interaction, where it plays a central role in the generation of meaning, providing visual clues about roles, practices and activities that lead to the establishment of shared vocabularies and meanings that enable embodied knowing. In this respect, the way in which we handle the lived experiences of bodies in action and interaction is centrally important to self and identity. The body is therefore socially inscribed and central to the generation of meaning. This idea was taken up by O'Loughlin (1998, 279) as the communicative body as 'that for which gesture, body orientation and proximity are the vehicle through which meanings are expressed. Thinking is undeniably embodied.'

Bodies that matter: Butler

By asserting that bodies matter, Butler (1990, 8) critiques Foucault's discursive determinism, whereby the corporeal is 'inscribed on the surface of the event, traced by language and dissolved by ideas'. According to Butler, the Foucauldian representation of the body references an unagentic powerless body that is acted upon and subject to coercion and manipulation. In response, Butler (1993) introduces the concept of embodiment by arguing gendered identity is embodied action that 'does not exist outside its doings; rather its performance is also a reiteration of previous doings that become intelligible as gender norms' (Nayak and Kehily, 2006, 467). In effect, when we perform (in our professional or vocational life or in education at any level), we enact and do gender. The body according to Butler acts a medium where acts or desires are created on the surface of the body (Butler, 1990, 136), where they are read by others.

Bodies that practise: Schatzki, Reckwitz

The practising body is a present theme in practice theories, which acknowledge that the body both references and expresses the conditions of life, serving as both actor and medium. This theme is located in the work of Schatzki (1997; 2002; Reckwitz, 2002) and the epistemologically oriented work of Gherardi (discussed in a later section).

Working from a theoretical perspective, Schatzki (2002, 3) brings the body into play in practice theory and provides a context for the composition of the body by noting that practice is an 'embodied materially mediated array of human activity centrally organised around shared practices and understanding'. By Schatzki's account, bodies are always present and central to intelligibility, reference the conditions and struggles of life and bring the discourse and relationships of the social site into discursive visibility. It is through the performance of bodily actions that the performance of other actors in constituted or effected (Schatzki, 1997, 44). The body in this version of practice theory is located not only in the practical sense of 'doings' but also through the concept of 'general understandings' that establish a contextually nuanced ambience in relation to 'senses of the worth, value, nature, or place of things, which infuse and are expressed in people's doings and sayings' (Schatzki, 2012, 16).

Reckwitz's (2002, 250) view of practice situates bodies as a 'routinised way in which bodies are moved, objects are handled, subjects are treated, things described and the world is understood'. According to Reckwitz, practice theory views and positions bodies in a different way:

> Practices are routinized bodily activities; as interconnected complexes of behavioural acts they are movements of the body. A social practice is the product of training the body in a certain way: when we learn a practice, we learn to be bodies in a certain way (and this means more than to 'use our bodies'). A practice can be understood as the regular, skilful 'performance' of (human) bodies. This holds for modes of handling certain objects as well as for 'intellectual' activities such as talking, reading, or writing. The body is thus not a mere 'instrument' which 'the agent' must 'use' in order to 'act', but the routinized actions are themselves bodily performances (which does not mean that a practice consists only of these movements and of nothing more, of course). These bodily activities then include also routinized mental and emotional activities which are – on a certain level – bodily, as well.
>
> (Reckwitz, 2002, 251)

Body as an unfinished state: Shilling

Shilling's body of work posits that due to its participation in society, the body is always in an unfinished state and is therefore always in a state of becoming, leaving the possibility for identity to be in continual flux. Pointing to the relationship between technology and the body, Shilling (1993, 5) argues that the relationship between the two act to transform bodies and the more that knowledge and expertise are expanded then the more uncertain we become as to what the body is and what its boundaries are.

Theorising the body in library and information science

In LIS, there are currently no theories of corporeality or embodiment that are derived from an information perspective. However, a growing number of researchers working in the information practice area are interrogating the enactment of embodiment and the body as information source by drawing from philosophical, psychological and social theory literature to make claims about embodiment. Literature associated with this field has been reviewed by Lloyd (2006; 2017), Lloyd and Olsson (2019) and Cox (2018), which while identifying the potential areas for research also highlight that embodiment and the body as research object continue to remain an absent presence within this field. Research that is currently drawing from social theories of embodiment and the body includes Lloyd's research with firefighters (2006), ambulance officers (2009), nurses (Bonner and Lloyd, 2011), refugees (Lloyd, 2017) and, most recently, the COVID-19 pandemic (Lloyd and Hicks, 2021), Olsson's study of theatre professionals (2010) and Veinot's (2007) study of hydroelectric vault inspectors' embodied information practices. The role and relationship between information literacy and the embodied experiences of a sadomasochist and live action role play community (LARP) was explored by Harviainen (2015). This research led to the finding that actors in this specialised setting develop highly refined information literacy practices, thereby enabling a high-level skill that, in turn, ensures safety in practice. Embodiment, meaning-making and transgender experiences have recently been investigated by Huttunen and Kortelainen (2021). This was followed by Huttunen's (2022) doctoral work, which focused on embodied information and the experiences of transgender people in Finland. A study of the information practices of the Ballet Folklórico de México highlighted the role of sociocultural information that is displayed while dancing, something that supports novice learning and enables embodiment of both expert and novice through repeated enactment and interaction with ambient information (Vamanu and Terronez, 2022).

LIS researchers have also drawn upon a psychological perspective and the concept of embodied cognition in their work on information behaviour. Embodied cognition rejects the dualism of the mind/body split. In critiquing the tendency to generalise or minimise the role of the body in understanding information behaviour and information practice, Lueg (2014; 2020) attempts to bring the body and corporeal information into dialogue with LIS, which has traditionally relegated the body and corporeal information to a secondary site and source. The importance of corporeal information in ultra-marathon running and embodied cognition was identified by Gorichanaz (2018). Emotional and embodied needs and desires have been highlighted by Keilty and Leazer (2014), whose work recognises that the body remains secondary and largely absent in research that focuses on information need. Polkinghorne's (2021) doctoral research explored embodied information practices in everyday food activities, leading the author to propose embodied mutual constitution as a theoretical concept.

Theoretical questions

The concept of embodiment and inclusion of the body as source and site challenges the dualism established by earlier theorists and shifts the focus towards the interrelatedness of bodies' intra- and interaction qua society. The impact of this idea positions the body and bodily experiences centrally by drawing attention to action and interaction – our bodies in reflection and in relation to other bodies and materiality. Thus, making the body a site of knowledge and source of information from which we read the body and learn from it as it references lived experience (Merleau-Ponty, 1962). The interdependence between physical experiences, material practices, resources, practice and social spaces is pivoted around the body, which couples together the social and epistemic modalities (Lloyd, 2006). This view enables ontological, epistemological and methodological questions about information, knowledge and ways of knowing to be asked.

Information is viewed as 'any difference which makes a difference' (Bateson, 1972, 459) and to make sense, information must be referenced against the ontological and epistemological settings of the context in which people position and are positioned. Ontologically, against the knowledges that shape the setting and ways of knowing and epistemologically, in relation to interaction with others who are co-present and co-participating in the ongoing performances and the material objects of the setting (Lloyd, 2014, 87). It has been suggested by Barad (1996, 179) that knowledge is always a view from somewhere which suggests that bodies work at both ontological and epistemological levels and this has implications for understanding and researching how information literacy happens in practice.

Knowledge is grounded in an ontological belonging in terms of what is known and how it is known and what is possible to know (i.e. what is sanctioned and what ways of knowing are legitimised). Ontologically, the body represents a site of corporeal knowledge that reflects how actors understand the nature of the reality that connects them to truth claims of the social site and a shared semantic space of language. Ontology is tied to claims of truth about the nature of reality which means that, in terms of information literacy research, it is critical to acknowledge there are numerous ways of understanding how ontologies operate. The ontological space may reference anti-positivist/anti-foundational reality as it is subjectively and intersubjectively experienced. Alternatively, it may represent an objectivist/positivist ontology where reality is understood to exist independently. In this respect, engaging with the concept of embodiment and corporeality open us up to questions about how the body is situated and understood reflexively and reflectively as a source.

Embodiment is the enmeshment of the corporeal, emotional, sensory and sentiment dimensions of the lived experience. In relation to information literacy, embodiment operates ontologically by drawing attention to questions about the nature of knowledge as it emerges in the context of specific practices or communities. This opens us up to questions that explore the nature of information and knowledge such as what information/knowledge counts in this setting. Many theorists question what exactly the body is, arguing that the body represents a social construction and is, therefore, ontologically open to interpretation

(Nettleton, 2001). In this respect, the body operates ontologically by referencing the nature of being, becoming and reality, which are inscribed upon the body and become central to embodied performances associated with social and cultural values.

Epistemologically, we know the world through bodies that interact with circulating discourses and power relations that constitute and shape the social. The concept of embodiment operates epistemologically by drawing attention to questions of how we know and what is worth knowing. Gherardi (2009) links bodies via the practice/knowledge nexus. The body acts to capture and disseminate knowledge: 'knowledge is not an object captured by means of mental schemes; rather it is a practice and collective activity and is acquired not only through thought, but also through the body and sensory and aesthetic knowledge' (Gherardi, 2009, 354). The epistemological position opens information literacy research up to questions about the ways of knowing that are privileged, prioritised and operationalised within the setting at both subjective and intersubjective levels.

Methodologically, the theme of absence, which has predominated in the embodiment literature, has become an avenue of both ontological and epistemological enquiry and has led to questions about the importance of embodied knowledges to an understanding of the lived experience (Leder, 1992). Until we understand absence and make it part of our research agenda, we will continue to marginalise the information experience. This, in turn, has implications for understanding the myriad of cultural ways in which information literacy practice emerges for individuals and communities – and whom information literacy practice privileges when it is delivered in an educational setting. Acknowledging the ontological and epistemological dimensions of the lived experience enables researchers to make methodological choices that foreground new versions of information literacy practice.

Recognising the primary contribution of embodiment and the body in the lived experience allows researchers to move beyond the boundaries of a focus on textual practices, which prioritises structural considerations over agentic and experiential concerns, towards a remit that recognises that knowledge and information are not solely the privilege of the epistemic modality. Instead, they emerge through interactions, actions, reactions, doings and undoing that form part of the rich and complex experience of everyday life. Broadening the remit acknowledges that bodies matter as site and source of knowledge and information that may not be articulated but is, none the less, important to understanding how people develop ways of knowing that inform their information literacy practice. Embodiment also reminds us that information literacy practice is not generic but has spatial and temporal elements (i.e. it is contextual and situated and emerges over time).

Focusing on the ontological and epistemological dimensions enables researchers to deepen their understanding of the complex layering of knowledge and information in everyday life and the role that information literacy practice plays in (a) weaving the paths, nodes and edges (Lloyd, 2003) that constitute information landscapes and (b) the performance of the practice as it untangles complex information environments. The depth of this approach to untangling information literacy practice moves researchers closer to understanding the role that information and knowledge play in the shaping of identity and the role of inscription in shaping the bodies as they practise. Acknowledging corporeality and embodiment also leads to distinct theoretical questions about how the body operates ontologically and epistemologically as a site of knowledge and source of information. How is embodied knowledge developed over time and then operationalised internally and externally? How does this impact on learning and instructional practices?

Surfacing the body: doing body work in information literacy practice

To return to the questions posed at the beginning of this chapter – in what ways do theories of embodiment and of the body disrupt current discourses and practices about information literacy and help to shape a deeper understanding of the complexity of the practice? What happens when bodies are foregrounded as information site and source and brought into thinking about information literacy? What do we gain when we bring the body into view?

The theory of information literacy practice (ToIL), which was proposed in 2017 (Lloyd, 2017), operates both ontologically and epistemologically by foregrounding the influences of the social and corporeal upon information, knowledge and ways of knowing. The concept of embodiment is central to the theory of information literacy because it is through the body that information literacy is enacted as a practice inherent in the site of the social (Schatzki, 2002) connecting people to the social, epistemic/instrumental and corporeal dimensions that reference being in the world (Lloyd, 2021). The theory originated to disrupt dualist discourses in the information literacy field that privilege textual representation of knowledge and ways of knowing related to information literacy while absenting other forms – and to reorient researchers towards understanding the ontological and epistemological elements of the practice. To unpack the theory in relation to embodiment, information literacy is:

1. A practice that is enacted in a social setting. The practice is shaped by the sayings and doings of the setting that enable it to come into view physically through action and semantically through discourse and language about why things (practices, skills, activities) happen. The enactment of information literacy emerges as people in practice connect with embodied knowledges afforded to them by the setting via knowledges that are enculturated, encoded, embedded, emotional, sentient, or sensory (ontological view).
2. Composed of a suite of activities and skills that reference structured and embodied knowledges and ways of knowing relevant to context (an epistemological view). The operationalisation of information literacy is enacted by doing the practice of information literacy (e.g. accessing specific types of information, evaluating information according to the sanctioned pathways agreed by the community or by reflecting on action). Successful enactment of information literacy practice is dependent on access to embodied knowledges that reference the history and

trajectory of developing knowledge and expertise temporally and spatially.
3 The development of information literacy practice occurs when actors engage with information environments that shape their contexts, reflect and draw upon their embodied performances and the performances of other actors engaged in the same project. Drawing from the knowledges afforded by context coupled with sentient and sensory knowledges, actors construct their information landscapes by establishing the paths, nodes and edges of ways of knowing. The practice of information literacy is therefore the performance of emplacement.

The aim of the theory of information literacy is to disrupt the established reductionist documentary discourses of information literacy by surfacing the body and corporeality as a significant source of information and knowledge from lived experience that is required to make sense of people and materiality that constitute the world. A feature of this disruption is the recognition that sentient and sensory information/knowledge are intricately enmeshed with encoded, enculturated and embedded knowledges. Embodiment is therefore informational and bodies offer up critical, often unarticulated, or unexpressed, sources of information and knowledge that emerges only at the moment of practice (Bonner and Lloyd, 2011) to inform practice and practising and reveal the histories and trajectories that shape the lived experience.

Embodiment represents knowledge that is acquired by doing and by subjecting or being subject to experiences with knowledges (our own and others) derived from enculturation, encoding or embedded performance (Blackler, 1995). It is only ever partially explicit but references our tangible interactions with practices and performances over time and space. Embodiment is the enmeshment of the corporeal, emotional, sensory and sentiment dimensions of the lived experience. Upon this view embodiment is a construction and subject to the various discourses that construct, deconstruct, emplace and disrupt the body in-practice and as-it-practises.

When foregrounded in research, theories of the body and embodiment become central to a richer understanding of information literacy as a practice that is enacted in social setting and composed of activities and skills that enrich a 'way of knowing' (Lloyd, 2017). It is the corporeal modality that enables the coupling of the epistemic and social modality. Acknowledging the active presence and contribution of the body as site and source, Leder reflects:

> ... in a significant sense, the lived body helps to constitute this world as experienced. We cannot understand the meaning and form of objects without reference to bodily powers through which we engage them – our senses, motility, language, desires. The lived body is not just one thing in the world but a way in which the world comes to be.
>
> (Leder, 1992, 35)

Employing theories of embodiment as a lens from which to understand information literacy draws attention to the body and makes it and the knowledges, trajectories, histories and privileges inscribed upon it visible. In this respect, research into embodiment and corporeality draws attention to the inscription of power, of privilege and how access to information is often predicated on unequal ways of knowing (e.g. refugees, women, the information-poor, marginalised and disabled groups).

Ontologically, as site and source about the nature of reality as it is referenced, and epistemologically, the body acts as a source of performative knowledge. Acknowledging that embodied knowledge references tangible practices or actions over time and space but is only ever partially explicit (Blackler, 1995, 1024) alters us, methodologically, to consider ways to capture the enmeshment of the corporeal, emotional, sensory and sentient dimension of the lived experience. This acknowledgement alters the nature of information literacy research and widens the scope of situational research to include the intangible outcomes derived from tangible practices, performances or actions over time and space. Embodiment is, therefore, subject to the various discourses that construct, deconstruct, emplace and disrupt the body in the practice. Moreover, these theories broaden the boundaries of the information practices discourse 'by demonstrating that embodied practices, like linguistic ones, are products of social construction' (Olsson and Lloyd, 2017, para. 38), thus referencing the sociocultural discursive communities through which they are enacted.

Conclusion

Humans are their bodies and bodies are storehouses of knowledge and information that can be known inwardly and represented and referenced outwardly. Bodies are therefore important sites of knowledge and sources of information that must be surfaced when attempting to understand the complex social practice of information literacy.

However, the notion of the absent presence is reflected in the corporeal gap, which continues to exist while embodiment and corporeality are reduced to secondary knowledge and bodies remain largely invisible in the LIS field. Theories have the capacity to enrich our narratives about information literacy practice. Embodiment can act as a theoretical lens that alerts researchers to the complex ways in which the body acts spatially and temporally as an information source and site of knowledge. This, in turn, contributes to a deeper understanding of how and why information literacy happens and the contribution this practice makes to the construction and enactment of our everyday lived experience. An embodied approach does not detract from a centralising documentary discourse for the field. Instead, it acknowledges that by nature, the ubiquity of information places demands on the field which, in turn, create challenges to develop a broader understanding of social life and how its enactment is made visible.

References

Barad, K. (1996) *Meeting the Universe Halfway: quantum physics and the entanglement of matter and meaning*, Duke University Press, 39–70.

Bates, M. J. (2018) Concepts for the Study of Information Embodiment, *Library Trends*, 66 (3), 239–66.

Bateson, G. (1972) *Steps to an Ecology of Mind*, Jason Aronson Inc.

Berger, P. L. and Luckman, T. (1966) *The Social Construction of Reality: a treatise in the sociology of knowledge*, Anchor Books.

Blackler, F. (1995) Knowledge, Knowledge Work and Organizations: an overview and interpretation, *Organization Studies*, 16 (6), 1021–46.

Bonner, A. and Lloyd, A. (2011) What Information Counts at the Moment of Practice? Information practices of renal nurses, *Journal of Advanced Nursing*, 67, 1213–21.

Butler, J. (1990) *Gender Trouble*, Routledge.

Butler, J. (1993) *Bodies That Matter*, Routledge.

Cox, A. M. (2018) Embodied Knowledge and Sensory Information: theoretical roots and inspirations, *Library Trends*, 66 (3), 223–38.

Crossley, N. (1995) Merleau-Ponty, the Elusive Body and Carnal Sociology, *Body & Society*, 1 (1), 43–63.

Crossley, N. (2001) The Phenomenological Habitus and its Construction, *Theory and Society*, 1 (30), 81–120.

Davies, B. (2000) *A Body of Writing, 1990–1999*, Rowman & Littlefield.

Descartes, R. (1634) *Discourse on the Method and the Mediations*, (trans. F. E. Sutcliffe), 1974, Penguin.

Durkheim, E. (1938) *The Rules of Sociological Method*, Macmillan.

Foucault, M. (1977) *Discipline and Punishment*, (trans. Alan Sheridan), 1995, Vintage Books.

Foucault, M. (1984) Nietzsche, Genealogy, History. In Rabinow, P. (ed.) *The Foucault Reader*, Pantheon Books.

Gherardi, S. (2008) Situated Knowledge and Situated Action: what do practice-based studies promise? In Barry, D. and Hansen, H. (eds) *The Sage Handbook of New Approaches in Management and Organization*, Sage, 516–27.

Gherardi, S. (2009) Knowing and Learning in Practice-Based Studies: an introduction, *The Learning Organisation*, 16 (5), 352–9.

Giddens, A. (1986) *The Constitution of Society: outline of the theory of structuration*, Polity Press.

Goffman, E. (1983) The Interaction Orders, *American Sociological Review*, 48, 1–17.

Gorichanaz, T. (2018) Understanding and Information Constellations in Ultrarunning, *Library Trends*, 66 (3), 329–50.

Habermas, J. (1987) *The Theory of Communicative Action: lifeworld and system: a critique of functionalist reason*, Vol. 2, Beacon Press.

Hartel, J. (2018) The Case against Information and the Body in Library and Information Science, *Library Trends*, 66 (4), 585–8.

Harviainen, J. T. (2015) Information Literacies of Self-Identified Sadomasochists: an ethnographic case study, *Journal of Documentation*, 71 (3), 423–39.

Howson, A. and Inglis, D. (2001) The Body in Sociology: tensions inside and outside sociological thought, *Sociological Review*, 49 (3), 297–317.

Huttunen, A. (2022) *Friction and Bodily Discomfort: transgender experiences of embodied knowledge and information practices*, doctoral thesis, University of Oulu, Finland.

Huttunen, A. and Kortelainen, T. A. (2021) Meaning-making on Gender: deeply meaningful information in a significant life change among transgender people, *Journal of the Association of Information Science and Technology*, 72 (7), 799–810.

Kant, I. (1785) *Groundwork on the Metaphysics of Morals*, 1964 edn, Harper & Row.

Keilty, P. and Leazer, G. (2014) What Porn Says to Information Studies: the affective value of documents and the body in information behavior, *Proceedings of the American Society for Information Science and Technology*, 51 (1), 1–11.

Leder, D. (1991) *The Absent Body*, University of Chicago Press.

Leder, D. (1992) Introduction. In Leder, D. (ed.) *The Body in Medical Thought and Practice*, Kluwer Academic.

Lindh, K. (2015) *Breathing Life into a Standard: the configuration of resuscitation in practices of informing*, doctoral thesis (monograph), Division of ALM and Digital Cultures.

Lloyd, A. (2003) Information Literacy: the meta-competency of the knowledge economy? An exploratory paper, *Journal of Librarianship and Information Science*, 35 (2), 87–92.

Lloyd, A. (2006) Information Literacy Landscapes: an emerging picture, *Journal of Documentation*, 62 (5), 570–83.

Lloyd, A. (2007a) Learning to Put out the Red Stuff: becoming information literate through discursive practice, *Library Quarterly*, 77 (2), 181–98.

Lloyd, A. (2007b) Recasting Information Literacy as Sociocultural Practice: implications for library and information science researchers, *Information Research*, 12 (4).

Lloyd, A. (2009) Informing Practice: information experiences of ambulance officers in training and on-road practice, *Journal of Documentation*, 65 (3), 396–419.

Lloyd, A. (2010a) Corporeality and Practice Theory: exploring emerging research agendas for information literacy, *Information Research*, 15 (3).

Lloyd, A. (2010b) Framing Information Literacy as Information Practice: site ontology and practice theory, *Journal of Documentation*, 66 (2), 245–58.

Lloyd, A. (2010c) Lessons from the Workplace: Understanding Information Literacy as Practice. In Lloyd, A. and Talja, S. (eds) *Practising Information Literacy: bringing theories of learning, practice and information literacy together*, Centre for Information Studies, 29–49.

Lloyd, A. (2011) Trapped between a Rock and a Hard Place: what counts as information literacy in the workplace and how is it conceptualized?, *Library Trends*, 60 (2), 277–96.

Lloyd, A. (2014) Informed Bodies: does the corporeal experience matter to information literacy practice? In Bruce, C., Davis, K., Hughes, H., Partridge, H. and Stoodley, I. (eds) *Information Experience: approaches to theory and practice*, Emerald, 85–99.

Lloyd, A. (2017) Information Literacy and Literacies of Information: a mid-range theory and model, *Journal of Information Literacy*, 11 (1), 95–105.

Lloyd, A. (2021) *The Qualitative Landscape of Information Literacy Research: perspectives, methods and techniques*, Facet Publishing.

Lloyd, A. and Hicks, A. (2021) Contextualising Risk: the unfolding information work and practices of people during the COVID-19 pandemic, *Journal of Documentation*, 77 (5), 1052–72.

Lloyd, A. and Olsson, M. (2019) Untangling the Knot: the information practices of enthusiast car restorers, *Journal of the Association for Information Science and Technology*, 70 (12), 1311–23.

Lueg, C. (2014) Characterisations of Human Perception and their Relevance When Studying Information Behaviour, *Journal of Documentation*, 70 (4), 562–74.

Lueg, C. P. (2015) The Missing Link: information behavior research and its estranged relationship with embodiment, Journal of the Association for Information Science and Technology, 66 (12), 2704–7.

Lueg, C. (2020) To Be or Not To Be (Embodied): that is not the question, *Journal of the Association for Information Science and Technology*, 71 (1), 114–17.

Merleau-Ponty, M. (1962) *Phenomenology of Perception*, Routledge & Kegan Paul.

Nayak, A. and Kehily, M. J. (2006) Gender Undone: subversion, regulation, and embodiment in the work of Judith Butler, *British Journal of Sociology of Education*, 27 (4), 459–72.

Nettleton, S. (2001) The Sociology of the Body. In Cockerham, W. (ed.) *The New Blackwell Companion to Medical Sociology*, 43–63.

Nettleton, S. and Watson, J. (1998) (eds) *The Body in Everyday Life*, Psychology Press.

O'Loughlin, M. (1998) Paying Attention to Bodies in Education: theoretical resources and practical suggestions, *Educational Philosophy and Theory*, 30 (3), 275–97.

Olsson, M. R. (2010) All the World's a Stage – the information practices and sense-making of theatre professionals, *Libri*, 60 (3), 241–52.

Olsson, M. R. and Lloyd, A. (2017) Losing the Art and Craft of Know-How: capturing vanishing embodied knowledge in the 21st century, *Information Research*, 22 (4).

O'Neill, J. (1985) *Five Bodies: the human shape of modern society*, Cornell University Press.

Parsons, T. (1937) *The Structure of Social Action*, Free Press.

Pilerot, O. and Maurin Söderholm, H. (2019) A conceptual framework for investigating documentary practices in prehospital emergency care. In Proceedings of the Tenth International Conference on Conceptions of Library and Information Science, Ljubljana, Slovenia, June 16–19, *Information Research*, 24 (4), paper colis1931, http://InformationR.net/ir/24-4/colis/colis1931.html [(Archived by the Internet Archive at https://web.archive.org/web/20191217180352/http://informationr.net/ir/24 4/colis/colis1931.html].

Polkinghorne, S. (2021) *Exploring Everyday Information Practices: embodied mutual constitution of people's complex relationship with food*, doctoral thesis, Swinburne University, Melbourne.

Reckwitz, A. (2002) Toward a Theory of Social Practices: a development in culturalist theorizing, *European Journal of Social Theory*, 5 (2), 243–63.

Schatzki, T. (1997) Practices and Actions: a Wittgensteinian critique of Bourdieu and Giddens, *Philosophy of the Social Sciences*, 27 (3), 283–308.

Schatzki, T. R. (2002) *The Site of the Social: a philosophical account of the constitution of social life and change*, Pennsylvania State University Press.

Schatzki, T. (2012) A Primer on Practices: theory and research. In Higgs, J., Barnett, R., Billett, S., Hutchings, M. and Trede, F. (eds) *Practice-Based Education: perspectives and strategies*, Springer, 13–26.

Shilling, C. (1993) *The Body and Social Theory*, Sage.

Shilling, C. (2001) Embodiment, Experience and Theory: in defence of the sociological tradition, *Sociological Review*, 49 (3), 327–44.

Shilling, C. (2009) The Embodied Foundations of Social Theory. In Ritzer, G. and Smart, B. (eds) *The Embodied Foundations of Social Theory*, Sage, 439–57.

Shilling, C. (2021) Embodiment. In *The Cambridge Handbook of Social Theory*, Cambridge University Press, 249–71.

Vamanu, I. and Terronez, M. (2022) Our Ancestors Passed This Down to Us for a Reason: information practices of Ballet Folklórico dancers in Mexican American communities, *Journal of Documentation*, 78 (6), 1213–27.

Veinot, T. C. (2007) The Eyes of the Power Company: workplace information practices of a vault inspector, *Library Quarterly*, 77 (2), 157–79.

Wacquant, L. (2004) *Body and Soul*, University of Chicago Press.

Weber, M. (1968) *Economics and Society*, University of California Press.

11
Variation Theory: Researching Information Literacy Through the Lens of Learning

Clarence Maybee

Introduction

The variation theory of learning is a theoretical framework that can guide information literacy research. The value of variation theory to information literacy research is that it can shed light on information literacy specifically in relationship to learning through the identification of patterns of variation that may enable learners to learn as intended. Developed from an educational research agenda (Marton and Booth, 1997; Marton, Hounsell and Entwistle, 1997; Marton and Tsui, 2004), variation theory is well suited to the study of information literacy in formal learning contexts. Grounded in the belief that reality is created through interaction between individuals and the world (Marton and Booth, 1997, 12–13) and that knowledge is awareness of phenomena created through such interactions (Marton, 1994), learning is defined as changes in awareness enabled by encountering variations or differences (Marton, 2014; Marton and Tsui, 2004). The theory focuses on specific parts of the learning process, including intentions for learning, how it is enacted in a classroom or other learning situations and the learners' lived experiences of learning. Variation theory allows for exploring the relationship between information literacy and learning in various ways, such as focusing on it as the sole outcome of a learning situation, or as a part of learning in a disciplinary learning context. Recognising that learning occurs in a myriad of contexts, variation theory may be adaptable to the study of information literacy outside educational settings, including playing a role in addressing information-focused challenges, such as misinformation, equitable access to information and so forth, facing the world today.

Variation theory
Origins
Variation theory guides research and practice that examines learning environments to reveal what students have learned, but also what was possible for them to learn within a

learning situation. The development of variation theory was directly informed by the research findings from studies applying the phenomenographic approach developed in the 1970s by Ference Marton and colleagues at the University of Gothenburg in Sweden. While there are different approaches to phenomenography, they all focus on identifying variations in human experience of the same phenomenon (Marton, 1981). This type of phenomenographic research was primarily developed to explore and describe learners' experiences in educational settings (Marton, Hounsell and Entwistle, 1997) The typical outcome from this kind of phenomenographic research, called an outcome space, is a set of categories that describe the varied ways of experiencing the phenomenon being studied. This type of research, which can be called the first branch of phenomenography, has been used to study information literacy. This research included the seminal study by Christine Bruce (1997) that introduced the seven faces model describing seven ways that university staff may experience information literacy:

1 information awareness
2 information sources
3 information process
4 information control
5 knowledge construction
6 knowledge extension
7 wisdom.

Focused on developing a research approach to identify students' experiences of the concepts being learned about in courses, phenomenographers were less concerned with metaphysical ideas (Svensson, 1997). However, over time phenomenographers have described the ontological and epistemological bases of phenomenography. While there is debate regarding the nature of the relationship, phenomenography is clearly influenced by the writings of phenomenologists, such as Martin Heidegger (1962), Merleau-Ponty (1962) and Husserl (1980) (see also Chapter 12 in this volume by Budd). Phenomenography maintains that experience is 'constituted as an internal relation between' a person and the world (Marton and Booth, 1997, 13). Because of this, phenomenography is referred to as *relationalist* or *constitutionalist* (Marton and Neuman, 1989).

Marton described the research aims of the first branch of phenomenography as finding and systematising the 'forms of thought in terms of which people interpret aspects of reality' (Marton, 1981, 180). Phenomenography is part of a group of differentiation theories that suggest that the way the world is constituted may vary between people (Marton, 2014, 55). Phenomenography adopts a second-order approach that aims to investigate phenomena through the first-hand experiences of research participants, not through the lens of the researcher (Marton, 1986). Phenomenographers maintain that there are a limited number of qualitatively different ways in which people may experience any phenomenon (Marton, 1994), which is supported by a substantial number of phenomenographic studies conducted since the 1980s (Marton and Pang, 1999). Reflecting what they learned from their research in the preceding two decades, Marton and his colleagues developed variation theory, which describes how encounters with variations may enable changes in awareness (Marton, 2014; Marton and Tsui, 2004). The move from methodological to theoretical concerns marked an important shift for the phenomenographic community (Marton and Pang, 1999).

Characteristics of the theory

The foundations of variation theory were introduced in the late 1990s (Marton and Booth, 1997) and expanded on over the next few years in two additional books (Marton and Morris, 2002; Marton and Tsui, 2004). Providing new insights from a decade of working with it, Marton (2014) refined variation theory in *Necessary Conditions for Learning*. Starting with the belief that there is no separation between a person and the world, the same ontological and epistemological perspectives that frame phenomenography underpin variation theory. While it is possible to frame such research through the lens of the researcher (Åkerlind, 2018), research guided by variation theory can also adopt a second-order approach that aims to reveal participants' first-hand experiences rather than those of the researcher. Following the idea that knowing is constituted as being aware of a phenomenon, then learning is facilitated by a change in awareness (Marton, 2014; Marton and Tsui, 2004). Learning is the discernment of varying ways of experiencing the phenomenon. To be more specific, it is not necessarily an entire phenomenon that is focused on in a learning situation. Instead, the emphasis is on an object of learning, which is comprised specifically of the parts of a phenomenon about which students are to learn.

An object of learning is comprised of aspects and features related to the phenomenon under study (Marton and Tsui, 2004). An aspect is a more general element of the object, while a feature is a specific type of aspect. For example, 'colour' is an aspect of a vehicle, but 'blue' is a feature of a blue vehicle. While an object of learning may be made up of several, only a subset of aspects and features are key for learners to discern. (To avoid confusion with approaches to information literacy underpinned by critical pedagogy discussed later in the chapter, the term 'key' will be used in place of the term 'critical', which is typically used by phenomenographers to describe the aspects and features that are necessary for learners to become aware.) The specific ways that key aspects and features need to be varied to enable learning is called a pattern of variation. The ways in which a teacher varies a topic through classroom interaction influences what the students may learn about the topic (Marton and Morris, 2002, 133).

Marton (2014) identified three types of variations. *Contrast* is when an aspect or feature is compared with something else. For example, the feature of peer review may be compared to another review process, such as editorial review. *Generalisation* occurs when two instances of an aspect or feature encountered at different points in time are experienced at the same time. A key feature of scholarly journal articles may be the 'genre' of the 'journal'. Students might be asked to identify instances when they have encountered this genre, such as magazines or trade publications. *Fusion* is a type of variation that happens when key aspects and features are focused on at the same time, such as when the feature of peer review and the feature of journal are focused on simultaneously to enable learners to develop an understanding of the concept of peer-reviewed journal.

An object of learning is comprised of three interrelated parts:

1 *intended* object reflecting the teacher's intent for the learning
2 *enacted* object illustrating the co-constructed learning by the teacher and the learners
3 *lived* object that describes learners' experiences or understandings after participation in the enacted object of learning (Marton, 2014; Marton and Tsui, 2004).

The intended object defines the variations (that is contrast, generalisation, or fusion) of which the teacher wants students to become aware. The enacted object is the variations that students were exposed to during a learning experience, such as a classroom lesson, group project or so forth. The lived object reflects the variations of which the learners became aware. A comparison of the three parts of an object of learning may reveal the alignment between intended variations and those highlighted during enactment, which can be used to explain differences between a teacher's intentions and students' learning.

Applications in research

Variation theory began being used around the turn of the 21st century to guide a new type of research, which has become a branch of phenomenography (Rovio-Johansson, 1999; Runesson, 1999). This research goes beyond identifying how students conceptualise phenomena to illuminate what students have learned, but also what it is possible to learn within a specific learning situation. This kind of research became possible because variation theory can explain learning. The power of variation theory in revealing how learning may occur is demonstrated in a study by Vikström (2008), who researched seven-to-twelve-year-old children's different ways of understanding cellular respiration and photosynthesis after being exposed to these concepts in classroom lessons. Six secondary school teachers worked with the researcher to identify the intended object of learning and then each taught a lesson to different groups of students. While the lesson plan outlined the intended object of learning, the examination of videotaped classroom lessons revealed the enacted object of learning and interviews with select students revealed the lived object of learning.

In Vikström's research, the students' understandings of cellular respiration and photosynthesis were closely related to their teacher's presentation of the concepts. While in one classroom the students were not able to discern the function of sugar and oxygen within the plant, in another the students were aware that sugar is used as a building material, but the function of oxygen was still unclear. Suggesting that students' maturity was not a factor in the outcome, the classroom with the youngest students was the only one in which the students expressed a complex understanding of cellular respiration and photosynthesis that aligned with the group of teachers' intentions.

While a phenomenographic study that is guided by variation theory aims to uncover information about an object of learning, variation theory may also be used to create teaching interventions and study the outcomes of these interventions. This research draws from an approach called 'lesson studies', in which groups of teachers collaboratively design a lesson to address difficult material and then observe it being implemented (Lewis, 2000, 2). Referred to as 'learning study', phenomenographic researchers adopted a similar approach using variation theory to frame their methods (Davies and Dunhill, 2008). Teachers are introduced to types of variation and use their own experiences of teaching and learning to determine key aspects and features of the object of learning to design lessons that enable variations necessary for the intended learning to occur (Pang, Linder and Fraser, 2006). Based on the students' awareness of the key aspects and features, the lessons are revised until the students learn as intended.

Whether conducting a phenomenographic study guided by variation theory or a learning study, the object of learning is the research object. When concepts related to information literacy are the object of learning, they may be studied and illuminated using variation theory. However, as discussed in the following section, variation theory's view of learning may also provide us with insights into the relation between information literacy and learning about other subjects.

Variation theory and information literacy
Studying the relationship between information literacy and learning

The primary intersection of variation theory and information literacy is that both are concerned with learning. Information literacy research that is grounded in variation theory has a different focus and outcome from studies that examine information literacy from other perspectives, such as those exploring it as part of a practice (Lloyd, 2010; 2012; also see Chapter 2 by Lloyd in this volume), or its role in navigating or disrupting hegemonic structures (Tewell, 2015; Whitworth, 2014b; also see Chapter 7 by Johansson). In research that is guided by variation theory, the object of research is an object of learning, which is comprised of intentions for learning, an enactment of learning and lived experiences of learning (Marton, 2014; Marton and Tsui, 2004). The outcome of such research is new understandings about how learning is experienced and how it may occur. Applying variation theory in information literacy research suggests that the researcher is interested in how information literacy may be learned or how it relates to learning more generally.

Variation theory research aims to identify a pattern of variation that can be replicated to enable new learners to experience variations necessary to learn as intended. When applied to information literacy research, the application of a phenomenographic approach guided by variation theory reveals how an object of learning related to information literacy may be experienced. Studying information literacy in this way requires recognising that reality is created through interaction between individuals and the world (Marton and Booth, 1997, 12–13) *and* that knowing is awareness of the phenomena created through these interactions (Marton, 1994). In line with earlier phenomenographic methods

(Marton, 1986), a second-order perspective that places participant voice to the forefront may be adopted in the study of information literacy guided by variation theory. Thus, the voices of those experiencing information literacy, be they students, teachers, information professionals and others, would be brought to the fore through such research. Applying variation theory to information literacy research requires an acknowledgement that individuals or groups of people may experience information literacy in various ways. The premise that information literacy is experienced differently by distinct people demands research that uncovers these differences.

Phenomenographic research would tend not to frame a study using a specific information literacy model, such as the Association of College & Research Libraries' (2015) *Framework for Information Literacy for Higher Education* or the Society of College, National and University Libraries' (2011) *Seven Pillars of Information Literacy*, because doing so could limit understanding of participants' experiences to elements that aligned with the chosen framework. By not limiting the investigation based on existing frameworks, the continued study of it using phenomenography can uncover changes in how information literacy is being experienced over time.

Research aligned with the first branch of phenomenography has shown that educators (Bruce, 1997; Webber, Boon and Johnston, 2005; Williams and Wavell, 2007) as well as students (Edwards, 2006; Lupton, 2008; Maybee, 2007; Parker, 2006) experience information literacy in a variety of ways. For example, information literacy experiences may focus on things such as finding information, critical thinking or building a knowledge base. A comparison of findings from these studies suggest that educators and students' experiences of information literacy may be seen as either focusing on using information (such as assessing, evaluating, analysing) or as an outcome that results from the use of information (such as constructing knowledge, developing a critical awareness) (Maybee, 2015). Lupton's (2008) research found three ways that students experienced information literacy in relationship to learning:

1 linearly (students learned techniques and then later applied them)
2 cyclically (students applied techniques and then later learned from the generated information)
3 simultaneously (students considered using information and learning about the subject one and the same).

The idea of a simultaneous focus on using information and learning is a central tenet of the informed learning model developed by Bruce (2008). Informed learning is an approach to information literacy that is focused on using information in disciplinary learning environments. Bruce suggests that 'information and information use could be regarded as mediators between learning intent and learning outcomes' and that '[b]eing aware of the role of information and its uses becomes an avenue for improving learning' (Bruce, 2008,

15). Providing a framework for information literacy education, informed learning is guided by three principles:

1. build on learners' previous experiences of using information to learn
2. emphasise learning to use information and disciplinary content simultaneously
3. foster new awareness of both using information and disciplinary content (Bruce and Hughes, 2010).

Grounded in the relational perspective that also underpins variation theory, informed learning emphasises the variations in how individuals or groups may experience the use of information while learning about a subject. As such, it can be used to frame information literacy in phenomenographic studies guided by variation theory (for example see Maybee et al., 2017).

Information literacy may be related to learning in various ways. Some aspects of information literacy could be an object of learning that is not related to any other learning. By contrast, as outlined by informed learning, with its simultaneous focus on using information and learning (Bruce, 2008), an object of learning could contain aspects of information literacy that were part of the learning intended to occur within a broader disciplinary learning experience. For example, learners might need to learn to engage with biological information in a particular way to understand how biologists frame biological research questions. A researcher could be interested only in how the learners engaged with the biology literature, or they may also be interested in how that engagement with the literature informed the learners' understanding of how biologists frame biological research questions. A researcher studying information literacy using a phenomenographic approach guided by variation theory would need to determine how their construction of information literacy informs the object of learning that is the object of research.

Variation theory describes learning as comprised of an act, which might include memorising, interpreting and such, that is directed towards a subject, such as formulas, concepts and so forth (Marton and Tsui, 2004). While it may seem counter-intuitive if thinking of it as its own distinct activity, information use may also be considered the 'act' part of learning. Locke (2009) and Lupton (2008) each mapped the act and the subject that emerged from their analysis of student experiences of information literacy as they studied three different academic subjects: education, music and tax law. The outcome of their research revealed that across and within the different subjects, students experienced various ways of using information (act of learning) that was directed towards different types of subject-focused learning. In Locke's study (2009) of students in an education course, one experience involved using information to conduct research (act) to create new disciplinary knowledge (subject), while another experience focused on using information responsibly (act) to understand the concept of community (subject).

An object of learning is comprised of key aspects and features that may be varied by being contrasted, generalised, or fused (Marton, 2014). Studying an object of learning using a phenomenographic approach guided by variation theory in which information literacy is the act of learning would require identifying the key aspects and features related to both using information (act) and the content (subject). For example, my doctoral study focused on a university writing course in which the teacher wanted her students to write papers that described a language and gender topic as the culmination of research that evolved over time (Maybee, 2015; Maybee et al., 2017). She wanted the students to understand the language and gender topic in a new way resulting from tracking the topic's development of one research study building upon another to bring new insights to light. There were three key aspects and features of which the students needed to become aware so that their lived experiences aligned with the intended experience of the teacher. Associated with information literacy, the students needed to become aware of the concept of a *sequence of research* (act). They also needed to become aware of a *thesis statement* (subject) and the idea of a *claim* (subject). These three features and aspects were first separated so that the students could become aware of them individually. Then they were fused, so that all three could be experienced simultaneously. When experienced simultaneously, the students were intended to experience them as one, that is: a thesis statement that made a claim based on a sequence of research.

Framing the object of learning in a study guided by variation theory as 'information use', such as assessing, evaluating or analysing information, would only enable the research to reveal the intended, enacted and lived experiences related to that specific information use. Such a study would be unlikely to reveal new knowledge related to learning about a subject that may have been occurring during the same learning experience, as it was not designed to uncover it. To understand how information literacy relates to the learning of other things (such as disciplinary facts, theories, concepts and so forth), the object of learning must entail aspects and features related to both information use and learning associated with the purpose of using that information. A likely outcome of such research would be that some learners would be focused solely on information use, while others would be focused on subject-related learning. However, we cannot know how information literacy may be related to subject-focused learning in a specific context unless we scope our research to specifically explore this relationship. To understand how information literacy relates to learning, applying the theoretical guideposts and methodological tools provided by variation theory is useful.

New pathways for studying information literacy

Phenomenography, including the branch that frames an object of research using variation theory, provides a purposeful lens through which to examine information literacy. A strength of variation theory is that it enables us to examine information literacy as it relates to learning. Yet, as with any theory, the application of variation theory limits what can be understood through research. Variation theory grew out of phenomenographic research that focused on understanding the varied experiences of students in different formal learning environments (Marton, Hounsell and Entwistle, 1997). The theory frames an object of learning as comprised of three parts: (a) intended, (b) enacted and (c) lived. Therefore, variation theory lends itself to the study of learning in classroom settings where a teacher sets intentions that are followed by an enactment of learning through lessons that result in students' lived experiences of learning (Marton and Tsui, 2004). In contrast to its utility in formal learning environments, variation theory is ill-suited to the examination of social or societal structures or systems. In part, this results from phenomenographic research that is guided by variation theory being focused on identifying the experiences of a member of a group or groups of people. The groups examined through such studies are frequently comprised of the students in the same classroom in a school or university. Exploring information literacy outside educational settings requires considering the implications of applying variation theory to other units of analysis.

Future development of variation theory should focus on the adaption of the theory to study information literacy as an object of learning in other contexts where learning occurs. Such development is necessary for variation theory to support the study of information literacy as it relates to compelling information-focused challenges facing the world today, such as the dissemination of disinformation and misinformation, the equitable distribution of information and so forth. Of course, undertaking such development requires (a) framing the contexts under investigation at sites where learning occurs and (b) acknowledging that there is value in uncovering the various ways that individuals or groups experience information literacy within these learning contexts. Applying a phenomenographic approach guided by variation theory to study information literacy can only take place when changes in awareness indicating that learning has occurred are observable. The intended object of learning must be identifiable, which in many settings may require a broader understanding of intent. For example, studying information literacy in a social media environment would necessitate identifying changes in awareness (lived object of learning) resulting from engagement with social media posts, but also require identifying the intentions for learning of the person or entity making those posts. It is certainly possible to conceive how variation theory could be used to shed light on a myriad of learning interactions that occur outside formal educational settings.

It has been suggested that the phenomenographic research could be adapted to take on a critical perspective (Whitworth, 2014a). While this was referring to the first branch of phenomenography, it is worth considering the possibility of applying a critical lens to the phenomenographic approach guided by variation theory. This could occur in one of two ways. First, variation theory may be applied to help understand students' experiences in learning situations where the intended object of learning focuses on learning critical concepts, such as structural racism or queer theory. In an information literacy context, variation theory may inform teaching that enables learners to build on their current experiences to become aware of aspects and features of information literacy that are grounded in critical perspectives. Second, data collected from a phenomenographic study could regularly be examined from a critical perspective to identify power dynamics within and across different experiences of an information literacy-related object of learning. Given the emphasis on revealing the first-hand experiences of those involved in a learning situation (Marton and Tsui, 2004), applying a critical framing to the analysis could be viewed as contrary to the principles of phenomenographic research. However, as with any learning theory, variation theory makes assumptions (based on earlier phenomenographic research findings) about the nature of learning. As suggested by Whitworth (2014a), one may also view power dynamics as a constant element of any information literacy-related object of learning and therefore, researchers could look to uncover it in the analysis of learning situations.

Another line of inquiry for phenomenographic research guided by variation theory is the influence that information literacy may have on the learning of disciplinary knowledge. This was foreshadowed in a phenomenographic study that occurred prior to the creation of variation theory, which found that high school students' experiences of using information were intricately linked to how they experienced the subject they were studying (Limberg, 1999; 2000). The study focused on the students' varied experiences of information seeking as well as their experiences of the topic they investigated when completing an essay. The findings suggested that the students' understandings of the subject content influenced how they searched for information. It also suggested that their prior experiences of information seeking influenced both their approach to searching as well as what they learned about the content.

A similar finding to Limberg's (1999) recognition of the connection between information seeking and subject learning emerged from my dissertation research (Maybee, 2015; Maybee et al., 2017). This research used variation theory to investigate information literacy in a higher education classroom. In this study, the intended object of learning detailed specific ways that students needed to learn to use information. To experience the object of learning in the way the teacher desired, it was necessary for the students to become aware of how a language and gender topic could be seen as having developed over time as new research built on previous findings. The essay they wrote needed to reflect an understanding of how the topic they chose to explore could be understood as the current instantiation of the topic based on its evolution through research. Having them explore the scholarly literature on a language and gender topic to trace how the related research evolved over time resulted in the students coming to understand the language and gender topic in a new way. The findings suggest that the very specific way the students used information shaped their understanding of the topic they investigated. Whether in the classroom or beyond, the potential of using a phenomenographic approach guided by variation theory to study information literacy is in intentionally examining the relationship between information literacy and learning.

Conclusion

The variation theory of learning provides a useful lens through which to investigate information literacy. Variation theory guides research that aims to understand how people learn to use information, but it also enables us to see the connection between information literacy and learning about a subject. Whenever learning is occurring through engagement with information, variation theory offers us an appropriate theoretical lens and methodological tools with which to investigate that occurrence. Nevertheless, there is room for further exploration into how the theory can support evolving interests of the information literacy research community. Building on findings such as Limberg's (1999) and Maybee (2015), there is great promise in new research that explores the influence of specific ways of using information on what can be learned. The ability of variation theory to enable us to understand the relationship between information literacy and learning allows for research of interest to many fields concerned with what fosters and influences learning.

References

Association of College & Research Libraries (2015) *Framework for Information Literacy for Higher Education*, www.ala.org/acrl/standards/ilframework.

Åkerlind, G. S. (2018) What Future for Phenomenographic Research? On continuity and development in the phenomenography and variation theory research tradition, *Scandinavian Journal of Educational Research*, 62, 949–58.

Bruce, C. S. (1997) *The Seven Faces of Information Literacy*, Auslib Press.

Bruce, C. S. (2008) *Informed Learning*, American Library Association.

Bruce, C. S. and Hughes, H. (2010) Informed Learning: a pedagogical construct for information literacy, *Library and Information Science Research*, 32, A2–A8.

Davies, P. and Dunhill, R. (2008) 'Learning Study' as a Model of Collaborative Practice in Initial Teacher Education, *Journal of Education for Teaching*, 24, 3–16.

Edwards, S. L. (2006) *Panning for Gold: information literacy and the net lenses model*, Auslib Press.

Heidegger, M. (1962) *Being and Time*, SCM Press.

Husserl, E. (1980) *Phenomenology and the Foundations of the Sciences: third book, ideas pertaining to a pure phenomenology and to a phenomenological philosophy*, Martinus Nijhoff Publishers.

Lewis, C. (2000) Lesson Study: the core of Japanese professional development, Invited address, Special Interest Group on Research in Mathematics Education, American Educational Research Association Meetings, New Orleans.

Limberg, L. (1999) Experiencing Information Seeking and Learning: a study of the interaction between two phenomena, *Information Research*, 5, http://informationr.net/ir/5-1/paper68.html.

Limberg, L. (2000) Is There a Relationship Between Information Seeking and Learning Outcomes? In Bruce, C. S., Candy, P. C. and Klaus, H. (eds) *Information Literacy Around the World: advances in programs and research*, Centre for Information Studies, Charles Sturt University.

Lloyd, A. (2010) *Information Literacy Landscapes: information literacy in education, workplace and everyday contexts*, Chandos.

Lloyd, A. (2012) Information Literacy as a Socially Enacted Practice: sensitising themes for an emerging perspective of people-in-practice, *Journal of Documentation*, 68, 772–83.

Locke, R. A. (2009) Learning Information Literacy: qualitatively different ways education students learn to find and use information, Master's thesis, Griffith University.

Lupton, M. (2008) *Information Literacy and Learning*, Auslib Press.

Marton, F. (1981) Phenomenography: describing conceptions of the world around us, *Instructional Science*, 10, 177–200.

Marton, F. (1986) Phenomenography: a research approach to investigating different understandings of reality, *Journal of Thought*, 21, 28–49.

Marton, F. (1994) Phenomenography. In Husén, T. and Postlethwaite, T. N. (eds) *International Encyclopedia of Education*, Pergamon, 4424–29.

Marton, F. (2014) *Necessary Conditions for Learning*, Routledge.

Marton, F. and Booth, S. (1997) *Learning and Awareness*, Lawrence Erlbaum.

Marton, F., Hounsell, D. and Entwistle, N. J. (1997) *The Experience of Learning: implications for teaching and studying in higher education*, 2nd edn, Scottish Academic Press.

Marton, F. and Morris, P. (eds) (2002) *What Matters? Discovering critical conditions of classroom learning*, Acta Universitatis Gothoburgensis.

Marton, F. and Neuman, D. (1989) Constructivism and Constitutionalism: some implications for elementary mathematics education, *Scandinavian Journal of Educational Research*, 33, 35–46. https://doi.org/10.1080/0031383890330103.

Marton, F. and Pang, M. F. (1999) Two Faces of Variation, paper presented at 8th European Association for Research for Learning and Instruction (EARLI) conference, Göteborg, Sweden.

Marton, F. and Tsui, A. (2004) *Classroom Discourse and the Space of Learning*, Lawrence Erlbaum.

Maybee, C. (2007) Understanding our Student Learners: a phenomenographic study revealing the ways that undergraduate women at Mills College understand using information, *Reference Services Review*, 35, 452–62.

Maybee, C. (2015) Informed Learning in the Undergraduate Classroom: the role of information experiences in shaping outcomes, Doctoral dissn, Queensland University of Technology. https://eprints.qut.edu.au/89685.

Maybee, C., Bruce, C. S., Lupton, M. and Rebmann, K. R. (2017) Designing Rich Information Experiences to Shape Learning Outcomes, *Studies in Higher Education*, 42, 2373–88.

Merleau-Ponty, M. (1962) *Phenomenology of Perception*, Humanities Press.

Pang, M. F., Linder, C. and Fraser, D. (2006) Beyond Lesson Studies and Design Experiments: using theoretical tools in practice and finding out how they work, *International Review of Economics Education*, 5, 28–45.

Parker, N. J. (2006) Assignments, Information and Learning: the postgraduate student experience, PhD thesis, University of Technology, Sydney, Faculty of Humanities and Social Sciences.

Rovio-Johansson, A. (1999) *Being Good at Teaching: exploring different ways of handling the same subject in higher education*, Acta Universitatis Gothoburgensis.

Runesson, U. (1999) Teaching as Constituting a Space of Variation, paper presented at the 8th European Association for Research for Learning and Instruction (EARLI), Göteborg, Sweden.

Society of College, National and University Libraries (2011) *SCONUL Seven Pillars of Information Literacy: core model for higher education*, www.sconul.ac.uk/page/seven-pillars-of-information-literacy.

Svensson, L. (1997) Theoretical Foundations of Phenomenography, *Higher Education Research and Development*, 16, 159–71.

Tewell, E. (2015) A Decade of Critical Information Literacy: a review of the literature, *Communications in Information Literacy*, 9, 24–43, https://doi.org/10.15760/comminfolit.2015.9.1.174.

Vikström, A. (2008) What is Intended, What is Realized and What is Learned? Teaching and learning biology in the primary school classroom, *Journal of Science Teacher Education*, 19, 211–33.

Webber, S., Boon, S. and Johnston, B. (2005) A Comparison of UK Academics' Conceptions of Information Literacy in Two Disciplines: English and Marketing, *Library and Information Research*, 29, 4–15.

Whitworth, A. (2014a) Nurturing Information Literacy Landscapes: networks, information literacy and the need for a critical phenomenography. In Rayne, S., Jones, C., de Laat, M., Ryberg, T. and Sinclair, C. (eds) *Proceedings of the 9th International Conference on Networked Learning*, University of Edinburgh.

Whitworth, A. (2014b) *Radical Information Literacy: reclaiming the political heart of the IL movement*, Chandos.

Williams, D. A. and Wavell, C. (2007) Secondary School Teachers' Conceptions of Student Information Literacy, *Journal of Librarianship and Information Science*, 39, 199–212.

12
Information Literacy: What Consciousness and Cognition Can Teach Us

John Budd

Introduction

To begin with, there is the need to determine just what 'theory' offers to the research into a field such as information literacy. No one expresses this more cogently and eloquently than Habermas:

> The mediation of theory and praxis can only be clarified if to begin with we distinguish three functions, which are measured of different criteria: the formation and extension of critical theorems, which can stand up to scientific discourse; the organizations of processes of enlightenment; in which such theorems are applied and can be tested in a unique manner by the initiation of processes of reflection carried on within certain groups toward which these processes have been directed; and the selection of appropriate strategies, the solution of tactical questions and the conduct of the political struggle. On the first level, the aim is true statements, of the second, authentic insights and on the third, prudent decisions.
>
> (Habermas, 1973, 32)

The last sentence is particularly applicable to the discussion of consciousness and cognition, and, indeed, the entirety of the contents of this volume. The importance of 'theory' is to enable 'praxis' to become as effective as possible. For example, Richard Haass (2023) says that, to participate fully in a democracy, the citizenry must first be informed (this is number one in his list of people's obligations). The very idea of theory may seem a bit foreign, but when we connect it to work on consciousness, we see that the *practice* of information literacy can flourish. That is the message Habermas leaves us with; in the present instance, the theory of consciousness can lead to a more complete understanding with how individuals can think *through* information. That is, people who think critically are able to employ information to make reasoned decisions. What follows in this introductory section is the debate regarding consciousness, where it resides and how it works.

There has been something of a tradition among many neuroscientists and philosophers of mind to adopt a monist position regarding the brain. That is to say, there is an explicit use of Cartesian dualism (the view that there is both a body and a spirit or soul and that the mind resides in the soul, even as the brain is a part of the physical body). Those who argue for a kind of dualism hedge their bets and define the two components of mind and consciousness very carefully, as we will see later. The upshot is that the vast majority of scientists and philosophers believe that the mind is a product of physical phenomena. Distinctions do not stop there, though. A number of individuals adopt an even more limited view of the brain, either as a metaphor or as, perhaps especially, a literal fact. That view is of the brain as a computer. As was just stated, some adopt a metaphorical equivalence, such as, 'what's missing, at least in part, is an appropriate metaphor to help us think about how the brain communicates within itself. I propose that the internet is that metaphor' (Daniel Graham, 2021, ix). He quotes Patricia Churchland and Terry Sejnowski, who write, 'Nervous systems and probably parts of nervous systems are themselves naturally evolved computers. . . . They represent features and relations in the world and they enable an animal to adapt to its circumstances' (Churchland and Sejnowski, 1992, 7).

The equivalence between brain and computer is shared by others; William Lycan uses the physical objects hardware and software to draw similarities between the brain and computers (Lycan, 1987, 46–7). Paul Churchland speaks against dualism as he invokes computer architecture as typifying the human brain: 'The dualistic approach to mind encompasses several quite different theories, but they are all agreed that the essential nature of conscious intelligence resides in something *nonphysical*, in something forever beyond the scope of science like physics, neurophysiology and computer science' (Churchland, 1988, 7). Michael Gazzaniga refers to work in computer simulation and says (regarding the human brain):

> And voilà! Once wiring-cost-minimization was added, in both changing and unchanging environments, modules immediately began to appear, whereas without the stipulation of minimizing costs, they didn't. . . . These simulation experiments provide strong evidence that selection pressures to maximize network performance and minimize connection costs will yield networks that are significantly more modular and more evolvable.
>
> (Gazzaniga, 2018, 96)

and he makes his stance abundantly clear by saying, 'I am and to this day remain, committed to the idea that physical mechanism can and will explain almost everything' (p. 226). Michael Graziano makes a connection between progress in computer technologies and our understanding of consciousness: 'As our information technology has improved, the information content of the mind has become less mysterious, while at the same time the act of being conscious of it, of experiencing anything at all, has become more remote and seemingly unsolvable' (Graziano, 2019, 5).

WHAT CONSCIOUSNESS AND COGNITION CAN TEACH US

The foregoing provides examples of what can be called the computational, or information-processing approach, to the brain and the mind. The brain is essentially a computer which processes information provided primarily by stimuli, such as visual excitation. Even some who take a more mechanistic idea of the brain recognise that the problem of explaining consciousness is complicated and must acknowledge some factors that can tend to confound us. Daniel Dennett is one such individual; he states:

> The conscious mind, it seems, cannot just be the brain, or any proper part of it, because nothing in the brain could
>
> (1) be the medium in which the purple cow is rendered;
> (2) be the thinking thing, the I in 'I think, therefore I am';
> (3) appreciate wine, hate racism, love someone, be a source of mattering;
> (4) act with moral responsibility.
>
> An acceptable theory of human consciousness must account for these four compelling grounds for thinking that there must be mind stuff.
>
> (Dennett, 1991, 33)

He spends the remainder of his book responding to those questions on the basis of materialism.

Graziano presents probably the most explicit assessment of the monistic and brain-centred locus of consciousness:

> The most commonly suggested brain structure for consciousness is the cerebral cortex, the part of the brain that expanded most in human evolution. A second common suggestion is the thalamus. . . . [T]he thalamus is closely connected to the cortex and information constantly resonates between the two, each part of the thalamus communicating mainly with a specific part of the cortex.
>
> (Graziano, 2019, 65)

This idea is the most specific that may exist when it comes to 'locating', or 'situating' consciousness. As can be expected, such a stance regarding consciousness could have an impact on thinking and practice in information literacy. If the physicalist viewpoint were to be adopted, then there would be a similar way of acting in information literacy.

Philosophers of mind such as Owen Flanagan suggest an alternative materialist stance. According to him, constructive naturalism:

> . . . is the position I am to defend. Like the anticonstructivist and the eliminativist, I think that naturalism is true. Against the anticonstructivist and principled agnostic, I maintain that there is reason for optimism about our ability to understand the relation between consciousness and

the brain. We can make intelligible the existence of consciousness in the natural world.

(Flanagan, 1992, 2)

He also maintains, as do others, that not every mental event is a conscious one, but every conscious event is a mental one.

Some in the information science (IS) field (writ large) also offer a computational position. Victor Rosenberg, for example, has said, 'There is no doubt that a large portion of human behavior associated with information is deterministic, even computer-like' (Rosenberg, 1974, 264). Some, though, adopt a divergent point of view, such as Belkin and Robertson:

> 'IS has up to now regarded [text and its structure] as its major concern; some interest has been shown in [the image-structure of the recipient], but study of this phenomenon has largely been concentrated in psychology or education. [The image-structure of the sender] remains virtually virgin territory.
>
> (Belkin and Robertson, 1976, 202)

The observation of Belkin and Robertson illustrates that Rosenberg's concept is insufficient.

Daniel Graham (2021, viii) takes a somewhat different view from those who adopt the computational view: 'Neuroscientists typically see the job of a given part of the brain – single neurons, neural circuits, or brain regions – as computing something.' Graham is also a materialist, but his concentration on the communicative processes within the brain sets his work apart from his colleagues. In fact, while one may disagree with the limitations of his metaphor, his focus on communication opens some new possibilities, unthought of by those represented so far. In evaluating theory – an important task for any practitioner – there must be a consideration of alternatives so that praxis will be able to achieve genuine goals of student learning, as will be shown.

Not everyone is a materialist – or at least not everyone is of the materialist bent that has been described thus far. John Searle may be the most prominent critic of what might be referred to as the 'received view', previously described, that has typified thought about consciousness and cognition (and the mind in general). He offers objections to contemporary materialism as it can be defined as manifest in several ways: logical behaviourism, black-box functionalism, strong artificial intelligence and other ways (Searle, 1992, 53). Instead, he states:

> Every conscious state is always *someone's* conscious state. . . . Subjectivity has the further consequence that all of my conscious forms of intentionality that give me information about the world independent of myself are always from a special point of view. The world itself has no point of view, but my access to the world through my conscious states is always perspectival, always from my point of view. [italics in original]
>
> (Searle, 1992, 94–5)

He is identifying a way of thinking that should typify information literacy education and student learning. When, in relating what information literacy *is* to students, instructors emphasise that it means thinking beyond the *self*, that are letting students know that the world is a complex place and that thinking *through* information is essential. This is, in part, related to the ACRL *Framework*'s tenets of authority and the evaluation of sources. Students learn to evaluate both who is speaking and what is being said. This is a function of consciousness and connects that to information literacy. It is also at the very heart of the ACRL *Framework for Information Literacy*; the objective is to help students (and others) to become *active* receivers of information and information seekers. Searle's words provide a proper segue to the next section.

Consciousness, cognition and information literacy

While there are difficulties associated with materialism, that does not mean that one should adopt a dualist point of view; that would be unproductive. It does mean that there is cause for scepticism regarding a mechanistic perspective of the brain. For example, Alvin Goldman is of the opinion:

> Once we acknowledge the need for qualitative properties, . . . we realize that we can get a much simpler model of mentalistic self-ascription by dispensing with the functional roles entirely. Why not adopt a very different model in which the concepts of headache, itch and so forth are representations of qualitative characteristics, not functional roles at all?
>
> (Goldman, 1993, 87)

Goldman expresses open-mindedness with respect to the qualitative aspects of being and is willing to admit that there are phenomena that are not limited to the brain. This is a theme that will be explored in some detail shortly: the entirety of the body is responsible for what we call consciousness.

What Goldman is speaking of has direct and immediate pertinence to theory of information literacy. The job for information literacy is indeed to bring together the object (that *thing* that is the object of instruction) and the self (the student, by means of instruction). In fact, it is time to turn our attention to information literacy and the discovery (creation?) of what it is. There are numerous attempts to define information literacy, but one will suffice for the current purposes, proffered by Natalie Greene Taylor and Paul Jaeger:

> Information literacy is a constantly refined practice of processing, accessing, understanding, critically evaluating and using information in ways that are relevant to one's life. Information literacy relies on a social structure that promotes the agency of individuals in their communities and in the legal, political, educational, communication and economic structures in their lives. Practicing information literacy is an iterative learning process that occurs throughout an individual's lifetime.

> Information literacy encompasses not only foundational literacies (reading/prose, writing/document, numeracy/quantitative) but also aspects of digital literacy (technology skills and ethics) and media literacy (critical analysis of nontextual content). In many cases, information literacy is closely associated with data, scientific, health, civic and other context-specific literacies.
>
> (Greene and Jaeger, 2022, 5)

The definition is broad and inclusive. And, while Greene and Jaeger's overall work is somewhat grounded in cognition, the definition does not explicitly mention consciousness. What will follow will be critical thought relating to information literacy, plus some particular emergent ideas on consciousness and cognition.

A place to begin is Annemaree Lloyd's suggestion regarding just what *kind* of practice information literacy is comprised of:

> Theme 1. Information literacy is enacted as a negotiated practice;
> Theme 2. Information literacy is enacted through practice architectures;
> Theme 3. Information literacy is enacted through the affordances of activities;
> Theme 4. Information literacy is enacted in ways of knowing.
>
> (Lloyd, 2012, 774–7)

Lloyd pointedly discusses the complexities of practice, especially in Theme 4. That theme is in keeping with an examination of consciousness as a means to enhance the practice of information literacy. She concludes her work, 'Embedding this rethinking of information literacy in ontological and epistemological terms, we are able to understand how information literacy happens and how that happening differs between settings' (Lloyd, 2012, 781). She demonstrates an anticipation of the unity of information literacy with consciousness and cognition that is at the heart of this chapter. She also echoes the thoughts of James Elmborg, who, in a classic piece, says that the nature of information is 'the product of socially negotiated epistemological processes and the raw material for the further making of new knowledge' (Elmborg, 2006, 198). As has already been shown in a preliminary way, ontology (the study of what *is*) and epistemology (the study of knowledge) are foci of both consciousness and cognition. As I have stated, using these experiences of learning 'transcend the often-used scales that concentrate on *skills* (that is, the abilities to construct a search, retrieve possibly relevant items and use the retrieved items as part of a task)' (Budd, 2020, 1379).

The foregoing ideas build upon Annie Downey's notion that, 'The prime function of education is to create knowledge and truth and learning to read texts, images and other documents is fundamentally about learning to understand the meaning of such things in order to develop knowledge and find truth' (Downey, 2016, 39). There is not space here to delve deeply into information literacy as the discovery of truth, but, as we have already seen, knowledge plays an integral role in information literacy and its connection to consciousness and cognition. E. J. McCoy says, 'Information literacy requires an understanding of how you are thinking about and evaluating the information that is being found and consumed; this is a metacognitive act that can be explicitly taught and practiced in the information literacy classroom' (McCoy, 2022, 42). The growth of knowledge is a defining human endeavour, just as it is ineluctably foundational to education. Information literacy is much more than a skill set; it is a way of thinking and, as we will see, of being. For example, the article by Leah Graham and Panatiogis Takis Metaxas (2003) illustrates that students who have *technical* proficiency tend to be fooled by misinformation; they lack a critical capacity to interpret and use information effectively. Recent work in the fields of neuroscience and the philosophy of mind show us that there is more to consciousness and knowledge than the ability to perform specific tasks. This is the message that Downey and others are attempting to transmit with their visions for information literacy. An instance of such an effort is reported by Mandi Goodsett and Hanna Schmillen, who examine librarians' evaluation of their thinking about instruction: 'It was particularly instructive to hear librarians describe information literacy and critical thinking as completely overlapping' (Goodsett and Schmillen, 2020, 103). 'Critical thinking' can be seen as a kind of stand-in for consciousness as librarians and other educators use the term. It may even be linked to metacognition. The term may be employed in assessment of information literacy programmes in general, as Teresa Neely and Simmona Simmons-Hodo point out when they say that a query designed to prompt students for a summary of a publication 'is an excellent example for assessing students' ability to read critically and identify the key focus of a particular passage' (Neely and Simmons-Hodo, 2006, 74)

The development of knowledge depends on consciousness and cognition, to be sure, but these phenomena are not simply activities of the brain. Communication, both within and without the individual brain, is also important. That, in part, is what information is about. The process of sharing that which gives shape to knowledge is a communicative one and the communication is of a particular kind. Andrew Whitworth recognises this necessity: 'The central argument of [his] book is that, since its emergence in the 1970s, IL has constructed and then institutionalised itself around a *monologic* approach that stands in a fundamental tension with the *dialogic* nature of learning, knowledge-formation and the use of language' (italics in original) (Whitworth, 2014, 1). Whitworth draws substantially from the concept of dialogism as articulated and developed by the early-20th-century literary theorist, Mikhail M. Bakhtin. Bakhtin maintained that the discourse of the natural sciences tends to be monologic, that the communication, more often than not, is a speaking *to* instead of a speaking *with*. While the sciences may have adopted a more contingent attitude recently, we can see from the works quoted in the first section of this chapter that the communication can be 'authoritative', and sometimes admits to little or no doubt. In the dialogical scenario, communication recognises that there is a two-way aspect, that, as Whitworth points out, such things as learning and knowledge depend upon dialogue to reach full realisation. Michael Holquist writes: 'In dialogism, the very capacity to have consciousness is based on *otherness*. . . . [I]n dialogism consciousness *is* otherness' (italics in original) (Holquist, 1990, 18). In other words, there is an element of phenomenology in dialogism and, by extension, in such things as consciousness and cognition. This assertion will now be explored further.

It is an appropriate time to turn back to discussion of consciousness and cognition, this time with special attention to phenomenological aspects of the mind. Smith and Thomasson present the place of phenomenology in this context:

> ... the goal of phenomenology is not to record the 'feel' of one's own mental states, but rather to explicate the essential types and structures of conscious experience as lived (from the first-person perspective), thus the logical or conceptual relations among experience types, with the focus on the intentional or representational structure of experience. Accordingly, the methods of phenomenology do not rely on 'peering inwards' at one's passing stream of consciousness.
> (Smith and Thomasson, 2005, 9)

A key concept in this view is 'experience', especially lived experience, or lifeworld. The conscious person experiences the world, including stimuli of all sorts, in a complex subjective manner. As we will see in the next section, this lifeworld is 'embodied'; the entirety of a person's being is part of the reception of the stimuli that come from the world. Intentionality is another key element of the full phenomenological experience. Gallagher and Zahavi write that 'all psychical, i.e. mental, phenomena exhibit intentionality, no physical phenomena do, which is why [Franz Brentano] can claim not only that intentionality is the defining mark of the mental, but also that the physical and the psychical are distinct realms' (Gallagher and Zahavi, 2012, 125. This may seem to smack of dualism, but it only recognises the distinction between the mental and the non-mental worlds.

In short, phenomenology addresses human experience and the things (and the ways things) are presented to us through that experience. The phenomena that are presented are complex; they are not mere things without meaning but are interpretable objects that enter our consciousness (frequently within contexts associated with other objects within our consciousnesses). In information literacy terms, an individual conceives of some need for information (which may be an assignment to write about the meaning underlying a certain poem) and then conceptualises a search strategy for use in a database. The individual has to infer some intentionality within the 'mental space' of the poem in order to translate the space into search terms. Perception – the transformation of simple visual, auditory, or other stimuli – constitutes fodder for meaning. The manner of perception is part of being; it is not just the things that an automaton might come across and react to. Perception is part of interpretation, and, as such, contributes to our consciousness and thinking about the object(s) perceived. While there is not space here to describe it fully, it must be said that there is an essential distinction to be made between the natural attitude and the phenomenological attitude. The natural attitude can be said to be naïve absorption of what is presented to a person; little interpretation or conscious cognition takes place. The phenomenological attitude is marked by a perception of the world *as it affects our perception of the world and its meaning*. In the phenomenological attitude there is a withholding of judgement, a conscious assessment of what is perceived and comprehended. In phenomenology there is much to see, but even more to understand. This is a sketch of phenomenology, but there are many works which can elucidate precisely what is meant by it and how it has an impact on the ways we are conscious of the world and how we translate the perception into action. Gallagher and Zahavi offer a very helpful observation, one that is especially pertinent to the theoretical construct set forth in this chapter: 'another way to characterize the difference between contemporary mainstream analytic philosophy of mind and phenomenology is by noting that whereas the majority of analytic philosophers today endorse some form of naturalism, phenomenologists have tended to adopt a non- or even anti-naturalistic approach' (Gallagher and Zahavi, 2012, 125).

If we look for a succinct assessment of phenomenology in the study of the mind, we can turn to Tim Bayne and Michelle Montague:

> Consciousness is rich. There are experiences in the five familiar sensory modalities: vision, audition, olfaction, gustation and touch. There are bodily sensations of various kinds: itches, tingles, cramps, pains and experiences of hunger, thirst and drowsiness. There are the conscious states associated with emotions and moods, such as feelings of elation, despair, boredom, fear and anxiety. Each of these kinds of conscious state has a distinct phenomenal character; there is 'something it is like' to be in such states.
>
> (Bayne and Montague, 2011, 1)

The 'something it is like' is a key concept in phenomenology. Humans have the distinct ability to ponder and discern what their physical sensory apparatuses are doing at a given time and to comprehend the conscious effects of those apparatuses. It means that a person understands what it is like to be in pain and to site the locus of the pain. Further and more importantly, it means that a person has the ability to comprehend the source and kind of intellectual stimulus to which she is subjected. The spur to read further about a topic is one such stimulus; what information literacy helps to do is see information itself as a stimulus to thinking. This is an essential quality that human beings possess and it is what enables people to understand signs of all kinds, including the complex signs of texts and documents.

Phenomenology does not remove doubt and scepticism from our conscious minds, but it helps to provide a general cognitive mechanism that allows us to confront doubt and to remove at least some of it. Taylor Carman helps to clarify the predicament by pointing out: 'The phenomenological alternative to eliminativism is to insist that although we can be wrong about some features of our perceptual experience, we can also be reasonably certain about others' (Carman, 2005, 68). Carman goes even further, stating that, 'I think [Daniel] Dennett's view is not just false, but incoherent' (Carman, 2005, 69). The incoherence is grounded in Dennett's actual denial of the existence of consciousness. For instance, for Dennett, qualitative experiences (that is, those that are not the products of direct physical stimuli) are not objects internal to the mind or consciousness. Carman and many other neuroscientists and philosophers reject this view and include qualitative experience and perception as part and parcel of the conscious and cognitive processes. Perception affects not only what we are conscious of, but how our consciousness is shaped by perceptions. The perceptual stimuli are evidence of the phenomenology of the mind. Perception includes the physical world, but it also extends to the mental. For example, as one reads, say, a novel or poetry, one's consciousness is affected and one becomes aware of something heretofore unknown and not thought of prior to the reading. This is directly related to information literacy and will be explored further.

It is evident that a number of theorists are of the opinion that consciousness is not merely a physical thing but is something more than that. Galen Strawson states this eloquently: 'Many philosophers talk in a strongly reificatory way about our mental states as if they were things in us, rather than things – states – we are in and this (mixing in with the whole behaviourist folly) has led many to find it natural to conceive of belief dispositions, preference dispositions and so on as mentally contentful entities. . . quite independently of our present experience' (Strawson, 2005, 57). In other words, Strawson critiques the 'received' view of consciousness, wherein all activity and content resides within the brain. As we are becoming aware, there is an extension that relates to the external world and perception of that world, plus the entirety of the human body and being. A sense such as a belief is more than a physical entity residing in the brain; it is, as Strawson says, a disposition, an inclination based on complex factors, both within and without the brain. Do note, none of the foregoing denies the activity of the brain and the neural system. It does mean that there is more at work than just neural activity.

Many of the examples used by neuroscientists and philosophers of mind have to do with the natural world and perception of that world. The theorists being spoken of in this section make the point that perception is more complicated than simply the physical phenomenon of visual sight and the brain's usage of the visual apparatus to form 'thoughts' about what is seen. When it comes to the likes of information literacy, it is more than the physical world that is in play; documents, images, speech and other things are absorbed by the human senses and thought mechanisms. As Richard Tieszen states, 'it is believed that naturalism has no place for abstract objects. Abstract objects, after all, do not have spatial extension and are not in the causal nexus like physical objects, are either timeless or omnitemporal and so on' (Tieszen, 2005, 183). Ideas, which are abstract objects, are the fodder of information literacy. For example, when searching for documents on a given topic, a student is frequently looking for certain concepts that are included in the documents. The formation of thoughts about the kinds of ideas that are, in large part, the content of information literacy instruction requires a more delicate and complex kind of perception. In the next section we will delve deeply into the abstract objects as they form essential aspects of information literacy.

One additional point at this time helps to set the tone for what is to come and which is integral to the theoretical foundation that is set forth in this chapter. Terry Horgan presents a key observation related to the abstract objects that Tieszen speaks of:

Another common line of argument is epistemological. People normally have special and especially strong, epistemic access to their own current, occurrent, thoughts and wishes. The claim is that the best explanation of the distinctive form of epistemic access invokes cognitive phenomenology: phenomenal character is *self-presenting* to the experiencing agent, in a way that non-phenomenal internal states are not; and the best explanation of people's special epistemic access to their own occurrent epistemic states is that these states have proprietary, non-sensory, cognitive phenomenology. Since phenomenal character is self-presenting, cognitive phenomenology provides special and especially strong, epistemic access to one's present occurrent cognitive states. [italics in original]

(Horgan, 2011, 58)

Abstract objects fit into Horgan's programme; the self-presenting aspect necessarily extends beyond the simple physical model of the aforementioned dynamics. Something much more complicated is at work – both for the instructor and for the student. For this theory to be efficacious, the teachers must accept that the epistemic states of the students are dependent on the teachers' own epistemic and phenomenological states.

As has been stated previously, there are some difficulties with the received materialist viewpoint. What this section of the chapter has presented can be described as a middle ground between the strong materialist outlook and a more modified physical point of view. In fact, consciousness and thought can certainly be seen as physical, but there are subtleties and nuances that render the kind of phenomenological position more tenable. Even some who adopt a physicalist stance can admit to some need for allowances. Damasio is one such thinker; he is of the opinion 'Without consciousness – that is, a mind endowed with *subjectivity* – you would have no way of knowing that you exist, let alone who you are and what you think. . . . There is indeed a self, but it is a process, not a thing and the process is present at all times when we are presumed to be conscious' (italics added) (Damasio, 2010, 4, 8). The very idea of self is one that transcends the material brain and extends to the entirety of the physical being as subject. Damasio is not alone in questioning the firm materialist stance (as Searle critiqued it). Others suggest related points that, while not denying physical being, call also for extensions.

One individual who fits this profile is David Papineau, who writes: 'Even those, like myself, who are persuaded that the mind is identical to the material brain, will surely admit that they sometimes hanker for some further understanding of *why* brain activities should yield conscious feelings' (italics in original) (Papineau, 2002, 145). He further says that there are many theorists who adopt an ontologically monist view that conscious states are material, while simultaneously holding a conceptually dualist stance, wherein there is a special set of phenomenal concepts (Papineau, 2002, 5). In a slightly more recent work Papineau elaborates on what he means by conceptual dualism: 'Nevertheless we have two quite different kinds of concepts for thinking about conscious/material properties, which I will call 'phenomenal' and 'material' concepts. . . . Phenomenal concepts are most easily thought of as akin to demonstratives, or even quotational terms' (Papineau, 2003, 206).

He adds, 'I take subjects' first-person phenomenal reports to provide a kind of observational data-base for research into the material referents of phenomenal concepts' (Papineau, 2003, 207). An interpretation of Papineau can hold that, while perception is of material objects, there are phenomenal concepts in the mind. Papineau and others, do not admit to the perception of abstract objects, though (see above). So, while he claims to be a conceptual dualist, there are desiderata that must be accounted for.

Other philosophers, such as Colin McGinn, are more sceptical than Papineau. McGinn claims, 'I argue that the bond between the mind and the brain is a deep mystery. Moreover, it is an ultimate mystery, a mystery that human intelligence will never unravel. Consciousness indubitably exists and it is connected to the brain in some intelligible way, but the nature of the connection necessarily eludes us' (McGinn, 1999, 5). While he does not invoke phenomenology, some of his observations are in keeping with the phenomenological point of view. He writes, 'Thought is clearly not the same as reality. A thought is something that goes through a person's mind, while reality in general does not (although thoughts are also one part of reality)' (McGinn, 1999, 31–2). McGinn maintains that, in a very real sense, science does not 'speak' of consciousness with an appropriate grammar. That is, there are limitations to the language of, mainly, neuroscience, that does not account for the difficulties of understanding thought and consciousness. Knowing something is not immaterial, but its materiality is more complex than can be captured by scientific speech.

Theory and praxis of information literacy

To get us started, we can refer to Anthony Chemero, who speaks to the idea of phenomenological realism, that 'allows us . . . to say that conscious experiences are genuinely existing aspects of animal-environment systems' (Chemero, 2009, 198). Individuals explore affordances (the quality that defines possible uses) as a means to connect with the environment, including other individuals. One unresolved aspect is whether embodied cognition includes a representational component. Chemero explains, 'Mental representations . . . are parts of explanations of behavior and their existence is vindicated and their proposed properties are confirmed by the success of explanations that call upon them' (Chemero, 2009, 50). A representation is then (mostly) accurate as a picture of what is supposed to be represented. A representation of a tree emulates an actual tree; a representation of dance emulates people engaged in dancing. Chemero urges that we accept the traditional form of representationalism, arguing that an opposing stance cannot imbue embodied cognitivism with the phenomenological fullness it requires. Weissenberger and colleagues emphasise that 'Representation has an inherent semantic quality; in order for a representation to capture what is ostensibly represented, meaning must be discerned in what is represented. The competing theory is eliminativism, which denies the semantic necessity and avers that neurological psychology is all that is required to conceive of something adequately' (Weissenberger, Budd and Herold, 2018, 712).

WHAT CONSCIOUSNESS AND COGNITION CAN TEACH US

Ezequiel Di Paolo and Evan Thompson provide a kind of précis of the theoretical construct articulated in the previous section:

> (1) We have seen that enactivism, unlike other approaches, attempts to provide a principled definition of the body as a self-individuating system. The concept of autonomy is what allows us to provide the definition. Thus, what is meant by 'body,' for the enactive approach, is not the body as a functional system defined in terms of inputs and outputs – as it is for functional cognitive science – but rather the body as an adaptively autonomous and therefore sense-making system.
>
> (2) Cognition, in its more general form, is sense-making – the adaptive regulation of states and interactions by an agent with respect to the consequences for the agent's own viability.
>
> (3) Without a body, there cannot be sense-making. Moreover, sense-making is a bodily process of adaptive self-regulation. The link between body and cognition is accordingly constitutive and not merely causal. To be a sense-maker is, among other things, to be autonomous and precarious, that is, to be a body, in the precise sense of 'body' that the enactive approach indicates.
>
> (Di Paolo and Thompson, 2014, 76)

We can now examine just how information literacy benefits from this theoretical approach.

A place to begin is with the opinion of Stephen Brookfield, who claims that the purpose of education is the creation of knowledge and truth (Brookfield, 2005). The phenomenological project is designed to accomplish these goals. It is an epistemological means to the growth of knowledge, in particular, with the uncovering of truth being a principal path to knowledge. The means is made apparent through the interpretation of the ACRL information literacy *Framework*, the tenets of which are:

> Authority Is Constructed and Contextual;
> Information Creation as Process;
> Information Has Value;
> Research as Inquiry;
> Scholarship as Conversation;
> Search as Strategic Exploration.
>
> (ACRL, 2021, 7)

Interpretation is key here; one may take issue with the specifics of application of these tenets, but their existence is in keeping with the theoretical stance stated above. For example, scholarship is – or should be – a conversation among participants. There is an implicit, if not explicit, process whereby individual scholars and researchers build upon one another's work by recognition of the phenomenological principle of many selves communicating and learning.

The fundamentally phenomenological attitude and method suggests a position that instructors can adopt as they prepare for information literacy instruction. This includes the critique of materialism by Searle, the scepticism of McGinn and other things, in addition to the directly phenomenological writings. It is evident that the strong materialism described in the first section of the chapter is inadequate for information literacy instruction (and, indeed, for learning generally). Information literacy and learning rely on the fundamental awareness and understanding that are not mechanical but are more phenomenological in their connection with the informing objects. The weak materialists have something to tell us about information literacy, as they relate the complexities of consciousness and the application of consciousness and cognition to learning. Consciousness, according to these theorists, includes critical factors and acumen. The perception that is part of consciousness leads to awareness and, eventually, understanding. We can turn to a few additional points to relate the application of the phenomenological theory to the praxis of information literacy instruction and learning.

Before turning to those remaining points, we can look at a variation on the definition of information literacy, offered by Elmborg:

> In order to provide a working definition of information literacy, we must navigate two competing visions of the library. In one vision, the library retains its status as neutral purveyor of information and information literacy is based on students mastering the libraries' tools and systems. In this vision, information literacy is reduced to mastering a set of library skills with traditional tools. In another more ambitious vision, the library becomes a site for student empowerment, a place where students create genuine questions and construct their own answers. In this vision, the library's role in perpetuating disciplinary classifications and organizing and disseminating authoritative knowledge becomes part of what students must understand to be information literate, but only part.
>
> (Elmborg, 2002, 455–6)

Elmborg elaborates on his definition by claiming that the target of information literacy is to help shape student consciousness (p. 456). That is a very important statement and one that affirms the theoretical stance that is presented in this chapter.

To return to the aforementioned points, we can examine the place perception has in information literacy instruction and learning. Alva Noë, drawing on the philosophy of Maurice Merleau-Ponty, makes the statement that perception is *active*; it is not something that happens to us, it is something that we *do*. What we do determines what we perceive and, moreover, what we do – what actions we take – in response to the perception (Noë, 2004, 1). In keeping with what Chemero and others say, Noë asserts: 'If perception is in part constituted by our possession and exercise of bodily skills . . . then it may also depend on our possession of the sort of bodies that can encompass those skills. To perceive like us, it follows, you must have a body like ours' (p. 25). The embodied cognition is more than a tacit acceptance of the phenomenological theoretical position. Consciousness and cognition do not simply reside in the brain, but are also tactile, auditory, olfactory, etc. The entirety of being is part of the whole, which is the phenomenological attitude and experience. In fact, *Being* is a fundamental component of phenomenology. Unfortunately, space does not allow for the elaboration of this idea within the present chapter.

To use the remaining space, there are two aspects of the phenomenological method that must be mentioned. Gallagher and Zahavi render these two aspects accessible; one is:

> The purpose of the epoché is not to doubt, neglect, abandon, or exclude reality from consideration; rather the aim is to suspend or neutralize a certain dogmatic attitude towards reality, thereby allowing us to focus more narrowly and directly on reality just as it is given – how it makes its appearance to us in experience. In short, the epoché entails a change of attitude towards reality, not an exclusion of reality. . . . Importantly, the epoché does not involve and exclusively turn inward.
>
> (Gallagher and Zahavi, 2012, 25)

(Epoché is the suspension of judgement, or the process of setting aside assumptions.)

They also address phenomenological reduction, which is opposed to strong materialism: 'The epoché and the reduction can be seen as two closely linked elements of a philosophical reflection, the purpose of which is to liberate us from a natural(istic) dogmatism and to make us aware of our constitutive (i.e. cognitive, meaning disclosing) contribution to what we experience' (Gallagher and Zahavi, 2012, 27). Information literacy instruction and learning depend on these two elements for awareness and understanding; teachers need to become fully cognisant of them so as to be able to communicate them to their students and to help the students perceive fully what they may expose themselves to.

To wrap up, I can reiterate my description of some years ago of the framework of phenomenological cognitive action:

> In summary, this framework consists of:
> - Phenomenology – the intersubjective relationship of students' intentional search for understanding through the statements, images, or voices of others and the teachers' engagement of students in those searches.
> - Cognition – students' ways of thinking about the academic (primarily) challenges they face (through their assignments, papers they write and explorations they undertake in all of their course work) and also the introduction of metacognitive processes that can help them respond to the challenges.
> - Action – the students' direct interaction with complex discourse (what others write, say and show) and the resources that can help them locate the discourse.
>
> (Budd, 2009, 4–5)

This programme actually anticipates the above interpretation of the ACRL *Framework* through the complexities of consciousness and cognition. In particular, it affirms such elements as conceiving of scholarship as a conversation. The connections offered here emphasise a dialogical nature to reading, thinking and reacting to information. These elements are at the heart of information literacy. It also presents a means by which information literacy can achieve its deepest goals and objectives.

References

ACRL (Association of College & Research Libraries) (2021) *Framework for Information Literacy for Higher Education*.

Bayne, T. and Montague, M. (2011) Cognitive Phenomenology: an introduction. In Bayne, T. and Montague, M. (eds) *Cognitive Phenomenology*, Oxford University Press, 1–34.

Belkin, N. J. and Robertson, S. E. (1976) Information Science and the Phenomenon of Information, *Journal of the American Society for Information Science*, 27, 197–204.

Brookfield, S. (2005) *The Power of Critical Theory: liberating adult learning and teaching*, Jossey-Bass.

Budd, J. (2009) *Framing Library Instruction*, ACRL.

Budd, J. M. (2020) Information Literacy and Consciousness, *Journal of Documentation*, 76, 1377–91.

Carman, T. (2005) On the Inescapability of Phenomenology. In Smith, D. W. and Thomasson, A. L. (eds) *Phenomenology and Philosophy of Mind*, Oxford University Press, 67–89.

Chemero, A. (2009) *Radical Embodied Cognitive Science*, MIT Press.

Churchland, P. M. (1988) *Matter and Consciousness*, rev. edn, MIT Press.

Churchland, P. S. and Sejnowski, T. J. (1992) *The Computational Brain*, MIT Press.

Damasio, A. (2010) *Self Comes to Mind: constructing the conscious brain*, Pantheon.

Dennett, D. C. (1991) *Consciousness Explained*, Little, Brown.

Di Paolo, E. and Thompson, E. (2014) The Enactive Approach. In Shapiro, L. (ed.) *The Routledge Handbook of Embodied Cognition*, Routledge, 68–78.

Downey, A. (2016) *Critical Information Literacy: foundations, inspiration, and ideas*, Library Juice Press.

Elmborg, J. (2002) Teaching at the Desk: towards a reference pedagogy, *portal: Libraries and the Academy*, 32, 455–64.

Elmborg, J. (2006) Critical Information Literacy: implications for instructional practice, *Journal of Academic Librarianship*, 32, 192–99.

Flanagan, O. (1992) *Consciousness Reconsidered*, MIT Press.

Gallagher, S. and Zahavi, D. (2012) *The Phenomenological Mind*, 2nd edn, Routledge.

Gazzaniga, M. S. (2018) *The Conscious Instinct: unraveling the mystery of how the brain makes the mind*, Farrar, Straus & Giroux.

Goldman, A. I. (1993) *Philosophical Applications of Cognitive Science*, Westview Press.

Goodsett, M. and Schmillen, H. (2020) Fostering Critical Thinking in First-Year Students through Information Literacy Instruction, *College & Research Libraries*, 83 (1), 91–110.

Graham, D. (2021) *An Internet in Your Head: a new paradigm for how the brain works*, Columbia University Press.

Graham, L. and Metaxas, P. T. (2003) 'Of Course It's True; I Saw It on the Internet': critical thinking in the internet era, *Communications of the ACM*, 46 (5), 71–5.

Graziano, M. S. A. (2019) *Rethinking Consciousness: a scientific theory of subjective experience*, W. W. Norton.

Greene, N. T. and Jaeger, P. T. (2022) *Foundations of Information Literacy*, American Library Association.

Haass, R. (2023) *The Bill of Obligations: the ten habits of good citizens,* Penguin Press.

Habermas, J. (1973) *Theory and Practice*, (trans. Viertel, J.), Beacon Press.

Holquist, M. (1990) *Dialogism: Bakhtin and his world*, Routledge.

Horgan, T. (2011) From Agentive Phenomenology to Cognitive Phenomenology: a guide for the perplexed. In Bayne, T. and Montague, M. (eds) *Cognitive Phenomenology*, Oxford University Press, 57–78.

Lloyd, A. (2012) Information Literacy as a Socially Enacted Practice: sensitizing themes for an emerging perspective of people-in-practice, *Journal of Documentation*, 66, 77–83.

Lycan, W. G. (1987) *Consciousness*, MIT Press.

McCoy, E. J. (2022) Teaching and Assessment of Metacognition in the Information Literacy Classroom, *Communications in Information Literacy*, 16, 42–52.

McGinn, C. (1999) *The Mysterious Flame: conscious minds in a material world,* Basic Books.

Neely, T. and Simmons-Hodo, S. (2006) Evaluating Information. In Neely, T. (ed.) *Information Literacy Assessment: standards-based tools and assignments*, American Library Association, 72–95.

Noë, A. (2004) *Action in Perception*, MIT Press.

Papineau, D. (2002) *Thinking about Consciousness*, Oxford University Press.

Papineau, D. (2003) Could There Be a Science of Consciousness?, *Philosophy of Mind*, 13, 205–20.

Rosenberg, V. (1974) The Scientific Premises of Information Science, *Journal of the American Society for Information Science*, 25, 263–69.

Searle, J. R. (1992) *The Rediscovery of the Mind*, MIT Press.

Smith, D. W. and Thomasson, A. L. (2005) Introduction. In Smith, D. W. and Thomasson, A. L. (eds) *Phenomenology and Philosophy of Mind*, Oxford University Press, 1–15.

Strawson, G. (2005) Intentionality and Experience: terminological preliminaries. In Smith, D. W. and Thomasson, A. L. (eds) *Phenomenology and Philosophy of Mind*, Oxford University Press, 41–66.

Tieszen, R. (2005) Consciousness of Abstract Objects. In Smith, D. W. and Thomasson, A. L. (eds) *Phenomenology and Philosophy of Mind*, Oxford University Press, 57–78.

Weissenberger, L., Budd, J. and Herold, K. (2018) Epistemology beyond the Brain, *Journal of the Association of Information Science and Technology*, 69 (5), 710–19.

Whitworth, A. (2014) *Radical Information Literacy: reclaiming the political heart of the IL movement*, Chandos Publishing.

13
Information Literacy Theorised Through Institutional Ethnography

Ola Pilerot

Introduction

Imagine the following scene: a student, let us call her Laura, participates in an information literacy class at a university. She has just started her bachelor programme and is generally a bit unsure about how she is supposed to act in order to be perceived as a good student. The librarian who teaches the class talks widely, accompanied by a PowerPoint-presentation, about the importance of students being able to determine their information needs, access information effectively and efficiently, being critical about information and information sources. Not only should one be able to understand the economic, legal and social issues surrounding the use of information, but there is also the need for accessing and using information in an ethically and legally correct way. The student is overwhelmed. Hardly anything of what the librarian says is of the sort that Laura usually thinks of when she is trying to find information on the web or elsewhere. It feels as if she has entered a world foreign to her.

From a research perspective, taking an analytical approach, the imagined scene functions as an illustration of how two traditions of approaching information literacy collide. Even if it is likely that Laura has not approached the concept of information literacy before experiencing the event in the university library described above, she probably has an idea of what it means to be able to find and use information in a purposeful way. However, this activity is not something that she consciously has formulated or put into words before.

This collision between two different ways in which information literacy is being understood can be described with the help of a distinction suggested already in the 1980s by the literacy researcher Brian Street. He distinguishes between an *autonomous* and an *ideological* approach to studying and understanding literacy (e.g. Street 1984; 2006). The former is grounded on an assumption that literacy – autonomously – will have beneficial effects beyond particular literacy events. The autonomous approach anticipates, in Street's (2006, 1) words, that '[i]ntroducing literacy to poor, "illiterate" people, villages, urban youth etc. will have the effect of enhancing their cognitive skills, improving their economic prospects, making them better citizens, regardless of the social and economic conditions that accounted for their "illiteracy" in the first place.' The ideological approach, on the other hand, conceives of literacy as inseparable from the context in which it is enacted. Literacy, according to this approach, is seen as embedded in social practices with their respective socially and historically developed epistemological traits. To be literate in one sphere of life is thus, according to the ideological approach, different from being literate in another sphere, which, by the way, explains why advocates of this approach speak in terms of literacies, in the plural. Literacy practices and meanings of literacy are linked to the issue of what constitutes worth knowing in a certain social practice and how knowledge and identity are performed by the people in the community of practice where literacy is enacted.

The distinction suggested by Street is recognisable also in the area of information literacy research and practice. In particular, it has been an ongoing, even if sometimes latent, struggle between two contrasting camps, where one can be represented by the American Library Association's issuing of the standards for information literacy, which, in the words of James Elmborg (2017, 62), 'were committing information literacy to a vision of "autonomous literacy"'. The other camp can be represented by a number of researchers whose work has as a common denominator a theoretical approach, more or less grounded in sociocultural and practice theories (see Chapter 2 by Lloyd) and where many subscribe to the notion of information literacies (e.g. Lloyd, 2010; Limberg, Sundin and Talja, 2012; Pilerot, 2016), i.e. an approach that to a great extent resembles what Street (1984; 2006) has termed an ideological approach.

The student, Laura in the introductory scene, entered into the sphere of academia and met a librarian who seems to have given voice to an autonomous approach to information literacy. More specifically, this approach seems autonomous because it is presented as a set of skills that can be transferred and put into use in any context. In that way, it appears as general and decontextualised in character. Being new to higher education, Laura did not immediately grasp the practices and meaning assigned to information literacy in this context. Even though Laura is the only student mentioned and included in the opening scene, she is not alone. There are also other students participating in the same class who are likely to experience a similar sense of uncertainty or even confusion. This dilemma clearly connects to the overarching question to be addressed in this chapter, namely: how is information literacy, as a concept and as a normatively prescribed practice, shaped into its form in a given social context? More specifically, what contributes to establishing individual and collective assumptions and understandings that motivate the people in the setting to enact, teach and promote information literacy in a certain way?

Using theory for understanding information literacy is something that one can do with different purposes. How one employs theoretical reasoning depends largely on what one is striving to accomplish. In this chapter, the aim is to suggest a theoretically informed mode of inquiry that discovers how local information literacy practices are shaped through the *ruling relations* to constellations of discourses and knowledge regimes located elsewhere, in other places and times. This is done through introducing and outlining the critical and explorative approach of *institutional ethnography*. The kind of theoretically infused research approach suggested here contributes to shedding light on processes of ruling and enables a resistance to information literacy efforts that risk becoming too broad and generic in character, including such teaching arrangements that neglect to attend to the specifics in the actual setting where information literacy is taught.

Institutional ethnography is a mode of inquiry and discovery that turns against the reification of the social – that is, it opposes reduction of the social to notions such as structure or system (Smith, 2005, 59). In a sense, it thereby avoids positioning theory as the governing principle of inquiry. One could therefore find it contradictory to suggest institutional ethnography as a topic for a book on theories for information literacy. However, if theory is conceived as a device that allows for a certain explanatory perspective that guides the researcher on what to look for and how to describe and understand that which is under study, institutional ethnography has the potential to offer a lot.

About institutional ethnography

Institutional ethnography was coined by the Canadian sociologist Dorothy Smith in the early 1980s and has since then been further developed by Smith and a growing number of other authors from a variety of the social science disciplines. Smith's (2005, 29) suggestion that it should be seen as a 'method of inquiry into the social' is often echoed in the literature (e.g. Norstedt and Breimo, 2016). A slightly more elaborated description presents institutional ethnography as a 'critical theory/methodology, with a particular focus on people's everyday lives and how their lives are organized and coordinated by institutional forces' (Kearney et al., 2019, 17). Already before Smith came up with the name of the approach, she worked for a long time along the lines of what eventually would become institutional ethnography. In a paper from the early 1970s she asserts that the 'social organization and production of the knowledge itself is the focus of inquiry' (Smith, 1974, 257). This suggestion is still resonating well with the gist of institutional ethnography as it has been developed by Smith and others over the years.

The actual term institutional ethnography will be discussed in more detail further on in the chapter. However, the notion of *institutional* implies that the approach seeks to elucidate how knowledge, values and discourses reside in, co-ordinate, characterise and mutually shape collectively identified and established spheres of society or, in institutional ethnography terms, institutions, such as the market, healthcare, higher education, etc. *Ethnography*, on the other hand, mainly signals two things: in order to explore these institutions, the inquiry needs to start locally, where people are attending to their sayings and doings and the texts and documents that not only contribute to co-ordinating activities but also serve to connect the local to the extra-local, i.e. settings beyond the local. The other thing concerns the outcome of the study, which consists of an account of the participants' sayings and doings, grounded in interviews, observations and analysis of documents and artefacts.

Nowadays, the literature on institutional ethnography is very rich. The recent publication of the *Palgrave Handbook of Institutional Ethnography* (Luken and Vaughan, 2021), a volume comprising nearly 600 pages with contributed chapters from nearly 40 authors, illustrates the growing engagement in this research approach. Smith's own oeuvre consists of more than ten books and numerous articles and book chapters.

Originally, Smith (e.g. 1987) described institutional ethnography as a method of inquiry beginning from women's experiences of being locked out from many areas of life. She experienced this herself in the late 1960s in connection with her work as a recently graduated academic at a sociology department. At the time, she was a single parent engaged in the women's movement when it became apparent to her how the mainstream mode of male-dominated sociology avoided issues that concerned the kind of experiences that characterised her own life outside academia. These experiences, in combination with her readings of Marx, spurred her towards 'a new social science that would not start with concepts or imagination, but that would start with actual people, their work, and the conditions of their lives' (Kearney et al., 2018, 294). They also led her to the kind of standpoint theory she operates with, according to which knowledge must be seen as socially situated and grounded in experiences (cf. Harding, 2009).

The influence from Marx leads institutional ethnography to taking as its point of departure the lives, materials and actualities of people that for different reasons are silenced and marginalised, thereby privileging a standpoint of people's experiences. In a related vein, institutional ethnography is also profiled as an insider's sociology (Smith, 1992) or a sociology for people (but not of people) (Smith, 2005). These rubrics signal a theoretical as well as a methodological position. From a theoretical perspective, it is asserted that the researcher cannot step outside society. In contrast to mainstream sociology that, according to Smith, aspires to depict its study objects from an Archimedean point, an outside view supposedly providing a true picture, she claims that '[t]here is no other way than beginning from the actual social relations in which we [all] are participants' (Smith, 1992, 94). From a methodological perspective, this viewpoint is related to institutional ethnography's emphasis of the ethnographical. In addition to Marx's materialism, it has been highlighted (Campbell, 2003) that institutional ethnography also draws on Mead's theory of the self, language and meaning, Bakhtin's reasoning on speech genres and Garfinkel's ethnomethodology (cf. Smith, 1999).

The writings on institutional ethnography and the works of Smith are not yet widely used within the area of information studies. A few articles present empirical studies that have employed institutional ethnography as a theoretical and methodological framework (e.g. Kizhakkethil, 2020; Green and Johnston, 2015). Others suggest institutional ethnography for specific purposes, such as Ocepek, who, in an exploration of everyday information behaviour as a theoretical concept, argues that it is a framework that contributes to shedding light on 'the nuances of the everyday world' (Ocepek, 2018, 398). In a related vein, Dalmer (2019) proposes that institutional ethnography is useful for reframing health information practices research. There is also a small number of contributions offering general introductory overviews of institutional ethnography in relation to information studies (e.g. Stooke, 2005; 2010; Dalmer, Stooke and McKenzie, 2017).

It is not possible within this chapter to account for and provide a justification for all possible avenues according to which information literacy could be theorised with the help of institutional ethnography. However, its orientation towards people, their doings and sayings, and, in particular, its focus on the role of texts and documents, makes institutional ethnography a suitable approach for information literacy research. The following section of this chapter presents an account of a set of key concepts. These can be used for elucidating how documents and other material objects, as well as discourses, with their varying rationalities and logics, contribute to the shaping of information literacy as it is presented, perceived and enacted in a given context.

Core elements of institutional ethnography for the understanding of information literacy

More specifically than previously indicated, the notion of institution in institutional ethnography refers to a bundle of document- and text-mediated relations that taken together encircle a specific established and predominant set of ordered social actions and procedures. According to Smith, institutions are 'forms of social organization that generalize and universalize across multiple local settings' (Smith, 2005, 42). In this sense, for example, mass media, the market, health care and education are institutions even though they obviously are distributed over a number of different sites and contexts. Considering information literacy an institution with its particular literature, generalised values, practices and traits, a multitude of sites and contexts are brought to mind. These are spanning over broad and general instances, such as workplaces and leisure, to more specific locations, such as schools and libraries, media-, communication- and information studies departments, ministries of education, governmental bodies, publishers, think tanks and so forth. Among the tasks of the institutional ethnographer is to explore the practices and processes that contribute to co-ordinating what is going on in these locations (cf. Smith, 2006).

The perspective taken here entails a focus on the ways in which constellations of people interact with their material surroundings, including texts, documents and other material objects. Through a theoretically grounded perspective in line with the main tenets of institutional ethnography, the subsequent sections offer a strategy for producing a 'cartography' of information literacy as an institutionalised phenomenon. It is argued that information literacy is shaped not only in the local contexts where it is observably practised, but also by its interrelated connections to trans-locally positioned complexes of governing and shaping forces. What is going on in the room where the teaching librarian is talking about the importance of identifying one's information needs cannot be completely disconnected from, for example, the policy makers' office at the governmental body.

Returning to the introductory scene with Laura, the newly embarked bachelor student, the cartography is outlined through identifying and mapping these connections as they are materialised through objects such as documents that convey, for example, ideologies, logics and rationalities; modes of control and standardisation; and rules and regulations. Likewise, material arrangements and tools such as information and communication technologies (ICTs), classification systems, platforms, algorithms, furnishing, etc., also function as connections between places that are distributed in time and space. Smith (2005, 226) explains that the 'project of mapping institutions always refers back to an actuality that those who are active in it know (the way that the phrase YOU ARE HERE works on a map). A map assembles different work knowledges, positioned differently and should include, where relevant, an account of the texts coordinating work processes in institutional settings.' Since the map in this chapter is represented in text, the metaphor of a cartography is the preferred term (cf. Latour, 2005, 16).

A fundamental idea in institutional ethnography is that social practices are 'organized by and co-ordinated with what people, mostly unknown and never to be known by us, are doing elsewhere and at different times' (Smith, 2001, 160–1). From an ontological perspective, this can be viewed as a spatio-temporal arrangement comprising a wide web of what Smith (e.g. 2005) describes as 'the ruling relations'. These relations co-ordinate activities 'across and beyond local sites of everyday experience' (Smith, 2002, 45). The ruling relations should not primarily be seen as a mode of domination but as a way of organising society. In Smith's words, they are 'forms of consciousness and organization that are objectified in the sense that they are constituted externally to particular people and places' (Smith, 2005, 13).

The mass production of texts and documents of all sorts is thus a fundamental condition for the ruling relations, since this has enabled 'access to words from beyond those spoken locally' (ibid.). The transportation of documents and ideas over long distances, both geographically and temporally, opens up for ways of doing and decisions taken locally, which are grounded in trans-locally developed discourses and systems of knowledge. Throughout the literature on institutional ethnography, not the least in Smith's own work, the emphasis is on texts as mediators of the ruling relations even though there is also a line of reasoning in some institutional ethnography texts regarding other material objects as 'yielding sets of instructions for how to act towards [them]' (Smith, 1990, 42). In this chapter and in line with this latter line of reasoning, the notion of text is extended to also comprise the wider notion of documents, which often comprise elements other than texts and other material objects that have the potential to function as connectors of the ruling relations. In institutional ethnography, and in particular in this chapter, the ethnographic exploration of texts, documents and other mediating objects is key. This is because, as Smith (2001, 159) puts it: 'exploring how texts mediate, regulate and authorize people's activities expands the scope of ethnographic method beyond the limits of observation: texts are to be seen as they enter into people's local practices of writing, drawing, reading, looking and so on. They must be examined as they coordinate people's activities.'

Documents of various sorts constitute a fundamental resource for the identification of the generalisability of institutional regimes, that is, the predominant characteristics in terms of practices and values and what counts as valid knowledge. Observations and interviews with people in the local setting under study, in turn, are crucial for discovering how the institutional regime contributes to co-ordinating, enabling and constraining, locally enacted practices. The constitution and implications of the ruling relations between, on the one hand, documents, discourses and systems of knowledge and, on the other hand, local practices, is of prime interest to the institutional ethnographer. In other words, through the method of ethnography, with specific attention to documents, the institutional ethnographer is engaged in discovering how people's everyday practices are 'hooked into a larger fabric not directly observable from within the everyday' (Smith, 2005, 39).

In addition to the prominent position of documents, the notion of discourse is also central to institutional ethnography (e.g. Smith, 2005), in particular the co-ordinating power of discourses (see also Chapter 5 by Hicks and Chapter 3 by Hirvonen in this volume). Institutional ethnographers acknowledge Foucault's conception of discourse, where knowledge does not primarily reside in the individual but is located externally, infused in practices, thereby forming imposed and coercing subjectivities in the shape of regulating orders. The example of such an order in focus for this contribution is information literacy in the way it has become institutionalised as a societal imperative formulated, expressed and enacted on various levels through discourses and activities such as teaching, policy-making and research.

A tentative critical cartography of an autonomous approach to information literacy

The student Laura has encountered a discourse through engaging in a practice that is somehow familiar, since it is about talking, thinking, writing and acting together with others, but still new to her in the sense that it involves 'frames, concepts and categories' (Smith, 2005, 225) that she is not accustomed to. The tools she is supposed to use in the classroom are in a way recognisable. There are computers, books and other texts in various formats, there is a teacher – the librarian – and other students, but there is a certain twist to it that makes things foreign, both the actual objects and the terms – the *bibliographic databases*, the *discovery tools*, the *academic genre*, the way in which the librarian *speaks*, the *terms* and *concepts* she uses. Together these things seem to make up a complex entity that is hard for Laura to penetrate and decipher. What makes the situation even more critical for her is that she knows that her performance somehow will be assessed. According to the tenets of institutional ethnography outlined above, the institution of information literacy has taken a certain shape in the location where Laura is supposed to be a good student (cf. Worthman and Troiano, 2019). This shape can be explored through identifying the ruling relations underpinning it. The following cartography is indeed not exhaustive but comprises a set of exemplars that can be followed up in order to get into sight how local information literacy practices are shaped through the ruling relations to trans-locally positioned constellations of discourses and knowledge regimes. In the following sub-sections, a selection of features that together form the tentative cartography is thus introduced.

The standards and the 'list approach' to information literacy

Already from the introductory scene, it can be discerned that there are certain expectations or demands on the students who participate in the session. They are supposed to develop a certain type of information literacy that includes a set of specific skills, which are more or less pronounced by the librarian. On one of the many slides that the librarian shows, there is a bullet-point list that dictates what it means to be an information-literate student. It may not be bibliographically referenced in the presentation, but here is an example of a certain stance to information literacy that is mediated through a text that circulates widely through the institution of information literacy and that has come to function as a ruling relation into this particular site. As such, it contributes to co-ordinate and shape the specific practices taking place in the site. Informed by and in line with the content of the presentation, the librarian has designed certain work tasks for the students, highlighted specific areas to which the students are supposed to turn their attention and introduced particular terms and concepts that characterise this stance.

When the institutional ethnographer traces the origins of this particular text, he or she will likely end up with one of the editions of the American Library Association's standards for information literacy or with any other of the numerous publications that the standards have influenced other authors to produce. (It should however be noted that the standards too are a result of prior research and debate.)

In the institutional ethnographer's quest for exploring the shape of IL, it is not enough only to look for texts and documents that mediate ruling relations. There must also be a focus on how these play out in the form of concrete, concerted sayings and doings in the local context under scrutiny, but the search for documents in this way 'expands [as Smith notes] the scope of ethnographic method beyond the limits of observation' (Smith, 2001, 159).

The idea of studying documents in context with the aim of exploring the practical implications of these documents for information literacy is not new. One such example is Pilerot and Lindberg's (2011) study of policy-documents issued by prominent organisations such as IFLA and UNESCO. They concluded that the export of a Western information literacy model focused on text-based information sources and ICTs into non-Western contexts that to a great extent lack ICTs, runs the risk of turning the organisations' educational aspirations for information literacy into an imperialistic project. However, the institutional ethnography approach suggested in this chapter offers opportunities for a richer analysis, since it includes a focus on both documents *and* the practices co-ordinated and shaped by the documents.

Tutorials

Even if not explicitly mentioned in the introductory scene, it is well known that formalised education for information literacy in higher education often includes the use of various interactive digital tools, such as games, quizzes, films and tutorials, that are expected to support the students' development of information literacy (e.g. Pinto et al., 2020). These must not necessarily be regarded as documents, but still as material objects that yield instructions for how to be interacted with. As stated previously in the chapter, objects of this kind also have the potential to function as connectors of the ruling relations. Regarding, for example, tutorials for information literacy, it has been shown in previous research (Sundin, 2008) that these tend to imply approaches to information literacy that are different from each other. According to an institutional ethnography perspective, the tutorials also give rise, depending on how they are designed, to different expected actions among those who use them. Accordingly, a design of a tutorial inevitably privileges a certain view that in turn obstructs other possible viewpoints. An example of how a certain view may be communicated through a digital tutorial concerns the specific feature of quizzes, which can be said to underscore a certain understanding of information literacy as concerning something that is either right or wrong. This is a dichotomous view on information literacy emerging from some sort of scale displaying the results of the skills of the person that takes the quiz. In line with an institutional ethnography perspective, this can reasonably be seen as a manifestation of a general idea permeating a capitalist society exposed to competition, which through tutorials and similar items seeps into local contexts of teaching, namely that students should be assessed and measured concerning their perceived levels of information literacy.

Course syllabuses and other steering documents

In the opening paragraph of this cartography, the ACRL's standards for information literacy were brought up as a potential intermediary of a ruling relation. Another set of documents that make their mark on what is going on in classrooms (and elsewhere) throughout the university consists of authoritative and controlling course syllabuses and other steering documents. These documents represent what Smith (2001, 173) describes as standardised and standardising genres. Both course syllabuses and steering documents such as ordinances for higher education are normative in character, prescribing certain activities and, in particular in the case of syllabuses, dictating certain texts that students are supposed to read. The concept Smith (Smith and Schryer, 2008) suggests for explaining this arrangement, when authority and control is exercised through documents, is *documentary governance*. An important feature of documentary governance relates to the material aspects of documents. Despite the assumption that most often it is the content that people are interested in when they are interacting with documents, '[n]ew technologies of writing and reading create new possibilities for coordinating work and other activities' (Smith and Schryer, 2008, 115). As has been indicated above, when documents travel along digital infrastructures throughout the networked society, texts become reproduced all over the place and at different times, which contributes to the stretching out of the ruling relations. In this way, documents and the content they carry are separated from face-to-face communication and become charged with a certain discursive force, making them into general ideas and concepts rather than local statements situated in the particular context in which they reach the reader. What this arrangement does, how documentary governance plays out in a certain setting, needs to be investigated when the shape of information literacy is explored.

Marketisation and commodification of academia

Another feature of interest in the fictitious introductory scene, which relates to yet another societal institution (in the institutional ethnography sense of using the term), namely the market, concerns the literature and the tools for finding the literature, that the students are expected to work with while at university. As the qualifier to literacy in this case is information (and not, for example, media or digital), an analysis of what shapes information literacy must necessarily take into consideration the characteristics of the information the students are expected to develop literacy in relation to. That both universities and their libraries are trying to withstand forces of commodification and marketisation is not new (e.g. Giroux, 2016; Levinsson, Norlund and Beach, 2020).

In her article on 'The McDonaldization of Academic Libraries' and their various efforts to respond to the aforementioned forces, Karen P. Nicholson asserts (with reference to Quinn, 2000) that libraries employ '"just-in-time" approaches to collection development – including a greater reliance on interlibrary loan and document delivery services, [and] standardized approaches to information literacy instruction'. They 'focus on quantity, such as inputs (like financial resources, number of staff, gate counts, number of volumes) and outputs (for instance, circulation stats, online transactions), as a surrogate for quality'. Furthermore, there is a 'growing predictability of academic libraries' collections resulting from the use of approval plans and journal aggregator databases' (Nicholson, 2015, 328). That the market finds its way into the institution of information literacy becomes visible through the libraries' ambition to regulate, standardise and slimline its collections and services. Following the fundamental principles of institutional ethnography, where a core assumption is that there is a linkage between, on the one hand, documents and material arrangements and, on the other hand, social organisation (Smith, 2001), the outlined scenario must be accounted for when exploring the shape of information literacy in this setting.

Yet another observation can be made regarding ruling relations related to tools for retrieving literature in this setting. In a call for the 'decolonisation' of scholarly communication, Jonathan P. Tennant (2020, 1) shows how Clarivate Analytics' Web of Science (WoS) and Elsevier's Scopus platform display 'an alarmingly warped version of reality: research from Africa, South America, and major parts of Asia is almost non-existent'. Both WoS and Scopus are clearly biased against research from non-Western countries, research published in languages other than English. They also demonstrate a clear emphasis on research from the sciences at the expense of research from the arts, humanities and social sciences. By limiting and orientating students toward a certain kind of literature, this too is more than likely to contribute to the shaping of the kind of information literacy that is enacted in the setting in question.

Other possible focus points for the institutional ethnographer exploring information literacy in context

For practical reasons, a cartography needs to be restricted to a manageable set of items, in particular here, in this chapter, since its main purpose is to illustrate the idea of mapping the institution of IL, but also in real-life research projects, where the researcher always needs to make decisions regarding what to focus on. Many more items could have been included because they bear a possibility of functioning as connectors of ruling relations in the context under scrutiny. Such examples include – but are certainly not limited to – discourses and practices concerning active learning, for instance manifested through specifically designed furnishing – e.g. so-called active learning classrooms – and pedagogies (cf. Hicks and Sinkinson, 2021). Especially from a library perspective, it could also be fruitful to interrogate intellectual tools such as bibliographic classification systems, which 'contribute to the promotion of identity and values of the institutions in which they are to function in a way that goes beyond their bibliographical function' (Hansson, 2021, 1). On a larger scale, there are also reasons to ponder the forces brought in motion by ubiquitous algorithmic platforms and search engines, which constantly and in all spheres of life contribute to shaping the ways in which information is sought and used (e.g. Haider and Sundin, 2019).

In summary, the argument is that information literacy, according to this tentative institutional ethnography analysis, emerges as a phenomenon that is anchored and enacted in its local context but to a great extent is shaped by ruling relations mediated by conglomerations of texts and documents and other material objects. By applying an institutional ethnography lens, it becomes visible how information literacy appears in the light of and is being shaped by, features such as ideologies (e.g. neoliberalism), ways of governing (e.g. corporate management in HE) and accountability and assessment practices in higher education (e.g. curriculum development and assessment of individuals). In Smith's words, this can be explained as if '[t]he various agencies of social control have institutionalized procedures for assembling, processing, and testing . . . the behaviour of individuals so that it can be matched against the paradigms which provide the working criteria of class-membership' (Smith, 1990, 12). Or, more specifically, in the case of Laura, the working criteria of being a good, information-literate student according to the autonomous approach to information literacy. The institution of information literacy in this particular setting, 'its conceptual organization, forms of social action, authorized actors and sites, and so forth, are concerned precisely with creating an order, a coherence' (p. 44) that matches the ruling relations and according to which people in the setting are expected to act.

Returning to Street's (1984; 2006) distinction between an autonomous and an ideological approach to information literacy, it is worth mentioning that also the latter approach, the ideological, would not be able to fully escape being shaped and co-ordinated by the ruling relations. However, institutional ethnography studies of the kind suggested here contribute to shed light on the processes of ruling, which, in turn, enables a conscious resistance to information literacy efforts that are too broad and generic in character, that is, such teaching arrangements that do not attend enough to the specifics in the actual setting where information literacy is taught.

Institutional ethnography studies are in many ways similar to a number of other theoretical approaches employed for studying information literacy. They share, for example, an interest expressed by representatives for sociocultural theory in explicating 'the relationships between human action, on the one hand, and the cultural, institutional, and historical contexts in which this action occurs, on the other' (Wertsch, 1998, 24). They also resemble a practice-theoretical approach in the urge to elucidate social phenomena 'without losing touch with the mundane nature of everyday life and the concrete and material nature of the activities with which we are all involved' (Nicolini, 2012, 9). What mainly makes an institutional ethnography approach specific for studies of information literacy is its accentuation of a bottom-up perspective – 'a sociology from people's standpoint' (Smith, 2005, 1) – and its focus on the ruling relations as mediated by documents and other material objects.

Concluding discussion

After having outlined the tentative cartography of information literacy, the remaining part of this chapter is aimed at pinpointing the connections between institutional ethnography as a theory and the study object of information literacy. The concluding discussion thus serves to illuminate institutional ethnography's ontological assumptions concerning information literacy studies, the enablers and constraints of institutional ethnography for information literacy research and its repertoire of methods.

Ontological and epistemological assumptions – people, activities, contexts, knowledge and learning information literacy

From an ontological perspective, institutional ethnography provides a conceptual framework for attention to actualities, of how the social exists, is configured and co-ordinated. As is mirrored in the starting point for this chapter, it takes people and their concerns with real-life issues as its point of departure. In this sense, institutional ethnography can be viewed as a standpoint theory (cf. e.g. Harding, 2004). Peoples' doings and sayings, their positioning in the world, their interactions with material objects are viewed as concrete actions inseparable from context. In line with what Street (1984; 2006) terms an ideological approach to information literacy, institutional ethnography views information literacy as a phenomenon that is embedded in social practices, which display their respective socially and historically developed epistemological traits. Epistemologically, institutional ethnography builds on the idea that knowledge is derived from interaction with others and with the material surroundings. It is never neutral and always local in the sense that there is no general knowledge, which is held to be true by all over all time and space (cf. Bowker, 2010). A key feature with institutional ethnography, however, is its dual analytical perspective, where the local always is seen as connected to the extra-local. This is where the ruling relations come into the picture. It has already been clearly stated throughout the chapter that documents and texts serve as mediators of these relations that connect sites over space and time. Institutional ethnography does not aspire to assess individuals' (or groups') information literacy, but if it would communicate an approach to what it might mean to be information literate, it would be emphasised that the ability to identify and trace the ruling relations in context constitutes a fundamental, critical ability. Learning information literacy in this sense implies a wider perspective that stretches beyond certain information sources and prescribed practices for finding and making use of information. It requires that the learner casts a critical gaze upon society at large (cf. Andersen, 2006).

Enablers and constraints of institutional ethnography for information literacy research

Through its awareness of power structures, which are made visible through the identification of discourses, rationalities and ideologies, mediated through documents and objects and conceptualised as the ruling relations, which infuse the practice of information literacy, institutional ethnography enables an understanding of information literacy as a politically charged concept and practice (see also Chapter 1 by Buschman and Chapter 6 by Rivano Eckerdal in this volume). At the same time, it also comprises a focus on lived experience, bodies and material arrangements. The connections between the local and the extra-local calls for the institutional ethnographer's attention. On an analytical level, the theory thus presupposes the researcher to work according to an oscillating mode, which includes certain moves that can be described as zooming in and out in relation to the study object (cf. Nicolini, 2009). It is a matter of simultaneously operating with close-ups and views from a distance. The crux is to highlight doings and sayings in practice and relate these to the ruling relations. This big task requires a lot from the institutional ethnography researcher and indicates some of the potential pitfalls with institutional ethnography. By aiming for the 'full picture' concerning what contributes to shape information literacy in context, the researcher runs the risk of being entrapped in too broad overarching analyses that miss out on the minute nuances in practice.

Repertoire of methods

This theoretical stance implies a certain repertoire of methods. Perhaps the most obvious feature of this repertoire is the ethnographic aspirations. The researcher needs to delve into the context under study, but this can be done in more than one way (cf. Smith, 2006). Interviews are widespread in institutional ethnographies, but rather than treating them as sources about individual experiences, the institutional ethnography interview serves to 'reveal the "relations of ruling" that shape local experiences' (DeVault and McCoy, 2006, 15). Participant observation is also put forth as a method for institutional ethnographies. Diamond (2006, 45) particularly highlights how observations can help to accentuate 'the presence of the author and the author's embodiment [as well as enhancing institutional ethnography's] goals of incorporating place, time, motion and the presence of larger social organization within local situations'. A continuous focus on documents and texts is among the trademarks of institutional ethnography and implies that the researcher is required to identify and scrutinise these, both as they take place in practice and as located elsewhere but with a connection to the context under study. In the tentative cartography above, it has also been shown how the researcher can work with previous research, which is not necessarily conducted in the tradition of institutional ethnography, in order to underscore certain aspects of the ruling relations as contributors to the shaping of information literacy in context.

The shaping of information literacy according to institutional ethnography

In the introduction, two overarching questions were posed: how is information literacy, as a concept and as a normatively prescribed practice, shaped into its form in a given social context? And what contributes to establishing individual and collective assumptions and understandings that motivate the people in the setting to enact, teach and promote information literacy in a certain way? According to the approach of inquiry outlined in this chapter, information literacy is a socially shaped, institutionalised phenomenon anchored and manifested in multiple settings. Since individual local settings always are connected through the ruling relations, as these are mediated through documents and other material objects, these manifestations of information literacy are inseparable from practices, discourses and values prevailing in society at large. Interaction among people and with the things used, the texts consulted and the documents that are allowed to underpin information literacy provide its certain shape. The examples of features included in the cartography suggested in this chapter are all potential contributors to the shaping of information literacy. The concept and practice of information literacy is value-laden. There is always a normative dimension. Depending on who is talking about or advocating information literacy, the different features that potentially contribute to shaping information literacy are emphasised in varying degrees. According to an idealistic discourse, information literacy is empowering and employed or enacted for good causes. But when information literacy – for example in the shape of a certain learning and teaching arrangement, as in the fictive opening scene of this chapter – is scrutinised through the lens of institutional ethnography, it becomes visible how information literacy might always be approached and enacted differently. In addition to introducing and outlining a set of central tenets of institutional ethnography, this chapter has shown how information literacy can be related to features such as marketisation and commodification, digital technologies and algorithmic logics (Gaw, 2022), politics and forms of governing, material configurations and other specific logics and rationalities.

References

Andersen, J. (2006) The Public Sphere and Discursive Activities: information literacy as sociopolitical skills, *Journal of Documentation*, **62** (2), 213–28.

Bowker, G. (2010) All Knowledge is Local, *Learning Communities: international journal of learning in social contexts Australia*, 2, 138–49.

Campbell, M. (2003) Dorothy Smith and Knowing the World We Live in, *Journal of Sociology & Social Welfare*, 30 (1), 3–22.

Dalmer, N. K. (2019) Considering the Local and the Translocal: reframing health information practice research using institutional ethnography, *Aslib Journal of Information Management*, 71 (6), 703–19.

Dalmer, N. K., Stooke, R. and McKenzie, P. (2017) Institutional Ethnography: a sociology for librarianship, *Library and Information Research*, 41 (125), 45–60.

DeVault, M. L. and McCoy, L. (2006) Institutional Ethnography: using interviews to investigate ruling relations. In Smith, D. (ed.) *Institutional Ethnography as Practice*, Rowman & Littlefield, 15–44.

Diamond, T. (2006) 'Where Did You Get the Fur Coat, Fern': participant observation in institutional ethnography. In Smith D. (ed.) *Institutional Ethnography as Practice*, Rowman & Littlefield, 45–63.

Elmborg, J. (2017) Lessons from Forty Years as a Literacy Educator: an information literacy narrative, *Journal of Information Literacy*, 11 (1).

Gaw, F. (2022) Algorithmic Logics and the Construction of Cultural Taste of the Netflix Recommender System, *Media, Culture & Society*, 44 (4), 706–25.

Giroux, H. A. (2016) Public Intellectuals Against the Neoliberal University. In Denzin, N. K. and Giardina, M. D. (eds) *Qualitative Inquiry Outside the Academy*, Routledge, 35–60.

Green, L. and Johnston, M. (2015) Global Perspectives: exploring school-based Brazilian librarianship through institutional ethnography, *School Libraries Worldwide*, 21 (1), 1–18.

Haider, J. and Sundin, O. (2019) *Invisible Search and Online Search Engines: the ubiquity of search in everyday life*, Routledge.

Hansson, J. (2021) Bringing Political Upheaval and Cultural Trauma into Order: a document-theoretical approach to the social significance of bibliographic classification systems, *Proceedings from the Document Academy*, 8 (2), 1–22.

Harding, S. G. (2009) Standpoint Theories: productively controversial, *Hypatia*, 24 (4), 192–200.

Harding, S. G. (ed.) (2004) *The Feminist Standpoint Theory Reader: intellectual and political controversies*, Routledge.

Hicks, A. and Sinkinson, C. (2021) Participation and Presence: interrogating active learning, *portal: Libraries and the Academy*, 21 (4), 749–71.

Kearney, G. P., Corman, M. K., Gormley, G. J., Hart, N. D., Johnston, J. L. and Smith, D. E. (2018) Institutional Ethnography: a sociology of discovery – in conversation with Dorothy Smith, *Social Theory & Health*, 16 (3), 292–306.

Kearney, G. P., Corman, M. K., Hart, N. D., Johnston, J. L. and Gormley, G. J. (2019) Why Institutional Ethnography? Why now? Institutional ethnography in health professions education, *Perspectives on Medical Education*, 8 (1), 17–24.

Kizhakkethil, P. (2020) 'You Make Me Miss Pune So Much': memory making and documenting in a Virtual Zenana, *Aslib Journal of Information Management*, 72 (4), 687–703.

Latour, B. (2005) *Reassembling the Social: an introduction to actor-network theory*, Oxford University Press.

Levinsson, M., Norlund, A. and Beach, D. (2020) Teacher Educators in Neoliberal Times: a phenomenological self-study, *Phenomenology & Practice*, 14 (1), 7–23.

Limberg, L., Sundin, O. and Talja, S. (2012) Three Theoretical Perspectives on Information Literacy, *Human IT: Journal for Information Technology Studies as a Human Science*, 11 (2).

Lloyd, A. (2010) Framing Information Literacy as Information Practice: site ontology and practice theory, *Journal of Documentation*, 66 (2), 245–58.

Luken, P. C. and Vaughan, S. (2021) *The Palgrave Handbook of Institutional Ethnography*, Springer.

Nicholson, K. P. (2015) The McDonaldization of Academic Libraries and the Values of Transformational Change, *College & Research Libraries*, 76 (3), 328–38.

Nicolini, D. (2009) Zooming In and Out: studying practices by switching theoretical lenses and trailing connections, *Organization Studies*, 30 (12), 1391–418.

Nicolini, D. (2012) *Practice Theory, Work and Organization: an introduction*, Oxford University Press.

Norstedt, M. and Paulsen Breimo, J. (2016) Moving Beyond Everyday Life in Institutional Ethnographies: methodological challenges and ethical dilemmas, *Forum: Qualitative Sozialforschung/Forum: Qualitative Social Research*, 17 (2), Art. 3.

Ocepek, M. G. (2018) Bringing Out the Everyday in Everyday Information Behavior, *Journal of Documentation*, 74 (2), 398–411.

Pilerot, O. (2016) A Practice-based Exploration of the Enactment of Information Literacy Among PhD Students in an Interdisciplinary Research Field, *Journal of Documentation*, 72 (3), 414–34.

Pilerot, O. and Lindberg, J. (2011) The Concept of Information Literacy in Policy-Making Texts: an imperialistic project?, *Library Trends*, 60 (2), 338–60.

Pinto, M., Fernández-Pascual, R., Caballero-Mariscal, D. and Sales, D. (2020) Information Literacy Trends in Higher Education (2006–2019): visualizing the emerging field of mobile information literacy, *Scientometrics*, 124 (2), 1479–510.

Quinn, B. (2000) The McDonaldization of Academic Libraries?, *College & Research Libraries*, 61 (3), 248–61.

Smith, D. E. (1974) The Social Construction of Documentary Reality, *Sociological Inquiry*, 44 (4), 257–68.

Smith, D. E. (1987) *The Everyday World as Problematic: a feminist sociology*, Northeastern University Press.

Smith, D. E. (1990) K is Mentally Ill. In Smith, D. E., *Texts, Facts, and Femininity: exploring the relations of ruling*, Routledge, 12–51.

Smith, D. E. (1992) Sociology from Women's Experience: a reaffirmation, *Sociological Theory*, 10 (1), 88–98.

Smith, D. E. (1999) Telling the Truth after Postmodernism. In Smith, D. E. *Writing the Social: critique, theory, and investigations*, University of Toronto Press, 96–130.

Smith, D. E. (2001) Texts and the Ontology of Organizations and Institutions, *Studies in Cultures, Organizations and Societies*, 7 (2), 159–98.

Smith, D. E. (2002) Institutional Ethnography. In May, T. (ed.) *Qualitative Research in Action*, Sage Publications, 17–52.

Smith, D. E. (2005) *Institutional Ethnography: a sociology for people*, Rowman Altamira.

Smith, D. E. (ed.) (2006) *Institutional Ethnography as Practice*, Rowman & Littlefield.

Smith, D. E. (2021) Exploring Institutional Words as People's Practices. In Luken, P. C. and Vaughan, S. (eds) *The Palgrave Handbook of Institutional Ethnography*, Springer, 65–78.

Smith, D. E. and Schryer, C. F. (2008) On Documentary Society. In Bazerman, C. (ed.) *Handbook of Research on Writing: history, society, school, individual, text*, Lawrence Erlbaum, 113–27.

Stooke, R. (2005) Institutional Ethnography. In Fisher, K. E., Erdelez, S. and McKechnie, L. (eds) *Theories of Information Behavior*, Information Today, 210–14.

Stooke, R. (2010) Investigating the Textually Mediated Work of Institutions: Dorothy E. Smith's sociology for people. In Leckie, G. J., Given, L. M. and Buschman, J. (eds) *Critical Theory for Library and Information Science: exploring the social from across the disciplines*, Libraries Unlimited, 283–94.

Street, B. V. (1984) *Literacy in Theory and Practice*, Cambridge University Press.

Street, B. V. (2006) Autonomous and Ideological Models of Literacy: approaches from new literacy studies, *Media Anthropology Network*, 17, 1–15.

Sundin, O. (2008) Negotiations on Information-seeking Expertise: a study of web-based tutorials for information literacy, *Journal of Documentation*, 64 (1), 24–44.

Tennant, J. P. (2020) Web of Science and Scopus are Not Global Databases of Knowledge, *European Science Editing*, 46.

Wertsch, J. V. (1998) *Mind as Action*, Oxford University Press.

Worthman, C. and Troiano, B. (2019) A Good Student Subject: a Foucauldian discourse analysis of an adolescent writer negotiating subject positions, *Critical Studies in Education*, 60 (2), 263–80.

Conclusion: Alerting Us to Difference

Alison Hicks, Annemaree Lloyd and Ola Pilerot

Theory is a critical element of research, providing the intellectual scaffolding that is necessary for its development, implementation, analysis, interpretation and critical evaluation. Theory provides the necessary concepts that can be employed to describe a phenomenon or practice as it is experienced and/or performatively enacted. Knowledge from theory is always a view from somewhere (Barad, 1996) and the knowledge provided by social theory draws attention to certain forms of knowledge and ways of knowing, i.e. different contexts, different concepts and different truths (Lloyd, 2005). Theory makes visible our standpoint or our assumptions and beliefs – our ontological and epistemological positions – and it scaffolds our decisions about methodology (Lloyd, 2021,18).

The theories presented in this book provide us with a range of perspectives and concepts that enrich our understanding of information literacy practice. The ontological and epistemological emphasis acts to alert us to differences and centre the lived experience of the practice. Overall, however, the broad palette of social theories makes a claim for the situatedness of the experience of information literacy. This is realised through a focus on the conditions of social life, including the sociomaterial aspects of practice, power, social dynamics and the role of epistemic narrative structures that promote specific forms of discourse and actions via a web of ruling relations.

Nevertheless, silences remain – with chapters exploring the sufficiency of democratic theory (on which the premise of information literacy as central to citizenship is built) and the critical contribution of corporeal information and intra-actions to ways of knowing. Pointing to the need for further research, these silences also have implications for teaching practices. If information literacy is understood as a political practice and a cultural tool, educational delivery must be carefully and critically understood in terms of hegemonic power and positionality – as well as through an acknowledgement that there are multiple sources of information and consequently, multiple ways of knowing.

The wider theoretical landscape

One of the overarching aims of this book was to reflect on the theoretical landscape of information literacy, with the goal of drawing out observations related to how theory contributes to and shapes information literacy research. Analysis of the various chapters in this book make clear that work with theory can be done in many different ways and there is great variation in strategies employed by the authors when theorising information literacy. This plays out on many different but often interrelated levels. On one level, we see more or less elaborated theoretical frameworks where the authors strive for employing a wide and encompassing perspective, including e.g. societal and political dimensions in their analyses (see for example Buschman's chapter on democracy and information literacy and Rivano Eckerdal's contribution concerning plural agonistics). In contrast, there are those theories that are developed from one or a few central concepts (for example Lloyd and Folk) where the theoretical line of reasoning is grounded in and supported by a manifold variety of social theories but still centred on the key concept in question (e.g. embodiment or equity mindset). We can thus see differences with regards to the degree in which authors zoom in or out (cf. Nicolini, 2009) in relation to their study objects. However, other contributions (like Pilerot's and Hirvonen's) work with theories where one of the main purposes is to enable an oscillating position that moves between where the action is (cf. Layder, 2006) and a zooming-out perspective, thereby striving to encompass both close-ups of information practices and an overarching view, which serves to capture the discursive and ideological dimensions that enable, constrain and mutually shape these practices. A similar ambition can be seen in the chapter by Haider and Sundin, where information literacy researchers are urged to interrogate the co-constitution of information practices and the systems and platforms in relation to which these practices are enacted.

Yet another difference concerns the ways in which the authors approach information literacy and its plausible goals. Whereas for example Maybee's chapter on variation theory and Folk's presentation of information literacy through an equity mindset take a pedagogical or instructional approach to information literacy, which serves to assist learners in developing information literacy, Hicks' contribution on positioning theory and Lloyd's on practice theory are aiming for an understanding of how information literacy is enacted as a situated practice. Other contributions tend to be dispersed over this scale, leaning towards either the pedagogical or the situated. These two positions can also be described in terms of either an objective or a subjective stance to information literacy. Pedagogical approaches to information literacy are often grounded in an objective stance, whereas the situated position tends to subscribe to the idea that knowledge and meaning-making can be discerned through studying information interactions in communities of practice. Another position that is seen within this book is the ideological approach to information literacy. This is visible in Rivano Eckerdal's chapter, where information literacy framed through the notion of plural agonistics is used as a political concept with the potential to avoid antagonism between different political or ideological standpoints. Johansson's chapter on critical literacy and critical design also has an ideological edge when it emphasises that theory can be used for highlighting normative-ethical considerations when striving to support critical information literacy practices among individuals and in society at large.

Chapters in this book also enable us to draw out observations related to thematic areas of interest within information literacy's theoretical landscape. In the introduction to this volume we surveyed existing theoretical work in the field to identify that, to date, this literature is organised around themes relating to the tension between agency and enactment; the legitimacy of information; the moral imperative of information literacy; the socially situated shape of information literacy and marginalisation. We continued this work in the conclusion, with each editor reading, coding and drawing out themes across the 13 chapters of this book. We now add the following four themes to our initial list (Table 2 on p. xvii):

- discourse and power
- decentring language
- privilege as critical reflection on teaching information literacy practice
- revisioning the premises on which information literacy is constructed.

These themes are represented in Table 3 and explored in detail below.

Table 3 *New themes within theoretical information literacy research*

6. Discourse and power	Hirvonen, Chapter 3; Hicks, Chapter 5; Folk, Chapter 8; Pilerot, Chapter 13
7. Decentring language	Johansson, Chapter 7; Haider and Sundin, Chapter 9; Lloyd, Chapter 10; Pilerot, Chapter 13
8. Revising the premises on which information literacy is constructed	Lloyd, Chapter 2; Buschman, Chapter 1; Bezerra and Schneider, Chapter 4; Rivano Eckerdal, Chapter 6; Budd, Chapter 12
9. Privilege as critical reflection on teaching information literacy practice	Folk, Chapter 8; Maybee, Chapter 11; Budd, Chapter 12

Themes
6. Discourse and power

One of the first new themes to emerge from the chapters of this book is the use of theory to explore the organising role that discourse plays within information literacy practice. Zeroing in on language use, which forms a much smaller-scale focus than usual within information literacy research, this theme also centres how discursive practices privilege certain (normative) views and perspectives. Pilerot's chapter, for example, employs institutional ethnography to illustrate how information literacy practices are shaped in relation to 'ruling relations', which refer to institutionalised discourses that are co-ordinated through documents and other material objects. Illustrating how the use of this theory/methodology helps to establish the 'predominant characteristics [of information literacy] in terms of practices and values and what counts as valid knowledge', the chapter nevertheless warns how regulation necessarily also 'impose[s] and coerce[s] subjectivities'. Ideas are extended through Hirvonen's chapter, which uses mediated discourse theory to explore the relationship between discourse and action further. Pointing out that accounts of information literacy often focus on meaning at the expense of structure, the chapter illustrates how a focus on mediated human action moves research 'from a microanalysis of social action to broader sociopolitical-cultural analysis' while facilitating insight into the often 'unnoticeable' ways in which information activity is shaped. In contrast, Hicks' chapter draws upon positioning theory to focus more concretely on the ways in which people adopt or reject discursive constructions that impact their broader information needs. Recognising that unevenly distributed opportunities for participation determine 'who can come to know . . ., develop a subject position . . . and move towards full participation' within an information environment, this chapter also introduces a more overt focus on how possibilities of action are built into a site or setting.

7. Decentring language

A second new theme that develops from within these chapters is the use of theory to decentre language, including information literacy's traditional emphasis on textual modalities of information. Drawing on research that has long advocated a decoupling of information literacy from documentary practice, this theme also emerges in relation to more recent attempts to introduce material and non-human ontologies into considerations of practice. Corporeality and the body provide one of the key strands within this theme, with Lloyd's chapter turning to social theories of embodiment to reflect on how the body disrupts current information literacy discourse. Arguing that information experience will continue to be marginalised 'until we understand [bodily] absence', this chapter further highlights how a corporeal focus references access to denied forms of knowledge as well as histories of privilege and inequality. A second overlooked strand within this theme is the material, which is explored within Sundin and Haider's chapter through the lens of sociomaterial theory. Recognising the materiality of both physical and digital artefacts, Haider and Sundin establish the need for information literacy to have a less detached relationship to objects, given that current algorithmic information infrastructure 'challenges traditional notions of, for example, trust, agency, intentions and even knowledge'. These ideas are further developed in Johansson's chapter, which draws from critical design theory to advocate the inclusion of 'feelings or tangible effects of inclusion and exclusion, oppression, marginalisation and discrimination' within considerations of critical literacy. Bringing a sociomaterial focus to the work of information system authorities, this chapter encourages information literacy's continued transgression beyond assumed boundaries of practice.

8. Revising the premises on which information literacy is constructed

Another new theme that is noted in the chapters of this book is the use of theory to challenge and revise how we currently conceive of information literacy. Information literacy has historically been developed on an ad hoc basis, emerging in relation to instrumental workplace and academic demands rather than through theory-driven conceptualisation. Chapters consequently draw upon theory to challenge taken-for-granted assumptions within information literacy narratives, including its underlying propositions. Buschman's chapter, for example, draws upon democratic theory to challenge the oft-mentioned link between information literacy and civic participation (e.g. Goldstein, 2020), including by unpacking how democratic values are often at odds with 'how information systems are designed, how people actually seek information, how they think, decide and identify as citizens'. Rivano Eckerdal's chapter similarly questions the expectation that information literacy will automatically promote democracy by using plural agonistics theory to demonstrate that 'there are conflicts for which there will not ever be any rational solution'. Theory is also used to challenge who we consider to be information-literate, with Bezerra and Schneider's chapter drawing on critical theory to argue that linking information literacy to economic demands positions creators of addictive online environments as information-literate, since their critical thinking is 'successfully oriented to shape information to their needs (or, for that matter, the profit needs of the companies they work for)'. Echoing some of the concerns raised in the introduction about the moral imperative of information literacy, these chapters extend this work by providing a robust rebuttal to some of the many unquestioned axioms that have come to be associated with information literacy practice.

9. Privilege as critical reflection on teaching information literacy practice

A final new theme that emerges from the chapters of this book is the use of theory to position privilege as a site for critical reflection upon information literacy teaching practice. Privilege is not a new theme within critical approaches to information literacy practice, which has considered both information privilege (Booth, 2014) and, less commonly, white privilege in the classroom (Rapchak, 2019). However, authors from this volume extend the theoretical reach of these ideas by situating privilege more firmly within professional reflexivity and responsibility. Thus, Folk's chapter uses the theoretical concept of equity mindset to position privilege as embedded within teaching expectations, arguing that the increased disaggregation of equity gap data, for instance, would lay the groundwork for transformative pedagogy. Similarly, Maybee's chapter highlights how variation theory's focus on the object of learning might complement critical work by facilitating analysis of the impact of privilege within small-scale contexts. Chapters also go beyond the classroom to explore how privilege impacts the design of learning objects, including library and information systems. Situating privilege in relation to issues of representation within both academic and everyday contexts, these chapters also draw more overt attention to positionality as well as broader ethical imperatives.

Looking to the future

We started this book recognising that theory has often had a poor reputation in information literacy discourse. Various bibliographic studies have noted the lack of theoretical literature in the field (Sproles, Detmering and Johnson, 2013), while the broader domain of information science has occasionally seemed to question the place of theory in information literacy research by labelling emerging conceptual work as merely 'currently fashionable' (Julien and Williamson, 2011). Research has also been curtailed through the perception that theoretical discussions are 'largely of no interest to practitioners' (Julien and Williamson, 2011). Chapters of this book challenge these ideas by drawing attention to information literacy's rich theoretical heritage. While the relative volume of theoretical information literacy literature may still be low, the introduction to this book as well as its ensuing chapters provides compelling evidence of the scope of theoretical information literacy work as well as the many meaningful contributions that this literature has made to the field. The more nuanced picture also reminds of the dangers of relying on purely quantitative bibliographic descriptions of the field (cf. Hicks et al., 2022).

Contributions to this book further dispel the perception that theoretical concerns are the unique purview of scholars rather than practitioners. Chapter authors comprise a wide range of librarians (and ex-librarians), while individual contributions draw on practitioner research and concerns, particularly in chapters that explore critical theory topics. And, while the theories presented in this book focus more on the shape of information literacy rather than how we teach for it, it is hoped that each chapter's careful exploration of key theoretical and methodological implications will make conceptual work accessible to those for whom it has previously been closed off. Importantly, this volume will also contribute to the theoretical education of scholars from outside the field of information literacy. For too long, considerations of information literacy theory have been restricted to Kuhlthau's information search process (e.g. Fisher, Erdelez and McKechnie, 2005; Julien and Williamson, 2011; Sonnenwald, 2016), despite critique from information literacy scholars (Tuominen, 1997). The range of theories presented in the preceding pages provides evidence of the limitations of this perspective and we hope that this conceptual work will also influence broader ideas within library and information science.

At the same time, this volume's focus on theory also risks reigniting certain debates regarding the status of information literacy. In particular, the establishment of a firmer theoretical base may, for some, be taken as evidence that information literacy forms its own discipline, an idea that has been sporadically floated by Johnston and Webber since the late 1990s (Johnston and Webber, 1999; 2006; Webber and Johnston, 2017). Within this reasoning, the establishment of Lloyd's (2017) *Theory of Information Literacy*, as well as the reliance on theory from other 'soft knowledge domains' (Johnston and Webber, 2006) may be seen to confirm that information literacy should be understood in disciplinary terms (Johnston and Webber, 2006; Webber and Johnston, 2017). However, this volume's emphasis on bringing authors from different backgrounds together to focus on a common problem means that we continue to position information literacy as a field within the broader discipline of library and information science. While we agree that information literacy does fulfil some of the criteria of a discipline, as laid out (and updated) in Webber and Johnston (2017), we consider that it also lacks core components of disciplinarity, namely, specialist terminology and methods as well as original theories that attempt to explain the essence and composition of the practice in terms that take information as the central phenomenon into account.

In sum, the aim of this book has been to introduce readers to theories and theoretical concepts that are currently being applied to the analysis of information literacy. We encouraged authors to explore how their selected theory opens information literacy up to analysis, but also to examine what the theory neglects, including the assumptions that it makes about people, activities, contexts, knowledge, or learning. We also tasked chapter writers with considering how their selected theory shapes the methodological choices we make as researchers of information literacy practice. The range of theories presented in the preceding pages provides evidence of the success of this approach and we believe that this volume will continue to influence both theoretical and applied information literacy research for the foreseeable future.

References

Barad, K. (1996) Meeting the Universe Halfway: realism and social constructivism without contradiction. In Hankinson Nelson, L. and Nelson, J. (eds) *Feminism, Science and the Philosophy of Science*, Springer, 161–94.

Booth, C. (2014) On Information Privilege, *Info-mational*, https://infomational.com/2014/12/01/on-information-privilege.

Fisher, K. E., Erdelez, S. and McKechnie, L. (eds) (2005) *Theories of Information Behavior*, Information Today.

Goldstein, S. (ed.) (2020) *Informed Societies*, Facet Publishing.

Hicks, A., McKinney, P., Inskip, C., Walton, G. and Lloyd, A. (2022) Leveraging Information Literacy: mapping the conceptual influence and appropriation of information literacy in other disciplinary landscapes, *Journal of Librarianship and Information Science*, https://doi.org/10.1177/09610006221090677.

Johnston, B. and Webber, S. (1999) Information Literacy as an Academic Discipline: an action research approach to developing a credit bearing class for business undergraduates. In Klasson, M., Loughridge, B. and Loof, S. (eds) *New Fields for Research in the 21st Century: Proceedings of the 3rd British Nordic Conference on Library and Information Studies: 12–14 April 1999*: Borås, Sweden, Swedish School of Library and Information Studies, University College of Borås, 183–97.

Johnston, B. and Webber, S. (2006) As We May Think: information literacy as a discipline for the information age, *Research Strategies*, **20** (3), 108–21.

Julien, H. and Williamson, K. (2011) Discourse and Practice in Information Literacy and Information Seeking: gaps and opportunities, *Information Research*, **16** (1).

Layder, D. (2006) *Understanding Social Theory*, 2nd edn, Sage.

Lloyd, A. (2005) Information Literacy: different contexts, different concepts, different truths?, *Journal Of Librarianship and Information Science*, **37** (2), 82–8.

Lloyd, A. (2017) Information Literacy and Literacies of Information: a mid-range theory and model, *Journal of Information Literacy*, **11** (1), 91–105.

Lloyd, A. (2021) *The Qualitative Landscape of Information Literacy Research: perspectives, methods and techniques*, Facet Publishing.

Nicolini, D. (2009) Zooming In and Out: studying practices by switching theoretical lenses and trailing connections, *Organization Studies*, **30** (12), 1391–418.

Rapchak, M. (2019) That Which Cannot be Named: the absence of race in the framework for information literacy for higher education, *Journal of Radical Librarianship*, **5**, 173–96.

Sonnenwald, D. H. (ed.) (2016) *Theory Development in the Information Sciences*, University of Texas Press.

Sproles, C., Detmering, R. and Johnson, A. M. (2013) Trends in the Literature on Library Instruction and Information Literacy 2001–2010, *Reference Services Review*, **41** (3), 395–412.

Tuominen, K. (1997) User-Centered Discourse: an analysis of the subject positions of the user and the librarian, *Library Quarterly*, **67** (4), 350–71.

Webber, S. and Johnston, B. (2017) Information Literacy: conceptions, context and the formation of a discipline, *Journal of Information Literacy*, **11** (1).

Index

American Library Association (ALA), information literacy (IL) 60
antagonism, plural agonistics 92–4
autonomous approach to IL research 215–16, 221–6
   course syllabuses and other steering documents 223–4
   critical cartography of an autonomous approach to IL research 221–6
   focus points 225–6
   list approach to IL 222
   marketisation and commodification of academia 224
   Scopus 224
   standards 222
   tutorials for IL education 222–3
   Web of Science (WoS) 224

Bayne, T., phenomenology 205
Belkin, N. J. 200
Bezerra, A. C. *et al.*, critical information literacy (CIL) 61–2
body and embodiment 165–78
   absenting the body 168–9
   argument for the body 165–7
   body work in IL practice 176–8
   bringing the body into view 169–70
   Butler, J. 171
   epistemological dimension 174–6, 178
   Foucault, M. 170–1
   Goffman, E. 171
   key theorists 170–2
   Leder, D. 177
   Merleau-Ponty, M. 170
   ontological dimension 174–6, 178
   privileging the mind in early theory 168–9
   Reckwitz, A. 171–2
   Schatzki, T. 171–2
   Shilling, C. 172
   theoretical questions 174–6
   theories of embodiment 168–70
   theorising the body in LIS 173
   theory of information literacy (ToIL) 167–8, 176–8

Capurro, R., critical information literacy (CIL) 59
CD *see* critical design
chains of equivalences, plural agonistics 105–6
CIL *see* critical information literacy
citizenship, libraries and IL 14–15
civic republicanism 4–7
civil society, libraries and IL 16
cognition and IL 201–8
cognition theory xvi
community, libraries and IL 16
consciousness and IL 201–8
critical and speculative design (CSD) *see* critical design
critical assumptions, information literacy 135–40
critical design (CD) 111–26
   associative design 114
   on being and knowledge 115–18
   central concepts 114–15
   critical literacy 111–26
   'design-for-research' methods 121–2, 123–4
   empirical studies 125–6
   focus 118–19
   future work 125
   innovative disciplinary crossovers 125
   methodological consequences 119–22

origins 113–14
overview 113–14
'research-for-design'-oriented focus of studies 120–1, 123
speculative design 114–15
theoretical and empirical attention 125
theoretical questions 115–22
critical information literacy (CIL) 57–68
approaches 61–4
Bezerra, A. C. *et al.* 61–2
Capurro, R. 59
concentration or suspension of everyday life 62
credibility dimension 63
critical consciousness 64
critical perspective 58–61
criticism dimension 63
dimensions 62–3
Elmborg, J. 64–5, 66–7
ethics dimension 63
IBM (company) 60–1
influences 63–5
instrumental dimension 62
relevance dimension 62–3
Schneider, M. 62–3
taste dimension 62
Tewell, E. 66–7
theoretically informed praxis 57–8
United States National Commission on Libraries and Information Science 59–60
criticality theory xvi
critical literacy 111–26
on being and knowledge 115–18
defining 112–13
'design-for-research' methods 121–2, 123–4
empirical studies 125–6
focus 118–19
future work 125
innovative disciplinary crossovers 125
methodological consequences 119–22
'research-for-design'-oriented focus of studies 120–1, 123
theoretical and empirical attention 125
theoretical questions 115–22
critically reflective approaches to IL, positioning theory 79–81
critical race theory, information literacy 143

decentring language 235, 236
deficit mindset 132–3
democracy and information literacy 1–16
current democracy 11–12
democratic politics 13–14
democratic theory 4–10
the empirical and the normative 11–16
Jefferson, Thomas 2
Kranich, Nancy 1–2, 3
libraries and democracy 1–2, 3
libraries and IL 14–15
reset 11–16
democratic institutions, plural agonistics 96–7, 98–100
democratic paradox, plural agonistics 95–7
democratic theory
civic republicanism 4–7
disengagement and the nature of contemporary engagement 7–8
public spheres 9–10
Dennett, D. C. 199
Di Paolo, E. 209
discourse and power 235–6
discourse theory xvi
diversity mindset 133

Elmborg, J.
critical information literacy (CIL) 64–5, 66–7
defining IL 210
the empirical and the normative, democracy and IL 11–16
epistemological assumptions, institutional ethnography 226–7
epistemological dimension, body and embodiment 174–6, 178
epistemological position
mediated discourse theory (MDT) 47–51
practice theory view to IL 33–4
equality, libraries and IL 14
equity mindset 131–45
deficit mindset 132–3
defining 132–5
diversity mindset 133
equity-minded sense-making 134–5
information literacy, critical assumptions 135–40
methodologies 143–5

INDEX

power dynamics 142
theories 140–3
ethics
  critical information literacy (CIL) 63
  plural agonistics 101–2
ethnography, institutional *see* institutional ethnography

fake news 3–4, 8–10
Flanagan, O. 199–200
Foucault, M., body and embodiment 170–1
Framework document, information literacy 137
future development, variation theory 191–2
future work 238–9
  critical design (CD) 125
  critical literacy 125

Gazzaniga, M. 198
Goffman, E., body and embodiment 171
Goldman, A. I. 201
Gonsher, I., critical design (CD) 119
Google Search 157–8
Graziano, M. S. A. 199
Greene, N. T. 201–2

Habermas, J., IL research 197
hegemony, plural agonistics 94–5
Horgan, T. 206–7

IBM (company), critical information literacy (CIL) 60–1
identity, plural agonistics 103–5
ideological approach to IL research 215–16
IFLA (International Federation of Library Associations) 4
institutional ethnography 215–28
  autonomous approach to IL research 215–16, 221–6
  characteristics 217–19
  constraints 174–6
  core elements 219–21
  course syllabuses and other steering documents 223–4
  critical cartography of an autonomous approach to IL research 221–6
  discourse 221
  enablers 174–6
  epistemological assumptions 226–7

focus points 225–6
fundamental idea 220–1
ideological approach to IL research 215–16
list approach to IL 222
marketisation and commodification of academia 224
methods repertoire 227–8
ontological assumptions 226–7
original purpose 218
Scopus 224
shaping of IL 228
standards 222
tutorials for IL education 222–3
Web of Science (WoS) 224
International Federation of Library Associations (IFLA) 4

Jaeger, P. T. 201–2
Jefferson, Thomas 2

Koch A. 2
Kranich, Nancy, libraries and democracy 1–2, 3

Leder, D., body and embodiment 177
legitimacy of information xvii, xviii–xix
libraries and IL, democracy and IL 14–15
list approach to IL 222
Lloyd, A. 202

Malazita, J. W., science and technology studies (STS) 117
marginalisation xvii, xx
marketisation and commodification of academia 224
material dimension of practice, positioning theory 78
materiality theory xvi
MDA (mediated discourse analysis) 39–40, 48–9
MDT *see* mediated discourse theory
mediated discourse analysis (MDA) 39–40, 48–9
mediated discourse theory (MDT) 39–52
  core elements 39–43
  discourses in place 42–3
  epistemological position 47–51
  historical bodies 42–3
  IL as a mediational means 43–4

IL from an MDT perspective 43–7
IL in a nexus of practice 44–6
interaction order 42–3
mediated discourse analysis (MDA) 39–40, 48–9
methodological position 47–51
nexus analysis 48–51, 52
ontogenesis of IL practices 46–7
ontological position 47–51
principle of communication 41–2
principle of history 42
researcher tasks 49–50
site of engagement 41
social action 41, 42–3
Merleau-Ponty, M., body and embodiment 170
Mill, John Stuart 5
Montague, M., phenomenology 205
moral imperative of IL xvii, xix
moral imperative of information literacy xvii, xix
Mouffe, C., plural agonistics 91, 92–9, 101–7, 108, 109
multimodal data, positioning theory 78

neutrality, plural agonistics 103
next steps xx–xxi
nexus analysis 48–51, 52

ontological assumptions, institutional ethnography 226–7
ontological dimension, body and embodiment 174–6, 178
ontological position, mediated discourse theory (MDT) 47–51
ontological questions, practice theory view to IL 32–3
overview of this book xiii–xv

Peden W. 2
phenomenographic research 204–5
    variation theory 188–92
plural agonistics 91–109
    antagonism 92–4
    chains of equivalences 105–6
    consensus and compromises 100–1
    core elements 92–7
    democratic institutions 96–7, 98–100
    democratic paradox 95–7

ethics 101–2
hegemony 94–5
identity 103–5
information literacy 97–107
limitations 107
Mouffe, C. 91, 92–9, 101–7, 108, 109
neutrality 103
passionate decisions 98–9
politics 101–2
researching IL with an agonistic view 106–7
politics, plural agonistics 101–2
positioning theory 71–85
    barriers to practice 76
    central concept 72
    critically reflective approaches to IL 79–81
    enhancement by other theories 84–5
    flawed theory? 83–4
    foundational positioning theory work 72–3, 78, 80
    interpreting and explaining IL 82–4
    within LIS 74
    material dimension of practice 78
    methodological choices for IL research 81–2
    modes 72–3
    multimodal data 78
    origins 73–4
    overview 72–3
    social action 77–8
    understandings of IL 75–81
practice theory xvi
practice theory view to IL 27–35
    creating information landscapes 32
    defining practices 29–31
    epistemological position 33–4
    explaining IL 35
    information and knowledge 31–2
    methodological perspective 34
    ontological questions 32–3
    practice theory landscape 29–31
    site ontology 31
    theoretical questions 31–2
    waves of practice theory 30–1
privilege as critical reflection on teaching IL practice 235, 237–8
Public Library Association 4
public spheres 12, 15
    democratic theory 9–10

diminution of public spheres 9–10
libraries and IL 16

Reckwitz, A., body and embodiment 171–2
researching IL with an agonistic view, plural agonistics 106–7
revising the premises on which IL is constructed 235, 237
Robertson, S. E. 200

Schatzki, T., body and embodiment 171–2
Schneider, M., critical information literacy (CIL) 62–3
Scollon, Ron 41–6, 49–50
Searle, J. R. 200–1
Shilling, C., body and embodiment 172
Smith, D. W. 204
social action
    mediated discourse theory (MDT) 41, 42–3
    positioning theory 77–8
socially situated shape of IL xvii, xix–xx
social theory xiii
sociocultural contexts, information literacy 137–9
sociocultural theory xvi
sociomateriality 149–62
    becomings 153
    configurations 153–4
    core elements 151–5
    definitional ambiguity 160–2
    entanglement and co-constitution 152
    information infrastructure 150–1
    infrastructure 154
    key notions 151–5
    materiality 154–5
    materiality in IL research 155–6
    methodological choices 159–60
    performativity 153
    punk approach 160–2
    theoretical questions 155–9
    understandings of IL 156–9
sociopolitical theory xvii
sociotechnical theory xvii
standards and the 'list approach' to IL 222

tension between agency and enactment xvii, xviii

Tewell, E., critical information literacy (CIL) 66–7
themes from theoretical literature xvii–xx, 235–8
    decentring language 235, 236
    discourse and power 235–6
    legitimacy of information xvii, xviii–xix
    marginalisation xvii, xx
    moral imperative of IL xvii, xix
    privilege as critical reflection on teaching IL practice 235, 237–8
    revising the premises on which IL is constructed 235, 237
    socially situated shape of IL xvii, xix–xx
    tension between agency and enactment xvii, xviii
theoretical landscape 233–5
theoretical research to date xv–xvii
theorising the body in LIS 173
theory and praxis of IL 208–12
theory employed in IL research xv–xvii
theory of information literacy (ToIL) 27–8, 30–1
    body and embodiment 167–8, 176–8
theory of information literacy practice xiii
Thomasson, A. 204
Thompson, E. 209
ToIL see theory of information literacy
tutorials for IL education 222–3

understandings of IL
    positioning theory 75–81
    sociomateriality 156–9
United States National Commission on Libraries and Information Science, critical information literacy (CIL) 59–60

variation theory 183–93
    applications in research 186–7
    characteristics 185–6
    future development 191–2
    and IL 187–92
    new pathways for studying IL 190–2
    object of learning 185–6, 189–90
    origins 183–5
    phenomenographic research 188–92
    relationship between IL and learning 187–90
    types of variations 185–6

245